What is Free Speech?

FARA DABHOIWALA

What is Free Speech?

The History of a Dangerous Idea

ALLEN LANE
an imprint of
PENGUIN BOOKS

ALLEN LANE

UK | USA | Canada | Ireland | Australia
India | New Zealand | South Africa

Allen Lane is part of the Penguin Random House group of companies
whose addresses can be found at global.penguinrandomhouse.com

Penguin Random House UK
One Embassy Gardens, 8 Viaduct Gardens, London SW11 7BW

penguin.co.uk

First published 2025
001

Set in 10.5/14pt Sabon LT Std
Typeset by Jouve (UK), Milton Keynes
Printed and bound in Great Britain by Clays Ltd, Elcograf S.p.A.

The authorized representative in the EEA is Penguin Random House Ireland,
Morrison Chambers, 32 Nassau Street, Dublin D02 YH68

A CIP catalogue record for this book is available from the British Library

ISBN: 978-0-241-34747-8

For Harriet and Kate,
my favourite speakers

And for Jo,
again and always

Contents

Introduction

What is the history of free speech? And why should anyone care?

I'd never thought about it myself until a few years ago, when a book I had written was translated into Chinese and I was invited to mainland China to speak about it. The book was a history of sexual attitudes, and I was used to readers around the world responding to it in different ways. But this time, something else happened, too. Though my contract prohibited any changes, the translation was censored – when the proofs arrived, I noticed that various things were missing. It turned out that an editor had removed them because in his view they were 'not appropriate'. When I pushed back, the editor-in-chief became involved. Eventually, I was told by email that the publishers had referred my complaints to 'the officials at the Press and Publication Bureau' in Nanjing, who had the final word. Those government censors agreed to reinstate a few of the cuts, but insisted on retaining the others.

In China, censorship was hard to ignore. Every newspaper, broadcaster and publishing house was owned by the state and expected to advance its ideological mission; millions of invisible monitors sanitized all online behaviour around the clock. As I travelled around, it dawned on me that I was witnessing something of a historical novelty. In the face of the internet, supposedly the most liberatory technology of free expression ever invented, the Chinese Communist Party seemed to have unleashed every tool previously devised to control opinion, as well as some totally new ones – and it was winning.

This was not supposed to be happening. For decades, western politicians had proclaimed that greater economic freedom would inevitably lead Chinese society to become more politically liberal, too. At the start of the twenty-first century, they were equally certain that the spread of the World Wide Web would speed up this process. Across the globe, free speech was meant to advance hand in hand with free trade. It might be true that the Chinese were trying to tame the internet, American president Bill Clinton quipped in 2000, but that would never work – 'Good luck! That's sort of like trying to nail Jell-O to the wall.'

Yet I was not entirely surprised by what I found. My trip took place in 2015, when Hillary Clinton was widely presumed to be the likely next president of the United States. A decade earlier, the best-selling Chinese edition of her memoir had been secretly censored by its publishers, who had rewritten and removed many passages on politically sensitive topics. These actions were outrageous, Clinton said when she found out, but also 'increasingly futile' – in the age of cyberspace, Chinese citizens would surely be ever more able to access the truth for themselves.

I'd noticed this story because, as it happened, the same, highly distinguished Chinese press that had done this to her book was now publishing mine. And then, on my final evening in China, I found myself having dinner with one of their senior editors. As we sat talking, it emerged that he was none other than the translator of Clinton's book, the very person who all those years ago had expurgated her text. I was transfixed, and eagerly tried to pump him for information. What was it like to be a censor, I wanted to find out. How did one know where the line was between the permissible and the impermissible – what words and topics were off limits, or not? What happened when the political situation changed and the guidelines altered? How did the officials at the Press and Publication Bureau communicate with him? (Mainly by phone, it turned out.) As my questions came tumbling out, he smiled condescendingly. We don't really use the word 'censor', he corrected me. When we work on a text, we prefer to think of it as 'tailoring'. A little snip here, a cut there, some patching up, and look – now it fits much better.

It struck me that this was exactly how official censors in eighteenth-century Europe had also often conceived of their work: as a kind of helpful, editorial collaboration with authors, intended to improve rather than diminish their text. The word 'censor' itself, both in its original Roman usage, and when resurrected in post-medieval Europe, simply described a public-spirited official whose job was to supervise the community's morals. What's more, for centuries, before 'liberty of the press' and 'free speech' became prominent ideologies, people everywhere had taken for granted that speech, writing and printing should be publicly regulated. In pre-modern courts, ordinary men and women were continually suing each other for speaking or writing bad words; their governments likewise routinely policed such things for the greater good. No one conceived of freedom of expression as a fundamental personal right. So why – and exactly when – did this change? What was the history of free speech?

Frustratingly, when I got back home to Oxford and tried to find books on the subject, it turned out that, although endless volumes had been written on censorship in every time and place you could think of, the history of free speech as a modern concept had attracted almost no attention – except from Americans fixated on their First Amendment. But then contemporary uses of the term appeared equally unclear – it mainly seemed to be a slogan that people brandished to gain publicity, or denounce their opponents.

These things were on my mind a few months later when, in the summer of 2016, I moved to America to take up a new job. Before long, I woke up one day to find that the citizens of my new homeland had not, after all, elected Hillary Clinton to be their next president. Instead, they had chosen a dangerously unhinged demagogue – a man who appeared to have catapulted himself into the most powerful office in the world mainly by broadcasting outrageous and hateful lies to tens of millions of people on social media. His elevation to the presidency only made this problem worse. No one could stop it, it seemed – it was all bound up with the sacrosanct right to free speech. Of course, the whole world was full of dangerous, lying demagogues. But the way that Americans talked about 'free speech', indeed obsessively celebrated it, was remarkably different from how it was conceived of in Britain, or Europe, or indeed in India, China, Indonesia, or anywhere else that I knew of. Why was this? When had these cultural differences come about? And how, I began to wonder, might tracing the history of free speech help me make sense of its contours in the modern world?

*

Now that I am myself an American citizen, I've come to understand how my compatriots think about free speech. But I am also still an Englishman, as well as Indian by inheritance, and I grew up in Cold War Europe. So I'm keenly aware of how differently cultures around the world treat freedom of expression; of how globally distinctive the current American approach is; and of the extent to which this is not a matter of reason but essentially of faith. The meaning of the First Amendment is a complicated legal doctrine, but it is also a kind of secular religion, with its own shifting dogmas and hagiography.

None of these things can be easily explained if you study the history of free speech only as a national question. Given how much had already been written about the evolution of American free-speech ideas, for example, I didn't presume I'd uncover anything new. But to my surprise I did, almost immediately – partly just by approaching the evidence in a comparative way. To see what is different, you need to compare cultures with one another, and explore how their historical trajectories overlap or diverge. And there's another reason why a transnational approach is essential. The liberties of speech and of the press have always been international concepts, constantly borrowed and reinvented across borders. Whenever people invoked these freedoms in the past, they were invariably comparing their own situation to what had happened elsewhere, in other times and places. We still do that. Free speech means different things in different cultures, but it's also an archetypal global concept, which requires a global history.

That doesn't mean a comprehensive history of freedom of expression in every period and place – that would be an unreadable book. It would also be unwritable, because there is no single history of free speech. Despite our widespread desire to see the history of free speech as a story of intellectual progress, and despite the sophistication of its various theorists over the ages, it has always been a weaponized mantra, rather than a completely coherent concept. That is precisely why we can never agree on its exact definition. Free speech is not a natural condition and censorship unnatural, as treatments of these subjects often imply. Nor is it the case, as is usually presumed, that freedom of speech is basically a matter of what can be freely said. Its contours are never defined only by content. Nor, finally, is liberty of expression simply what arises from reducing restrictions. On the

4

contrary, it is itself a deeply artificial concept. Both its theory and its practice always have a distinctive shape of their own. To trace that changing form, as this book will do, requires more than simply charting shifting taboos about particular words and ideas. It is also, always, about uncovering the unequal distribution of power: who can speak, and who is silenced; whose voices are amplified, and why. And it is about how these imbalances have been affected by the changing media landscape over the past five hundred years and more – from societies that were mainly oral, through the invention and spread of printing, right up to the global media revolutions of our own times. Those are the deeper, more illuminating questions about the history of free speech that this book will pursue.

In order to answer them, I have highlighted what seemed to me the most significant themes and episodes in the invention and spread of this slippery yet ever-appealing set of ideals. Laws and their enforcement are key indexes of how cultures define and practise liberty of expression – as well as of the distribution of power within those societies. Judicial developments thus play an important role in the story. Yet this is not a book about legal history but about the politics of free speech more generally, and its evolution over time – especially as an ideal. As will become clear, the theory of free speech has always lagged behind its practice – greed, technological change and political expediency invariably outpace lawmakers and philosophers.

Free speech is a dangerous idea for two reasons. One is its potential to unsettle orthodoxy, give voice to rebels and iconoclasts, and rouse people to action. That is why we tend to celebrate it. But the other reason is more troubling. Throughout history, this resonant ideal has also been perpetually manipulated by the powerful, the malicious and the self-interested – for personal gain, to silence others, to sow dissension or to subvert the truth.

Freedom of expression also can take many forms – from clothing and behaviour to film, music, cartoons and art of all kinds. But its modern history is especially bound up with the medium of print. In the eighteenth and nineteenth centuries, when free speech exploded into a globally influential ideology, the printing press was the most powerful technology of communication the world had ever seen. For that reason, laws and discussions about expression always focused especially on the liberty of printing. The final chapter of this book explores how that privileging of the press influenced attitudes to speech itself, and to later mass media like radio, television and the internet. Until then, we will be focusing largely on the spoken, written and printed word.

My argument also pays special attention to the anglophone world – setting it in a comparative framework, and drawing out its peculiarities. That is not just because some of the earliest and most influential models of speech and press freedom were developed there, but also because globally, in our own time, American media companies have come to dominate the online marketplace of communication. However we feel about this, all of us would benefit from understanding when, why and to what extent the English-speaking world evolved a distinctive outlook towards speech, and from contrasting this with the historical trajectories of other cultures.

Finally, the book approaches its subject at different scales of enquiry, at times zooming in to analyse in detail crucial individuals and ideas, at others panning out to survey broader topics and questions. The opening three chapters take us from the world before free speech to the invention of the modern concept in the early eighteenth century. Then, over the next four chapters, we'll explore how this ideal was manipulated to different effect in contrasting global settings, by various kinds of speakers: in the white-supremacist slave societies of the Caribbean and North America; in the poor, intellectually peripheral kingdoms of Scandinavia, which nonetheless passed the world's first free-speech laws; in France and the United States, whose intertwined early free-speech history had remarkable, far-reaching consequences, unnoticed until now; and by women and men, slavers and abolitionists, conservatives and radicals, fighting for different causes across Europe and America. The final chapter of the book, which explores the momentous history of changing twentieth-century American views and laws, also does so comparatively – especially by highlighting the enduring but underappreciated influence on American attitudes of international socialist and communist critiques.

The main reason for examining the subject in this way is to show that, wherever one looks, liberty of speech was never a stable concept either in theory or in practice, but always shaped by changing local priorities. Just as free speech has no single meaning in the present, so too in the past; one cannot analyse its evolution using fixed comparative categories. On the other hand, press and speech liberty was not a completely free-floating set of ideas: it also developed powerful intellectual lineages, which persist up to the present. Some of the chapters therefore explore in depth how this process of reinvention and appropriation took place at critical turning points. For example, one of the reasons for the distinctiveness of anglophone practices was the extraordinary sway of two key English texts: an eighteenth-century collection of anonymous essays entitled 'Cato's Letters', which essentially invented the modern ideal of political free speech, and the nineteenth-century treatise *On Liberty* by the philosopher John Stuart Mill, which developed it further in various original ways. In both cases, their arguments appeared to contemporary and later readers to be compellingly authoritative – yet they were, in fact, secretly shot through with personal prejudices and intellectual flaws that tell an ominously different story.

As we shall see, before the modern concepts of press and speech liberty were first conceived, people for millennia had thought very differently about the power of expression, and many of those presumptions still partly inform our outlook today. Ideals of free speech also evolved at different times for different purposes. There were ancient conceptions of it – as channelling God's voice, or boldly advising a ruler. There was a Renaissance, scholarly version, which underpinned the academic exchange of the Republic of Letters, as well as a Protestant one, centred on freedom of conscience. But the most consequential ideal was the right to speak out on matters of public concern. That was the last kind of free speech to be fully theorized, and it took diverse forms across European cultures, even as everywhere it was acknowledged to be the most obviously important. That type of expression – political speech, loosely defined – remains at the core of how we think about free speech around the world today, and it will therefore be the main focus of this book.

Whatever their differences, all modern models of free speech were originally western creations. Non-European cultures before 1700 had sophisticated cultures of oral, written and printed communication; some had long tolerated, even encouraged, freedom of religious expression, frank royal counsel and other forms of outspoken debate. But the specific concepts and practices traced in this book, especially that of liberty of speech and of the press as political rights, were invented in Europe and exported from there. How they came to be imposed and interpreted in different circumstances around the globe is therefore also a story about imperial practices and their legacies into the present. What did it mean for European settlers to claim liberty of speech while keeping other-skinned populations in bondage, denying them an equal voice, or purporting to 'civilize' them? How did people at the time make sense of this? What did freedom of speech signify to natives, slaves and anti-colonial activists? And what have been the lasting, postcolonial effects of this history? These general questions are examined throughout, and in detail in the two penultimate chapters, which trace the history of free speech in India from its colonial beginnings to its present, postcolonial state. Because I have chosen to focus on those places where the ideas of freedom of speech and of the press were earliest and most influentially taken up, the scope of my analysis leaves out later developments in the Far East, Africa and Latin America: I hope that historians of those parts of the world will be able to extend and correct my hypotheses as necessary.

In exploring these varied issues, my main intellectual stimulus has been the brilliant work of philosophers, lawyers, literary critics, feminist scholars and other thinkers who in recent decades have analysed questions of free speech and censorship in the present, including Catharine A. MacKinnon, Frederick Schauer, Jeremy Waldron, Ronald Dworkin, Robert Post, Stanley Fish and Rae Langton, among many others. These writers often vehemently disagree with one another, and I with them; and sometimes their work centres on topics, such as pornography, with which this book is only glancingly concerned. But part of my aim has simply been to apply their general insights to the study of history.

The traditional, commonsensical notion of free speech is that the more freedom of expression the better, both for individuals and for society – because speech is harmless, compared to action, and free debate advances truth. Likewise, we tend to presume that censorship restricts personal liberty; that it is usually imposed by governments; that it targets unwelcome ideas; and, in short, that it is an unnatural and undesirable practice. By contrast, most of the modern theorists I have mentioned take a rather different view – as, indeed, did many intelligent observers in the past. For example, they treat speech as a form of action, rather than making a strict separation between the two. (As Voltaire once explained to a friend, 'I write in order to act'.) They also tend to be attuned to the fact that authority and dominance take many different forms, not just those exercised by the state. They explore how the voices of the powerful in society can overwhelm those of the powerless, and how this is equally true of norms and laws about freedom of expression. The creation and interpretation of rules about 'free speech' is a perennially mutable and politicized process: freedom is never equally distributed. Nor is censorship only exercised by governments: formal and informal rules about expression are ubiquitous. We label such restraints 'censorship' when we disapprove of them, but in truth they are inescapable. That is because they are inherent in ordinary social norms and differentials of power, but also for a more fundamental reason. Communication itself always depends on rules and restrictions, simply to be intelligible – even when you're just talking to yourself in the shower, you're obeying some of those. Freedom requires constraint.

These are some of the intellectual approaches that have inspired me. I hope that my analysis will in turn persuade general readers, as well as lawyers, philosophers and other students of modern free speech, that its history can help us better understand and navigate its conundrums in the present. For my ultimate purpose, reader, is not to tell you *what* to think about free speech, but *how* to think about it, as a global as well as a local matter – to explain how we got into our current predicament, to show that history complicates our contemporary presumptions, and to suggest that it also raises new questions, and possibilities, for the future.

I

The Power of Speech

For most of history, freedom of speech as we understand it today was not an intelligible concept, let alone an ideal. Sometimes, as we'll explore, people aspired to 'speak freely', outside the bounds of normal convention, for example when warning about imminent peril. But that was an exceptional mode, with its own long-established rhetorical rules. Overwhelmingly, pre-modern societies stressed the dangers, rather than the benefits, of outspokenness.

That was because they knew that words were powerful. In every culture in the world, speech was used to summon supernatural forces, through spells, curses, oaths, vows, prayers, blessings and incantations. In every culture, too, bad words could foment political discord and social disorder, divide families and injure reputations. Of course, even in largely illiterate societies, talking had always been understood to be an action of a particular kind. The moral code of the ancient Zoroastrians of Persia distinguished 'good thoughts, good words and good deeds' from one another, as having different effects in the world. So, too, sixteenth-century Europeans knew, as Shakespeare put it, that 'words are but wind': they were slippery and undependable things. But the overriding fact that everyone took for granted was that speech could be immensely potent, and should be carefully used. Every ancient civilization had taught this. 'A word is a bird,' an Assyrian proverb warned, 'once released, no man can recapture it.' 'All things are founded on speech,' cautioned the earliest Indian law code. 'A man who steals speech is guilty of stealing everything.' 'Be a craftsman in speech,' an Egyptian ruler was instructed, two thousand years before the birth of Christ, for 'the tongue is a sword to a man, and speech is more valorous than any fighting.'

These were the principles that Jews and Christians inherited and perpetuated in their own Near Eastern and European cultures over the centuries that followed. At the heart of medieval Christianity was the ritual of transubstantiation, whereby the pronouncing of magical utterances turned wine and bread into the very body and blood of Christ. The Bible too was full of warnings about the force of speech. 'Death and life are in the power of the tongue,' said the Book of Proverbs. 'The tongue is a fire, a world of iniquity,' warned the apostle James. 'The tongue can no man tame; it is an unruly evil, full of deadly poison.' Other scriptural passages compared it to a scourge, a rod, a razor, a sword, a bow, an arrow, a deep pit or a burning fire – words were dangerous and deadly weapons.

As a result, the public policing and punishing of speech was a central feature of every pre-modern Christian society. Spoken words could be treated as crimes against another person, against the whole community, against the government or against God himself. By the middle ages, this was taken for granted. An English law of 1275 declared it a crime to 'tell or publish any false news or tales' that might create discord between the king and his people, on pain of imprisonment or worse. In 1378, the so-called Statute of Gloucester likewise prohibited slander, 'false news' or 'horrible and false lies' uttered against any noble or great officer of the realm. Ordinary men and women, too, frequently defended themselves at law against the bad words of others. Suits for defamation, 'scolding' and the spreading of false tales were extremely common in all kinds of courts throughout the later middle ages; verbal injury was punished as strictly as physical violence, and sometimes more. In medieval Iceland, where poetry was seen as an especially potent form of language, special laws restricted not only mocking verse but also unwanted adulation – if a man wrote an unsolicited love poem to a woman, she could have him punished for it. Most serious of all, in every community, were bad words against God: heresy and blasphemy, the two greatest injuries to divine authority, were both essentially crimes of speech.

The policing of expression was further tightened in the sixteenth and seventeenth centuries. The fracturing of Christianity into many opposing churches during the Reformation and Counter-Reformation created a new fixation with discovering and suppressing heterodoxy. As a result, both Catholics and different varieties of Protestants devoted themselves to continually monitoring and correcting the thoughts and words of their congregations. If you were to get tipsy in a tavern, as Alexander Champion of Wiltshire did one day in 1612, and speculate that heaven and hell were like your table and bench – so that, look, you could step from one to another! – that single slip could land you in the local church court for blasphemy. And, as everyone knew, if you persisted in serious heterodoxy, you would be executed: that's what happened to thousands of European men and women who were burnt at the stake during the sixteenth and early seventeenth centuries.

Secular governments, too, were increasingly intrusive about people's views. As monarchs in this period expanded their powers of warfare, taxation and religion, they likewise sought to wield ever-closer control over the opinions of their subjects, even inventing the usefully vague new crime of 'sedition' (essentially, disloyal speech) to facilitate this. Because verbal disaffection might easily infect others, it had to be rooted out. In Thomas More's *Utopia* (1516), it is a capital offence to discuss public affairs outside the assembly. Shortly afterwards, at the height of Henry VIII's political and religious changes, more than a hundred English men and women were executed in the space of just six years, for uttering supposedly treasonous or 'seditious' words. (More himself ended on the scaffold in 1535 on similar grounds – for refusing to swear a new loyalty oath.)

That was an exceptionally savage episode. But the underlying principle was shared by all European governments of the sixteenth and seventeenth centuries: it was imperative to punish disloyal speech. Indeed, we mainly know about popular political opinions in this period because men and women by their thousands got into trouble for expressing them. If you were unwise enough to speculate publicly about your king or queen's person or policies, you were liable to be arrested, pilloried, flung into jail, fined ruinously large amounts of money, or worse – a Scottish law of 1585 made spoken or written 'reproach, or slander' of the monarch or their laws a capital offence. In 1579, when the puritan (that is, zealously Protestant) lawyer John Stubbs dared write a pamphlet criticizing Queen Elizabeth's marriage negotiations with a French prince, he and his printer and publisher were punished by having their right hands chopped off at the public marketplace in Westminster. In later decades, laws against insubordinate criticism were extended to cover any 'magistrate or other public person', as well as the monarch and the government in general.

Beyond religious deviance and political criticism, many other kinds of expression were also dangerous. Spells and curses had been feared since time immemorial; the uttering of such bad words also lay at the heart of many seventeenth-century witchcraft prosecutions. In Scotland, statutes in 1551, 1561, 1567, 1609, 1645 and 1649 made cursing and swearing punishable by fines, public shaming and even death. Similar legislation was passed in England and its overseas colonies throughout the seventeenth century (including in Ireland – where the practice of malediction was so ingrained, not least among the Catholic clergy, that it remained a central feature of daily life well into the twentieth century). Ordinary communities also regularly punished women and men whose loose, unbridled tongues marked them out as 'scolds' and 'barrators': by 1600, every town and village in England was supposed to have installed a 'cucking-stool' for that purpose. In Scotland, they used the 'branks' – an iron cage and gag locked around the head of the offender. Bad words could not be allowed to disorder the harmony of the community.

Nor could they be tolerated between individuals. From the later sixteenth century onwards, interpersonal suits for defamation and slander became even more common than they had been in the middle ages, flooding the courts. Everyone agreed that insulting or insubordinate speech could seriously damage a person's standing in the community and was a breach of the peace. When, in January 1640, a Salisbury tailor got into an argument with one of his clients about a long-overdue bill, and had the temerity to assert that 'he was as good a man as the other', he soon found himself in court for this, condemned to pay damages. It was not just the honour and credit of monarchs and governors that needed to be publicly policed and defended against opprobrious words, but that of all reputable citizens – every year, thousands of men and women resorted to law to do just that.

In practice, of course, the pre-modern regulation of speech, as of other kinds of behaviour, was always patchy. Pre-modern communities and governments did not have infinite powers of surveillance or enforcement. Their world was full of noisy, loose, insubordinate, heterodox and otherwise dangerous talk that went unpunished or unnoticed. The exact limits of the law were fluid, changeable and frequently contested. Its reach inevitably constrained some people more than others: the words of shop women and servants were more obviously inhibited and liable to be punished than those of aristocrats. Nonetheless, this was also a world in which people in general thought very differently about words, actions and liberty. Instead of valuing freedom of expression, their main preoccupation was to limit it.

WORDS AS WEAPONS

Underlying this outlook was an age-old recognition of the power of words and the dangers of unbridled speech. As the Old Testament declared, 'The stroke of the whip maketh marks in the flesh: but the stroke of the tongue breaketh the bones.' Until the eighteenth century,* it was a commonplace that speaking ill of someone or something could be *more* harmful than any physical action. As Robert Burton put it in *The Anatomy of Melancholy* (1621), 'a bitter jest, a slander, a calumny, pierceth deeper than any loss, danger, bodily pain or injury whatsoever'. 'Many times a *scorn* cuts deeper than a *sword*,' the poet and preacher John Donne agreed.

In largely face-to-face cultures, where personal reputation was everything, verbal and physical violence were therefore commonly conflated or conjoined. Aside from the security of property, an early seventeenth-century legal treatise explained, the twin aims of the law were to protect persons against bodily harm and to preserve 'their good names from shame and infamy' – defamation was equivalent to assault. For Thomas Hobbes, likewise, it was a foundational principle of human society that no one should be permitted to 'declare hatred or contempt of another', 'by deed, word, countenance, or gesture'. On such grounds, some early law codes permitted a man to kill another outright in response not just to physical assault but also to a severe insult. In medieval Iceland, for example, 'if a man calls another man womanish or says he has been buggered or fucked . . . [he] has the right

---

* What changed then is explained in Chapter 10.

to kill.' In later centuries, the same connection between verbal and corporal aggression was manifested in the conventions of the personal duel. The ritualized exchange of spoken, written and printed words was central to its conception of how personal honour was injured and defended; so was the basic point that a person's reputation was as valuable as their life; so too the intimate overlap between rhetorical and physical combat.

It was equally taken for granted that disorderly speech between individuals disrupted the community: it was not just a private but a public problem. Many laws epitomized this. A much-invoked English Act of 1551 penalized quarrelling in a church or churchyard. Defamation cases were sometimes brought by public prosecutors, on behalf of the community, rather than by the injured party. In the 1650s, the puritan government of Oliver Cromwell went so far as to prohibit not just overt insults and abuse, but all 'provoking words or gestures': any language that gave offence could be prosecuted. As the record makes clear, those enforcing such laws drew a direct connection between neighbourly discord and seditious speech against the state itself. European colonies across the oceans operated on the same basis, so that the founding laws of Pennsylvania in 1682, for example, prohibited not just 'offences against God, as swearing, cursing, lying, profane talking [and] obscene words', but also stipulated that 'all scandalous and malicious reporters, backbiters, defamers and spreaders of false news, whether against magistrates, or private persons, shall be ... severely punished, as enemies to the peace and concord of this province', as would anyone who 'shall abuse or deride any other for his or her different persuasion and practice in matters of religion'.

The principles underpinning this world view were rehearsed at length by many popular moralists of the sixteenth and seventeenth centuries. The first basic fact that they stressed was that speech was a physical act – and that, of all the parts of the human body, the tongue was by far the hardest to control. It was 'subject to more errors, slips and failings, than the hand, or any other member of the body', explained the puritan Edward Reyner, and needed constant watching and bridling. Like many others, he pointed out that God had created the lips and teeth as a physical guard, 'to keep the tongue in, and hath shut it up in the mouth as in a cloister ... to teach it modesty, and keep it under restraint, and make it slow to speak' – and yet that was not enough. 'Like a wild pampered horse', 'a cage full of unclean birds' or 'the chariot of the Devil', it often broke loose and created havoc.

Controlling your tongue was therefore a difficult, lifelong struggle. Ideally, one's speech should always be modest, reverent, truthful and sparing – learning when to keep silent was central to all codes of correct behaviour. But, in reality, both the temptations of the devil and the inherent corruption of human nature meant that tongues were perennially slipping out of control. As a result, evil words were everywhere: 'swearing, blaspheming, cursed speaking, railing, backbiting, slandering, chiding, quarrelling, contending, jesting, mocking, flattering, lying, dissembling, vain and idle talking overflow in all places'.

This was a serious problem, because pre-modern people took for granted that evil talk did real damage. It didn't just injure individuals: it poisoned the whole community. Bad words were like an infection: they defiled both speaker and hearers. Words could also provoke supernatural power. Spells brought out the devil; oaths summoned God; blasphemies assaulted him. History was full of men, women and children whose 'offending tongues' had been divinely punished by horrible deaths – the evil organ swelling up in their mouths to choke them, or bitten off, or eaten up by worms; or their whole bodies smitten with leprosy, swallowed up by the earth, consumed by fire or eaten alive by bears.

This focus on the physicality of bad words explains why their punishment often focused on the defective limbs that had allowed them to escape into the world. Just as Stubbs and his accomplices had been made to lose the hands that had written and published disloyal expressions, so not hearing the truth, and speaking ill instead, was to be punished by cutting off a person's ears, or nailing these to the pillory, or by 'burning in the face with letters, or by gagging his two jaws in painful manner, and so he cannot speak any words . . . or by burning through his tongue, or perchance cutting off his tongue', as an English judge advocated in 1577.

Nowadays, we don't tend to believe that human nature is intrinsically corrupt, or that spells can summon the devil. Physical mutilation seems to us a cruel and abhorrent punishment. Yet it's hard to deny the more basic pre-modern truth about the potency of words. Speech is an action; words do have consequences. They can be at least as damaging as physical blows. Anyone who has ever parented a teenager, or lived through a painful break-up, or been the victim of verbal abuse, knows this – words can leave deep and lasting scars. And this is not just a matter of damage to individuals, but to our society as a whole. All cultures of the past, and most in the present, acknowledge the fact that the repetition of harmful words and lies can poison public discourse: it can perpetuate sexual and racial discrimination, fuel religious persecution, sow social and political division, undermine legitimate political and scientific authority, or pave the way for violence. In other words, our modern distinction between words and actions, and their supposedly different potency, is just a convenient myth. As we shall see in the course of this book, it makes the ideology of free speech possible, but it's also an inherently unstable fiction. If we want to understand the history of free speech, it's best to be clear from the outset about that problematic fact.

HIERARCHY AND AUTHORITY

Another foundation of our current free-speech attitudes is that everyone's voice deserves an equal hearing. In the political and social worlds of the past, people tended to presume the opposite. Everybody took for granted that human societies were naturally hierarchical, and that the speech of higher persons had greater authority than that of their inferiors. As well as instilling the importance of verbal discipline and civility in everyone, early Hindu codes of law and ethics sharply distinguished between the speech rights of different castes. The speech of a Brahmin, the highest rank, was more powerful than that of a lower person; that person in turn 'should never say anything unpleasant to [the Brahmin] or use harsh words against him'. A low-caste man who spoke disdainfully of higher castes would have 'a red-hot iron nail ten fingers long . . . driven into his mouth'; for 'grossly abusive words . . . his tongue shall be cut off'; if he dared dispute with higher castes about law or ethics, 'the king should pour hot oil into his mouth and ears'.

An analogous mindset is visible in the earliest known English law about words. In the year 695 CE, when the Anglo-Saxon king Wihtræd of Kent set down his law code, he decreed his own word to be 'incontrovertible': it was to be accepted without any oath or formality. The same was true of the word of a bishop. But below them was a strict hierarchy of status: the lower you were, the more trouble you had to go to in order to prove yourself. And no provision at all was made for the voice of any woman, child or slave. In 1215, Magna Carta, the great English charter of rights, likewise decreed that a woman's testimony was inadmissible at law in any case of criminal death, save that of her own husband.

Similar principles continued to hold sway in the sixteenth and seventeenth centuries. Every act of personal communication, whether oral or written, was calibrated according to status. When addressing another person, you would always consider their relative rank and tailor your language accordingly. 'If inferior persons write to you,' the Yorkshire gentleman William Wentworth advised his son Thomas in 1604, and *if* 'it be fit to return them answer', then 'either do it by word of mouth, or cause one of your servants to write to him your answer' – to write back in person to a subordinate would be demeaning. In similar vein, in his best-selling Elizabethan guide to conversation, William Perkins reminded his readers that 'our elders and betters ... must [always] have leave and liberty to speak first'; that 'young men and women [are] only to speak when they are asked'; and that 'servants and children' should never answer back. These were pretty universal principles. Aztec youths in sixteenth- and seventeenth-century Mexico were taught essentially the same things about 'good speech'.

Among these many intersecting hierarchies of status that of sex was the oldest and most obvious. Other things being equal, male speech was more authoritative, and more permissible, than that of women. In all the religious, social and legal codes that Near Eastern and European men drew up over the centuries, the basic notion that women should hold their tongue was a perennial theme, as was the presumption that they, as the weaker sex, were more prone to dangerously loose and ungoverned talk. The Bible itself ordered that women must 'keep silence in the churches: for it is not permitted unto them to speak' nor 'to teach, nor to usurp authority over the man, but to be in silence'. In this world view, verbal restraint was a mark of female virtue, garrulousness or 'freedom' of speech in a woman signified immodesty, and many subjects were 'improper' for female conversation. In almost the earliest text of European literature, Homer's *Odyssey*, the hero's son sharply admonishes Odysseus's grief-stricken wife Penelope, when she speaks out publicly in a gathering of men: 'Mother, go back up to your chamber, and busy yourself with your own work, the loom and the distaff, and bid your handmaids attend to their own tasks; but speech will be the business of men.' Penelope obeys, as Homer tells us in the next verse: 'She took to heart the clear good sense in what her son had said.' Female speech was always less free than that of men; female outspokenness more 'unnatural' and disorderly. Of the many sexist presumptions that our modern world has inherited from the distant past, this is surely one of the most deeply embedded and perniciously enduring.

In practice, of course, as far back as we can see, all these hierarchies of speech were also continually being challenged and subverted. When writing on their own behalf, women were perfectly capable of pointing out that stereotypes about their conduct were but male slanders and fantasies – this was a central theme of European feminist argument at least as early as Christine de Pizan's *Book of the City of Ladies* (1405). In fiction, the many tensions between male and female speech norms were rich subjects for comedy and contemplation. In real life, too, queens, female aristocrats and other powerful women spoke publicly in ways that crossed the gender divide. In 1648, in the midst of civil war, the rich and well-connected Maryland settler Margaret Brent, acting as executor for one late governor and legal representative for another, addressed the new colony's Assembly 'and requested to have vote in the house for herself – and voice also'; being denied, she 'protested against all proceedings in this present Assembly, unless she may be present and have vote'.

Less exalted women, too, expressed strong political opinions. They also continually raised their voices in public to abuse each other – or to sue over such defamation. The limits of female speech were constantly tested and reinscribed by women themselves, as well as by men. Small wonder that her sex prized talk, as the erudite Bathusa Makin summed up in 1673: 'It is objected against women, as a reproach, that they have too much tongue: but ... the tongue is the only weapon women have to defend themselves with, and they had need to use it dextrously.' In short, the reason that so much effort had to be put into policing words was that, even in a world that generally deprecated freedom of speech, supposedly inferior people constantly spoke irreverently and out of turn.

The same tension was fundamental to pre-modern politics. This was a world in which, in theory, authority always came from above. Only a tiny minority of propertied men participated in national government, and only a handful of the monarch's closest councillors were even permitted to *discuss* royal policy. Those who dared libel a ruler were therefore 'enemies of common society'. As the English government official Sir Thomas Smith memorably put it in 1583, the mass of the population 'have no voice nor authorit[y] in our commonwealth'. 'No account is made of these [people],' he explained, 'but only to be ruled, not to rule other[s].' A century later, when the journalist Henry Carr was convicted for publishing an unauthorized weekly newspaper, the royal judges affirmed 'that no person whatsoever could expose to the public knowledge anything that concerned the affairs of the public, without license from the king ... it is unlawful, whether it be malicious or not'. Yet in practice, as everyone was well aware, people at all levels of pre-modern society did constantly discuss political affairs, and often critically.

Time and again in the pre-modern world, the popular circulation of rumours led to riots, insurrections and social disorder. For most educated contemporaries, this confirmed ancient stereotypes about the ignorance of ordinary people, and bolstered the hierarchical principle that politics should be conducted in secret: even debates in parliament were meant to be strictly confidential. As the brilliant scholar and courtier Francis Bacon put it, 'matters of state ... are no themes or subjects fit for vulgar persons' (even if they liked to think that 'now-a-days there is no vulgar, but all [are] statesmen'). Among the core powers of any sovereign, and key to avoiding civil war, as Hobbes explained in his *Leviathan* (1651), written in the midst of just such a conflict, was that of judging 'what opinions and doctrines are averse, and what conducing to Peace' and of regulating public speech and printed books accordingly.

As a consequence, 'free' speech was mainly thought of as something negative, which disrupted the social, political, religious and cosmic order. People should be publicly punished for bad words, the Queen's Council ordered in 1587, 'for the example of others and restraining that liberty of speech'. A few years later, despairing about the difficulty of suppressing 'malicious pamphlets' that were received as if they were 'the flying sparks of truth', Bacon worried that 'they carry with them a presence and countenance of liberty of speech'. 'The ordinary precursors of civil war', an early seventeenth-century French ambassador agreed, were 'cartoons, defamatory libels' and 'free speaking'. Even King James, who prided himself on allowing 'convenient freedom of speech', issued repeated proclamations in the 1620s against 'the inordinate liberty of unreverent speech' among his subjects – not just the vulgar, but 'every [one] of them, from the highest to the lowest'.

The contrary idea, encapsulated in the proverb *vox populi, vox Dei* ('the voice of the people is the voice of God'), was sometimes invoked by religious polemicists, authors of complaint literature and political theorists. 'Not without good reason is the voice of the people likened to that of God,' argued Machiavelli, 'for public opinion is remarkably accurate in its prognostications.' But he, too, warned against the dangers of slander and public misjudgement, and conceded that 'common opinion' saw the multitude as fickle and easily led astray.

In consequence, all pre-modern governments put huge efforts into restricting and controlling political information and opinion, whether spoken, written or otherwise. Printing presses in this period almost invariably operated under licence; their output was meant to be vetted before publication. Historians usually describe all this as 'censorship'. But that's a rather anachronistic way of interpreting it. Because in the pre-modern world, even when they were mouthing off, people usually didn't presume that they had a *right* to liberty of expression. On the contrary, they largely accepted and agreed with the principle of speech regulation, and enthusiastically participated in it. Partly that was because they believed, much more strongly than we do, in the existence of absolute truth and error. Yet their ultimate concern was not to combat falsehood but to maintain social harmony. Whereas we tend to celebrate freedom of expression as invariably advancing the truth, they saw the relationship between speech and truth as more complicated. For them, speech was not a simple right, but a complicated ethical matter. The permissibility of spoken or written words always depended on their exact circumstance: who was speaking, who was listening, what was the tone and intention of the words, and what was their medium. The words themselves were always only part of the answer; the ultimate judgement was contextual.

For example, though it was generally held that lying was always wrong, many serious theorists of religion and politics also argued that it was sometimes necessary for people to dissimulate and deceive. The notion that speech should be used to conceal the truth was especially developed among persecuted religious groups, such as the medieval Waldensians, the English Lollards, the crypto-Jewish *conversos* of Spain, and underground Catholic and Protestant minorities after the Reformation. But it was also routinely endorsed by leading political commentators, such as Machiavelli, Montaigne, Bacon and Justus Lipsius, on the grounds that dissimulation was an essential tool for rulers and courtiers. As Montaigne observed in 1580, 'truth for us nowadays is not what is, but what others can be brought to accept'.

More generally, it was also a well-established principle that speaking candidly was sometimes wrong, or even criminal. Perkins's *A Direction for the Government of the Tongue* included a chapter about the many occasions when it was necessary to conceal the truth. One should never reveal anything hurtful, dangerous or secret, and always keep quiet about 'the infirmities and sins of our neighbours' – 'if any truth be to the hindrance of God's glory, or of the good of our neighbour', it must be concealed. No one should presume to speak of 'things unknown, things which concern us not, things above our reach'. Instead of individual rights, this outlook prioritized the social fabric. Words, like other actions, should be used to bolster charity and civility, rather than to destroy them. Holding your tongue was as vital as using it. 'Be rather silent than speak ill of any man, though he deserve it,' Elizabeth Jocelin summarized the conventional sentiment in 1622. In the eyes of the law, too, words that created disorder were punishable even if accurate. Truth was not a sufficient defence for anyone sued in the church courts; nor against a charge of sedition. On the contrary, veracity was commonly treated as an aggravating factor – after all, a true accusation was more likely to cause a breach of the peace than a false one.

On the other hand, people in the pre-modern world were also acutely focused on the dangers of untruth. That was why they saw the regulation of speech and print as a vitally necessary safeguard against forgery, falsehood and misrepresentation – what one seventeenth-century observer described as 'that great and immoderate liberty of lying'. Policing expression was about protecting individuals against the damage caused by malice and defamation; it was an ethical struggle to maintain the cohesion of civil society; and it was also about upholding truth and fighting back against lies.

Indeed, the most rigorously policed and suppressed texts in Elizabethan and Jacobean England were not those that set out reasoned religious and political arguments, but ones that trafficked in scurrilous slanders and outrageous conspiracy theories. It was the underground tracts that portrayed Queen Elizabeth as a lustful whore, who had borne many bastards; or 'revealed' that her favourites were adulterers and murderers; or 'exposed' leading churchmen as secret sodomites; or whipped up endless panics about covert plots and uprisings. The same kinds of wild rumours and slanders dominated the world of verbal 'seditious words'. These stories were notoriously popular. They spread like wildfire, they were very hard to suppress, and they didn't just poison people's minds: they motivated them to action. As everyone knew, revolts and risings were invariably provoked and accompanied by popular rumour-mongering.

In early July 1628, for example, just a few years after his accession, a report of the death of King Charles I began to circulate in the borderlands of England and Wales. When the tale reached the town of Llanelli, it set off a mass panic. More than a hundred of the town's inhabitants, apparently under the illusion that a Spanish army had also landed on the coast, set off across the countryside to raise the alarm, 'crying most fearfully' along the way. As they marched, they were joined by more recruits, and the story was elaborated to the effect that the king had been poisoned by the Duke of Buckingham, who had staged a coup and seized the throne for himself. When the crowd swarmed into Swansea, the local authorities immediately sent word of the king's death to the county's chief inhabitants, and publicly announced the news in the market square, where it was greeted 'with a general lamentation of the whole people, who gave out that they feared that the papists would rise up in arms and kill them in their sleep'. By the end of the week the news had spread as far as Cornwall, and much of the south-west coast appears to have been on the alert for invasion and rebellion.

That's just a single instance of how powerfully disruptive a completely baseless political rumour could be – one week in the never-ending pre-modern onslaught of fake news. The story that the Duke of Buckingham was a serial murderer, who had killed his rivals and then successively poisoned both James I and Charles I, was secretly promoted by the undercover propaganda networks of the British monarchy's foreign enemies. It paved the way for the grisly murder of Buckingham's supposed accomplice, Dr John Lamb, and for Buckingham's own very public assassination a few weeks later, in August 1628. It also directly influenced the parliamentary politics of the 1620s, the growing public mistrust of Charles I, and the bitter divisions of the civil wars in the 1640s. In short, it was a slanderous lie whose perpetuation had enormous consequences.

Over the past few decades, historians have uncovered a huge amount about European popular political consciousness from the middle ages through to the eighteenth century. It's clear that, in pre-modern society, people of all ranks talked about news and politics all the time, that they had strong opinions about it, and that this fact was vitally important to the conduct of politics. Historians invariably celebrate these findings, just as they applaud the growth of manu-script and printed news and commentary in this period – as signs of the vitality of popular political opinion, and of the expansion of the public sphere. We see in these developments the origins of our own democratic culture.

And yet what we tend to overlook is that the overwhelming currency of popular political discourse was not reasoned debate but hateful lies and conspiracy theories, inflammatory misinformation, crazy rumours and outright fakery. Politicians themselves often believed and fuelled such falsehoods, as part of their own attempts to pacify or win over public opinion: they actively created forgeries, spread rumours and inflamed people's delusions about conspiracies and cover-ups. Ordin-ary people in turn often trusted this flood of untruth because it seemed plausible – usually such stories embroidered on a few established facts, threw in some topical fears and confirmed existing prejudices. As a result, people supposed they were being given a glimpse into the hidden reality of politics, when in reality they were swallowing a toxic stew of propaganda and untruth.

So when we celebrate the growth of the public sphere, or the failures of pre-modern censorship, or the rise of public opinion, what we're often describing is the growing political influence of a deluded and hugely misinformed public. As recent research has shown, for example, it was the increasing hold of rival conspiracy theories that caused the final breakdown of politics across the British Isles in the 1640s, and the ensuing carnage of the civil wars, in which hundreds of thousands of people lost their lives – precisely the kind of disastrous chaos that the ideology of speech regulation had always warned about, and been intended to prevent.

Out of this cataclysmic breakdown in the regulation of speech and print there eventually emerged new practices and ideas about freedom of expression, as we'll see shortly. The ideal of political free speech developed first in the anglophone world because of the precocious peculiarities of English politics in the late seventeenth and early eighteenth centuries. Yet that in turn was only possible because by 1700 there had already emerged, across Europe, a new theory of *religious* free speech – as part of efforts by intellectuals and rulers, in the fractured world of post-Reformation Christendom, to enable religious enemies to live alongside each other without violence. As we shall see next, the rise of this doctrine was itself a momentous social and intellectual development, which undermined some of the traditional, age-old principles of speech regulation.

2

Tolerating Words

Before 1500, across Christian Europe, religious plurality was a largely unthinkable concept. Even though popular religious practice was never uniform, deviations from the Church's orthodoxy were meant to be treated as error or heresy – dangerous untruths that could not be allowed to spread. The Protestant Reformation of the mid sixteenth century, which fragmented Christendom into ever more numerous warring sects, did not immediately change this basic outlook, but merely multiplied it – each religious group continued to presume that it possessed the sole truth, and to condemn deviant ideas. This led to more than a century of intense bloodshed, not just between Catholics and reformers, but also between the many different Protestant groups that emerged. Yet, in the longer term, the predicament of constant religious strife also gave rise, mainly among Protestants, to new ideas about the potential benefits of allowing differing religious ideas to be freely aired within a single society.

PLURALITY AND TRUTH

This development built upon a much older classical and Judeo-Christian tradition of valorizing the frank speaking of truth. In both the Old and New Testaments, it was clear that God sometimes spoke through prophets, martyrs and saints – and that they in turn could communicate directly with him. For such people to speak out boldly, irrespective of the circumstances, was a sign of virtue and of divine inspiration. From the earliest days of the Church, Christians high and low invoked that model whenever they were minded to deliver potentially unwelcome messages to those in power. In sixteenth-century Scotland, some local congregations even decreed that, to prevent the festering of secret 'back-bite and slander' against parish elders, there should be special biannual occasions when 'every man shall have liberty to speak', to criticize their leaders openly.

These long-standing religious notions of prophesy, jeremiad and reproof overlapped with the secular idea, first developed in Athens in the fifth century BCE, of free speech as a sign of independence – the liberty of the free citizen or the virtuous philosopher to speak their mind on matters of public moment. Such forms of truthful out-spokenness in religious or civic matters (referred to in Greek as *parrhesia*, in Latin as *licentia* or *libertas*) developed into familiar medieval and Renaissance genres of rhetoric. Yet this was a very different concept of 'free speech' from our modern one, and was applied primarily to the question of how best to counsel a superior. In 1523, it was this humanist ideal of frank counsel that inspired Thomas More, as Speaker of the House of Commons in England, to ask the king for his 'gracious licence and pardon' that every member of parliament should 'freely ... and boldly ... declare his advice', without having to fear 'your dreadful displeasure'. This was the origin of parliamentary 'freedom of speech and debate', as it became known. Until the very end of the seventeenth century, this liberty was conceived of as a special, temporary privilege granted to chosen counsellors to deliberate frankly and in secret, in order to offer the monarch their honest advice. On occasion this outlook spilled over into arguments about the exact boundaries of frank counsel or complaints about censorship, especially when unwelcome warn-ings were delivered publicly or in print. But its general conception of free speech was part of the language of hierarchy, duty, deference and decorum – far removed from the modern notion of universal, in-dividual rights.

In the aftermath of the Reformation, however, some zealous Chris-tians developed new ideas about religious freedom of expression. This began with Protestant reformers attacking the Catholic Church's edicts against 'heretical' books, and its other attempts to silence them, which they portrayed as attempts to suppress 'God's holy truth' because it threatened the papists' 'manifest idolatry and palpable abomination'.

It's true that, for their own part, most Protestant groups were also keen to enforce conformity, in order to prevent the spread of error: in 1554, for example, John Calvin instigated the execution of his rival reformer Michael Servetus for publishing heretical ideas. Yet, partly in reaction to such episodes, a few reformed thinkers began to develop a more radical critique of religious censorship. 'To kill a man is not to defend a doctrine, but to kill a man,' argued the influential writer Sebastian Castellio, himself a refugee from both the Catholic Inquisition and the intolerance of Calvin's Geneva: persuasion and debate were the proper responses to heterodoxy. The popular German spiritualist Sebastian Franck went further, arguing that, ultimately, only God could judge the difference between true and false religious beliefs: humans, who could presume no such certainty, should leave each other in peace.

In the face of religious fragmentation, a few sixteenth-century governments, too, experimented with toleration. To ensure peace, economic prosperity and political stability, some allowed private freedom of conscience; others permitted public worship by significant minorities. In Transylvania, the four largest denominations (Catholic, Lutheran, Calvinist and Unitarian) were given equal liberty, on the principle that 'faith is the gift of God' and could not be imposed. In the religiously diverse multi-ethnic republic of Poland–Lithuania, the Warsaw Confederation of 1573, drawn up soon after the horrific Bartholomew's Day massacre of Protestants in France, enjoined peace and cooperation between confessional groups, given the 'great dissidence in the affairs of the Christian Religion in our country, and to prevent any sedition for this reason among the people such as we clearly perceive in other realms'.

These developments were more prudential than principled. But in the newly created Dutch Republic, which experimented with various degrees of practical toleration in the aftermath of a largely Protestant rebellion against Spanish Catholic overlordship, the polymath humanist Dirck Volkertszoon Coornhert in 1582 went so far as to propose a complete liberty for 'the writing, publishing, printing, selling, having, and reading of tracts and books' on religious subjects. 'Freedom,' he wrote, 'has always consisted chiefly in the fact that someone is allowed freely to speak his mind,' and truth was no respecter of status or authority. Lies and errors should certainly be refuted, but this could never be done by force, only by countering them 'verbally or in writing . . . [with] the divine and all-powerful truth herself'. Repression and censorship, by contrast, might 'suppress lies and heresies for a while', but ultimately were 'not just useless, but harmful', because they only made the forbidden ideas seem more interesting and potent, and undermined confidence in the authorities.

Implicit in assertions like those of Castellio and Coornhert were two novel presumptions about conscience and human nature that gained ground in Protestant theological debates from the later sixteenth century onwards. Both helped advance a more explicit case for spiritual freedom of expression. The first was that one's inner convictions could never be changed by force but only through persuasion; the second, that individuals could (and, indeed, should) find their own way to religious truth, and might do so through different routes. Nowadays these seem like unexceptionable views. Yet before 1700 they directly repudiated conventional Christian teaching, which for centuries had stressed the weakness of people's minds and consciences, the necessary guidance of scripture, laws and teachers, and the dangers of religious divergence.

In the middle of the seventeenth century there was also an important practical impetus, which shifted the centre of discussion to the English-speaking world. In 1641, during the civil wars, England's system of governmental print control, which had allowed only a limited number of presses to operate, and required all controversial texts to be approved before publication, broke down. Amid the chaos of combat, a multitude of new religious sects sprang up, and a tsunami of popular religious discussion flooded off London's printing presses. This novel liberty, and repeated efforts to rein it in, forged a fresh connection between freedom of expression and freedom of conscience. The two things were not equally valued: to its advocates, the ultimate aim of liberty of conscience was never diversity, but truth. As the puritan MP Francis Rous explained: 'I contend not for variety of opinions; I know there is but one truth. But this truth cannot be so easily brought forth without this liberty.' The hope was that with 'free trading of truth set on foot, and liberty given to try all things', errors would be exploded, 'straying brethren' set right and Christians united. We all know that 'there is but one truth', agreed the brilliant puritan politician Sir Henry Vane the Younger, 'which ever thrives best in fair and open debates': despite their fallen nature, all humans 'cannot but see good and light when it comes forth, and be in some part convinced of it'.

In the view of such thinkers, Christ's gospel permitted only 'gentle exhortation and friendly admonition' to be used against religious error. Because of their stress on the primacy of 'inner light' as a spiritual guide, and their millenarian beliefs about the 'discovery' of religious truth, they often argued that no one should be punished for sincerely following their conscience, even if it led them into error. Conscientious idolaters were less sinful than mere conformists, urged Vane, for at least they possessed a genuine spirit of inquiry. The influential London merchant and controversialist Henry Robinson took a similar view. Everyone had a perfect right to 'teach or publish erroneous doctrines, which they in their own opinion thought had been sound', and in any religious dispute every party deserved equal 'liberty of speech, writing, printing, or whatsoever else'. To be sure, he conceded, the establishment of such freedom would throw society into a great 'confusion' of divergent religious ideas – but that was preferable to hypocritically forcing people into mere outward conformity to things they did not truly believe. Besides, he mused in 1643, drawing on his own experience of living abroad among Catholics, Jews and Muslims, how could anyone ever be persuaded to change their beliefs and acknowledge error, except in a free exchange of ideas?

Robinson was friendly with many other mid-century advocates of religious free expression, including Roger Williams, William Walwyn and John Milton. Around this time, Milton, an erudite poet and schoolmaster in his mid-thirties, had made a disastrous, short-lived marriage to a teenager he barely knew, Mary Powell. After a few weeks living together, she returned for good to her parents' home. Milton, ever the academic, responded to this personal trauma by publishing a series of learned theological tracts on why a husband should be allowed to divorce his wife if their marriage had broken down (because it was always *her* fault). When these were denounced in parliament as examples of dangerous, unlicensed religious speculation, his anger turned against the whole system of pre-publication print control.

The resulting critique of religious censorship that Milton produced in 1644, a pamphlet entitled *Areopagitica*, was the first detailed treatment of the subject in English. Addressing parliament using the rhetoric of *parrhesia*, it developed the idea that pre-publication licensing was itself a popish invention, aimed at keeping people in the dark. Like previous authors, Milton claimed that such restraint was not just harmful but unnecessary, for in open debate truth always prevailed: 'Let her and Falsehood grapple; who ever knew Truth put to the worse, in a free and open encounter?' But he went further in implying that almost all kinds of knowledge, not just overtly religious writing, was spiritually beneficial – arguing for the benefits of allowing even erroneous and immoral ideas to circulate. This was because truth 'may have more shapes than one', and 'faith and knowledge thrives by exercise ... where there is much desire to learn, there of necessity will be much arguing, much writing, many opinions: for opinion in good men is but knowledge in the making'. Above all, 'the knowledge of good is so involved and interwoven with the knowledge of evil' that exposure to bad books and immoral opinions was actually essential: only by actively engaging with and rejecting vice could one forge true virtue and understanding. 'The liberty to know, to utter, and to argue freely according to conscience' was therefore the greatest freedom of all.

Though his synthesis of them was brilliantly provocative, Milton's basic ideas were hardly original. The saying that 'there is no book so bad that you cannot get some good from it' dated back to the Roman author Pliny, and was a much-rehearsed humanist cliché. But in this case its invocation served a deeply spiritual doctrine. For Milton, as for other puritans who advocated 'free debate', only opinions 'probable by scripture' deserved airing in 'free and lawful debate'. Nor did their testing involve reason so much as divine inspiration. As his hero Henry Vane put it, mere 'fleshly wisdom' or 'natural reason ... will not know what opinion to follow' – 'all the struggling of ... natural understanding' could never divine God's purpose. Instead, 'the light within us must be our guide, to lead us into all that understanding of the Scripture, or other truths, which are fitting for us to know'. It wasn't a capacity given to everyone; it certainly had nothing to do with rights. You had to wait for the Holy Spirit to enter into and enlighten you.

RELIGIOUS AND SECULAR SPEECH

None of these stirring ideals had much immediate effect beyond radical Protestant and sectarian circles. Though considerable liberty of conscience prevailed in England from the 1640s until the restoration of the monarchy and state church in 1660, Milton's views on freedom of expression were extreme, and there is no record of anyone paying them the slightest bit of attention during his own lifetime. Censorship remained widely acceptable; new laws were regularly passed to enforce it. For several years after publishing *Areopagitica*, ironically enough Milton himself worked as a government licenser of printed works.

All this began to change towards the end of the seventeenth century. In 1685, after decades of failed attempts to enforce religious uniformity, the accession of the openly Catholic King James II to the throne, and thus the headship of the staunchly Protestant state church, created a novel constitutional crisis. As part of their power struggle, both the new king and his political opponents tried desperately to win the support of the country's influential minority of Presbyterians, Congregationalists and other Protestant sects. After the invasion and deposition of James in 1688 by William of Orange, his Dutch Protestant son-in-law, in what became known as the 'Glorious Revolution', the English parliament a few months later reluctantly legalized a degree of nonconformity, to shore up support for the new regime by such religious dissenters.

Shortly afterwards it also abandoned the system of pre-publication licensing. Partly this happened because of increasing resentment against the printing monopoly of the London Stationers' Company, but more generally it reflected a lack of agreement about how to control the public discussion of religious doctrine in the new tolerationist environment. In 1695, when the licensing law came up for renewal, members of parliament couldn't agree on a workable solution: and so it simply lapsed. At this point the intellectual arguments for religious free expression, though increasingly prominent, were still deeply controversial. Many orthodox Christians continued to regard tolerance of heterodox ideas as dangerous to the state church. Greater print freedom, likewise, was often condemned for fuelling irreligion. In practice, too, the immediate consequence of toleration was not greater concord but increasingly open religious conflict.

Yet slowly but surely the official establishment of religious plurality did elevate its principles into mainstream presumptions: over time, in the English context, they became explanations of the status quo, rather than radical challenges to it. Milton's *Areopagitica* gradually became a canonical text, after its author's late celebrity and posthumous reputation led to its being rediscovered and popularized by several later seventeenth-century religious and political freethinkers. Similar authority accrued to the writings of John Locke, who in 1689 set out what rapidly became one of the most influential of all European defences of freedom of conscience and expression – not because its claims were original, but because it so fluently repackaged for a general audience all the main lines of Protestant reasoning developed by earlier advocates of toleration.

Locke's *Letter Concerning Toleration* and its three sequels first of all reasserted the premise that Truth (for him, too, a capitalized female entity) always prevailed in open discussion, and that pre-publication censorship, by contrast, only helped to perpetuate falsehoods: 'She is not taught by laws, nor has she any need of force to procure her entrance into the minds of men ... if Truth makes not into the understanding by her own light, she will be but the weaker for any borrowed force.' On the other hand, though continuing to cleave to the presumption that there was in fact 'but one Truth, one way to Heaven', Locke also adopted the position that ultimately it was unknowable, visible only to God. That was one reason why freedom of religion was essential. The other was that beliefs could never be changed by force, and were in any case harmless things – laws and governments should address only outward actions, not inner thoughts. In consequence, Locke advocated a complete freedom for all 'speculative opinions', even 'false and absurd' ones, for 'the business of laws is not to provide for the truth of opinions, but for the safety and security of the commonwealth'. Indeed, he argued, reversing conventional wisdom in the same way as some sixteenth-century tolerationists had done, it 'is not the diversity of opinions (which cannot be avoided), but the refusal of toleration to those that are of different opinions (which might have been granted) that has produced all the bustles and wars, that have been in the Christian world, upon account of religion' – diversity of opinion itself was inevitable, beneficial and harmless.

Both the theory and practice of religious toleration differed considerably across European cultures. In England and its North American colonies, ideals of free expression were from the outset closely bound up with freethinking about religion, as they were too for many writers of the French Enlightenment. But in other places, Protestant as well as Catholic, religious uniformity remained central to national identity long beyond 1700, so that, as we'll see, freedom of speech did not automatically include, or derive from, religious toleration. What's more, even in the most spiritually permissive cultures, there were always two obvious ways in which the freedom of religious speech was limited.

One of these was the question of whose speech should be permitted. The orthodox view remained that women had no place in religious debate, let alone in teaching men. Yet the history of Christianity also included plenty of female prophesy. During and after the Reformation, some radical strands of Protestantism gave further impetus to feminine outspokenness. Women were prominent among separatist sects in seventeenth-century Britain, Holland and New England, such as the Baptists and Quakers, whose doctrines stressed the spiritual equality of the sexes and the ultimate authority of inner conscience. Many such congregations allowed women to debate, vote and prophesy – sometimes even to preach. Yet this remained only a marginal and widely deprecated phenomenon. In 1763, after James Boswell heard a woman preaching at a Quaker meeting, Dr Johnson compared the phenomenon to a dog walking on its hind legs: 'It is not done well; but you are surprised to find it done at all.' In the following century, this deep-seated bigotry against women preaching and publicly debating spiritual matters was to become one of the chief targets of early campaigns for women's rights on both sides of the Atlantic.

The other strong limit on religious free speech was that of tone and content. Advocates of religious liberty invariably stressed that such freedom could never extend to insult. 'Reproachful language, against either men or opinions', should be punished, argued William Walwyn, for 'though reason and argument is allowable and necessary for the finding out of truth, yet reviling railing, bitter taunts, and reproaches, tends to the disturbance of civil peace.' Nor would they permit words that might injure the 'public good' or 'civil society' – a prohibition they usually also extended to spiritual doctrines, such as Catholicism or atheism, which were perceived to have dangerous political implications. Coornhert had strictly excluded anything 'slanderous' or 'seditious': his concern was only 'the improvement of the church'. The overriding aim of puritan writers such as Rous, Milton and Vane was likewise to advance the spiritual enlightenment of God's people. For them, liberty of conscience obviously excluded anything contrary to 'the manifest good of societies' or 'public peace' – such as 'the doctrines of the Papists', 'open superstition', expressions 'impious or evil absolutely either against faith or manners' or anything 'mischievous and libellous'. Such toxic ideas should be prohibited and punished. Locke took the same view: freedom of expression could never extend to 'opinions contrary to human society, or to those moral rules which are necessary to the preservation of civil society'. For him, that meant anything from promiscuity to Catholicism to atheism: even advocating religious intolerance was beyond the pale. In short, no theorist of religious freedom would allow speech that they presumed might provoke social disorder; all of them would punish opinions that they deemed to be dangerous.

As a result, over and over again, both in Europe and its overseas colonies, the most self-consciously tolerationist religious communities ended up censoring, banning and expelling people whose expressions of religious zeal strayed too far. In the 1650s, the English puritan regime proudly enacted one of the most tolerant policies in Europe, readmitting Jews (who had been horribly persecuted and then expelled in the thirteenth century) and allowing all Protestants to worship as they pleased. But most of them abhorred the aggressively unconventional behaviour of the Quakers, the fastest-growing new sect, who distinguished themselves partly by their radical, spiritually inspired attitude to speech and communication – interrupting sermons, condemning the use of oaths, reviling other Christians as fools and idiots, refusing to use titles or to remove their hats in deference to social superiors, referring to everyone as 'thee' and 'thou' rather than the more respectful 'you', and even going unclothed in public as a metaphor of spiritual nakedness. When, in this shameless vein, their leader James Nayler rode into Bristol on a donkey one day in October 1656, seeming to mimic Christ's entry into Jerusalem, he was therefore immediately arrested, and many outraged MPs sought to have him summarily put to death. Only after weeks of impassioned debate on the matter did they give up on his execution – instead settling for boring through his tongue with a red-hot poker, branding his forehead with the letter B (for Blasphemer) and having him publicly pilloried, whipped through the streets and then imprisoned at hard labour. He died not long afterwards. In Massachusetts, fears of Quaker anarchy led similarly to the public flogging, mutilation, banishment and execution of its proselytizers.

The principle of limiting religious free speech according to the prevailing orthodoxy has proved to be impressively long-lasting, even in those societies ostensibly most committed to religious toleration. Across the western world, prosecutions for atheism and blasphemy persisted throughout the eighteenth, nineteenth and twentieth centuries. Indeed, several US state constitutions still, on paper at least, bar atheists from holding office. As late as the 1990s, a non-believing professor of mathematics in South Carolina had to spend years battling at law to be allowed to serve as a notary public; while it took until 2016 for a New Jersey driver to be allowed to keep her vanity licence plate '8THEIST', previously deemed 'offensive to good taste and decency'. Meanwhile, in 2023 the United States Supreme Court ruled that religious liberty of speech allows public businesses to discriminate against certain types of customers – for example, if a fundamentalist Christian business owner is opposed to gay marriage. The question of how far religious freedom of speech and action should extend is obviously far from settled.

This is not a new problem. From the moment that the ideals of liberty of conscience and expression first became influential, they were taken up, manipulated and extended in all sorts of novel ways. In the seventeenth and eighteenth centuries, even arguments for sexual promiscuity were often derived from ideas about religious toleration – despite the urgent attempts that authors like Locke repeatedly made to prevent such (to their mind) dangerous misappropriations of their ideas. No matter how firmly the theorists of religious toleration sought to distinguish between permissible spiritual discussion and impermissible social and political controversy, the distinction between divine and secular subjects was, ultimately, unstable – it rested more on the power to define what was legitimate than on anything else. Soon after 1700, in fact, the rhetoric of religious liberty was to be cleverly hijacked to advance a radically new and momentous argument: the right to political freedom of speech.

3

Inventing Free Speech

Walk into the grand, marbled halls of the United States Capitol in Washington, DC, and you are in the world's greatest centre of power. Every day, the legislators in this building take decisions that affect the lives of millions, sometimes billions of people, within the US and around the globe. Its architecture is meant to convey the dignity of that task – and also to impress upon American lawmakers that they are part of a glorious history. Everywhere there are statues, inscriptions and other reminders of the proud democratic traditions of this pioneering nation, born in a revolution of liberty two hundred and fifty years ago.

In the Senate's part of the building, the walls commemorate important events in the early years of the republic. Over in the House of Representatives' wing, the decor exalts legislative landmarks. At the apex of its central corridor is depicted the nation's foundational law, the constitution. Beside a mural captioned 'The First Federal Congress, 1789' are vignettes of a preacher and a printer, to symbolize the First Amendment. And beneath these images is an explanatory quotation: 'Without Freedom of Thought there can be no such thing as Wisdom & no such thing as publick Liberty without Freedom of Speech'.

It's a rousing and entirely appropriate statement – those lines are taken from the ultimate source of the First Amendment's conception of free speech. Who composed them? The inscription explains – 'Benjamin Franklin 1722'. Type the quote into any internet search engine, and page after page of results will whole-heartedly concur: the sixteen-year-old Franklin coined this sentence in a newspaper column he published in July 1722. What a precocious genius he must have been! It's a favourite 'Founding Fathers' Quote': you can purchase an embossed version of it online.

But in fact the teenaged Franklin didn't come up with these words. He was actually quoting someone else. Delve a little deeper and even the internet will soon disclose that. Scholars have always known who composed this text, as did Franklin's contemporaries. Yet the true story of how and why it came to be written has never been told before. It reveals both how political freedom of speech first came to be conceived of as a mechanism for truth, an antidote to falsehood and the foundation of all liberty – and that, ironically, this new and powerful theory was itself a deliberately mendacious fiction. That, as we shall see, is a paradox whose consequences we are still living with.

CATO'S LETTERS

Between 1720 and 1723, two ambitious London journalists, Thomas Gordon and John Trenchard, published a series of anonymous newspaper articles that came to be known as 'Cato's Letters'. Their paper's editor gave them that name, linking their ideals to those of the famously uncorruptible Roman senator Cato the Younger, who had led the opposition to the tyranny of Julius Caesar.

Trenchard and Gordon's column was an instant hit. Their continually quoted and reprinted collection of around 140 essays became one the most influential Anglo-American works of the eighteenth century. Its overall political theory was fairly derivative. Mainly it purveyed easily digestible nostrums about personal liberty, religious freedom, the limits of government and the nature of knowledge, drawn from weightier recent writers such as Algernon Sidney, Charles Davenant and John Locke, as well as older heroes of republican thought such as Machiavelli. Yet at its heart was a novel set of arguments about freedom of speech and the press. No one before 'Cato' had ever put forward an essentially secular ideal of free speech as a popular political right, let alone made it the very foundation of all liberty. Here is the stirring opening of his first column on the subject, published in the *London Journal* on 4 February 1721 (in all, Cato devoted four essays to the concept, as well as various passing references):

Without freedom of thought, there can be no such thing as wisdom; and no such thing as public liberty, without freedom of speech, which is the right of every man, as far as by it, he does not hurt or control the right of another: And this is the only check it ought to suffer, and the only bounds it ought to know.

This sacred privilege is so essential to free governments, that the security of property, and the freedom of speech, always go together; and in those wretched countries where a man cannot call his tongue his own, he can scarce call anything else his own. Whoever would overthrow the liberty of the nation, must begin by subduing the freeness of speech; a *thing* terrible to public *traitors*.

It is not often one can date a major intellectual shift with such precision. But in this case it is well established that the idea of political liberty of speech as an individual right was first widely discussed in the English-speaking world, and that Cato's was at once its earliest and most celebrated model. This 'daring and well-developed theory of free speech' suddenly 'burst upon the scene', marvels the leading American historian of the subject, like 'a flashing star in an orthodox sky'. Due to its originality, scope and popularity, 'no eighteenth-century work exerted more influence' on British and American ideas about freedom of speech and print. Though countless later writers tackled the topic, they all – whether agreeing or disagreeing – trailed in Cato's wake. Until the publication of John Stuart Mill's *On Liberty* in 1859, it was probably the most important English-language text on the subject.

But how did two little-known journalists suddenly manage to invent an entirely new way of thinking about politics and public debate? For various reasons, this remains an unexplored puzzle. Though the text of Cato's Letters has been much studied, not much has previously been discovered about its authors, and scholarly analyses of their work invariably focus on its overall relationship to eighteenth-century political trends, rather than its specific propositions about speech. Historians of print, meanwhile, tend to note Trenchard and Gordon's new arguments about freedom of expression without interrogating their oddity. Yet, as we shall see, what is puzzling is not just that Cato's theory of speech was so innovative, and its authors' motives so obscure: it is also that it ignored exactly the issues that were highlighted by every other contemporary commentator. Its presumptions about free speech match those of our time, but not those of their own.

To appreciate this, we need to recall that the pre-modern world Trenchard and Gordon were born into had taken a very different view of speech and its regulation, but that by 1720 those age-old presumptions were coming under pressure from new religious, political and technological developments. The previous chapter charted the first of these – the rise of religious liberty. What other changes around this time made possible Trenchard and Gordon's invention of political free speech?

LIBERTY OF THE PRESS

There were two. One was the emergence in later seventeenth-century Britain of a new kind of populist national politics, organized around the world's first-ever enduring political parties, the conservative 'Tories' (who stood for divine-right monarchy and coercive religious uniformity – the so-called 'High Church' position) and the more progressive 'Whigs' (who favoured limits on royal power and toleration for Protestant sects). This transformation greatly enhanced the status of the English parliament as the chief arena of public debate. After the revolution of 1688 a new English Bill of Rights accordingly upgraded the traditional 'freedom of speech and debates' of members of parliament to a constitutional entitlement. Previously it had been only a privilege, granted by monarchs – who had not scrupled to punish members whose speech displeased them. But even the new concept of a right to free parliamentary debate remained predicated on the ancient rhetorical ideal that rulers deserved honest counsel from their chosen advisers during the sitting of their representative body – not at all on the idea that every citizen had a right to address the public.

In fact, as far as the general population was concerned, the new structure of politics created a great paradox. On the one hand – with two rival political parties now constantly appealing to public opinion, more frequent elections than ever before, and the introduction in the 1690s of new forms of public finance, like government bonds and traded stocks, whose fortunes were sensitive to public opinion – the verdict of the people at large became more important than ever. Yet, on the other hand, especially given that the vote was still restricted to only a small minority of propertied men, the rise of party politics itself sharpened the age-old mistrust of popular judgement as irrational and easily swayed – especially by the lies and disinformation of the other side. Were the people behaving as a rational 'public', or a misinformed 'mob'? That became the perennial, critical question.

The second major change, which compounded this problem, was the largely inadvertent breakdown of pre-publication licensing. The consequence of its abandonment in 1695 was not just a surge of religious polemic (whose dangerous tendencies parliament tried to restrain by passing a new Blasphemy Act in 1698), but also a great explosion of printed daily and weekly news, and its eager exploitation by political partisans. Previously such press freedom and appeals to public opinion had only obtained during periods of political breakdown, notably in the 1640s, when embryonic ideas of political free speech were occasionally put into print. Now they became the norm, on a vastly greater scale than ever before. English political discourse rapidly became the most unrestrained and fast-paced in the world.

All this made 'liberty of the press' into a fashionable new phrase. By and large, early eighteenth-century English men and women grew to accept that these novel circumstances were here to stay. They became addicted to argumentative newspapers and pamphlets. And they were often proud that the English press was now 'freer' than in other places. Its champions gradually came to reinterpret the end of licensing as a natural consequence of the revolution of 1688 – part of the progression from tyrannical absolutism to superior, parliamentary monarchy. In 1706, for example, the radical journalist John Tutchin used this patriotic argument to justify his own constant muck-raking attacks on the government of the day. Freedom of expression, he explained to the readers of his paper, the *Observator*, epitomized the superiority of English liberty over French 'vassalage':

> here we dare speak and write the Truth, this is an essential part of our freedom; there they dare not speak or write their minds . . . we are slaves neither in body or mind. We breathe in a free air, we think free,

we are neither pen nor tongue tied, and yet are under restrictions of law; neither has an unbounded liberty.

Yet it was obvious not only that such arguments tended to be self-serving, but also, as Tutchin's one-time colleague Daniel Defoe observed in 1720, that the explosion of newspapers had created a wave of 'false news' – 'forgery, infamy and absurdity' masquerading as fact. It had allowed the art of political lying to reach such heights, noted Jonathan Swift, that mere plodding reality no longer stood a chance: 'Falsehood flies, and Truth comes limping after it ... Like a man who has thought of a good repartee, when the discourse is changed, or the company parted.'* No early eighteenth-century commentator on press freedom failed to notice 'the mischiefs that proceed from the abuse of it, in the daily propagation of news and scandal', lies and misrepresentation.

In addition, although pre-publication censorship had been abandoned, governments retained many ways of controlling the press. Both Tories and Whigs regularly reaffirmed the laws against 'spreading false news, and printing and publishing of irreligious and seditious papers and libels', as a royal proclamation of 1702 put it. Beyond these two loose parties (which, like the population at large, demonized Catholicism) loomed the shadowy counter-revolutionary threat of 'Jacobites' – those who clandestinely worked to return the deposed James II and his descendants to the throne, through intermittent plots and serious rebellions in 1715 and 1745. In this febrile context, pretty much any political criticism could be deemed 'seditious', even if true, and writers and printers were regularly harassed, arrested, put on trial and imprisoned (or even executed, as happened in 1693 and 1719 to the publishers of Jacobite tracts). Until the later 1710s, serious efforts were intermittently made to reintroduce some form of prior censorship, and in 1737 a new Theatre Licensing Act permanently muzzled political criticism from the stage, by giving the government absolute power to censor plays and close theatres. Throughout John Locke's lifetime (1632–1704), the great argument he and others championed,

---

* Swift's equally memorable analogy for why governments controlled the publication of dangerous ideas was that 'a Man may be allowed to keep Poisons in his Closet, but not to vend them about as Cordials'.

that truth would emerge out of free debate, was still largely confined to the spheres of scholarship and religious toleration – and even there it remained contentious.

Nor was there yet any substantive legal or philosophical doctrine of political free speech. Works of political theory ignored the concept, and even radical writers showed little interest in defining its principles. At most, like Tutchin and Defoe, they distinguished vaguely between 'liberty of the press', which was beneficial because it allowed people to discuss public affairs, and, on the other hand, press 'licence' or 'licentiousness', which was to be punished because it spread harmful ideas, slander or lies. Though this distinction was endlessly discussed, it remained essentially a matter of subjective judgement. In the 1640s, a few writings by leaders of the so-called Leveller movement had gestured towards a principled theory of political press liberty. So did a smattering of late seventeenth-century paraphrases of Milton's *Areopagitica*. But none of these passing remarks amounted to a fully worked-out doctrine of political free speech, especially compared with how elaborately the theory of religious freedom of expression was debated and developed.

Of the handful of theorists of free speech before 1720 who even considered the realm of politics, rather than religion, the deist lawyer Matthew Tindal went furthest, when in 1698 he described liberty of expression as not just a spiritual but also a 'civil' and 'natural right', a safeguard of political as well as religious liberty – albeit only in passing, in an argument mainly about freedom of conscience. Most contemporary observers would have regarded this as misguided sophistry. To them, the national parliament was the proper guardian of 'the people's rights', and the only legitimate forum for 'liberty and freedom of speech'. Unrestrained publishing brought not 'liberty' but the chaos of unchecked insult, misrepresentation and the multitude's 'deluded' and 'ignorant' criticisms. No private person's 'natural rights' could trump those of the community: preserving peace, order and comity. When Tutchin was convicted of seditious libel in 1704, the Lord Chief Justice, Sir John Holt, dismissed his 'plausible pretences of defending the rights and liberties of the people' by instructing the jury that, even though the *Observator* had not defamed any particular minister by name, nonetheless its attacks could not be tolerated: for, if writers and printers could not be punished 'for possessing people with an ill opinion of the government, no government could subsist . . . this has always been looked upon as a crime'. This became a famous, if controversial, legal maxim. It built on Holt's previous rulings affirming that judges, not juries, were to decide whether written words were libellous; and that writing such words was always criminal, even if they were never published, or were not intended maliciously, or were in fact true.

The upshot was that 'liberty of the press' remained but an empty, cynical catchphrase: politicians loved to trumpet it in opposition, yet on gaining power invariably trampled all over it. As historians these days point out, 'Nothing could be further from the truth [than] that the early eighteenth century witnessed the emergence of the freedom of the press.' Even the idea was inconceivable: people had essentially no intellectual tools, 'no language to justify the free press'.

THE IMPACT OF JOURNALISM

That is why Trenchard and Gordon's declarations about free speech were so extraordinary. Almost everything about their claims was unprecedented: their breadth, their essentially secular conception, their unconditional valorizing of public judgement. Such audaciousness was typical of their journalism, and it helps explain why Cato's Letters, begun in the midst of an economic and political crisis, were an instant sensation. It turned their first home, the *London Journal*, into the most widely read paper in Britain. More than a dozen collections of the Letters were published even while the essays were still appearing; for decades thereafter, they were endlessly reissued, copied, quoted and translated across the world.

Their success partly derived from their hot new format. A newspaper column could reach thousands of readers immediately, grow its audience over time, and be reprinted without limit by other papers – as well as having an enduring afterlife in book form. In all these ways, Trenchard and Gordon's ideas reached a mass audience, and stayed current for decades, as few books or pamphlets could.

Cato's premises, too, were informed by the greater practical freedoms that the English press now enjoyed. Instead of having to argue against the system of pre-publication licensing, Trenchard and Gordon, adopting Tutchin's rhetoric, set themselves up as the standard-bearers of the new liberties established since the revolution of 1688. Instead of as partisan agitators, they cleverly cast themselves as defenders of established freedoms – warning that these were now under threat from corruption and tyranny by over-mighty governors, and not only from Jacobitism. Just as advocates of religious liberty had long done, they constructed a mythical, self-congratulatory, patriotic history of free speech: in this case, one in which *political* liberty of expression had once flourished in the Roman Republic and was now reborn in England, the freest nation of the modern world.

They also wrote in a fresh, journalistic style: brief, witty and eminently quotable. In keeping with the rhetorical decorum of 'politeness', politicians were rarely identified explicitly: mostly, the argument was conveyed allegorically, and through seemingly neutral, timeless or historical propositions. All this was meant to imply that Cato was beyond the partisan fray, surveying it dispassionately from higher ground.

It proved to be a brilliantly successful tactic. Even while the Letters were still appearing, Gordon steadfastly pretended they never alluded to current events, but provided only 'general reasonings about public virtue and corruption'. They certainly couldn't be criticisms of government ministers, he maintained, tongue in cheek: for as they 'are levelled only at guilty men, 'tis impossible they should give any offence to the innocent managers of public affairs'. By the 1740s, observers of all political colours had come to presume that Cato's maxims were aimed generally 'against all bad administrations', rather than at particular parties.

Yet originally, they were, in fact, highly topical interventions. As the lead column of an avowedly partisan newspaper, they savagely condemned not only Tories, Jacobites and High Church principles, but also many ministers and policies of the current Whig government, especially its handling of the disastrous 1720 South Sea stock-market crash. Despite Trenchard and Gordon's purported disdain for 'faction or cabal', they were really peddling propaganda for their own strand of radical Whiggery.

Their first readers spotted this immediately. High Churchmen,

Tories and Jacobites attacked the Letters as 'a weekly defence of treason or sacrilege', whose writers 'endeavour to spread erroneous and unjust principles, and to poison the morals and loyalty of people'. Government supporters, for their part, worried that Cato's relentless 'vilifying [of] the Administration' and 'brooding of false news' would only buttress Tory and Jacobite propaganda among 'weak and ignorant people, who having no judgment of their own, are misled by a vogue' for easy slogans and 'political scandal'. Even the opposition Whig politician Robert Molesworth, whose own political principles matched those of Cato's Letters so closely that he was commonly presumed to be their author, privately agreed that they contained 'sometimes silly, sometimes false assertions and conclusions, frequently very bitter personal reflections and applications'.

Those topical allusions are no longer obvious, because to avoid prosecution for libel they were cleverly wrapped in allegory, innuendo and irony. Even 'when he is painting both King, and Ministry, in the most odious colours', noted one critic, Cato 'still says, with his usual irony, our King's most gentle government, and the virtuous administration of an uncorrupt Ministry'. Gordon, especially, loved sailing close to the wind, simultaneously winking at and disclaiming the real meaning of his 'historical' analyses. In 1721, he impudently dedicated a best-selling pamphlet on political corruption to the head of the government, the Duke of Sunderland, lauding his 'uncorrupt heart and clean hands': readers knew to infer exactly the opposite. Sunderland's successor, the notoriously greasy-handed Robert Walpole, got the same treatment. At the height of Cato's fame, Gordon went so far as to anonymously publish a scintillating essay on the art of 'Defaming an Administration'. As well as liberal use of the 'significant *Italic*', he explained, one could write in 'the Allegorical Mode' (of 'ambiguity or double entendre'); the Historical Mode; the Ironical Mode (very common 'this year or two past'); the Fictitious Mode (scaremongering about a made-up danger, such as 'suppressing the Liberty of the Press'); as well as the 'Foreign', the 'Categorical', the 'Hypothetical' or the shameless 'Lying Mode' – where, 'having set forth the blackness of corruption, and the punishment which it deserves', one immediately hastened to affirm 'that our present Ministers are guilty of none of the crimes before mentioned'.

Leading politicians were enraged by such impertinent criticism. 'Never was there a writer', marvelled one observer, 'that ever so insulted a government, and treated his superiors with so much contempt ... he reviles the Ministry in the most opprobrious terms, and represents them as acting with no other view, than to corrupt, impoverish and enslave the nation.' For all its deflection, Cato's language was indeed often incendiary. The Letters celebrated the assassination of Julius Caesar as a justified act; denounced the clergy as 'contemptible insects'; threatened Sunderland, Walpole and other MPs with popular vengeance; and attacked stock-market profiteers as 'vermin' fit for extermination. 'Hang them,' they urged, 'load all the gallows in England.' They longed to see 'a thousand stock-jobbers, well trussed up', the nation purged by 'letting out some of our adulterate and corrupt blood'.

Within months, a parliamentary committee against 'seditious libels' had summoned the *London Journal*'s printer and 'Mr Gordon, the reputed author of Cato's Letters'. To escape arrest, Gordon went into hiding; but the Letters continued to appear. Then, at his instigation, the *Journal* printed an explosive exposé of parliament's mismanagement of the South Sea affair. Overnight, in response, the government arrested the paper's printer, publisher, pressmen, retailers and street-hawkers, broke up its printing press, seized ten thousand copies and flung the editor, Benjamin Norton Defoe, into jail. Before long, Norton Defoe bent to pressure and became a government informant. His father, Daniel Defoe, commented angrily in his own paper that 'the young Defoe is but a stalking horse and tool', a scapegoat for the two 'champion scribblers' who had been baying for 'blood, the gallows, and heads upon poles'. But Trenchard and Gordon continued, undeterred. If anything, a dismayed government informant noted a few days later, the raids had only increased Cato's reputation as a fearless truth-teller, rather than a poisonous, rabble-rousing spreader of 'malicious and scandalous libels':

The general cry among the common people is of late, 'Oh! This is a fine paper! This paper contains nothing but truth! The man that writes this knows everything that's doing at court!' Therefore whatever person or thing it condemns (tho' never so sacred) is condemned by the suffrage of the giddy multitude; and last Saturday's paper is now become the general talk of not only this place [i.e. Birmingham], but Coventry, Warwick, etc. In every alehouse people have the *London Journal* in their hands, showing to each other with a kind of joy the most audacious reflections therein contained.

NOVEL ARGUMENTS

Recovering their original context allows us to see that, despite their rhetoric, Cato's Letters were intensely partial in intention and reception. The same was true of Trenchard and Gordon's arguments about free speech, which mainly justified their own practices. That was why Cato defined free speech only in terms of government censorship, waved away the dangers of slander and misinformation, and was so keen to separate 'public' from 'private' affairs, in order to create a special category of protected expression. It even explains their timing – Cato's two final essays on 'libels', basically arguing that no anti-governmental speech should ever be silenced, were a direct response to their own temporary de-platforming in 1722, when (as we shall see) their column was suddenly dropped by the *London Journal*. Their model of press and speech liberty was an essentially self-serving vision, masquerading as a neutral, universal one. Of course, corrupt motives don't necessarily lead to invalid arguments – but in this case they did. Trenchard and Gordon's theory was profoundly flawed.

The deeper question is not why, but *how* they managed to articulate it. Given that everyone agreed that slander and misinformation were dangerous, and that newspapers were making things worse, and given that the distinction between press 'liberty' and 'licence' was so untheorized, how did they justify their novel, radical argument that freedom of speech and of the press was the basis of all liberty, and should never be curtailed by government?

Though Trenchard was an experienced polemicist, he and Gordon were above all brilliant popularizers, rather than original thinkers. At first sight, their free-speech arguments seem entirely novel. But they weren't: the two of them had simply taken existing arguments about *religious* liberty of expression, and twisted these to fit political speech.

Trenchard and Gordon knew those religious arguments well: their previous writings had mainly been defences of toleration, and in Cato's Letters, too, this remained a prominent theme. Both came from nonconformist backgrounds, and they admiringly cited Milton, Locke (whom Trenchard may have known personally) and Tindal (with whom they were friendly). In their first newspaper, the best-selling *Independent Whig* (1720–21), they stood against the 'bold and dangerous falsehoods' of the clergy, and for 'liberty of conscience', 'freedom of thought' and 'the liberty of the press'. If only 'freedom of [religious] opinion' were allowed, Gordon later wrote, all religious conflict would cease: 'what a surprising glorious change would appear all over the world, and as it were a new creation, the beauty of liberty, the force of truth, captivating every rational beholder, and scattering their mortal enemies'.

By 1720, that was a conventional Whig way of thinking about religious truth and debate. What's more, contemporary discussions of politics and religion were already in various ways closely intertwined. Religious liberty had been a central political issue since the Reformation, and political speech in this period was saturated with arguments about religion. Nonetheless, existing justifications of religious free speech, like Locke's, depended precisely on distinguishing it from political speech. The former, they argued, was harmless but divinely inspired speculation, bound to lead the spiritually elect ever more closely to the truth, yet ultimately judgeable only by God; whereas the latter was a wholly different kind of talk – impelled by selfish, earthly motives, with potentially dangerous effects in the world. In Cato's Letters, Trenchard and Gordon were the first to simply ignore this careful distinction between spiritual and secular expression, and its underlying contrast between divine and human understanding. In civil society, too, they claimed, when 'all opinions are equally indulged, and all parties equally allowed to speak their minds, the truth will come out'. As in religious matters, so in politics: truth was irresistible, and impervious to falsehood:

'tis senseless to think that any Truth can suffer by being thoroughly searched, or examined into; or that the discovery of it can prejudice right religion, equal government, or the happiness of society in any respect: She has so many advantages above error, that she wants only to be shown, to gain admiration and esteem; and we see every day that she breaks through the bonds of tyranny and fraud, and shines through the mists of superstition and ignorance.

By hijacking Milton's millenarian idiom of spiritual inspiration, and extending it to the spheres of society and government, they founded a new theory of political speech.

In the same way, they reworked his radical Protestant conspiracy theory about self-interested priests shackling people's minds, by transposing it to the realm of politics and substituting 'governors' for priests. Throughout history, their argument became, rulers invariably plotted to brainwash and enslave their subjects. By contrast, a free people was always unbiased, united and infallible in its political judgements. It followed that any governmental restriction of speech was a sign of incipient tyranny; only complete liberty of speech allowed the truth to break through and the people to be free.

Though Trenchard and Gordon referred incidentally to free speech as 'the Right of every Man', they mainly thought of it not in terms of individual rights but those of 'the people' collectively – thereby eliding the basic problem that, by their own definition, liberty only meant the right to speak or act *without harming others*. Their assertion was that, in politics as in religion, the truth was always single: allow but proper freedom of discussion, and it would be revealed. It followed that the people, unless deceived, would always be united in their judgement. Despite conceding that one person's free speech ought never to injure another, that slander was 'a very base and mean thing', that it was necessary to punish personal libels as 'a sort of writing that hurts particular persons, without doing good to the public', and that press freedom should not extend to 'licentiousness of the press', let alone 'an uncontrolled liberty [for people] to calumniate their superiors, or one another', these passing caveats about the limits and dangers of free speech were never developed. Instead, without acknowledging the contradiction, they argued mainly in the opposite direction.

This was a deliberately misleading strategy. In reality, like every other informed observer, Trenchard and Gordon were fully aware that the political discourse of their age was easily corrupted. In several of their other anonymous writings, they too warned against 'the abuse of words', and allowing the 'poison' of dangerous ideas to 'infatuate the multitude'. It was easy, they cautioned repeatedly, to lead astray the 'ignorant many', 'the mob', 'the blind monster', 'the many-headed beast' of the common people.

Yet Cato's paean to free speech spoke only in laudatory terms of 'the people' and their infallible wisdom – drawing on a long tradition of populist polemics about the divine voice of the people, but giving it a new, sharpened theoretical edge. 'Misrepresentation of public measures is easily overthrown,' it blithely declared, 'by representing public measures truly.' The people were not interested in faction: 'they have no Interest, but the general Interest ... they never hate their governors, till their governors deserve to be hated ... The people, when they are not misled or corrupted, generally make a sound judgment of things.' Only the 'external delusion' and 'imposture' of rulers ever led them astray. In short, Trenchard and Gordon's solution to the intractable, age-old problems of political division and public misjudgement was to pretend that these weren't real problems at all.

Instead, their polemic conceived of free speech primarily as an antidote to governmental oppression. Tyrants, Tindal had argued in 1698, always tried to control the press, and made it 'a crime to talk, much more to write, about political matters'. Cato's Letters made this its central theme, building on Trenchard and Gordon's previous writings against corruption and autocracy, and their vision that rulers were always but 'trustees of the people'. 'Honest magistrates' welcomed scrutiny. 'Only the wicked governors of men dread what is said of them': freedom of speech was feared only by the corrupt and the guilty, for its purpose was to restrain the powerful from doing wrong. Without free communication, Tindal had opined, 'no other liberty can be secure' – 'secure but the liberty of the press, and that will, in all probability, secure all other liberty'. Trenchard and Gordon took this notion, and supersized it. 'Of Freedom of Speech: That the Same is Inseparable from Public Liberty' became the title of Gordon's lead essay, in which he described free speech as 'the great Bulwark of Liberty'.

Cato's bottom line was that even the publishing of malicious slander was 'an evil arising out of a much greater good ... rather many libels should escape, than the Liberty of the Press should be infringed'. This was a deliberately provocative claim. Since classical times, commentators had regarded 'libelling' as a serious evil, which poisoned personal relations and political discourse alike, and should therefore be strictly punished. Milton had repeatedly stressed this point, and so did all subsequent discussions. To libel a person was akin to assassinating them, warned the *Spectator* in 1712: 'this cruel practice tends to the utter subversion of all Truth and Humanity'. Trenchard and Gordon's lengthy attention to the phenomenon (to which they devoted three entire essays) reflects how central it was to contemporary debates about liberty of expression. Yet their basic response was, once again, to dismiss the problem out of hand. Because they conceived of free speech as always empowering the weak, and presumed that 'the judgement of the people ... does rarely err', it followed that even libels were, ultimately, beneficial. 'Guilty men alone fear them, or are hurt by them', for they 'seldom or never annoy an innocent man, or promote any considerable error'. Even if they did, that 'an innocent man should be now and then aspersed' was a price worth paying. In Cato's universe of communication, libellers were always less powerful than their targets, and liberty of expression always trumped the rights of individuals.

Indeed, the overall thrust of Trenchard and Gordon's argument was that freedom of speech could never be limited at all. Gone was any acknowledgement that some ideas might be too wrong or dangerous to be allowed to spread. It was true, they granted in passing, that mischievous writings might sometimes 'foment popular and perhaps causeless discontents, blast and obstruct the best measures, and now and then promote insurrections and rebellions'. But that, too, was worth it. Time and again, they fell back on the proposition that the benefits of free speech far outweighed the dangers. Echoing Milton, they asserted that vice and licence were in every sphere of life inseparable from virtue and liberty. For them, as masterful polemicists, it followed that *any* restraint was equivalent to the destruction of free speech: 'Are men's hands to be cut off, because they may and sometimes do steal and murder with them? Or their tongues to be pulled out, because they may tell lies, swear, or talk sedition?' No – if people were allowed to think and speak freely, they may reason wrongly, irreligiously, or seditiously, and sometimes will do so; and by such means may possibly now and then pervert and mislead an ignorant and unwary person; and if they be suffered to write their thoughts, the mischief may be still more diffusive; but if they be not permitted, by any or all these ways, to communicate their opinions or improvements to one another, the world must soon be over-run with barbarism, superstition, injustice, tyranny, and the most stupid ignorance.

It was all or nothing. Freedom of speech always led towards greater enlightenment; its restraint always presaged barbarism.

MONEY AND MANIPULATION

The rhetorical power of Trenchard and Gordon's theory derived from its repeated assertion of questionable but resonant certainties. Politicians always needed watching; the people were invariably right; free speech inevitably advanced knowledge; truth unerringly vanquished falsehood. It was brilliant journalism. Before long, it had attained the status of infallible wisdom: nowadays, these have become mainstream propositions.

Yet when they were first articulated, these specious claims were widely critiqued, both for dismissing the acute problems of slander and political misinformation, and for their many internal contradictions. In the early 1720s, none other than Matthew Tindal, who had always been more cautious in his arguments about press freedom, took particular umbrage at Trenchard and Gordon's insouciant dismissal of the dangers of a mis-informed public. In two lengthy manuscripts and a series of pamphlets, he dissected the falsehoods and 'infinite absurdities' of 'Cato the Journalist'. Let's be real, he urged: 'If the people are able to judge rightly in matters of truth as well as liberty, how come they everywhere to be enemies of both?' To Tindal, history and current affairs alike showed only too clearly that, in fact, 'the common people, upon every unforeseen accident, use their fears instead of their reason; they believe every absurdity, magnify every disagreeable apprehension, and are immediately capable of measures destructive even of their own welfare'. It was crazy to pretend they always discerned the truth. As for liberty, it was only enlightened rulers who had recently taken steps 'against persecution, priestcraft, and all civil and ecclesiastical tyranny': even so, the 'inexhaustible fund of stupidity in human nature' remained generally hostile to civil and spiritual liberty, in England as everywhere else.

At any rate, as Tindal acidly pointed out, Cato was so naïve and inconsistent (sometimes extolling popular judgement as infallible while elsewhere conceding its fickleness) that 'either he does not know what he says himself, or is the vilest of hypocrites'. Though pretending 'to disperse thick, and deceitful mists from before weak eyes', he was really no more than an artful conspiracy theorist, spreading irresponsible, dangerous lies about the people's supposed rights, flattering their 'great discernment, penetration, and right judgment', and constantly hinting at government plots 'wholly to enslave us'. Despite their endless invocation of 'Liberty', the real effect of Cato's Letters was plainly 'to deceive, or mislead unthinking people'.

Thus, ironically enough, Tindal, the first serious exponent of political freedom of speech, dismissed Cato's Letters, which built upon his principles, as 'highly criminal' – 'libels pernicious to the State' that could not be 'long permitted with impunity'. His own view was that speech, writing and printing were powerful instruments for ill as well as for good: it depended on how they were wielded. As he'd already cautioned back in 1698, a free press was 'the support of all our liberties', but if abused could become 'an engine to destroy them all'. In fact, he argued, the advent of print had mainly served to oppress, rather than to liberate, ordinary people. His reading of history was that 'most countries in Europe maintained their freedom tolerably well till the invention of printing': it was precisely their rulers' acquisition of this powerful new tool of indoctrination that had first led their subjects to be 'by degrees gulled and cheated of their liberty'.

Tindal's annoyance was understandable, for apart from a few glancing references to the imperfections of the libel laws, Cato's Letters completely ignored the troublesome reality of how the media really worked. Its free-speech model made no mention of the taxation and harassment of newspapers, their cut-throat competition for readers, the government's monopoly over the postal network, the toxic spread of political lies, the problems of media partisanship, the difficulty of sifting truth from fiction, or the ways in which money and power continually undermined even the possibility of free and honest public communication.

All of these were, in fact, well-known problems. Over a century earlier, in the 1590s, Francis Bacon had already identified many of them in his manuscript treatises criticizing the power of slander and the employment of impoverished and ambitious writers to spread partisan lies. Traditionally, European rulers had sought to combat such problems, and to control public opinion, mainly by monopolizing the dissemination of information, and suppressing criticism. In England after 1695 that became increasingly difficult: whenever ministers took repressive action, a memo of 1722 complained, 'double the number of papers were sold upon it'. But though news was popular, it was also commercially risky: most of the seventy-plus new papers launched in the capital between 1719 and 1723 quickly failed. So, politicians soon developed a fresh tactic: covertly bribing authors and publishers to work for them. Instead of fighting against the burgeoning commercial market for news and opinion, they exploited it. Political 'falsehood and scandal' had become ubiquitous, noted the *Spectator* in 1712, because 'all sides are equally guilty of it ... every dirty scribbler is countenanced by great names, whose interests he propagates by such vile and infamous methods'. In short, spreading misinformation and propaganda for profit was intrinsic, not incidental, to the world's first 'free' press.

By 1720, this collusive system was well established. Walpole expanded it still further during his decades in office (1721–42), secretly funnelling thousands of pounds per year to writers, printers and publishers. Indeed, the deepest irony of Tindal's many anonymous critiques was that he attacked Cato's Letters in his capacity as a paid propagandist for the ministry. So obviously corrupt was political journalism that other critics presumed that Cato himself, too, wrote for money, rather than out of principle. As Daniel Defoe knowingly remarked in the summer of 1721, as rumours swirled of the government's impending action against the *London Journal*, columnists were often accused of writing maliciously or traitorously and seditiously, and the like, when perhaps the mistaken unhappy scribbler has had no sedition, or treason, or malice in his head, and the indictment ought only to have said greedily, covetously, and avariciously, the man having had no design at all, but merely to get a penny, and perhaps to buy him[self] bread.

All 'common Hackney writers' were corrupt, Gordon himself bluntly pointed out in the spring of 1723, in an anonymous column for another paper. Whether 'hirelings of a court' or 'pensioners of the multitude', they wrote for money, and could change their tune at the drop of a hat. Indeed, he noted, many critics of the government had recently 'made their peace, or their terms; and accordingly changed their warmest satires against some men, into fulsome panegyrics on the same persons'.

Yet Cato's Letters ignored all this. Their theory of political communication invoked a simple, neutral marketplace of ideas, in which the truth would always out – as long as evil rulers didn't suppress free speech. This was Trenchard and Gordon's final, deepest deception. Because in fact they were not just intimately familiar with how corrupt political writing really was, but deeply complicit in it.

THE PERSONAL AND THE POLITICAL

So was their publisher. In the autumn of 1720, when Thomas Gordon sent the *London Journal* the first, unsigned column of what would become Cato's Letters, its new proprietor was a young capitalist named Elizée Dobrée, junior member of a Huguenot merchant dynasty from the Channel Islands. Like Gordon, he was still in his twenties and unmarried. His paper, barely a year old, had started off specializing in foreign, not domestic, news and had always staunchly supported the government. Most of the work was done by its youthful editor, Benjamin Norton Defoe, the illegitimate son of Daniel Defoe. Floating some money in the fashionable new world of media start-ups was probably an amusing diversion at first, but just as Trenchard and Gordon began to write for his paper, Dobrée's prospects shattered. The one close relative on whose patronage he depended ('the only person of whom I expect something of consequence, and am much in his favour') lost his fortune in the South Sea debacle. Suddenly, all Dobrée had was his newspaper, and so, 'carried away by my extreme pain', he permitted Trenchard and Gordon's angry attacks on the perpetrators, and rejoiced at the *Journal*'s rising popularity.

Within a few months, as its circulation and advertising revenue soared, Dobrée felt secure enough to marry. Shortly after, he set about cashing in his unexpected windfall: he was a businessman, not an ideologue. Having failed to curb Cato's column through arrests and intimidation, Walpole's government instead simply bought off Dobrée, behind the backs of the *London Journal*'s writers and editor. In the end, Cato's insubordinate criticisms were silenced not by force but by money.

It took some time to negotiate the deal. But in September 1722, with Cato's Letters at the pinnacle of its success, Dobrée secretly switched sides, abruptly stopped running the essays, and sold the *Journal* to the government. Overnight, the nation's leading channel of political criticism turned into a ministerial mouthpiece, complete with a new lead column that exposed the folly of Cato's past pronouncements and redirected its readers' anger towards the threat of Jacobitism. Of Trenchard and Gordon's four essays directly on freedom of speech and of the press, Dobrée had published the first two. Their annoyance about being suddenly de-platformed inspired the second pair, a vindication of 'what are usually called libels', which appeared a few weeks later in the new paper they hurriedly launched, the *British Journal*. Loudly denouncing the government's 'extravagant, arbitrary, and violent' censorship, they continued publishing Cato's Letters until the summer of 1723. By then, Trenchard may already have been seriously ill; he died in December.

But their apparent defiance was a sham: Gordon had meanwhile also secretly begun working for the ministry. He was young, poor and ravenously ambitious: all he had was his skill as a writer, and it had always been for sale. When he'd first arrived, penniless, in London in the early 1710s, he'd started out as a low-level spy for the Tory leader and brilliant propagandist Robert Harley, before switching sides, trading on his pen as best he could. As one of his earliest critics noted, he was an unprincipled, mercenary hack, who lived in a constant 'state of dependency' – Trenchard was only his latest benefactor. Already in the summer of 1721, as the government was piling on the pressure against the *London Journal*, and a warrant was out for his arrest, Gordon had had 'constant overtures from men in power', clandestine meetings with government ministers, and 'many offers' of a secret pension in return for abandoning Cato's Letters and switching sides. In response, he delicately professed his esteem for the administration, his 'intention to drop politics', and his interest in an appointment to 'some post of credit in which [you] would always find me honest and grateful'. Trenchard, who was himself independently rich and famously incorruptible, privately mused that he'd not be surprised if his young friend sold out: 'if I could help the poor fellow to a creditable employment I should be willing to do it . . . Let him act how he pleases.'

Early in May 1722, Gordon took the plunge: leaving Cato's Letters temporarily to Trenchard, he began a secret apprenticeship with the administration. Up to this point, he'd written most of the Letters: now, he switched to government propaganda. For the launch of the *St James's Journal*, a new ministerial counterblast to opposition papers such as the *London Journal*, Gordon clandestinely provided a blistering lead editorial, attacking exactly the principles that Cato so passionately espoused. With equal eloquence, he now voiced the orthodox view of politics and print. Parliament was the true organ of the people's authority: it was dangerous nonsense to suppose that ordinary citizens themselves had 'capacity and opportunity to know thoroughly their own, and the National Interest'. Still less could private individuals presume to criticize public affairs – least of all the ignorant 'multitude', that 'confused herd of vagabonds'. In a remarkable passage (whose reference to himself looks like a coded mea culpa, addressed to those who had commissioned him), Gordon warned that it was easy but perilous for journalists to pander to the masses by defaming authority and talking up the people's supposed 'Sovereign and Sacred Authority'. That was how even innocent, well-meaning citizens were turned into angry, deluded populists:

> when I observe a worthy trader, without any natural malice of his own, sucking in the poison of popularity, and boiling with Indignation

against an administration which the journalist informs him is very corrupt, I am grieved that ever Machiavel, Hobbes, Sidney, Filmer, and the more illustrious moderns, *including myself*, appeared in human nature.

The following year, in the aftermath of a failed Jacobite plot, he published a still more overt retraction. 'Cato's Letter . . . on the present state of affairs', as he billed this anonymous pamphlet, hailed Walpole's 'wise and vigilant ministry' for having foiled the conspirators, and endorsed its every move. It even defended the indefinite maintenance of a standing army, a spectre of despotism against which Trenchard, and then Cato, had campaigned passionately for decades. Such restrictions of liberty, Gordon now declared, were a price worth paying to avoid Jacobite slavery. In hindsight, he confessed, he and Trenchard had been wrong to assume 'the Sense of the People', and to rail against Sunderland, Walpole, the management of the South Sea crisis, and other supposed signs of ministerial tyranny. In fact, the government had always behaved like 'Guardian Angels of the Land', while Cato's Letters, 'besides many of my [other] writings', had unwittingly played into the hands of the Jacobites, always intent on 'poisoning the minds of the people from the press'. 'We have too long been in an error,' Gordon concluded: the only honourable course was to acknowledge it, and 'to make atonement for the mischief'.

Shortly after this, Trenchard and Gordon did a covert deal: they ended Cato's Letters, in return for Gordon's secret employment by the administration. I saw Gordon the other day, Molesworth wrote sourly to an acquaintance: 'he has gained his point: and who would keep his honesty any longer than it would serve his turn?' Trenchard was fully complicit in this quid pro quo: indeed, the politics of Cato's Letters had from the outset also been shaped by his own secret motives and quest for preferment. In the end, as Gordon privately noted, his collaborator's main concern on his deathbed was 'about Mr Walpole's keeping his promise to me, and pressed me to write to him over and over the day before he died . . . He had it much in his head to see me settled and raised in the world . . . I hope Mr Walpole will keep his promise to me.'

He did. In the years that followed, Gordon rose to become the prime minister's most trusted secret censor, overseeing the work of other propagandists, and growing rich and fat over almost two decades in the pay of the ministry. To contemporaries it seemed clear what had happened. As political writers were essentially mercenary, 'following party only as hunger, conveniency, or ambition directs them', even the most outspoken early eighteenth-century advocate of free speech had been bribed to switch sides and shut up.

Modern scholars have tended to overlook or reject this view. Political theorists and historians of the First Amendment, oblivious to the venality of eighteenth-century media and politics, treat Cato's propositions as coherent, disinterested and sincere. Intellectual historians, meanwhile, protest that Gordon maintained his principles even after accepting Walpole's patronage, noting that he continued to publish prolifically, and wrongly supposing that, like Trenchard, he was already independently wealthy.

Yet what counts is that none of Gordon's writing after 1723 ever again criticized the government, let alone stirred up a mass audience. Revisiting the question 'Of Freedom of Speech' in 1728, he adopted the traditional perspective of rulers: honest counsel was better than flattery, safer to let the people grumble than to forbid it – yet for them 'tumultuously . . . to publish their mutual discontents and wrongs, and to inflame one another' was insupportable. His post-1723 view of press and politics was essentially the opposite of Cato's. Government and parliament were the true sources of authority. The people were easily misled. Most political writers were greedy, partisan scum, whose incessant 'libels' against authority were cheap, irresponsible and dangerous. For 'ungrateful and licentious language is followed naturally and too fast by ungrateful and licentious actions . . . and the one is often intended to introduce the other'. History proved that licentious speech was intolerable: 'unbounded liberty is as dangerous as unbounded Power'.

TRUTH AND CONSEQUENCES

That the first modern theory of political free speech was a self-serving tissue of deliberate fabrications, glaring contradictions and wilful omissions was not, of course, evident to the countless contemporary and later admirers of Cato's Letters, who read it in good faith as an epitome of political wisdom. But my argument has been that it was not *written* in good faith – and that the resulting omissions and contradictions created a deeply flawed model of free speech. Instead of addressing the many problems that bedevilled political communication, it deliberately concealed them. Unlike the concept of religious free speech that it so sloppily appropriated, it was not constructed over decades of painstaking, pan-European debate, but cobbled together by two hacks on a deadline. Though its many reprints canonized their text, it was never a rigorous work of political philosophy, just a brilliantly written series of polemical columns. That readability fuelled its immense success, but it also helps to explain why, on closer inspection, Trenchard and Gordon's free-speech theory is so full of holes.

That matters even today, because of its extraordinary influence. From the outset, both politicians seeking power and political writers defending their trade instinctively loved its populist, anti-governmental message. In England, Cato's free-speech rhetoric was eagerly taken up and developed in the 1730s by the *Craftsman*, Walpole's chief journalistic antagonist. As the next chapter will explore, its impact was especially profound in North America, where Cato's astonishing popularity was bound up with the emergence of the first colonial newspapers from the 1720s onwards. Many of these eagerly seized on Cato's essays, the boldest available defence of press freedom, to justify their own practices. Through endless quotation and exemplification, Trenchard and Gordon's words and ideals became commonplaces of colonial political and legal thought. When, at the outset of the American Revolutionary War in 1776, the rebellious states drew up declarations of their rights, the free-speech clauses they included, even if not consciously modelled on Cato's Letters, carried their unmistakable ideological imprint. The first and most influential, that of Virginia, declared that 'the Freedom of the Press is one of the great Bulwarks of Liberty, and can never be restrained but by despotic Government'. That sentiment, and the 'bulwarks of liberty' phrase, which countless other writers also adopted, including James Madison in his original draft of the Bill of Rights, came straight from Cato's first letter on free speech. In 1789, the First Amendment of the United States' constitution duly enshrined Trenchard and Gordon's template in what was to become the most powerful free-speech law in the world: the injunction that 'Congress shall make no law . . . abridging the freedom of speech, or of the press'.

Globally, as we shall see, the amendment's rhetorical absolutism and anti-governmental focus proved entirely anomalous. Even though liberty of speech and of the press have been just as prominently enshrined in hundreds of other constitutions around the world since the later eighteenth century, not a single non-American law has ever conceived of free speech in this way. Instead, they invariably balance the right to speak freely with the obligation to do so responsibly. As the French Declaration of the Rights of Man put it, also in 1789: 'The free communication of ideas and opinions is one of the most precious of the rights of man. Every citizen may, accordingly, speak, write, and print with freedom, but shall be responsible for such abuses of this freedom as shall be defined by law.'

That alternative approach has obvious drawbacks of its own. But it does foreground the uncomfortable truths that Trenchard and Gordon were so keen to avoid: speech can cause harm, and we, 'the people', often don't agree. Its formulation highlights that liberty of speech is never absolute, and can conflict with other fundamental values. And it takes a holistic view of rights, rather than presuming some overwhelmingly important distinction between the actions of 'government' and all other spheres of power.

That difference matters – for one thing, because of the idiosyncratic way the First Amendment is phrased, most speech in the United States is not in fact covered by it. Under American law, any private entity can censor, fire or punish people as much as it likes, for exactly the same forms of expression that any 'government' may not inhibit. No other culture sustains such a massively asymmetrical approach to private versus public power over personal expression.

Nowadays that is no longer just an American problem: these anomalies affect us all. The rise of the internet, and the overwhelming global dominance of US social media companies, have made it the case that, across the world, norms about freedom of expression online are based primarily on American beliefs in the nobility of the First Amendment, the overriding dangers of government censorship, and the truth-revealing properties of the marketplace of ideas. In this view, the correct response to lies, misinformation and hate speech is only ever – more speech. Worse still, though everything that social media companies do is shaped primarily by their greed for profit and market share, their own theories of speech and acceptable expression consistently – wilfully – ignore this most fundamental motive.

That is why it is helpful to understand how and why the right to political free speech was first invented. Doing so doesn't just illuminate how deeply flawed its first substantive theory was, and how its biases have carried over into the idiosyncratic American laws it inspired, as we'll be exploring later in this book. It also opens up ways of rethinking our present predicaments. Instead of being the antidote to misinformation and falsehood, the story of Cato's Letters suggests, free speech often amplifies it. Tension between freedom of expression and other principles is not necessarily dangerous, or the indicator of a slide towards tyranny and thought police, as Cato and his modern epigones would have us believe. Governments are never the only or even the most powerful arbiters of speech. A profit-driven media marketplace is not the best determinant of truth. And it is not a bad thing to be constantly balancing on slippery slopes, making difficult collective decisions about how to square incommensurable values, and revisiting those judgements over and over again. We may regret the time and effort that costs, just as we may disagree with the outcomes – but it is the inevitable condition of life in any divided yet democratic society.

4

The Shapes of Freedom

Whether as scholars or citizens, we are all accustomed to spotting censorship. We know it comes in different shapes: historians are used to cataloguing its contours across time and place. But in the case of freedom of speech and of the press, we usually don't think this way. Instead, we presume that freedom is simply what's left when censorship's artificial restrictions are removed. The one advances as the other retreats: freedom of expression is the natural, desirable inverse of censorship. Yet actually that is not true. As we saw in the previous chapter, free speech is not something that emerges straightforwardly from the lessening of restraint. It is itself a contrived, invented concept. It, too, always has a shape. It flows more easily in certain directions than in others; it often aggregates around existing forms of power. This is not just true of its practice, but equally of its theory.

From its earliest inception in Cato's Letters, the nominally neutral new ideology of free speech as a political right was in fact deeply prejudiced. That was not just true of how it defined speech, truth, libel and the media. It was also a matter of whose voices counted, and whose did not – especially in its conception of the differences between men and women, and its treatment of race and slavery. Those biases were intrinsic to the original text – and were to be sharpened further when its ideology was imported into the slave societies of the Americas.

As in every other text of this period, Cato's construction of the 'public' was strongly gendered. This fundamentally affected the definition of free speech. So too, like many political tracts of the seventeenth and eighteenth centuries, Cato's Letters continually condemned enslavement, the antithesis of liberty – 'slavery' was precisely what freedom of speech and print was meant to prevent. Yet at the same time, the text condoned the actual bondage of Black people. Its creators, Trenchard, Gordon and Dobrée, were personally connected to slave ownership in the Americas. Both in its original and most of its later eighteenth-century articulations, freedom of speech was a racialized ideology – in much the same way that early newspapers, the most self-conscious and celebrated exponents of press liberty in the anglophone world of the seventeenth and eighteenth centuries, were also important tools of enslavement and white supremacy.

In practice, free speech could take other shapes, too. From the outset it was always a contested ideal, which could be appropriated by the weak as well as the strong. Slaves, like women, had their own notions of liberty and could never be completely silenced. Yet both in its initial formulation and still more in its transplantation across the Atlantic, the new concept of free speech was always shadowed by the reality of racialized unfreedom.

MALE AND FEMALE SPEECH

Cato's Letters is a male text – written by men, about men, for men. Female subjects and voices are conspicuously absent from its countless references to ancient and modern examples, and from its entire 350,000-word philosophy of liberty. This was hardly unusual for an eighteenth-century political tract, but it profoundly shaped Trenchard and Gordon's theory of free speech.

Implicit in their text was a stark view of sexual difference. Women were disregarded because Cato's central theme, 'public liberty', was presumed to be a solely masculine concern. The work's many metaphors, similes and personifications were likewise almost exclusively male. Just once, Trenchard wrote a letter as 'A Woman', with a long reply by Cato, critiquing mercenary marriage and depicting wives as profligate and interested only in household matters. The essay's argument was that marriage, by providing men with domestic felicity, allowed them to focus on advancing public liberty and happiness. That was the only connection between women and public affairs.

This conceptual distinction between the public and the domestic also characterized Cato's model of free speech. Freedom of speech was foundational to 'public liberty' because it allowed private citizens, by definition men, to critique 'the administration of government'. Its ambit was to 'publicly' examine the transacting of 'public matters' and 'public proceedings' by 'public ministers'. Conversely, the realm of free speech did not extend to private affairs: to 'writing that hurts particular persons, without doing good to the public'; to speech about 'private and personal failings', or 'private offences'; or to libels 'against private men', or concerning 'purely personal' matters. All of that, Trenchard and Gordon affirmed, was not liberty but 'licentiousness', and rightly punishable. Even 'the private vices or weaknesses of governors' were off limits, unless they affected their public actions.

This was a deeply gendered theory. Cato took for granted that women did not engage with public affairs: their speech was entirely domestic, trivial and inferior. In 1724, Gordon's eulogy of his deceased co-author reproduced this hierarchy precisely. It extolled Trenchard's speech and writing as pellucid, rational and eloquent. And then it drew a contrast. As for women, 'he treated them with great niceness and respect; he abounded in their own chit-chat, and said a world of pleasant things'. In other words, while male discourse was 'strong, fine, and useful', and concerned with public welfare, female conversation consisted of sweet, airy nothings.

Yet to conclude only that the shape of Trenchard and Gordon's free-speech model reflected the intrinsic gendering of contemporary culture, notable though that is, would be to overlook a crucial additional point. Women's voices had always been part of the public sphere, even when they were theoretically excluded from it. For centuries before 1700, male and female speech alike had animated rumours, protests and other expressions of popular political opinion. The idea of women addressing the public through print may have been controversial in earlier ages, but by the early 1720s, when Trenchard and Gordon put forward their arguments, anglophone public discourse was far from being a solely masculine preserve. The same was true in France, where female authors and intellectual salons hosted by women had been well established since the previous century. In both countries women writers were increasingly commonplace in the world of print – and one of their major themes was the unjust male silencing of their sex.

Among the most brilliant of these voices was that of the poet Sarah Fyge, who in 1686, when still only fourteen or fifteen, wrote and published her first major work, a long attack on gendered stereotypes entitled *The Female Advocate*. Her later poems circulated for many years among like-minded writers before they were printed in 1703. They included 'The Emulation', which wittily juxtaposed the lifelong social subordination of women (and their sufferance of endless mansplaining), against their evident capacity to outshine men in wit and learning:

> [. . .] From the first dawn of Life, unto the Grave,
> Poor Womankind's in every State, a Slave.
> The Nurse, the Mistress, Parent and the Swain,
> For Love she must, there's none escape that Pain;
> Then comes the last, the fatal Slavery,
> The Husband with insulting Tyranny [. . .]
> But in this blessed Age, such Freedom's given,
> That every Man explains the Will of Heaven;
> And shall we Women now sit tamely by,
> Make no excursions in our Philosophy,
> Or grace our Thoughts in tuneful Poetry?
> We will our Rights in Learning's World maintain,
> Wits Empire, now, shall know a Female Reign [. . .]

'The Liberty', from the same collection, begins with a description of the gendered conventions that keep women from expressing themselves freely, before vowing to throw off such 'fetters' and 'manacles' – as all women secretly wish to do:

> My Sex forbids, I should my Silence break,
> I lose my Jest, cause Women must not speak. [. . .]
> My Pen if ever us'd imploy'd must be,
> In lofty Themes of useful Houswifery,
> Transcribing old Receipts of Cookery: [. . .]
> My daring Pen, will bolder Sallies make,
> And like my self, an uncheck'd freedom take;

Not chain'd to the nice Order of my Sex,
And with restraints my wishing Soul perplex:
I'll blush at Sin, and not what some call Shame,
Secure my Virtue, slight precarious Fame.
This Courage speaks me[: be] Brave, 'tis surely worse,
To keep those Rules, which privately we Curse:
And I'll appeal, to all the formal Saints,
With what reluctance they indure restraints.

'Wife and servant are the same, / But only differ in the name,' wrote another much-admired poet, Mary, Lady Chudleigh, around this time – for no husband allowed his wife to speak freely:

When she the word *obey* has said, [...]
Then but to look, to laugh, or speak,
Will the Nuptial Contract break.
Like Mutes she Signs alone must make,
And never any Freedom take, [...]
And nothing act, and nothing say,
But what her haughty Lord thinks fit,
Who, with the power, has all the wit.

As well as being poets, novelists and playwrights, women were also journalists, satirists, philosophers and essayists: among the leading political authors of the late seventeenth and early eighteenth centuries were Delarivier Manley, Susanna Centlivre and Mary Astell. In addition, women were central to the production and distribution of political discourse, as printers, publishers, booksellers and retailers of books and newspapers. Without their efforts, no one would have read Cato's Letters. What's more, women, like men, were avid and opinionated discussers of political news. As one of Trenchard's closest intellectual associates deplored in 1716, 'the ladies ... turn their heads to politics too much'. Throughout the eighteenth century, female authorship, readership and interest in politics would only increase. Thus, in putting forward their gendered model of speech and the public sphere, Trenchard and Gordon, though claiming to describe reality, were in fact concocting a wishful male fiction.

Their notion of public discourse as a separate, masculine domain was also fairly novel. Though 'private' and 'public' were concepts of growing fascination in eighteenth-century society, the presumption that they were essentially distinct was still far from dominant. The more traditional way of thinking stressed instead that personal and communal affairs were intimately intertwined, and that honest public conduct depended on virtuous domestic life. This was in line with the most fashionable early eighteenth-century model of elite discourse, 'politeness', in which female sociability and conversation were portrayed as beneficial to men, rather than as separate, inferior domains.

Were Trenchard and Gordon consciously repudiating this prevailing view of social and sexual relations? One remarkable piece of evidence suggests that they were. When the two of them started writing together, the most popular essayists and co-authors in the English-speaking world were Joseph Addison and Richard Steele. These men, in their massively successful periodicals, the *Tatler* (1709–11) and the *Spectator* (1711–14), had done more than anyone to popularize the ideals of politeness and superior female refinement. In other ways, too, their shadow must have loomed large, especially to the young, ambitious but penniless Gordon. Both were rich, successful politicians as well as best-selling authors; and Addison's hit play *Cato, a Tragedy* (1712) probably inspired the name of Trenchard and Gordon's column. So it's notable how forcefully Gordon responded in the summer of 1721 when a senior government minister, secretly meeting with him in hopes of flattering the youthful upstart polemicist into switching sides, invoked the towering example of the recently deceased Addison, saying he 'deserved a statue of gold for his endeavours to mend private and domestic manners'. To this, Gordon scornfully replied that

> Mr Addison wrote well upon little ordinary subjects relating to men and their wives, but to do good to the world he began at the wrong end, since whoever would mend mankind must begin with the public, and the methods of government, in which is contained all virtue or vice, happiness or misery, and that wherever the government is bad, private manners will be necessarily bad.

It was a strikingly self-confident repudiation of Addison's and Steele's authority and their underlying presumptions about gender and worldly affairs.

The distinction between the public and the private, and the differences between male and female language, were much-discussed themes throughout the later seventeenth and early eighteenth centuries. The *Spectator*, too, alongside its advocacy of polite conversation between the sexes, had stressed 'that men and women ought to busy themselves in their proper spheres, and on such matters only as are suitable to their respective sex'. Yet while decrying women's political partisanship as unfeminine, it also repeatedly acknowledged passionate female engagement with politics and other undomestic affairs.

Cato's Letters, by contrast, wilfully ignored this reality. In doing so, its new and influential theories of liberty and of political freedom of speech helped harden the presumption that politics was a solely masculine preserve. By 1800, it had become commonplace to distinguish between private and public domains of life, and to presume that these corresponded to essentially male and female areas. Though this ideology gained in strength, however, it was perennially contradicted by the actuality of female interest and participation in worldly affairs, and the impossibility of ever pinning down a clear division between the private and the public. The notion that there was such a thing as a distinct public sphere, that women were wholly absent from it, and that freedom of speech was hence inevitably only a male concern, was always only a self-serving argument, masquerading as a neutral description of the supposedly natural state of affairs. But that is how patriarchy works and continually, invisibly, reinforces itself. The history of free speech is part of that story.

FREEDOM AND BONDAGE

The essential purpose of free speech, Cato declared, was to prevent tyranny and bondage. Whenever oppressors managed to curb free expression, the people became 'enslaved', and their 'minds ... degenerated into all the vileness and methods of servitude: abject sycophancy and blind submission'. How to maintain liberty and avoid slavery was in fact the central theme of Trenchard and Gordon's entire political philosophy. Throughout their text, as in other contemporary works of literature and philosophy, slavery was a ubiquitous concept, the antithesis of English freedom. After all, argued Cato, most peoples across the globe (including 'all Asia and . . . all Africa') lived in 'enslaved countries', subject to the whims of tyrants: 'We are Men, and they are Slaves.'

How did Trenchard and Gordon's use of this idiom relate to the reality that their own society enslaved human beings? How did it affect their philosophy of free speech, which became so popular in the slaveholding societies of America? Similar questions have long been asked about John Locke's theory of liberty, which likewise employed the rhetoric of slavery and was widely read by colonial and revolutionary Americans. They have not been posed before about the obscure creators of Cato's Letters. But their lives and writings, too, were implicated in the enslavement of Black people across the North Atlantic world. From its inception, free speech was a racialized ideal.

By the 1710s, British readers and writers took colonial slavery entirely for granted. Trenchard and Gordon's great journalistic rival Daniel Defoe was among those who invested money in it and wrote propaganda on behalf of slave traders. As he declared in 1711, complaining about a recent rise in the cost of enslaved Africans, 'furnishing the plantations with sufficient supplies of Negroes at moderate prices' had long been 'a most profitable, useful, and absolutely necessary branch of our commerce'. The growing popularity of Cato's Letters between the 1720s and 1750s coincided with the continued British expansion of the transatlantic slave trade. London's newspapers openly celebrated 'the Negro Trade', marketed 'Black' and 'Negro' humans for sale, and advertised for the capture of local slaves who had managed to escape. On 16 September 1721, the *London Journal* opened with Cato's stirring pronouncement that 'men are naturally equal'; the next sheet updated readers with the happy news that hundreds of 'very fine slaves' had been loaded on to English ships off the coast of Africa and were on their way to the Americas.

Peoples who lived in liberty, like the Greeks and Romans, Gordon explained, were innately superior, 'another species of mankind'. Slaves, on the other hand, were but 'sheep': for 'they who are used like beasts, will be apt to degenerate into beasts'. He never differentiated between the vassals of tyrants and those of the Romans and other 'free' societies like his own. In a deeply hierarchical culture, where 'slave' could refer to an owned human being, or a victim of tyranny, or simply a morally inferior person, it was easy to slip from notions of English superiority to contempt for oppressed, 'slavish' nations, and thence to the presumption that some peoples or individuals were born to be slaves. Trenchard and Gordon's hero Algernon Sidney was among those who took for granted that 'the base effeminate Asiaticks and Africans, for being careless of their liberty, or unable to govern themselves, were by Aristotle and other wise men called slaves by nature, and looked upon as little different from beasts'.

Thus the text of Cato's Letters, too, repeatedly argued that unfree government was a species of slavery that corrupted even tyrants themselves ('A Prince of Slaves is a slave; he is only the biggest and the worst'), yet also casually condoned the slave trade – indeed portrayed it as a support to English liberties. One of Trenchard's eulogies to political freedom celebrated the industrious 'English planters in America, [who] besides maintaining themselves and ten times as many Negroes', generated such prosperity for their homeland: 'Such are the blessings of liberty.' Another lauded the economic benefits of 'colonies planted in proper climates, and kept to their proper business ... particularly many of our own colonies in the West-Indies' whose inhabitants balanced their exports by importing goods 'for themselves and their slaves'. These passages borrowed heavily from the arguments of his and Locke's old associate the Bristol merchant and West Indies trader John Cary, whose well-known *Essay on the State of England* (1695) had enthused about the slave trade as 'the best traffic the kingdom hath' and urged its expansion, given the cheapness of African slaves and the productivity of enslaved plantation labour across the Caribbean and North America.

There were also personal connections between Cato's creators and the business of slavery. Trenchard had served as a colonial administrator in Ireland and invested in the South Sea Company, which trafficked in slaves. His estate, where many of Cato's Letters were written, wound up in the hands of a millionaire whose fortune came from Jamaican slave plantations. Before he became a writer, Gordon almost emigrated to the Caribbean, too: in 1713 his then patron, the chief minister Robert Harley, an enthusiastic promotor of the slave trade, had proposed to send him as a spy to the East or West Indies.

In 1719, Gordon's *A Modest Apology for Parson Alberoni*, the best-selling satire that launched his literary career, became one of the first books to be (re)printed in Jamaica. And all three of his offspring were drawn into the empire. In 1740, his younger son, Bill, sailed to India on an East India Company ship. A decade later, his other two children emigrated to Jamaica, Britain's most profitable colony, the rich, brutal epicentre of its inhuman commerce. The youngest, Patty, married a sugar planter and became thereby the mistress (as her husband put it) of hundreds of 'Negroes, mules, horses, cattle', and other chattels. Her brother Tom, a barrister and justice of the peace, likewise ended up the rich and powerful owner of large numbers of slaves, the most valuable one of whom he named Cato. In 1760, he supported the bloody suppression of Tacky's Revolt, the largest uprising of enslaved people the British Empire had ever faced. He spent his life defending the interests of other slaveholders and the principles of slavery, in due course becoming the chief justice of Port Royal, the attorney-general of Jamaica, an assemblyman and a member of its ruling Council.

Jamaica was one of the foremost centres of print in the eighteenth-century English-speaking world: Tom Gordon amassed a library of two thousand volumes. It is likely that Cato's Letters were reprinted in its many local newspapers and imported in book form, as they were on the American mainland, though the surviving evidence is too sparse to know exactly how popular they became in the Caribbean. What is certain is that their racist implications took on additional force when transplanted across the Atlantic. In the early Americas, the ideology of free speech buttressed white supremacy.

For eighteenth-century white male colonists, freedom of speech was both a potent political ideal and a constant practical marker of their superiority over others. Their law and politics were transacted through oral rituals – such as the taking of oaths, the giving of evidence, the making of speeches, or the formal debate of policy – from which lesser human beings were automatically excluded. That meant women, Jews, Catholics and Quakers, as in Britain – as well as all people of colour. The words of mulattoes, Indians and free Blacks were always inferior to those of whites, while the mass silencing of Black people was central to slavery itself.

Indeed, racialized presumptions about speech came to be central to eighteenth-century definitions of humankind itself. That the eloquence of Africans proved their equal humanity was one of the arguments that critics of slavery put forward with increasing force. But other whites urged the opposite – that Black utterances were inherently inferior. Among those espousing this position was the philosopher David Hume. Setting out to prove in 1753 that all 'negroes' were 'naturally inferior to the whites', Hume dismissed a seemingly contrary West Indian example: 'In *Jamaica* indeed, they talk of one negro, as a man of parts and learning; but 'tis likely he is admired for very slender accomplishments, like a parrot, who speaks a few words plainly.' No Black voice could ever be more than a bestial squawk.

Hume's assertion became tremendously influential: it made him the favourite authority of white supremacists throughout the later eighteenth and the nineteenth centuries. Although he disdained to name him, the subject of his contempt was a free Black Jamaican, Francis Williams, who had been educated in England, was an accomplished Latin poet and owned slaves himself. In the early 1720s, Williams was living in London and so was doubtless familiar with Cato's Letters – in the autumn of 1721, Thomas Gordon even referred to him in one of them as an 'ingenious gentleman ... a *Black*', rejected by the Royal Society because of the colour of his skin. A generation later, Williams and Gordon's son Tom were fellow luminaries of Jamaica's capital, Spanish Town.

Contemporary descriptions of the younger Gordon often highlighted his rhetorical skill: he was 'famed in wordy war', 'the ablest speaker', 'eloquence [flowed] from his tongue'. That he made 'very moving' speeches when sentencing people to death was reported as far away as Boston. As the proud, self-confident heir of Thomas Gordon, and as a leading colonial lawyer and politician, he took for granted, like his British and North American counterparts, that freedom of speech was a cornerstone of liberty.

Williams, too, was legally skilled, assured and articulate. Yet exactly the same values that were admirable in a white man were unbecoming in a Black one. Because white West Indians were so invested in trying to make the distinction between slavery and freedom synonymous with the difference between dark and pale bodies, it was deeply aggravating to them that (as one leading planter complained) Williams 'had not the modesty to be silent' and instead publicly insisted that skin colour was irrelevant to intelligence ('virtue and understanding,' he wrote, 'have no colour; there is no colour in an honest mind, nor in art'). Barred because of his colour from practising law or holding public office, he instead opened a school for free Black children, instructing them in reading, writing, Latin and mathematics. White Jamaicans tried repeatedly to quiet his voice, but never with complete success. When, in 1730, the island's government passed a law degrading his legal rights (as a dangerously uppity Negro), Williams successfully petitioned the imperial authorities in England to overturn it. He knew that how words are received, and what force they carry, always depends on their audience, not just their author.

It was likewise because colonists essentially equated liberty of speech with white supremacy that they put so much effort into silencing enslaved people. In 1748, the very notion that enslaved Jamaicans might legitimately complain about their maltreatment was so repugnant to the island's white settlers that it inspired a satirical 'petition of negro slaves', whose form and content underlined how threatening the notion of their writing and speaking up for themselves was. Indeed, slaves were not normally permitted to read or write at all. Teaching them literacy was a terrible mistake, warned the London magistrate Sir John Fielding in the aftermath of Tacky's Revolt – exposure to such 'sweets of liberty' led directly to 'those Insurrections that have lately caused and threatened such mischiefs and dangers to the inhabitants of and planters in the islands in the West-Indies'. Instead, the enslaved were branded with the language of their oppressors, through marks of ownership burnt into their bodies and the forcible renaming of their persons. Their own speech was continually policed; they were often punished by being physically muted. As a young, recently arrived African on a Virginia plantation in the mid 1750s, Olaudah Equiano was terrified by the appearance of a Black house slave who moved around fixed in an iron muzzle, 'which locked her mouth so fast that she could scarcely speak; and could not eat nor drink'. Some slave owners ordered such equipment from London, others improvised their own degrading tortures. In Jamaica, in Tom and Patty Gordon's day, the overseer Thomas Thistlewood would sometimes force one slave to 'shit' in another's mouth and then 'immediately put in a gag whilst his mouth was full and made him wear it 4 or 5 hours'.

Yet even in such conditions of extreme violence and unfreedom, the words of enslaved men and women remained ever-present, irrepressible and potentially transgressive. Spoken words were both representations and actions: their utterance was the most ubiquitous way in which the boundaries between liberty and bondage were constantly reinforced or contested. In that sense, even the speech of the unfree was always free: though liberty of speech was theorized in exclusionary terms, the practice of speaking freely was much harder to constrain. And Black speech fuelled continuous Black resistance. In Jamaica alone, we know of major plots, involving hundreds and sometimes thousands of slaves, in 1673, 1676, 1678, 1685–7, 1690, 1745, 1760, 1766, 1776, 1791–2, 1808, 1815, 1819, 1823–4 and 1831–2 – as well as full-blown wars in 1728–39 and 1795–6 between the settlers and different bands of Maroons, the escaped slaves and their descendants who controlled semi-autonomous strongholds in the island's mountainous interior. As the British recognized, Black societies, too, put great store in oaths, orations and invocations, both between people and as a connection to the all-powerful spirit world. To be prevented from speaking, an Akan proverb warned, was akin to being murdered: to silence another unjustly was a grievous crime. If the British Empire was partly an oral creation – sustained through spoken as much as through written and printed words – then that was even truer of the spiritual, legal and political cultures that African slaves and their descendants created in their transatlantic purgatories. For all these reasons, slave owners obsessed about slave talk. They could never completely control it, yet feared its power to bind and inspire – for, as everyone knew, oaths and whispers bred insubordination, conspiracy and revolt.

Despite the profound imbalances of power in colonial societies, the ongoing effort to racialize freedom of expression was therefore persistently undermined by non-white defiance. Just as women's participation in public debate belied the misogynist claim that free speech was the exclusive preserve of men, so too the subaltern peoples of slave societies, by asserting their own liberties of speech and writing, challenged the colonists' attempts to treat their voices as essentially inferior. Long before he used his pen to attack the slave trade in the 1780s, Equiano's words repeatedly frustrated his white oppressors: they 'answered that I talked too good English. I replied, I believed

I did.' Enslaved men and women employed language all the time to subvert the rules of their bondage, to assert their own identities, to gain more agency than they were supposed to have. Rebellious slaves marshalled the power of talk and, even in the face of death, spoke out defiantly against white supremacy. Francis Williams refused to be quiet. One of his favourite pupils, a young free Black man called Brown, employed his talents as a writer to forge passes for escaped slaves. So, too, in the early 1730s, did two white servant boys ('one named John Done or Dun ... the other Charles') who aided the Jamaican rebel guerrillas.

None of this amounts to an explicitly articulated alternative ideal of free speech. It is much easier to see how people of colour and their allies reappropriated the general notion of liberty than it is to find equivalent theorizing about speech or print, at least before the last quarter of the eighteenth century.* And yet the impact of these subversive speech acts was nonetheless profound. In countless, mainly unrecorded ways, they continually destabilized white efforts to cement hierarchies of speech, freedom and race.

PUBLISHING AND POWER

The force of words is not intrinsic. It depends on their author, their audience – and their medium. Spoken utterances can be potent, as can handwritten documents. But ever since the invention of print,

---

* By 1773, as anti-slavery sentiments were increasing, it was possible for an enslaved Black man in Massachusetts to smuggle a written attack on slavery to the publishers of the *Boston Gazette*; for him to place the denial of literacy to enslaved people at the heart of their political predicament; for his argument to condemn white Americans for fearing 'Slavery' and demanding 'Liberty' and 'the Rights of Mankind' from Great Britain, yet blithely ignoring their own violent and illegitimate mass enslavement of others ('the slavery of black men is repugnant to the laws of a free constitution, [that] a set of men merely on account of their colour, may be bought and sold as chattels ... we have neither sold nor forfeited our liberty, and have as good a right to freedom as any of the Sons of Adam'); and for the paper's publishers actually to print this text in their columns – juxtaposing it on the page with an advertisement for a new edition of Locke's writings on liberty and slavery. This combination of events would have been scarcely conceivable in earlier decades.

techniques of mass communication have had the greatest reach. To understand the shape of free speech, in any age, we need also to attend to this fact. Which voices are amplified, how and why? The clout of the media is never evenly distributed.

As we saw in the previous chapter, Trenchard and Gordon's lofty theory of free speech was deliberately silent about the pervasive influence of money on writers and publishers – just as it was on the role of the media more generally, treating all communication, whether spoken, written or printed, as essentially equal. Their own actions told a different story. So did those of their publisher Dobrée, as first a facilitator and then a suppressor of political criticism – and so does the history of his and the column's intertwined afterlives in America.

The amazing American popularity of Cato's Letters began with its canonization by the first colonial newspapers. In 1719 there had been only one paper in North America; by 1733, there were a dozen or more. In colonial contexts, where extra cachet attached to metropolitan writers, and sensitivity to printed criticism tended to be more acute than in the home country, Cato's free-speech essays provided a prestigious, ready-made defence of political journalism itself. They were the first, the boldest and thus the go-to statement for any early eighteenth-century colonial printer or writer wanting to attract attention and assert their independence.

That was why Benjamin Franklin and his brother James reprinted them repeatedly when their *New-England Courant* ran into trouble with the Massachusetts Council in the early 1720s. So did Andrew Bradford, whose *American Weekly Mercury*, Philadelphia's first newspaper, took a similarly populist line. A decade later, in 1733, a faction of New York merchants and lawyers opposed to their new, assertive governor, William Cosby, decided to launch a newspaper to stir up popular hatred against him, and to counter the government-controlled *New-York Gazette*, printed by Bradford's father, William. The anti-Cosby clique hired the elder Bradford's former apprentice, the printer John Peter Zenger, to produce what became the first overtly partisan media channel in America, the *New-York Weekly Journal*.

The ensuing paper war between the *Gazette* and the *Journal*, culminating in Zenger's trial, became the foundational moment of American free-press ideology. The arguments it rehearsed about political speech were not original: they replayed the English debates begun by Cato in 1721 and already recycled by London's leading opposition paper of the later 1720s and early 1730s, the *Craftsman*. The difference was that, in America, Trenchard and Gordon's assertions gained much more sway than they ever did in England – even the *Gazette* defensively acknowledged their authority. In 1735, a jury acquitted Zenger of printing 'seditious libel', following the new logic of Cato's ideals (that truth could never be libellous, and that juries could judge this) rather than the established letter of the law. Through constant commentary, quotation and republication, Trenchard and Gordon's ideas took on a life of their own, becoming part of the mainstream of American political and legal thought. A few decades on, they influenced the free-speech and press provisions that most of the rebellious colonies included in their declarations of rights between 1776 and 1784, and thence the peculiar shape of the First Amendment itself.

The person most responsible for popularizing Cato's ideas in North America was the lawyer James Alexander, the founder and lead author of the *New-York Weekly Journal*. Trenchard and Gordon were his main intellectual inspiration. He launched his paper with a long essay on press liberty, purportedly by Cato himself, in which, saluting Gordon by name, he paraphrased his heroes' arguments for the 'colonies and plantations'. 'Truth will always prevail over falsehood,' he declared, and only tyrants and traitors sought to restrain print, for 'No nation ancient or modern ever lost the liberty of freely speaking, writing, or publishing their sentiments, but forthwith lost their liberty in general and became slaves. LIBERTY and SLAVERY! how amiable is one! how odious and abominable the other!' For weeks on end, Alexander republished Trenchard and Gordon's columns on speech and libel, together with his own commentary. When Cosby had Zenger arrested, Alexander immediately reran Cato's defence of free speech – and Lewis Morris Jnr (the son of his main co-conspirator, the powerful lawyer Lewis Morris Snr) declaimed it in the State Assembly. 'This is a state of slavery, and so no libel,' Alexander noted privately about his attacks on the governor. Even though Zenger's acquittal did not technically change the law, it certainly bolstered colonial press freedom, and Alexander's 1736 pamphlet account of it became the best-known early eighteenth-century American defence of libertarian free-speech ideals.

'Every man who prefers freedom to a life of slavery will bless and honour you,' Zenger's lawyer had appealed to the jury. Probably there were Black faces in the room when he spoke, for enslaved people made up a fifth of New York's population. Alongside its constant appeals to 'liberty' and denunciations of 'slavery', the *New-York Weekly Journal*, like most American papers, regularly advertised slave sales. Like other colonial printers, Zenger sometimes acted as a middleman in such trans-actions. Like them, too, he may well have owned and traded slaves, and used them in the production and distribution of his paper. When copies of the *Journal* were publicly burned on the governor's orders, it was an unfree 'Negro' man who carried out the task. James Alexander, an immigrant from Scotland, owned Black New Yorkers and helped his son become an enthusiastic shipper and trader of African slaves; Lewis Morris Snr, descended from Caribbean planters, and an equally 'devoted reader' of Cato's Letters, was the largest slaveholder in all of the northern colonies. Even to term this constant juxtaposition of slav-ery and liberty a 'paradox', as American historians habitually do, is to whitewash the truth. Keeping other humans in bondage was never in contradiction with early white Americans' views on freedom of speech or action: it sustained it. Alexander, one of the richest people in New York, spoke contemptuously of 'the pampered insolence of the slaves' who toiled all around him. 'Negroes', Morris Senior once warned his son, were inveterate thieves and 'both stupid and conceited': they were not fit to look after, or speak for, themselves.

Every day of their lives in the West Indies, Thomas Gordon's chil-dren, too, made manifest that free speech, as they understood it, was a racist ideology. We can only surmise how far Gordon himself would have approved of this interpretation of his writings. Neither he nor Trenchard ever crossed the Atlantic. But Elizée Dobrée did.

In the autumn of 1722, he'd had the world at his feet. Just a few days after surreptitiously transferring ownership of the *London Journal* to the government, Dobrée and his new wife, Eliza, proudly baptized their first child, Mary. Elisha (as he called himself in English) enjoyed his new proximity to the corridors of power, and used his profits to set up as a merchant banker in the City – the family career he had been trained for 'since my infancy'. Yet though he was fluent in French, had beautiful handwriting and could keep accounts, he was not very good at business. Soon he went bankrupt. He and his wife were forced to move to cheaper lodgings. They had more children. Casting about, he tried to restore his fortunes with a fanciful plan to recoin Guernsey's currency. But before his youngest turned two, he'd had enough. Leaving his family behind, he embarked for America.

He may have had some personal contacts there, for his extended family were in the business of buying and selling captive African people. Equiano mentions them in his famous autobiography: he was first brought to England on a vessel they owned; his enslaver knew them. In any event, Dobrée made for Charleston, South Carolina, the capital of continental slavery, and tried to set up as a trader. Things did not go well. Soon he was forced to flee south, to the brand-new colony of Georgia, the hardscrabble frontier of British settlement. But within days of his arrival in Savannah, his creditors caught up with him, and he was again declared bankrupt.

'I . . . came into these American parts in hopes to better my fortune,' he later wrote, 'but all in vain.' Despite concocting endless harebrained schemes to make money – planting exotic crops, exporting timber, building a ship, keeping cattle, panning for salt – Elisha Dobrée spent the rest of his life essentially living by his pen. He wrote letters and petitions, translated papers and cast accounts for others. Merchants, lawyers and local administrators employed him as a scrivener and bookkeeper, in their offices or for piece rates. He thought repeatedly about composing a manuscript newsletter, a weekly 'journal of events', for Georgia's Trustees, and begged them for employment as a clerk, accountant or other kind of 'penman' – as he was 'not strong enough for a sawyer or any hard-working trade'. Eventually, as his dreams of prosperity faded away, together with his hopes of ever seeing his family again, his skill as a writer was all he had left.

Whatever he thought of Trenchard and Gordon's idea that liberty of speech prevented 'slavery', he surely reflected on how his power as a scribe and his 'freedom in writing' elevated him, not just beyond less-educated whites but especially above the darker-skinned people held in bondage all around him. Half of Charleston's population was Black, yet South Carolina's laws, like those of other colonies, prohibited the movement of 'any Negro or slave' without a written 'ticket' from their owner, and empowered 'any white Person, to beat, maim or assault . . . [or] kill' any enslaved person who failed to produce one. It was illegal to counterfeit such a pass, or even to teach a slave to write. As in the West Indies, enslaved people were denied literacy, yet their lives could hinge on the production – or forgery – of letters.

Though Georgia had been founded without slavery, to encourage the industry of poor European settlers, its white colonists almost immediately began to complain that this infringed their 'rights', 'privileges', and 'natural liberties' as British subjects, making them 'greater slaves' than any 'poor Africans' would be. Following a vociferous campaign, slavery was legalized in 1750. Yet from the colony's inception, enslaved Indians and Africans had already been everywhere in Georgia: on the run to freedom in Spanish Florida; on hire from South Carolina; or illegally imported by settlers championing their own 'liberty of getting Negroes'. Dobrée personally relied on their forced labour. He did business with slavers. One of his closest companions on the American frontier, Francis Moore, had spent years with the Royal African Company, buying enslaved people on the Gold Coast. With the colony's 'most noted freeholders', Dobrée discussed drawing up a petition for Georgia's whites 'to have Negroes' too. He wrote himself to the Trustees in London, urging them to permit it. He criticized Savannah's governors for treating whites 'more like slaves than Christian freemen'. He was a weak, wheedling, endlessly self-pitying man, whose wife, Eliza, refusing to join him, dismissed him as 'whimsical', feckless and improvident. But, as was the case for most American colonists, racialized unfreedom buoyed up his own sense of liberty and self-worth.

The other ironic twist of Dobrée's later life was that, barely a decade after he had so successfully deployed the mercenary power of the press against others, first to attack the government and then to sell out his own journalists, he came to experience its negative effects for himself. He did not like it. In July 1734, Savannah's bailiff advertised Dobrée's insolvency in the new *South-Carolina Gazette*, the region's first newspaper. For months afterwards, Dobrée fumed about 'the great damage I suffered and still am like to suffer' from 'the advertisement in the Carolina Gazette, which spreads through all America'. He had been ruined, he spluttered: 'The discredit and ill character of persons thus advertised is a barbarous way of murdering a man in his reputation, the loss of which is one of the greatest loss[es] a person can suffer in this world.'

He was right about the reach of newsprint: even in London, people read about his latest dishonour. But when he opened the weekly *Gazette* in those lonely early months on the American frontier, he also would have found, alongside intermittent notices about his own bankruptcy, some startling reminders of the new free-speech ideals that he himself had helped usher into the world – and of the explicitly racialized shapes that such ideas of liberty and bondage were taking on in America. Just as he arrived in Charleston, the *Gazette* relaunched itself – with a précis of Cato's first letter on free speech. The *New-York Weekly Journal* circulated in the south, so, throughout 1734, Dobrée quite likely also followed its extraordinary championing of Cato's views. If not, just a few days after complaining about his own appearance in the *Gazette*'s columns, he would have read in them what was happening to Zenger and his paper. Over the page in the same issue was a report about a slave rebellion, an advertisement for a large slave plantation, and another offering a reward for the return of an escaped 'Negro man, named Cato' – a name very often given to slaves in the British colonies. The following year, when the *Gazette* reprinted the London Cato's first essay on free speech, extolling it as the foundation of public liberty and 'the right of every man, as far as by it he does not hurt or control the right of another', its next sheet advertised the usual cargoes of 'choice Negro slaves' and African 'runaways' called 'Flora', 'Sancho' and 'Sampson' – men and women whose speech was so unfree in the eyes of white people that even their own names had been taken from them.

The last trace I have been able to find of Dobrée is that, early in 1750, he wrote, witnessed and proved the will of a New York tavern keeper called Affy Crawford. That suggests he may also have known her recently deceased husband, Hugh, who a decade earlier as a New York constable had taken an active part in the bloodiest racial episode of that city's colonial history. Following a string of fires over several weeks in the spring of 1741, Manhattan's colonists feared their slaves were plotting to rise up against them. Along with a few suspect whites, more than two hundred enslaved and free Black men and women were swept up in the ensuing investigation. Scores were put on trial; thirty Black people were hanged or burnt at the stake; eighty-four more were sold into a living death as plantation slaves in the West Indies. Among those tried were four men named Cato. Three of these were executed; one lied his way to a pardon.

To warn his readers against Black people's 'great deal of craft; their unintelligible jargon' and their inveterate deceitfulness, the city's chief attorney printed the shackled speech of the almost twenty enslaved people who had been forced to testify. One of them, a teenager named Sawney or Sandy, initially refused to volunteer anything, even after he had been 'for a long time argued with' by the white jurymen. 'They told him, if he would speak the truth, the governor would pardon him . . . [and] save his life' – to which he answered: '*That the time before* [i.e. during an earlier uprising] *after that the Negroes told all they knew, then the white people hanged them.*' That had been in 1712, before Sandy was born: he must have been taught this lesson by his elders. In the face of white justice, Black people knew, neither truth, lies nor silence would necessarily save them. Dobrée was in New York at this time, working as a scribe in various government bureaus: the Customs House, the Treasury, the Naval Office, the Secretary's office. So he almost certainly lived through this episode, witnessed the executions, and knew those involved in its violent upholding of white liberty.

In fact, in almost twenty years criss-crossing the Eastern seaboard in search of work, from New York all the way down to Frederica, the southernmost outpost of British territory, Dobrée interacted, Zelig-like, with a remarkable collection of people: James Oglethorpe, the founder of Georgia, who for years employed him as his confidential scribe; Richard Peters, the leading Philadelphia intellectual and Secretary of Pennsylvania; John Wesley, the creator of Methodism, whom he impressed with his piety. But by far his longest association, probably the most enduring employment of his life, was with none other than James Alexander, the foremost American exponent of Cato's philosophy, mastermind of the *New-York Weekly Journal*'s partisan appeals for free speech and liberty – and a rich, untroubled exponent of actual human slavery.

When they first got to know each other, Alexander, as one of New York's leading attorneys, was helping to lead the slave trials and executions of 1741–2. For at least eight or nine years thereafter, he met intermittently with Dobrée, sent money to his wife in England, and paid him handsomely to copy thousands of pages of sensitive legal documents for him and his associates. By this time, New Jersey had become the main focus of his legal and political life: his friend Lewis Morris Snr, the other leader of the anti-Cosby agitation of the past decade, was now its governor. Alexander doubtless appreciated Dobrée's skill as a scrivener; among the surviving colonial records of those decades must still be untold numbers of anonymous documents – scribed letters, business accounts, legal minutes – in his clear and florid hand. Yet it is hard to imagine that was the only reason for his lengthy patronage of the man. Surely he also valued Dobrée as the former proprietor of the *London Journal* – the unsung third creator of Cato's Letters, whose ideals had so inspired him, and which he himself had done so much to popularize among his free, white, newspaper-reading, slave-owning fellow Americans.

LIBERTY AND SPEECH

In the autumn of 1739, a group of enslaved African men and women in South Carolina staged the most audacious bid for freedom that British colonists on the North American mainland had ever seen. On the outbreak of war with Spain, up to a hundred slaves escaped from their plantations, seized arms and ammunition, and tried to make their way south through Georgia, to liberty in Florida. Before they were hunted down and executed, they killed about twenty-five white settlers and alarmed thousands more. One reason why New Yorkers were so jittery about slave conspiracies in 1741 was the knowledge of what had happened in Stono, near Charleston, just a few months earlier.

Most of what we know about this event comes from a single, detailed, seven-page document composed in Savannah, Georgia, soon after it occurred. Without this text, the name of the rebels' captain, Jemmy, would have gone unrecorded, and so too the indelible image of their company marching along at daybreak 'with colours displayed and two drums beating', new recruits running to join them on the road, and all of them 'calling out Liberty' – Liberty, Liberty! Other contemporary accounts suggest the brutality of the white response. Dozens of rebels were shot, hanged or gibbeted alive (that is, lashed to a post and starved to death); some planters 'cut off their heads and set them up at every mile post they came to'. But this particular narrative was composed to sway public opinion in England: it was expressly sent to London to be published in the newspapers there. Though the rebels were 'shot on the spot', it stressed, this in fact redounded 'to the honour of the Carolina Planters . . . [who] did not torture one Negro, but only put them to an easy death'. That these 'Negro slaves' had been 'brought' from Africa, and were probably fellow Christians, was noted in passing; what mattered was 'the humanity' shown them by the colonists. Even when slaughtering other human beings for resisting enslavement, the superiority of white people shone through. This document was penned by Elisha Dobrée.

The enslaved rebels themselves had no newspapers, no pens, no paper. Their speech is lost to posterity – all but that single, exhilarating word they chanted together during their brief moment of freedom: 'Liberty!' They lived in a society that prized freedom of speech, writing and publishing primarily as markers of free, white, male, property-owning citizenship. Cato's Letters, its first and most influential model, consciously privileged certain types of speaker, and certain forms of speech, over others. Despite its universalist language, the gendered and racial shape of liberty was already implicit in Trenchard and Gordon's text, and in the lives of its creators. When those ideals were transplanted across the Atlantic, it was not hard for them to be racialized still further. The makers and consumers of early newspapers celebrated them for advancing unfettered speech, and so do modern historians: but they were also powerful tools of slavery and white supremacy. In addition to facilitating the slave trade, and endlessly reinforcing notions of non-white inferiority in their columns, another of their uses was to advertise and thus help recapture absconded slaves – a function pioneered not by colonial printers but already by seventeenth-century English papers. Newspapers were never neutral or universal conduits of opinion. And the shape that abstract values such as free speech take on, across time and space, is likewise always politicized. The free speech of some is established through the silencing of others.

Yet that also means the meaning of such terms is never completely settled. They can be appropriated, extended – or ignored. The asserting of ideals of free speech required a perpetual labour of indoctrination, because of the agency of those who contested its presumptions and, secretly or openly, raised their own voices and pens in defiance: servants, women, non-whites, slaves. 'Though he is my property,' seethed the Charleston enslaver Joshua Eden, whose Black man Limus had run away, with his 'saucy and impudent tongue ... he has the audacity to tell me [that] he will be free, that he will serve no man, and that he will be conquered or governed by no man.'

'Servitude mars all genius,' Cato's Letters had disdainfully asserted, 'nor is either a pen or a pencil of any use in a hand that is manacled.' That was the rhetoric of free people; but it was not true. The unfree could never be permanently silenced, and they themselves knew that. In the oral tradition of the Stono rebellion that was passed down by its enslaved survivors, its leader had been a slave – called Cato – who knew how to read and write. Long before the uprising, he used this power to write 'passes for slaves and do all he can to send them to freedom'.

That was what Francis Williams's favourite pupil, Brown, had done, too. And there were many like him. In the early summer of 1729, a few years after New York acquired its first newspaper, James Alexander placed an advertisement in its columns. He was in his late thirties, already a rich and powerful politician, the father of seven young children and stepchildren, the possessor of grand houses, large estates and many other human beings. To his great annoyance, one of them, a Black American his own age, 'a sensible cunning fellow' named Yaff whom he had acquired only recently, had dared to escape. Alexander offered a large reward for his recapture. His enslaved servant had absconded around 9 June, and the ad ran for weeks, until the end of July – perhaps that means that he managed to remain at large.

Yaff was literate: he had probably forged himself a pass to get away. He was wearing livery – he may have been Alexander's butler.

Who knows if he'd had the chance to browse in Alexander's library, the finest in New York, or if he had ever flicked through its prized volumes of Cato's Letters. No matter. He understood the power of words, and of writing. He'd already been sold twice in his life. He knew what freedom really was, that white people controlled its shape – and that he refused to let them.

5

Enlightened Experiments

The world's first laws explicitly upholding freedom of expression were not passed in Britain, Holland, France or America, but in the far north of Europe. In December 1766, the king of Sweden approved a revolutionary statute, 'Relating to Freedom of Writing and of the Press'. It opened with a ringing endorsement of 'the great advantages that flow to the public from a lawful freedom of writing and of the press':

> an unrestricted mutual enlightenment in various useful subjects not only promotes the development and dissemination of sciences and useful crafts but also offers greater opportunities to each of our loyal subjects to gain improved knowledge and appreciation of a wisely ordered system of government; while this freedom should also be regarded as one of the best means of improving morality and promoting obedience to the laws, when abuses and illegalities are revealed to the public through the press.

Before long, the new prince of Denmark–Norway followed suit. Sweden was an enemy country, so neither he nor any other Danish discussion of press freedom in the 1770s ever referred to its example, though it must have influenced them. 'We have decided to permit in our kingdoms and lands in general an unlimited freedom of the press,' a Danish proclamation of September 1770 declared. For

> we are fully convinced that it is as harmful to the impartial search for truth as it is to the discovery of obsolete errors and prejudices, when honest-minded patriots, zealous for the common good and the genuine welfare of their fellow citizens, are frightened and prevented, by orders or preconceptions, or deference to persons, from writing freely,

attacking abuses and uncovering prejudices, according to their insight, conscience, and conviction.

This sudden Nordic embrace of free expression was especially remarkable because these were cultures that had previously been highly repressive of critical speech. Unlike Britain, the Dutch United Provinces and North America, the northern kingdoms had few printing houses, strict censorship, authoritarian governments and hardly any political journalism. In Swedish law it had hitherto been a crime simply to write down any criticism of the constitution – even if you did so in private and never showed it to another person. Under the Danish and Norwegian codes, anyone writing or posting up 'any anonymous lampoon, or scurrilous paper, on any person of established character' would suffer life imprisonment with hard labour, or be executed.

So how did it come about that these two unlikely nations pioneered legalized freedom of expression? What did it mean for them – and how do their stories fit into the global history of free speech? To answer these questions, we need to start by surveying how, by the mid eighteenth century, intellectuals across Europe saw freedom of expression and liberty of the press not just as political and religious ideals, but as practical tools for advancing knowledge and promoting social progress.

THE FREEDOM OF PHILOSOPHIZING

The creators of the Scandinavian free-speech laws all shared several presumptions. The most basic one was that freedom of discussion advanced truth and learning. This was already a long-established scholarly principle. Since the middle ages, European universities, like their counterparts in Asia and Africa, had used staged verbal disputations to investigate controversial topics. Handling and exploding dangerous ideas in this carefully controlled arena – in Latin, within the walls of the university, under the guidance of orthodox professors, relying only on reasoned arguments – was meant to inoculate students and teachers against error, and advance correct understanding.* Rulers often also gave universities and scientific academies special responsibilities for the censorship and publishing of theological, philosophical and scientific texts.

The scholarly ideal of *libertas philosophandi* ('the freedom of philosophizing') also extended to international intellectual exchange through print and writing. In the fifteenth century, European humanists had coined the phrase 'the republic of letters' for their cross-border community of scholars. By 1700 this had become a well-known concept, often celebrated for its egalitarian commitment to freedom of expression. Here, for example, is how it was described in 1697 by someone who knew a lot about censorship, the great French philosopher Pierre Bayle – a man who spent most of his scholarly life as a refugee, exiled from his homeland because of its persecution of Protestants like him. The republic of letters, he wrote with feeling, was not like that. In the real world, rulers everywhere controlled what you could and couldn't say. The republic of letters, by contrast,

> is an extremely free state. The only dominion recognized is that of truth and reason: under their auspices, war can be innocently waged on anyone ... In relation to error and ignorance, every individual has the right to take up arms and may exercise it without asking permission from those that govern.

In other words, early theorists of scholarly free speech defined it as a separate sphere, beyond governmental control. Serious scholarly debate should be left unregulated, Bayle urged, because it was harmless. 'Showing the public, the faults, which are in a book' never hurt anyone. That was quite different from publishing harmful 'libels' or 'satires': even scholars should be punished if they did that, 'because satires divest a man of his reputation, which is a kind of civil

---

* Though sometimes this technique backfired: many notorious cases of religious heresy – from the middle ages through to the radical scepticism of the Edinburgh student Thomas Aikenhead, who in 1697 became the last person to be executed for blasphemy in the British Isles – were also provoked by the culture of university disputation.

homicide'. Proper scholarship or sincere religious speculation was one thing; slander or sedition quite another.

Even Baruch Spinoza, the most radical seventeenth-century theorist of *libertas philosophandi*, stressed this point. Freedom of philosophical speculation was 'absolutely necessary for progress in science and the liberal arts', he explained, but no one should speak or act against 'the laws of the authorities' or propound seditious doctrines: 'loyalty to the state is paramount'. That was also the view taken by the influential Prussian philosopher Immanuel Kant a century later. Reasoned public debate, he argued, 'must at all times be free, and it alone can bring about enlightenment' – yet such intellectual liberty was perfectly compatible with 'a lesser degree of civil freedom'. Sucking up to his learned but despotic monarch, Frederick the Great, Kant distinguished freedom of reasoning from political agitation. 'In the interests of the commonwealth', even scholars 'must conduct themselves passively in order that the government may direct them . . . Here one is certainly not allowed to argue; rather, one must obey.'

A perennial difficulty with justifying academic free speech in this way was, however, that the distinction between harmless scholarship and dangerous subversion lay essentially in the eye of the beholder. Bayle, Spinoza and Kant all defended scholarly free thinking as part of their own attacks on religious superstition, 'priestcraft' and intolerance – yet to Catholics and orthodox Protestants across Europe, such critiques, no matter how learned or decorously expressed, were deeply threatening. Bayle's works were widely proscribed. Spinoza was expelled from his Amsterdam Jewish community for teaching 'abominable heresies'; his writings were banned across Europe, and could only be printed clandestinely.

That the foremost early theorists of academic liberty were themselves deeply contentious writers was no accident, nor that the arguments for religious and scholarly free speech were very similar. Because religious questions were both central to scholarship and of the utmost political sensitivity, learned free speech was never an apolitical domain. On the contrary – attempts to classify it as such were themselves political statements. Like all definitions of free speech, they were assertions that their authors' own views should be exempt from constraint.

Even in the most spiritually tolerant of European nations, like England and the Dutch Republic, radical scholarly and religious speculation was thus never without risk. Writings that seemed to encourage irreligion, political disaffection, insubordination or sexual libertinism could still be banned, their writers and publishers punished, their careers destroyed. Elsewhere, more stringent censorship persisted – though so did the long-standing practices of printing works in one place to be sold elsewhere, in order to evade local controls, of applying different standards to texts in foreign languages and of circulating the most controversial materials only in manuscript. What appeared in print was, everywhere, a continual process of negotiation between authors, printers, censors, the clergy and secular governments – not just about particular texts, but about how best to channel the power of the printing press towards positive, rather than destructive, ends.

As the principles of religious and/or learned free speech came, to varying degrees, to be accepted by educated Europeans, this outlook also increasingly spilled over into their attitudes towards public discussion more generally. Even in the heartland of the Inquisition, learned readers wishing to read particular banned books could obtain an official permit to do so, and by the mid eighteenth century, the secular authorities of Italy's various states were increasingly defining press liberty in more permissive terms than the clergy had traditionally allowed. Scholarship itself was also ever more accessible. Bayle's best-selling works were all published not in Latin but in French, and then translated into English. New scholarly periodicals, like the popular *Nouvelles de la république des lettres* that he founded in 1684, allowed even amateurs to keep abreast of the latest scientific news, book reviews and debates, in English, German, Dutch, Italian or French.

As the editors of the *Encyclopédie*, the great monument of French Enlightenment thought, put it in 1753: 'we believe that the democracy of the republic of letters must extend to every subject, even to allow and suffer the worst criticisms, as long as they are not personal'. The simple proposition that open public debate would dispel error and bring illumination in every sphere of life – morality, agriculture, religion, trade, education, government – was intrinsically appealing to progressive Christians who believed that a similar spirit of rational, free enquiry had already reduced religious superstition and transformed scientific understanding of the world. The great engine of such progress was the printing press, whose liberation from censorship therefore became essential to the progress of humanity.

SPREADING ENLIGHTENMENT

What would such 'liberty of the press' look like in practice? Though Jean-Jacques Rousseau, the most influential European social theorist of the later eighteenth century, didn't address this question in particular, his ideas about human nature, social development and the 'general will' of the people profoundly shaped its international discussion. The popular French author Louis-Sébastien Mercier, for one, drew on them in several banned but best-selling works envisaging the enlightened future.

In the present, Mercier informed his readers, the truth was being stifled by tyranny, despotism and superstition. Censorship protected corrupt rulers from the popular outrage to which fearless 'philosophical writers', with their unerring ability to reveal injustice, would otherwise expose them. Yet everywhere, enlightened ideas were 'awakening Europe from its slumbers' – before long, society, law and politics alike would be guided by 'the pure lights of reason'. In Mercier's utopian year 2440, the *philosophes* of the eighteenth century have come to be worshipped as prophets whose writings had inspired the people to overthrow oppression and establish a truly rational society.

The citizens of the twenty-fifth century have destroyed most other texts from the past, because they were dangerously full of error – 'nothing leads the mind farther astray than bad books'. But they also celebrate liberty of the press as 'the true measure of the liberty of the people'. Because their government is just, it fears no criticism; and because the people are rational, 'very few absurdities are published'. Indeed, because the objective 'opinion of the public' is the best judge of vice and virtue, it automatically flushes out any work that might contain 'dangerous principles, such as are inconsistent with sound morality' – 'the public voice is the sole judge in these cases; and it is to that alone [that] regard is paid'. The author of any 'bad book' is made to wear 'a mask, in order to hide his shame, till he has effaced it by writing something more rational and beneficial to society'. Meanwhile, he is visited twice a day by two virtuous citizens, who use reason to convince him of his faults. All of them are men: in the perfect future, women would only be wives and housekeepers, never writers or citizens.

This enthusiastic vision presumed that liberating the printing press would create an enlightened public, united in its understanding of truth and rejection of error. As Rousseau had asserted, in a properly constituted society 'the common good makes itself so manifestly evident that only common sense is needed to discern it' – the general will was 'unchanging, incorruptible and pure'.

Yet in reality, spreading enlightenment was a hugely contentious project. The idea of questioning all received authority and reshaping society on the basis of free public debate remained abhorrent to most conservative thinkers, rulers and churchmen. And even self-consciously enlightened thinkers differed widely in their attitudes (so much so that the Enlightenment was in truth never a single project but made up of many strands and modes of thought). Despite his own constant struggles with censors and book burnings, Rousseau himself upheld the right of governments to police the circulation of ideas, the obligation of writers to obey existing law, and the need for people to be correctly educated. The general will was not the same as the opinion of the majority; nor was too much dissent and public debate a good thing, if it led to disunity or error. Freedom of expression, he argued, could be good or bad: it depended on the consequences. Responsible books, like his own, that advanced the common good deserved protection. But slander and abuse did not – nor obscene, subversive or otherwise 'dangerous' writings of any kind.

THE PRESS AND THE PUBLIC

Out of these different debates there had emerged by the mid eighteenth century two distinctive ways of thinking about print, freedom and politics. British and American oppositional writers (and many French ones, too) focused on the role of the press in holding rulers to account – by 1800, some English commentators referred to it as a new 'fourth estate', alongside the three traditional 'estates' of clergy, nobility and commons. Anglophone conservatives were more apt to complain that gutter journalism and cheap print were debasing politics and undermining social order. Yet they, too, invariably celebrated 'the liberty of the press' from government control as a key feature of their constitutions. As the traditionalist Oxford professor, judge and member of parliament William Blackstone put it in his massively influential interpretation of 1769, the essence of press freedom was simply the absence of 'previous restraints' – that is, of pre-publication censorship.

Many Scandinavian proponents of press liberty were inspired by such attitudes, as we'll see. But their outlook was also strongly influenced by the dominant outlook across Catholic Europe, Latin America, and the Germanic and the Eastern European world. This was that liberty of the press was not a fundamental right but a tool of government. It should be used to educate the population and modernize the nation, but not be allowed to undermine social or political stability. Certain political or religious subjects were too dangerous for the general population to discuss without proper guidance; only educated people could be trusted with greater freedom; and rulers should retain ultimate control over the boundaries of public debate. In this view, press freedom was entirely compatible with some form of prior restraint.

Whenever Italian intellectuals celebrated 'freedom of the press' or 'liberty to think and write', for example, they never had in mind the abolition of censorship, but only its transfer from the clergy into enlightened, secular hands. The philosopher Carlo Antonio Pilati's best-selling treatise *On Reforming Italy, or Rather Ways to Reform the Worst Customs and Most Pernicious Laws of Italy* (1767) exemplified this position. 'Books can do good, but also much harm,' he explained. The best way to get 'good books' into wide circulation, and to deny publication to those that contained 'intolerable errors', was to have all manuscripts reviewed by unprejudiced, enlightened state censors. By the mid eighteenth century, across Europe, the men (again, always men) who acted as official censors were themselves commonly writers and intellectuals who were sympathetic to the cause of enlightenment. Usually, they revised texts in collaboration and negotiation with authors, and regarded their own role as largely constructive, rather than punitive.

This conception of press freedom also appealed to rulers who were keen to modernize their nations without relinquishing absolute power – like the Holy Roman Emperor, Joseph II, the German-born empress of Russia, Catherine the Great, and her former lover, the anglophile king of Poland–Lithuania, Stanisław August. Censorship policy in such realms shifted frequently, as rulers succeeded each other, changed their minds or responded to political circumstances. Yet the language of their legal regulations often described it in terms of press 'liberty', and so did contemporary observers. The liberty of the pen, Voltaire wrote in 1768, 'is established in England as in Poland', as if the situation in those two countries was essentially comparable.

The most celebrated example of such a regime was that of Frederick the Great of Prussia, who throughout his long rule (1740–86) set himself up as the continent's most enlightened philosopher-prince – corresponding with leading intellectuals, sheltering controversial writers and encouraging learned debate. 'Nothing surprised me more, when I first came to Berlin' in 1775, a Scottish visitor noted, 'than the freedom with which many people speak of the measures of government, and the conduct of the King ... The same freedom appears in the booksellers' shops, where literary productions of all kinds are sold openly.' But this was always only liberty on the ruler's terms. 'Don't speak to me of your Berliner freedom of thought and expression,' the great dramatist and philosopher Gotthold Ephraim Lessing complained to a friend in 1769, shortly after he'd left Prussia for the more liberal metropolis of Hamburg:

> It consists solely of the freedom to ridicule religion as much as you like ... But let someone appear in Berlin to speak out for the rights of the subjects who wish to raise their voices against exploitation and despotism, as is already happening in France and Denmark: and then you will soon experience which nation is, even today, the most enslaved in Europe.

Because Germany was divided into countless smaller principalities, each with its own systems of law and censorship, it was, compared to the Dutch-, French- and English-speaking worlds, slower to develop a unified sphere of public debate. Until the 1770s, German discussion of press freedom was largely confined to scholars, and dominated by the views of its leading philosopher, Christian Wolff.

Wolff saw himself as a great champion of fearless rationalism. The exercise of reason, he argued, was the only sure path to ascertaining truth. In 1723, having scandalized his more orthodox colleagues at Halle University by extolling the moral capacity of non-Christians, he was stripped of his professorship and exiled from Prussia on pain of death. Only in 1740, after the accession of Frederick the Great, was he permitted to return. Despite this experience, his views on liberty of speech and of the press were pretty conventional. *Libertas philosophandi*, he repeatedly stressed, was a restricted sphere. It should steer clear of political questions. Nor should the freedoms enjoyed by scholars extend to the general public. Government censorship was essential, for ordinary people were not yet rational enough to be trusted to their own judgements.

Most later German theorists agreed. Even Karl Friedrich Bahrdt, who in 1787 defended press freedom as a 'human right', drew the line at revealing 'things that are not public and should not be publicized'. The secret workings of rulers and ministers, he emphasized, 'must remain absolutely excluded from the domain of the freedom of the press. For if writers were to begin to venture into things of this kind and speak about them before the public, this could become a danger to the state and undermine respect for the prince abroad.' Kant's conception of free speech ('it must not transcend the bounds of respect and devotion towards the existing constitution') emerged out of this intellectual tradition. In the aftermath of the French Revolution, a few younger German thinkers, such as Johann Gottlieb Fichte, flirted with a more populist, unlimited view of press liberty. But for most, freedom of speech could never trump obedience to the state.

This was because German theorists of press freedom were not just the subjects of absolute rulers but often their employees. As members of a tiny elite of enlightened scholar-administrators, helping to govern comparatively small, conservative nations with limited reading publics, the context of their debates, and their own social and political position, were very different from that of most French or anglophone writers of the later eighteenth century, who had easier access to large, receptive audiences, and who often championed press liberty in order to attack the government of the day, boost their public profile, ridicule their intellectual opponents, or profit from the sales of their own publications.

Beyond these various differences and inhibitions, though, most progressive eighteenth-century intellectuals, across Europe and North America, shared a general belief in what we might call the trickle-down theory of enlightenment. That is, if enlightened rulers and intellectuals showed the way, others would follow, and society as a whole would gradually improve. It was only lack of education that produced 'the gross ignorance and stupidity which, in a civilized society, seem so frequently to benumb the understandings of all the inferior ranks of people', observed Adam Smith: 'the more they are instructed, the less liable they are to the delusions of enthusiasm and superstition'. 'Learning to read and write raises us above the rabble,' the young Prussian lawyer Heinrich Friedrich Dietz agreed, in his *Apology for Toleration and Press Freedom* (1781). 'It is therefore a great duty of the educated mind to communicate its insights and knowledge to others, and thereby to seek to increase the number of wise and happy people in the state, and to diminish the great crowd of the mob.'

DOCTOR'S ORDERS

The Nordic free-speech laws of 1766–70 were a direct product of this growing international ferment over the printing press as an engine of social progress. The politicians who created them were all writers and intellectuals. Many had been educated at German universities, or inspired by their own experiences of living and working in other countries, especially England.

Denmark–Norway was an absolute monarchy – in theory its ruler, Christian VII, could decide everything unilaterally. But in practice he was a mentally ill young man who'd only recently ascended to the throne and had little interest in government. It was Johann Friedrich Struensee, the king's energetic new German physician, de facto chief minister – and also the secret lover of his English queen, Caroline Matilda – who pushed through the revolutionary press decree of 1770.

At the time of its implementation, the king was twenty-one, the queen nineteen and Struensee himself only thirty-three. But he was already an ambitious public intellectual, with experience of battling censorship in the cause of enlightenment. His father, Adam, was a leading Protestant clergyman, author and university professor, and Struensee grew up in a milieu dedicated to intellectual and religious tolerance – by the time he was a young adult, he privately scorned Christianity as a mess of irrational imposture. In his teens, he studied medicine at Halle, a centre of German Enlightenment and rationalist thought under Wolff's leadership – whose lectures he also attended. Upon graduating in 1757, he took a job as public physician in Altona, Denmark's second-largest city, right next to Hamburg.

Over the following decade, as well as maintaining a busy and innovative practice as a doctor, Struensee threw himself into local intellectual life, reading widely in several languages, writing regularly for learned and literary magazines, becoming friends with the region's leading (and often heterodox) writers and scholars, battling with them against the vicissitudes of Hamburg and Altona's different censorship regimes, and even starting up two periodicals of his own – a *Monthly Magazine of Usefulness and Pleasure* and the *Altona Monthly for the Promotion of Science, Arts, Taste, and Morality*. Both sought to combat superstition and spread enlightenment; both were soon shut down by the local censors. In vain, Struensee appealed in 1764 to the Danish chief minister, Count Bernstorff, to judge whether his efforts were 'harmful or beneficial to the public', and to be allowed to publish without such oversight – because, he argued, 'a censorship that is conceived of as corrective and used to rob me of the freedom, which all writers have, would not only insult my honour but also hinder the thing itself' – that is, the public good.

No, he was told in reply: 'publication and censorship go together as naturally as a dog and the cudgel its owner uses to punish it'. It was a painful episode, though it didn't stop him from continuing to publish his thoughts on the 'omnipotent pedagogical power of enlightenment'. In the later 1760s, Struensee translated Voltaire, cultivated aristocratic connections and eventually came to the notice of the royal court in Copenhagen, where his equally freethinking grandfather had been doctor to the previous king. In 1768, the increasingly unstable new teenaged monarch, who also adored Voltaire, passed through Altona and took Struensee on as royal physician for a lengthy tour of Germany, the Netherlands, England and France. In London, the young doctor met Samuel Johnson and other English writers; in Paris, leading *philosophes* such as d'Alembert and Helvetius; in Oxford and Cambridge he was given honorary degrees. By the time he arrived in Copenhagen in 1769, he had highly developed views on print liberty, and was also (to Bernstorff's chagrin) increasingly close to the king and the levers of power.

As soon as he grasped them, he set the press free. In the autumn of 1770, Struensee convinced Christian VII to sack Bernstorff, abolish the royal Council and essentially place all power in his own hands. His very first public act was the proclamation of 14 September that, with immediate effect, censorship was to be replaced by 'an unrestricted freedom of the press' throughout the realm. With it, he launched an intense campaign to radically transform every aspect of Danish society in accordance with enlightened principles. Over the next sixteen months, working at an astonishing pace, Struensee issued more than eighteen hundred decrees – curbing serfdom, abolishing torture, restricting the ill-treatment of enslaved people in Danish colonies, forbidding corporal punishment in schools, enhancing religious toleration, eliminating privileges of rank, reorganizing the court and government, rationalizing the criminal laws, and instituting hundreds of other educational, fiscal, social, military, medical, economic and agricultural reforms.

Denmark–Norway's press decree of 1770 was thus intended as the cornerstone of a much wider programme of governmental enlightenment. Its wording also illustrates the straightforward way in which a fairly typical mid-century European intellectual like Struensee regarded press freedom. Censorship inhibited progress; to liberate the printing press was to free the human spirit to advance on all fronts. Struensee never learned Danish, so he may not have known of the similar views that in recent decades had been expressed by local thinkers like Jens Schelderup Sneedorff and P. F. Suhm. But in any case, he didn't believe that the issue was complicated. The entire legislative order was expressed in a single handwritten sentence, taking up less than half a page of script; the royal memo that inspired it, jotted down by the king himself at a cabinet meeting with Struensee a few days earlier, had been shorter still: '3. Another order to the chancelleries: to give unrestricted permission to the press to print books without any censorship.' That was what happened when a progressive writer and man of science, who'd long chafed against censorship, suddenly found himself in a position of absolute power.

ANGLOPHILE INNOVATORS

The Swedish case was different. Its pioneering free-speech law, passed in 1766, was a much longer, more convoluted text: not the precipitous command of a single person, but a parliamentary statute whose passage was the culmination of decades of proposals, consultations and debates about press liberty among local politicians and intellectuals.

That was because in Sweden (which until 1809 included what is now Finland), a constitutional revolution in 1719–20 had placed all power with the Riksdag, composed of representatives of the country's four 'estates' – the nobility, clergy, citizens and peasantry. This parliament was supposed to meet every three years; in between, the nation was governed by a Council of State. The monarch was only a figurehead: when one king refused to sign his Council's orders, they simply created a rubber stamp of his signature, instead. Assisting the Council were the permanent administrative boards of major government departments. That of the Chancery, the Kanslikollegium, was in overall charge of censorship. The day-to-day vetting of religious literature was carried out by trusted clergymen of the national church; that of scholarly works by university professors; and that of secular texts by a special government department in Stockholm, headed by the chief censor. Written criticism of the constitution or government was forbidden, whether in manuscript or in print. As an official *Memorial on False and Erroneous Ideas* explained in 1752, 'ignorance is better than wrong ideas', and 'the idea that the Estates can err, is contrary to the fundamental law of the land'.

Despite this authoritarian system, we can trace the origins of Swedish ideas about press freedom back to the beginning of the eighteenth century. A key early figure was Count Carl Gyllenborg, the intellectually precocious scion of a leading family, who spent his formative adult years as secretary, Resident and finally Minister of the Swedish embassy in England. For almost fifteen years, between 1703 and 1717, he lived in London, revelling in its lively culture of print journalism, party-political intrigue, and freedom of discussion, publishing anonymous political pamphlets of his own, and developing a lifelong anglophilia. As well as becoming a Fellow of the Royal Society and marrying an English-woman, he greatly admired English drama, translated and wrote plays of his own, and made friends with leading authors, intellectuals and political polemicists like Jonathan Swift.

In 1722, back in Stockholm, Gyllenborg chaired a spirited discussion in the Kanslikollegium. The polymath Emanuel Swedenborg, who had also spent several years living in London during the previous decade, had recently been allowed to print a pamphlet on Sweden's economic crisis. Now, he wanted permission to advertise in the capital's new semi-official weekly paper, the *Stockholmske Post-Tidener*, asking readers for feedback on the subject. That could not be allowed, the board decided. As the former chief censor explained, it was unthinkable 'that private individuals should be allowed to deliver opinions in a matter of such general importance'. Yet the acting chief censor, Johan Rosenadler, had taken a different view. On matters that concerned everyone, 'from beggars to the rich', he reasoned, allowing the general public to air its views would help the next Riksdag formulate its policies. That was also the practice in England, Gyllenborg agreed, essentially making the same argument that Trenchard and Gordon had expounded in Cato's Letters just a few months earlier: 'In a free state no one should be prevented from public discussion of matters that concern everybody, especially as the truth thereby comes out and everyone becomes better informed as to the nature of the issue.'

In due course, Gyllenborg himself imported into Swedish politics many of the tools and tactics he'd learned about in England. Having become the leader of a political faction, he gradually shaped it into an organized party, with its own agents, whips, machinery of discip-line and publicity. During the 1738 election, he managed a team of paid writers who churned out clandestine manuscript pamphlets that ridiculed his political opponents as sleepy 'Night-Caps'. Henceforth, they became known as the 'Caps'; and his own party, which called itself the 'Hats', gradually consolidated its power. Towards the end of the 1739 Riksdag, Gyllenborg's young nephew Henning, evidently channelling his uncle's long-held views, duly proposed to his fellow legislators

> That every citizen without constraint or supervision may submit his thoughts to the free judgement of the public, which drives away the barbarian darkness in a country, encourages competition between cultured writers, through whom the truth more and more comes to the fore, and helps a free people to know itself, its strengths and its weaknesses.

Of course, he acknowledged, any publication that abused government, religion or good morals would still be punished; but perhaps it was time to lessen, or even abandon, prior censorship.

That was also the view of another prominent Swedish intellectual of this period, Anders Bachmanson, who was to become one of the leading Caps. He, too, had lived in London, in the early 1720s, and was deeply influenced by that experience. On his return to Stockholm in 1724, he applied in vain for permission to print a treatise on the latest British social and economic theories – including a chapter on the benefits of press liberty. For years he wrangled fruitlessly about its publication with Rosenadler the censor and with the Kanslikollegium. Eventually, in 1730, the work was printed without the offending part – though Bachmanson couldn't resist advertising in the text that its chapter on 'liberty' had been suppressed 'against the will of the author'. A few years later, in a book printed in Hamburg but also suppressed before publication, he devoted even more space to arguments for press freedom. Meanwhile, as a member of its 1727 session, Bachmanson too argued in the Riksdag against censorship.

Where did Bachmanson get his ideas from? His suppressed book of 1734, of which now only the manuscript survives, included a long final chapter that made clear his intellectual debts, and had been meant to introduce his Scandinavian readers to the most important foreign texts on the subject. They were all English. The earliest of them was one that he must have read soon after it first came out, when he was living in London. Perhaps it had also formed the basis of the now-lost chapter on press freedom that he'd drafted back in 1724.

It was Cato's first letter on free speech, printed in the *London Journal* of 4 February 1721.

By the middle of the century, Gyllenborg was dead, and his Hat party had come to regard the maintenance of censorship as a useful tool for maintaining their grip on power. In 1750, the government banned all public discussion of past or present policy, and punished the Uppsala University professor Johan Ihre for allowing the publication of academic theses in Latin that included political criticism. The Hats' leading theoretician, the scientist and bishop Johan Browallius, argued that all opponents of his party were traitors and tools of foreign conspiracy. His colleague Nils Wallerius, another great defender of orthodox religion, advised the librarian of Uppsala University that it was necessary to import into Sweden only a single copy of the works of David Hume and various other heterodox authors, for him to study and refute – such books 'should otherwise not be brought into the country and not be sold'.

Yet such strident defences of political and religious orthodoxy were partly provoked by growing pressure to ease censorship. In 1749 the Danish-Norwegian polymath Ludvig Holberg reported that many people in Sweden were now advocating 'to let authors write freely, as in England and Holland', though the majority was still against it. The government official Christian König, who'd studied abroad, argued in 1746–7 that scholars should be allowed publicly to discuss and critique actual and proposed laws and policies. In 1755, the Hats themselves took the unprecedented step of founding a weekly political newspaper, *En Ärlig Swensk* ('An Honest Swede'), in order to shape public opinion in their favour. This broached a host of political subjects whose very discussion had previously been forbidden. So did the increasing use of print by members of the Riksdag themselves. Most strikingly, the different estates began to publish their minutes and arguments when in dispute with each other, thus implicitly appealing to the judgement of the public at large.

The anonymous editor of *En Ärlig Swensk* was none other than the current chief censor himself, Niclas von Oelreich, a former university professor and librarian who took an increasingly permissive line, especially towards religious texts. He was only paid his censor's fee for works he approved, which may have influenced his decisions; he also gradually became disaffected with the Hats. 'Free peoples have the freedom and right to speak freely,' his newspaper now asserted. In 1756, he allowed Bachmanson (now ennobled and renamed Nordencrantz) to print an anonymous pamphlet, *Freedom in the Use of Reason, Pen and Print*. It was immediately banned by the government. But in 1760, as a leading member of the newly convened Riksdag, whose authority superseded that of the Kanslikollegium, Nordencrantz resubmitted the work to another censor and got it published at last – as well as a much longer, almost 700-page treatise advocating root and branch reform of Sweden's entire political system. He didn't propose the end of censorship, only greater freedom of political discussion – as in England, to whose example and authors he repeatedly referred. When the Council forbade this latter book's distribution, Nordencrantz successfully demanded that the text be examined by all 1,000 members of the Riksdag, to whom it was nominally addressed – thus ensuring that its arguments became very widely known. It proved to be the beginning of the end for the rule of the Hats, and for the existing machinery of press regulation.

SCIENTIFIC AND CIVIL LIBERTY

This was not the only spur. Just a few months earlier, Oelreich had been involved in another controversy about a free-speech pamphlet, this one written not by a politician but by an upstart young Finnish scholar, Peter Forsskål, whose career epitomizes the connections between Nordic free-speech debates and international scholarly trends. Forsskål had started out studying theology at Uppsala University, intending to become a clergyman, like his father. But then he learned Arabic and Hebrew, and came under the spell of Carl Linnaeus, the great botanist and zoologist – who later named a genus of nettles after him, in tribute to his prickly character. In 1753 Forsskål moved to Göttingen to continue his studies with the renowned orientalist and philosopher Johann David Michaelis. His three years there ignited a passionate interest in free speech. Partly this arose out of his academic work. He wrote and defended a Latin thesis, 'Doubts About the Principles of Modern Philosophy', which critiqued

Christian Wolff's dominant ontology as old-fashioned and insufficiently rational. He loved the cut and thrust of academic debate, and delighted in offending the sensibilities of powerful orthodox thinkers back home like Wallerius. But while in Göttingen Forsskål also began to conceive of liberty of speech as a matter of much broader, public importance – one of the necessary foundations for a truly free society.

That was partly because he found himself at a university that was as much English as German in its intellectual outlook. It had been founded in 1737 by George II of Great Britain, who was also the ruler of Hanover, to be a progressive centre of learning within his German territories. Forsskål found its atmosphere liberating compared to the intellectual climate in Sweden, and his professors encouraged this view. He and Forsskål had many discussions about the meaning of freedom, Michaelis later recalled, in which he had explained to his pupil 'that Swedish liberty was very different from what we called liberty. There [i.e. in Sweden], no one dared to express their opinions, let alone have them printed – that was what we called slavery.' 'If only in Sweden we had the freedom to think and to write that England and Germany enjoy,' Forsskål lamented on his return to Uppsala. Even though he never visited the British Isles, his aspirations for Swedish society were shaped by his perception of English press freedoms and civil liberties.

Another acquaintance of his who doubtless buttressed this view was the brilliant young Dutch publisher Elie Luzac, who had arrived in Göttingen as the university's new printer and bookseller just a few months after Forsskål. Michaelis was one of the people who had helped recruit him: he even helped him find the best location for his shop, where Luzac published and sold the latest works from across Europe. Over the previous decade, while based in Leiden, he had established himself as a central figure in the international republic of letters, becoming a renowned editor and printer of scholarly works and journals in several languages. He was himself an author and intellectual, with a lively interest in politics and current affairs as well as the latest scholarship. Just before he moved to Göttingen, one of his anonymous pamphlets was publicly burnt by the magistrates of Amsterdam, for arguing (with approving citations to Locke and many other English Whig theorists) that the people had a natural right to revolt against tyranny. Most eighteenth-century printers had firm opinions about press liberty, but few engaged with the question as deeply or publicly as Luzac.

In 1748, Luzac had published one of the most controversial works of the Enlightenment, the anonymous *L'Homme machine*, by his friend Julien Offray de La Mettrie, a French doctor who had fled to Leiden after his previous book on the same theme – the materiality of the human soul – had been banned in Paris. His new work created even more of a furore, due to its unmistakably atheist implications. The Dutch authorities ordered every copy of it to be confiscated and destroyed. Luzac was repeatedly interrogated about its origins, and heavily fined. Despite this (and his personal disagreement with its arguments), he refused to reveal the author's identity, and helped him escape to Prussia, where Frederick the Great added La Mettrie to his coterie of trophy intellectuals. Luzac clandestinely published further editions of *L'Homme machine*, as well as a best-selling pamphlet of his own on the subject (*L'Homme plus que machine*). He also engaged in spirited public and private debates about freedom of thought and the liberty of the press. The following year, again in French, he set out his views at length in the anonymously produced *Essay on the Freedom of Expression* (1749).

Luzac's treatise was essentially a work of Protestant moral philosophy, connecting liberty of thought to the freedom of conscience. Like his fellow Huguenot Bayle, to whom he referred, his main aim was to exalt the scholarly pursuit of truth through reasoned argument, and to condemn religiously based intolerance of such learned discussion. Without full freedom of religious and moral debate, it would be impossible to find truth; and, in the political sphere, if rulers were just, they had nothing to fear from criticism. Like Milton, Luzac argued that even intrinsically harmful ideas could have an ill effect only when taken up by minds inclined to vice: the problem was immoral people, not bad ideas. He also presumed that ideas were irrepressible, and that the general public ultimately would always distinguish truth from error (even if it might occasionally be led astray). At the same time, as a lifelong philosophical devotee of Christian Wolff, Luzac stressed that his model was only concerned with the expression of reasoned arguments in good faith. It didn't apply to other kinds of speech or writing, which could legitimately be censored: fiction, libels and lampoons, 'books full of indecent and injurious words', works that mixed arguments with insult and obscenity – or, he added mischievously, the ignorant and harmful pronouncements of clergymen about political affairs.

When Frederick the Great tried to persuade Luzac to move to Berlin, he demurred, noting privately that, by his own standards, even Prussian nobles were 'not accustomed to hearing free speech'. Instead, he dedicated his *Essay* to the English, the only nation in the world he believed enjoyed 'perfect' freedom of expression. His arguments about political free speech owed an unspoken but obvious debt to those of Trenchard and Gordon, which were well known in Holland. Indeed, Luzac was such a fan of their work that, during his time in Göttingen, one of his most ambitious projects was to commission and publish a grand, four-volume German translation of them. Forsskål must have known about this, too – its first part appeared around the same time that he was preparing his own dissertation, which was also published by Luzac.

So when Forsskål returned to Sweden a few months later, he was full of new ideas about press liberty. His first job was as a private tutor in the household of Johan Ihre, the Uppsala professor who'd been punished for allowing his students to express dissident political views in their academic dissertations. A few years later, secure in the knowledge that, through Michaelis's and Linnaeus's patronage, he was soon to embark on a scientific voyage abroad in the service of the Danish crown, Forsskål determined that he, too, would try to advance the cause of civil liberty in his homeland. To this end, in May 1759, he defended a thesis he had composed in the philosophy faculty at Uppsala, entitled 'On Civil Liberty' (*De libertate civili*). Unusually, it was written in Swedish; unsurprisingly, given its contents, he was refused permission to have it printed. When the Kanslikollegium upheld this decision, overruling his protest that it was insupportable 'in the land of freedom ... to live without the most tender part of freedom: to be allowed to speak and write about the flaws and benefits of the country', Forsskål decided to raise the stakes.

Without informing the Kanslikollegium, he submitted the text to the censor, Oelreich, accepted Oelreich's changes to the text, and had it printed as a public pamphlet. His publisher was Lars Salvius, the same radical bookseller and pamphleteer who a decade earlier had planned to do something similar with Ihre's students' political treatises. Though Oelreich had cut out Forsskål's most strident claims for free speech, such as 'the truth always wins when it is allowed to be challenged and defended equally', they all probably knew what would happen. On the day of publication, Forsskål hurriedly collected the entire print run of five hundred and distributed it to his friends, by post and hand. Within hours, the Kanslikollegium had summoned Forsskål and Salvius, read them the riot act, suspended Oelreich and ordered every copy of *Thoughts on Civil Liberties* to be rounded up and destroyed. But as only seventy-nine copies were ever confiscated, the text soon became widely known, and Forsskål remained undaunted. He now wrote directly to the king, defending his work's central proposition on press liberty. In any nation, he argued, there would always be discontented people, and

> there are only two ways of avoiding harmful consequences of discontent: one requires ink, the other blood. If the discontented are allowed to speak freely, they can be refuted, informed and transformed into an enlightened general public. Those who lose their arguments, lose their discontent and their inclination to rebellion as well.

Censorship, on the other hand, could only increase popular discontent. A few months later, Forsskål left Sweden for a scientific expedition to the Arabian peninsula: he would die there in 1763, at the age of thirty-one. Even in the midst of gathering botanical specimens thousands of miles away, he remained keenly interested in the advance of press liberty in his homeland. 'How fares the Riksdag and the freedom of writing in Sweden?' he enquired eagerly of Linnaeus in one of his last letters, sent from Alexandria in the autumn of 1761.

LEGISLATING FOR EXPRESSION

By 1760, there was therefore already considerable pressure to liberalize Swedish press policy, not least from printers and censors, and detailed arguments had been put forward by politicians and scholars. In autumn of that year, the Riksdag, still controlled by the Hats, duly set up a special committee, assisted by Oelreich, to liberalize censorship and permit greater freedom of public discussion – though with proper controls, given the ignorance of 'the lowliest congregation of a course populace', as their final report put it. Though no action was taken, political censorship grew increasingly lax, allowing the Caps' demands for change to be increasingly publicized. At the next election, held in the midst of an ongoing economic crisis, they ousted the Hats in a landslide. The new Riksdag that met in 1765 was, in consequence, full of members who had come to Stockholm eager to reform the constitution and enshrine freedom of expression in law – especially among the more radical so-called 'younger Caps' of the lower clergy and peasantry.

Though they were inspired by general enlightenment principles, Swedish discussions about free speech were always much less concerned with abstract notions of liberty and justice than with the overriding problem of how to lift their backward, peasant society out of poverty. Every Swedish or Finnish intellectual who advocated press liberty, from Swedenborg to Forsskål, was simultaneously engaged in projects for the development of natural knowledge or economic prosperity. This was the background against which the question of how legally to define 'freedom of writing and of the press' was first addressed. During a year and a half of meetings and debates, the members of the Riksdag systematically hammered out their collective answer. It turned out to be very different from the simple formulas that the lawmakers of Copenhagen, Philadelphia and Paris were soon to adopt.

The most detailed discussions took place in a committee whose most active member was an energetic young Finnish curate, amateur scientist and pamphleteer, Anders Chydenius, who had been deeply affected by Nordencrantz's recent writings. (He was also influenced by another Cap leader, Johann Arckenholtz, who had admired English and Dutch press freedom since his travels in those countries in the early 1730s; by his publisher Salvius; and possibly by Forsskål, his contemporary at Uppsala University.) This group studied all the materials it could find on press freedom. By the end of 1765 it had agreed 'to loosen the bonds by which freeborn Swedish talents have hitherto been fettered', because the enlightenment of society required 'the free use of pens and print', and because 'the fundamental advantage of such a freedom has been thoroughly experienced' in other nations, notably England. But it took many more months, until the final version of the law was agreed by the Riksdag and promulgated by the king on 2 December 1766, to decide on the details.

One point of vehement disagreement was whether the Riksdag's own proceedings could be published. This echoed debates in the English-speaking world since the seventeenth century. The Hats had long maintained that 'letting what is said here be laid before the public's judgement, perhaps at inns, in taverns, on street corners and in other places', would be a recipe for chaos. As one nobleman put it in 1761: 'The public consists of a multitude of feeble-minded persons who are not possessed of sufficient discernment for examining the affairs of the realm.' Even in England, another correctly pointed out, parliamentary debates remained confidential, and were not allowed to be published, so as to allow members to speak without inhibition. The concept of parliamentary free speech had always depended on secrecy – and on restricting the freedom of the press. But in Sweden in 1766, the holders of such opinions (which included most noble Caps) were outvoted by members who, swayed by Nordencrantz's arguments, took the opposite view – that 'the public is an enlightened judge, an impartial judge, and never makes its decisions on . . . loose grounds'.

The idea of actually abolishing censorship was still more contentious. For twelve months, no one even raised this possibility. Then, in April 1766, at a sparsely attended committee meeting, Chydenius suddenly forced the issue, arguing that press freedom was the main foundation of national liberty, that 'truths exercise a persuasive power over the human heart if they are simply allowed to irradiate it freely', and that censorship, 'being useless, unnecessary and harmful, should henceforth cease entirely'. After a fierce debate between him and Oelreich, those present voted by the narrowest possible margin to recommend abolition. Instead of settling the matter, this split the committee, which proceeded to draft two separate proposals for the Riksdag's larger 'Grand Deputation' to consider – one abolishing censorship, the other reforming its procedures. When the final votes were taken in the autumn of 1766, the former proposal squeaked through, despite the opposition of the estate of nobles – ironically enough, Chydenius himself had meanwhile been expelled from the Riksdag for having published a best-selling pamphlet criticizing its economic policy.

Even the passage of the 1766 free-speech law was, though, not really the end of censorship in Sweden. As the statute's final text made clear, its principle of press freedom essentially applied only to the sphere of economic and political debate. That was what most Swedish free-speech theorists had previously advocated – even the original, uncensored text of Forsskål's radical pamphlet had taken for granted that 'unlimited' freedom of writing still meant that 'serious punishment follows all writing which is indisputably indecent, contains blasphemy against God, insults private individuals and incites apparent vices'. In similar fashion, the Act of 1766 maintained pre-publication censorship for all texts that 'in any way touch upon' Christian doctrine. The government would continue to ban the import and sale of 'harmful . . . forbidden and corrupting books'. And the opening paragraphs of the law specified that, as well as the capacious category of 'Christian faith', press liberty also did not extend to many other untouchable spheres: the whole of 'Christian morality and its principles'; the fundamentals of the constitution; and the honour of the monarch, royal family, government officials, foreign heads of state, members of the Riksdag and, indeed, 'any upright citizen'. The writing or printing of anything that contravened these red lines remained punishable by heavy fines, 'severe physical punishment', or even death.

The abolition of pre-publication censorship had been a late, highly contested decision, but the opposite was true of all these restrictions, which were matters of unanimous consensus. Agreeing that all these subjects should be excluded from the liberty of writing and printing was the very first thing the committee decided when it began work in 1765. In the anglophone world, ideas about political freedom of speech overlapped with arguments for religious freedom; in Sweden, by contrast, the law admitted of no such connection, even if some of its proponents privately did. Chydenius himself enthusiastically supported the principle of enlightened autocracy, and, like König, Nordencrantz and Forsskål before him, lauded the example of the

Chinese, the richest nation in the world, whose conception of 'free-dom to write', he explained, was mainly intended to uphold the absolute power of their all-powerful emperor. Even before he and his colleagues turned to the question of censorship, their vision of free speech already had a distinctive, local shape.

FREEDOM AND RESTRAINT

The immediate effect of the pioneering Scandinavian free-speech laws was a dramatic explosion of printed debate. Hundreds of pamphlets and dozens of new periodicals were published in Sweden from 1767 onwards, and in Denmark after 1770. As if to signal the approval of the enlightened world, Voltaire himself publicly celebrated the estab-lishment of 'the freedom to speak to men with the pen' in Sweden, and later in Denmark: 'there is no freedom among men without that of explaining their thoughts'.

Yet within months, further laws were rushed out in both kingdoms to curb 'abuses' of the new liberty. In March 1767, a Swedish statute criminalized seditious speech that 'through the spread of suspicions and the dissemination of forged lies creates complaints, controversy and harmful discord between the citizens of the realm'. In Denmark, printed discussion during 1771 turned increasingly critical of Struen-see, portraying him as a usurping, power-hungry foreigner, and even attacking his adultery with the queen – who in July gave birth to a daughter widely presumed to be his. In response, Struensee issued a new edict against 'licentiousness', ordering that 'press freedom must not be abused'. This stipulated that all publications must carry the name of the printer or author, that writing anything contrary to 'exist-ing laws' remained illegal – and that insults, libels and 'incendiary writings' remained punishable under existing laws. It didn't help him survive. A few weeks later, in January 1772, he was ousted in a palace coup and quickly executed. In the aftermath, press liberty was grad-ually circumscribed, and formally abolished the following year.

Sweden's initial era of press freedom, too, ended in 1772, when King Gustav III seized power from the Riksdag and reinstituted a mon-archical autocracy. The monarch, who fancied himself an enlightened reformer, boasted to Voltaire that, under his new laws, 'press freedom is more extensive in Sweden than in any other country, more so even than in England' – in fact, he steadily curtailed it.

All the same, the ideal of greater press freedom lived on in both nations. Even some of Struensee's fiercest critics among the Danish intelligentsia continued to argue for it. In 1774, two years before the first American declarations of rights, the influential writer P. F. Suhm privately circulated with copies of his political novel *Euphron* a constitutional manifesto which proclaimed that everyone should have 'the liberty to think, speak, and write as he wants', subject only to laws against 'the misuse of this freedom', as well as guaranteeing unlimited liberty of religious belief and the right of petition. The question was no longer whether press freedom was feasible or desirable, only what form it should take.

In many other parts of the globe, by contrast, the ideal of press liberty remained irrelevant or unknown. In East Asia, where printing had been widely employed for centuries before its European invention, its use remained subject to governmental oversight. In the poorer regions of Europe, as well as across India, Africa, Australasia, the Ottoman Empire and much of the Americas, printing presses were still rare at this time. Apart from one or two brief experiments, not a single one was in use in Brazil until 1808, when the Portuguese royal family, fleeing to their giant transatlantic colony in order to escape Napoleon's invasion, brought with them a royal press. (The Brazilian opposition in turn relocated to London, and began using print from there.)

The broader significance of the pioneering Nordic free-speech laws was nonetheless international. Their history illustrates that by the mid eighteenth century, at least among literate Europeans and North Americans, press freedom had become a profoundly transnational concept. Its ideology was central to cross-border scholarly and public debates about enlightenment and social progress. Its practice, too, was henceforth always conceived of in international terms – people invariably defined press freedom by comparing its shape in their own town or nation with its contours elsewhere. In the Netherlands, which had no real indigenous tradition of debates about political freedom of expression, it was only the example of English press-freedom debates around John Wilkes in 1762–3, as well as a short-lived proposal later in the 1760s to introduce pre-publication censorship, that spurred the first serious vernacular defences of liberty of the press as an individual right (Elie Luzac was again a prominent voice, this time in Dutch). In 1770, news of the Scandinavian innovations was quickly reported by French, German, English, Scottish and Caribbean newspapers. A few years later, even though their detailed formulations differed, both American and French revolutionaries took a similar approach to enshrining press liberty in law. They drew on the same transnational set of ideas; and they, too, constantly invoked the examples of laws and freedoms in other nations.

As well as illuminating the international character of free-speech debates, the Scandinavian decrees were notable for being the first legal declarations to conceive of freedom of communication as a basic, individual right of all citizens. This, too, proved to be a lasting development. Though the Danish government in 1772–3 seriously considered reintroducing prior censorship, it never did. Instead, from this point onwards, no matter how restrictive, Scandinavian laws were always expressed as measures to uphold the noble ideals of press liberty and freedom of expression. Instead of presuming that speech and print should be regulated, they proceeded from the opposite premise: all expression was permissible, unless specifically excepted. In the course of the nineteenth century, this principle would gradually become the norm everywhere. Nowadays, even deeply repressive political regimes around the world pay lip service to it. In 1766, by contrast, it had been a novelty.

6

The Accidental Exceptionalism of
the First Amendment

There are really only two ways of approaching free speech as a personal right. The first is what we might call the 'balancing' approach – everyone is entitled to express themselves freely, but with certain limits. The earliest articulations of this idea, around 1700, defined it as the difference between 'liberty' of press or speech, which was valuable, and 'licentiousness', or excessive freedom, which was harmful. In this model, the right to free speech is always checked by a sense of its proper boundaries. 'Every person shall have the right freely to express and disseminate their opinions in speech, writing, and pictures,' says the first clause of Germany's constitutional guarantee of free expression, drawn up in 1949. 'There shall be no censorship.' But clause two then immediately specifies: 'These rights shall be limited by the provisions of the general laws, the legal regulations for the protection of young persons, and by the right of personal honour.' And a further article warns that it also does not apply to 'Whoever abuses the freedom of expression, in particular the freedom of the press', in order to undermine democracy. Like all rights, free speech comes with responsibilities.

The other way of thinking is what we might call the 'absolutist' or libertarian one. That's the view that, as the novelist Salman Rushdie put it in 2015, 'the moment you limit free speech, it is not free speech'. The most powerful expression of this model is the First Amendment of the United States' constitution: 'Congress shall make no law ... abridging the freedom of speech, or of the press.' No ifs, no buts, no mention of boundaries.

The contrast between the balanced and absolutist approaches is partly psychological. The former sees restrictions on expression as normal and necessary, the latter as suspicious and dangerous – a sign of creeping censorship, or of contemptible intellectual weakness. In Rushdie's words, 'freedom is indivisible ... the moment somebody says, "Yes, I believe in free speech, *BUT*", I stop listening'. 'I'm a free-speech absolutist,' people often proudly say – it feels good to stand for freedom, and against censorship.

In practice, of course, libertarian theories do usually acknowledge that free speech has limits. They don't defend falsely shouting 'FIRE!' in a crowded theatre, committing perjury or disseminating child pornography. So you'd be forgiven for concluding that the distinction between the two models is essentially rhetorical, a distinction without a substantive difference. One approach states up front that freedom of speech always has to be balanced against other considerations; the other maintains that liberty of expression is of paramount import-ance, and sorts out the details afterwards. They both end up balancing free speech against other considerations, just from different starting points.

But in fact there's more to it than that, because the rhetorical dif-ference also has two important practical consequences. In the first place, only under the absolutist model can the right of 'free speech' be legally extended to undermine labour unions, flood elections with unlimited amounts of corporate money, expose children to interactive video games involving extreme violence and killing, or permit the sale of animal-abuse movies – to mention just a few recent American inter-pretations of its far-reaching scope. Even when the US Congress and president specifically ban such things, those laws can be invalidated by the Supreme Court on the grounds that they limit 'speech'. Even the Court's justices themselves have recently begun to complain about such legal 'weaponizing' of free speech, but it is facilitated by the First Amendment's libertarian phrasing.

The second curious difference is that the American model, derived from the First Amendment, applies only to government control ('*Congress* shall make no law'). In any non-governmental university, employment, medium or public space, the constitutional right to free speech does not apply. The result is that exactly the same words or actions (displaying a bumper sticker, kneeling for the national anthem or expressing your political opinion) can be sacrosanct free expression in one context, but entirely unprotected in others – you can be punished, blacklisted or lose your job for it. This happens all the time. So the First Amendment's right to free speech is simultaneously much more expansive than that of any other culture, but also much narrower: in most circumstances, it's not applicable at all.

Why Americans follow the absolute rather than the balanced model is a historical accident. Both ways of thinking originated around 1700, and were represented in the world's earliest laws guaranteeing political freedom of expression. In fact, how exactly to frame the right to free speech soon became one of the most hotly debated legal and political questions in the world. Between 1750 and 1850, as written constitutions became all the rage across the globe, freedom of the press emerged as *the* most commonly enumerated constitutional right of all – more prominent even than freedom of religion, or popular sovereignty itself. (The freedoms of speech and writing were also often specified, though not quite as frequently.) The prominence of press liberty in these charters was no coincidence. By the later eighteenth century, print had come to be widely regarded as an indispensable tool of political communication and transparent government, while the printing press was also vital to the spread of constitutions themselves. Such documents may have been drafted in verbal debate, pen and ink, but it was print that disseminated and empowered them – locally, nationally and internationally.

For all these reasons, hundreds of laws guaranteeing free expression were passed after 1750. But only in one nation, the United States, did they ever follow the absolutist model: first in the revolutionary constitutions proclaimed by its rebellious colonies between 1776 and 1784, and then in the national Bill of Rights adopted by the first federal Congress in 1789, and implemented in 1791, after its ratification by the states. Collectively, these texts were among the most widely publicized and influential legal documents of their age: many of their provisions were copied around the world. But not their approach to freedom of expression. For well over two hundred years now, free-speech laws everywhere else have rejected the absolutist American template, and instead opted for the balancing approach.

Why is that? In the mountains of scholarship devoted to the origins of American free-speech doctrines, this remarkable fact is practically never mentioned. Instead, scholars of early American attitudes have focused obsessively on two related but more parochial issues: why the First Amendment was phrased the way it was; and what exactly early Americans understood by 'the freedom of speech, or of the press'. Over and over again, these questions have been explored by reference to the sparse documentation of the 1789 constitutional convention, the domestic newspapers, pamphlets and correspondence of the period, and the controversy over the partisan 1798 Sedition Act, introduced by the second president, John Adams, which made 'any false, scandalous, and malicious writing ... against the government' a federal crime, and sparked a national debate about the scope of the First Amendment – until Adams lost his bid for re-election in 1800, and the law expired at the end of his term, seemingly vindicating the more libertarian attitudes of its opponents.

Thereafter, most histories of free speech fast-forward to the aftermath of the First World War. For, as we shall see in Chapter 10, only in 1919 did the Supreme Court begin to apply the First Amendment to questions of speech and of the press, and only from 1925 onwards did it decree that this text governed local as well as federal law (using the post-Civil War doctrine of 'incorporation', based on the Fourteenth Amendment). Few scholars study the intervening period; and even those that do, tend to concentrate on national courts and disputes, rather than local ones.

Yet this focus on national debates and laws misses a lot about early US understandings of free speech. On the one hand, it has completely overlooked important foreign (that is, non-British) influences on American thinking. On the other hand, it blinds us to the significance of state laws before and after 1789. If, instead, we take a more comprehensive view, attending to the interrelationship of international, national and local law-making, a rather different picture emerges. It then becomes clear that, even in America, the balancing approach to free speech came to be widely embraced, early on – not just in discussions about the exact bounds of free speech, but as a matter of fundamental law. That was not yet the case in June 1789. At the time it was drafted, the absolutist phrasing of the First Amendment seemed the obvious way of framing the principle. But, as we shall see, even before the amendment had been ratified, that had started to change – Americans began to favour an alternative way of describing the constitutional right itself.

LOCAL DECLARATIONS

Why did America's white settlers, when drawing up their revolutionary constitutions, invariably describe free speech in absolutist terms? Here's how their earliest declarations of rights put it:

June 1776, Virginia:
'That the freedom of the press is one of the greatest bulwarks of liberty, and can never be restrained but by despotic governments.'

August 1776, Pennsylvania:
'That the people have a right to freedom of speech, and of writing and publishing their sentiments; therefore the freedom of the press ought not to be restrained.' And furthermore: 'The printing presses shall be free to every person, who undertakes to examine the proceedings of the legislature, or any part of government.'

September 1776, Delaware:
'That the liberty of the press ought to be inviolably preserved.'

These became the three standard free-speech templates of revolutionary America, quickly and widely publicized by its newspapers. Every other colony that issued such a declaration later in the 1770s simply copied one of these models.

The most basic reason for such phrasing was that, at this time, 'liberty of the press' meant something quite specific to the English-speaking settlers of North America – the right to print anything without prior government approval. Until the Scandinavian experiments of the 1760s and 70s, this kind of press freedom had been a uniquely Anglo-Dutch phenomenon. In North America, too, it was a comparatively recent innovation. As late as 1722, there were no printing presses anywhere on the continent, except in Boston, New London, New York and Philadelphia, and their operators were often harassed and censured by local governors and assemblies. But in the decades since the Zenger trial of 1735, American printing had expanded into a much more widespread, independent and potent political tool – increasingly critical in rallying opposition to British policies. By the later 1760s, as a result, colonial governors were fairly powerless to prosecute even the most seditious, libellous or mendacious writings.

Beyond the absence of government control, what exactly did press 'freedom' signify by the 1770s? In late 1774, responding to the British government's recent rescinding of local laws and liberties in Quebec and Massachusetts, the Continental Congress of the rebellious colonies publicly set out why 'freedom of the press' was for them an inalienable right:

> The importance of this consists, besides the advancement of truth, science and morality, and arts in general, in its diffusion of liberal sentiments on the administration of government, its ready communication of thoughts between subjects, and its consequential promotion of union among them, whereby oppressive officers are shamed or intimidated into more honourable and just modes of conducting affairs.

In other words, their main concern was with print's political functions: it enabled citizens to organize; it spread 'liberal' ideas of government; it held government officials to account.

The harder question, which had been debated across the English-speaking world since 1695, was exactly how far this freedom should extend. What about personal attacks, the spreading of rumours or the slandering of public officials? Should government officers be entitled to respectful treatment, or at least be safeguarded against subversive lies? And what about the national interest, and the dangers of treason, sedition and civil disorder?

There were two schools of thought on these matters. One, inaugurated by Cato's Letters, was essentially libertarian. Without press oversight, it argued, public figures would misuse their power. Abusive attacks were permissible if they conveyed the truth; lies could not hurt anyone who was truly honest; and ordinary people were the best judges of all these things – any aggrieved person could sue for libel, and juries should decide the merits of the case (rather than the presiding judge, as English law actually stipulated). By the 1760s and early 1770s, this outlook was commonplace among British political reformers. Those who opposed their government's policy towards the American colonies often argued that press freedom was being destroyed by the ministry's use of the libel laws to silence them.

In America itself, Patriot rebels celebrated the same ideology. The onset of their war against royal tyranny led to a flurry of reprintings of Cato's Letters on press freedom. When, in May 1776, a committee of Virginia delegates was tasked with drafting the first colonial 'declaration of rights', they simply epitomized Cato's well-known argument, complete with its famous dictum that 'freedom of speech is the great bulwark of liberty'. 'That the freedom of the press, being the great bulwark of liberty, can never be restrained but in a despotic government,' one of them scribbled on a paper that the planter George Mason, their most active member, had brought to their meeting. When presented with this formulation a few days later, the full state convention, which included James Madison and Patrick Henry, merely tweaked its grammar: their only substantive debate was over a different clause, whose wording (soon changed) had threatened to imply that Virginia's hundreds of thousands of enslaved people, too, might claim such 'inherent rights'.

The alternative, older view of the limits of free speech was more concerned with the dangers of 'licentiousness'. Its most influential English-language formulation was that of William Blackstone, whose authoritative *Commentaries on the Laws of England* (1765–70) summarized conservative legal orthodoxy: 'spreading false news' about any 'great man' was a crime against the public peace; so too were all 'libels' – that is, writings or pictures 'of an immoral or illegal tendency', especially 'malicious defamations of any person, and especially a magistrate', that might anger such a person, 'or expose him to public hatred, contempt, and ridicule'. Whether such accusations were true or false was completely 'immaterial . . . since the provocation, and not the falsity, is the thing to be punished criminally . . . [The] tendency which all libels have to create animosities, and to disturb the public peace, is the sole consideration of the law'. In punishing such abuses, Blackstone concluded,

> the liberty of the press, properly understood, is by no means infringed
> or violated. The liberty of the press is indeed essential to the nature

of a free state: but this consists in laying no previous restraints upon publications, and not in freedom from censure for criminal matter when published. Every freeman has an undoubted right to lay what sentiments he pleases before the public: to forbid this, is to destroy the freedom of the press: but if he publishes what is improper, mischievous, or illegal, he must take the consequence of his own temerity . . . To punish (as the law does at present) any dangerous or offensive writings, which, when published, shall on a fair and impartial trial be adjudged of a pernicious tendency, is necessary for the preservation of peace and good order, of government and religion, the only solid foundations of civil liberty . . . Neither is any restraint hereby laid upon freedom of thought or enquiry: liberty of private sentiment is still left; the dissemination, or making public, of bad sentiments, destructive of the ends of society, is the crime which society corrects.

In short, he argued, 'to censure licentiousness, is to maintain the liberty, of the press'.

Despite the great contrast between libertarian and balanced theories of free speech, the fact that the latter, too, rhetorically exalted an uninfringeable 'liberty of the press' meant that the division between the two approaches remained invisible in the language of American revolutionary constitutions. In fact, the two new state declarations issued in the early 1780s both borrowed Blackstone's widely read phrasing. 'The liberty of the press is essential to the freedom in a state; it ought not, therefore, to be restricted in this commonwealth,' declared the Massachusetts convention in March 1780. The following year, New Hampshire's delegates merged this with the popular 'inviolably preserved' clause (coined by Delaware in 1776), ending up with: 'The Liberty of the Press is essential to the security of freedom in a State; it ought therefore to be inviolably preserved.' Even when we can surmise that its drafters embraced balancing, Blackstonian attitudes, their constitutional language remained absolutist – because conservatives, too, maintained that press liberty was sacrosanct, and that punishing licentiousness did not infringe it.

The writers of these documents also never entertained the idea that freedom of expression should extend to their political opponents. If they had, they would have had to grapple harder with defining its exact limits. As it was, they took for granted that all 'Enemies of American Freedom' should be silenced: free speech was not for those diffusing 'wrong sentiments respecting the measures now carrying on for the recovery and establishment of our rights'. 'We see freedom of speech suppressed, the liberty and secrecy of the press destroyed, the voice of truth silenced,' a leading Loyalist politician complained in 1775; shortly afterwards, as if on cue, a group of armed Patriots destroyed his publisher's printing press. The men who did this were staunch believers in their own political free speech. They were led by Alexander McDougall, who just a few years earlier had himself been tried and convicted for criticizing New York's colonial assembly – an event that he and his supporters had built up into the greatest cause célèbre for press liberty since the Zenger trial.

Late in 1775, Connecticut outlawed all 'writing or speaking' against 'the United Colonies'. A few weeks later, Congress warned that 'well-meaning, but uninformed people in these colonies' were being 'deceived and drawn into erroneous opinions respecting the American cause' by 'unworthy Americans'. Soon, every colony had passed legislation criminalizing Loyalist political opinions. 'The liberty of the press hath justly been held up as an important privilege of the people,' a signer of the declaration of independence explained towards the end of 1776:

> It is indeed highly reasonable that the channels of information should be kept open for the benefit of the multitude; and no man holds this right in more sacred estimation than I do. But when this privilege is manifestly abused, and the press becomes an engine for sowing the most dangerous dissentions, for spreading false alarms, and undermining the very foundations of government, ought not that government, upon the plain principles of self-preservation, to silence, by its own authority, such a daring violator of its peace, and tear from its bosom the serpent that would sting it to death?

The same partisan outlook extended to disputes within the revolutionary camp. In January 1777, the revolutionary leader John Adam Treutlen served on the committee that drew up Georgia's new constitution, including its stirring injunction 'Freedom of the press, and trial by Jury, to remain inviolate *for ever*'. Barely six months later, as the state's first governor, he banned the arguments of other local Patriots who were 'UNLAWFULLY endeavouring to POISON the minds of the good people of this state against the government thereof . . . by letters, petitions and otherwise, daily exciting animosities among the inhabitants'. The new constitutions of several other states specified that liberty of conscience and worship could not extend to disturbing 'the good order, peace, or safety of the state' (Maryland, 1776), 'treasonable or seditious discourses' (North Carolina, 1776), or speaking 'irreverently or seditiously of the government of this state' (South Carolina, 1778).

Because of the apparent tension between the absolutist language of early American constitutions and the 1798 Sedition Act, scholars have long been obsessed with – and taken diametrically opposed views on – whether early Americans thought 'seditious libel' should be a crime or not. But that is a red herring. Not only was there no great consensus on that specific point, but there couldn't be: people's definitions of free expression were inevitably contextual and determined by political circumstance. From its earliest beginnings, the constitutional right to free speech always had an unstable, politicized meaning.

NATIONAL RIGHTS

This was the intellectual and political setting in which the First Amendment originated. But at first, in May 1787, when a convention convened in Philadelphia to draw up a national constitution, almost no one envisaged that this document should include any declaration of rights – least of all James Madison of Virginia, its most energetic draftsman. The idea was only mooted briefly, towards the end of the session. On 20 August, the youngest delegate present, twenty-four-year-old Charles Pinckney of South Carolina, proposed a national list of rights, including that 'the liberty of the press shall be inviolably preserved'. Without debate, the idea was referred to a committee; nothing came of it. Then, on 12 September, after the constitution's basic text had already been agreed and printed, and the convention was debating its final revisions, George Mason, the oldest of the Virginia delegates, suddenly spoke out. 'He wished the plan had been prefaced with a bill of rights,' he told the meeting, and what's more, that would be easy to accomplish: 'with the aid of the state declarations, a bill might be prepared in a few hours'. (As they all knew, he himself had drafted the very first such declaration, back in the spring of 1776.) But no state's delegation supported this idea, not even his own. Two days later, in the penultimate session, Pinckney had one last try, 'to insert a declaration "that the liberty of the press should be inviolably observed –"', but it was narrowly voted down. As Roger Sherman of Connecticut explained the conventional thinking: 'It is unnecessary – The power of Congress does not extend to the press.'

Pinckney himself soon came round to that view, too.* But Mason boycotted the constitution's signing, in protest at its flaws. 'There is no declaration of rights', he scribbled angrily on his copy of the printed text, 'and the laws of the general government being paramount to the laws and constitution of the several states, the declaration of rights in the separate states are no security.' He was particularly concerned about the lack of a 'declaration of any kind, for preserving the liberty of the press'. Almost immediately, his arguments found their way into print, and the omission of a Bill of Rights from the constitution became the central objection of a growing anti-Federalist campaign against its proposed form. Over the ensuing months, several state conventions delayed or agreed to ratification only on condition that the text be amended to add such a national charter of citizens' rights.

One of these was Virginia, where in June 1788 a powerful anti-Federalist lobby, led by Mason and the state's charismatic former governor, Patrick Henry, won their convention's agreement that 'among other essential rights, liberty of conscience and of the press cannot be cancelled, abridged, restrained, or modified by any authority of the United States'. They also got the meeting to advocate the immediate adoption of a national 'declaration or bill of rights asserting and securing from encroachment the essential and unalienable

---

* Bills of Rights in general, he concluded on his return to South Carolina, were problematic, for they 'generally begin with declaring that all men are by nature born free. Now, we should make that declaration with a very bad grace, when a large part of our property consists in men who are actually born slaves.'

rights of the people', and to recommend for this purpose a model text recently compiled by leading anti-Federalists. On the issue of press liberty, this proposal updated Virginia's existing 1776 declaration by merging it with the words of Pennsylvania's equally famous statement. The hybrid result, possibly composed by Mason himself, was this:

> That the people have a right to freedom of speech, and of writing and publishing their sentiments; that the freedom of the press is one of the greatest bulwarks of liberty, and ought not to be violated.

James Madison was a central actor in these heated debates, too: throughout the Virginia ratification convention, he led the opposition to Mason's proposals, just as he had the previous year at the Federal convention in Philadelphia. He'd always agreed it was 'essential' to prohibit state governments 'from controlling the press', just as they shouldn't infringe on religious freedom, trial by jury and other basic principles. But like other Federalists, he did not see the need for a national declaration of rights, and continued to oppose the idea even after the constitution had been ratified. 'For why declare that things shall not be done which there is no power to do?' asked Alexander Hamilton, in a 1788 defence of their position. 'Why, for instance, should it be said that the liberty of the press shall not be restrained, when no power is given by which restrictions may be imposed?' It would be an 'absurdity'. In any case, he argued, such declarations were pointless verbiage:

> What signifies a declaration, that 'the liberty of the press shall be inviolably preserved'? What is the liberty of the press? Who can give it any definition which would not leave the utmost latitude for evasion? I hold it to be impracticable; and from this I infer, that its security, whatever fine declarations may be inserted in any constitution respecting it, must altogether depend on public opinion, and on the general spirit of the people and of the government.

Though he agreed that constitutional rules were always but 'parchment barriers against the encroaching spirit of power', the persistent strength of anti-Federalist sentiment eventually persuaded Madison to compromise. In order to win a seat in the first House of

Representatives, he campaigned on a promise that the national constitution 'ought to be revised [to include] all essential rights, particularly the rights of conscience in the fullest latitude, the freedom of the press, trials by jury, security against general warrants etc.'. When the first United States Congress met in New York in the spring of 1789, he duly became the proposal's main champion. His draft Bill of Rights leaned heavily on the Virginia anti-Federalists' state-of-the art formulations; in his clause on freedom of speech and of the press, as in others, the only real change he made was to explicitly forbid the Federal government from restricting the right:

> The people shall not be deprived or abridged of their right to speak, to write, or to publish their sentiments; and the freedom of the press, as one of the great bulwarks of liberty, shall be inviolable.

Eventually, after some minor modifications in debates and committees, and the merging of several clauses into a single article, this prohibition emerged as part of the third amendment agreed by Congress:

> Congress shall make no law respecting an establishment of religion, or prohibiting the free exercise thereof; or abridging the freedom of speech, or of the press; or the right of the people peaceably to assemble, and to petition the government for a redress of grievances.

In 1791, because articles one and two had failed to be ratified by enough states, this duly became the first amendment.

How lawmakers altered the amendment's wording between the draft proposals and the text finally adopted on 25 September has been much scrutinized but need not detain us. The most significant change they made was that, though initially in 1788 the anti-Federalists had formulated freedom of speech and of the press as positive rights of the people, the final wording adopted in 1789 mandated only that 'Congress shall make no law' to abridge them. Instead of an affirmative guarantee of personal liberty, it became a negative prohibition enjoined upon the national government. The politics of this change go to the heart of the conflict between the Federalist and anti-Federalist visions of the United States. To Federalists like Madison, the power of the new national government, especially Congress, was the critical solution to the many differences between states. But to anti-Federalists the powers now presumed by the federal government were dangerously similar to those that the British imperial state had previously abused. That is why the First Amendment ended up with its odd shape – not a statement of citizens' rights, let alone one defending individual speech and press liberties against state and local governments, but only a safeguard against overreach by the *federal* government. The point of that wording, and the purpose of the text, was only to restrict the powers of the new, national Congress.

There's a deep irony here. As we shall see later in this book, the modern interpretation of the First Amendment has gradually turned this original meaning on its head: nowadays it is read precisely as a guarantee of individual rights, whose national character is supposed to trump any state or local restrictions on expression. But that was not at all the legal or political import of the clause in 1789.

Beyond this, all the other alterations of phrasing were essentially cosmetic. And, despite its last-minute stress on restricting Congress, the end result retained the libertarian essence of every American declaration about freedom of speech and of the press issued over the previous thirteen years. In the summer of 1789, there simply seemed to be no other conceivable way of formulating this particular ideal. Despite Americans' widely varying views on the exact scope of free speech in practice, everyone in the English-speaking world who sought to describe it as a right was trapped in the same absolutist rhetorical framework. But that was about to change.

TRANSATLANTIC DEVELOPMENTS

Nowhere were America's constitutional innovations and debates of the 1780s followed with greater interest than halfway across the world in France, the new nation's foremost ally, which had just begun to undergo its own revolutionary convulsions. And no one in France was keener to learn from the American example than the young Marquis de Lafayette, hero of the American Revolutionary War, 'adoptive son' of General Washington, friend of Franklin, Adams, Hamilton and Jefferson, and one of the leading reformers at the court of Louis XVI. He named his firstborn child 'Georges Washington', avidly devoured the latest American political treatises and developments, and endlessly discussed them with Jefferson (the US envoy in Paris since 1784), as well as with his own compatriots. Lafayette was the most celebrated of France's *américains* – writers and legislators inspired by America's example. His grand house in Paris became a central meeting place for French and American politicians. On the main wall of its study, as an inspiration to himself, he installed a copy of the American Declaration of Independence, engraved in gold letters, next to another, empty frame – 'waiting for the declaration of the rights of France', he announced.

In the eighteenth century it took several weeks for news to cross the Atlantic, by ship. Late in 1787, Lafayette finally received from Washington a copy of the federal constitution that had been agreed at Philadelphia in September. So did Jefferson, Virginia's former governor and delegate, who was in close touch with Madison and others about its ratification, and immediately urged them to add 'a bill of rights providing clearly and without the aid of sophisms for freedom of religion, freedom of the press' and other inalienable rights.

Lafayette, too, consulted with Jefferson before replying to Washington. 'I read the new proposed constitution with an unspeakable eagerness and attention,' he wrote back to the general, adding that, on reflection, 'I am only afraid of two things – 1st the want of a Declaration of Rights.' Yet that was not an insuperable problem, he continued, doubtless channelling the arguments of his 'dear friend' the envoy, for 'a bill of rights may be made if wished for by the people before they accept the constitution'. Soon he and Jefferson were meeting regularly to debate such a text's finer points with Thomas Paine, the great Anglo-American champion of liberty and democracy, who was visiting Paris to cheer on the new revolution in France. On both sides of the Atlantic, constitution-making was in the air. Here in France, too, Lafayette informed Washington: 'I am heartily wishing for a constitution, and a bill of rights, and wish it may be effected with as much tranquillity and mutual satisfaction as it is possible.'

By the spring of 1788, all of them were hopeful that a French national convention would soon be called and draw up a declaration of rights. After Louis XVI decreed in August that the Estates General would indeed convene the following year, Lafayette's circle began to discuss what form such a charter should take. In Paris, Jefferson informed his American correspondents in December, 'all the world is occupied at present in framing, every one his own plan of a bill of rights.' A few weeks later, he sent some examples of such drafts across the Atlantic, to help Madison with his own efforts. Perhaps for similar reasons, the Marquis de Condorcet published his own plan in English as well as French. When the Estates General eventually convened in May, Lafayette, with Jefferson's help, produced the first detailed proposal. On 11 July 1789, to thunderous applause, he presented this text to the newly formed National Assembly. More than thirty alternative models by other authors were also considered over the ensuing weeks before, in late August, the final text of the Declaration of the Rights of Man and of the Citizen was agreed.

Liberty of speech and print were prominent demands in almost every one of these proposals. Everyone knew about the absolutist, American approach to this issue. Some delegates gestured to it in composing their own clauses. America's state constitutions were endlessly translated, discussed and looked to for inspiration: even the Virginia ratifying convention's 1788 model Bill of Rights, whose wording became the template for the First Amendment, was published in French by leading *américains* in January 1789.

Yet in France these liberties meant something significantly different. For one thing, it was a matter of creating rather than preserving rights. French writers and readers by the 1780s were hardly muzzled, having developed many ways of evading and flouting print censorship. But they had to engage in such subterfuge precisely because press freedom in the anglophone sense did not yet exist. Just before the Estates convened, the crown renewed all its controls, including pre-publication censorship and police surveillance of printing. Nor did the French aspire to the degree of religious freedom that North Americans by the 1780s took for granted: as a result, their debates about liberty of expression were initially dominated by questions of religious disputation and the role of the national church. The declaration's eventual compromise on this front was the separate Article 10, agreed before press liberty itself was debated, specifying that 'No one should be troubled for his opinions, even religious ones, provided that their expression does not disturb the public order established by law'.

The political context, too, was crucially different. In the American revolution, about a third of the settler population of the thirteen colonies had wanted to remain loyal to Britain, and a further twenty per cent were people held in slavery. Several hundred thousand of the territory's original, native inhabitants still lived there, too. Yet though the Patriots probably represented less than half of the actual population, they had successfully portrayed their revolt not as a civil war but as a unified struggle against external tyranny. They proceeded to expel Loyalists, cast off monarchy and design a new form of republican government.

By contrast, the French in 1789 strove to fix their age-old political system, without destroying it. Their own solution to the danger of executive tyranny was mainly to reassert the ultimate sovereignty of the nation. Thus, the final text of the declaration never mentions the monarchy: the deputies of the National Assembly boldly envisaged themselves as the sovereign power, whose role was to balance individual freedoms against the public good. The result was that, not just in matters of expression but throughout the text of the declaration, the power of the law was continually invoked as a necessary restraint on personal liberties.

What's more, even though (or perhaps precisely because) the deputies were divided between conservative and more liberal camps, they sought consensus. Much more than those of the revolutionary Americans, their draft declarations of rights valued the harmony of civil society, the balance between entitlements and duties, the importance of the 'social contract', the law as an expression of 'the general will', and the difference between the state of nature, in which liberty was unrestrained, and human society, in which it was necessarily limited. Individual rights, for them, were not liberties to be protected *against* laws and governments, but to be defined by them.

A large number of them therefore sought to emulate British, not transatlantic, constitutional arrangements. 'The Americans', the Comte de Mirabeau explained to his fellow delegates, had deliberately framed their declarations of rights in simple terms, so as to appeal to 'the people, to whom only freedom matters'. But, as he noted perceptively, that made less for 'a declaration of human rights, than for a declaration of war against tyrants': it avoided all the hard questions about the exact relationship between natural rights and civil society. As the brilliant young lawyer Jean-Joseph Mounier proudly reminded the Assembly on 9 July, opening the debate on a declaration of rights, 'we should not forget that the French are not a new people, who've only recently emerged from the depths of the forests to form a civil association . . . ' – unlike the settlers of America, was the disdainful implication. Many others voiced similar sentiments.

Against this backdrop, and given an intellectual tradition in which press freedom had always been conceived of in a more nuanced fashion than in the anglophone worship of 'liberty of the press', the right to free speech was expressed very differently. In France, too, it was easy to jot down 'la liberté de la presse', without qualification, in a list of desirable basic rights. Early in 1788, Mirabeau himself had drawn up a declaration of rights for the revolutionary Dutch Patriots which copied the American state formula that 'the liberty of the press ought to be inviolably preserved'. But when it came to expressing this as a constitutional principle for their own nation, he and other francophone authors invariably took a balancing approach. What their Declaration of Rights would fix, Jefferson explained to John Adams, was 'the *degree* of liberty which may be given to the press'. 'No man can be molested for his opinions or the communication of his ideas,' began one of the typical draft texts that he recommended to Madison in January 1789, 'unless he violates the social order, or the honour of another, in which case he is subject to the law.' In June, when conferring with the delegates at Versailles on how to proceed, Jefferson proposed a similar formulation for their 'Charter of Rights': 'Printers shall be liable to legal prosecution for printing and publishing false facts injurious to the party prosecuting: but they shall be under no other restraint.' In the end, Lafayette scrapped a clause singling out 'calumnies' for punishment, but maintained the general principle that freedom of expression should never infringe on the rights of others.

The dozens of other proposals that were considered, and the subsequent debate in the Assembly, likewise took for granted that freedom of expression by any means was a natural but limited right, and focused mainly on how to express its proper boundaries. Should it stop at 'the rights of others', 'harm to others', 'the abusive use of this freedom', 'calumny or sedition', 'subjects prohibited by law', or leave the question to be determined by the text of the future constitution? Condorcet had initially thought it sufficient to prescribe that 'the press shall be free, and no penal laws shall be made, except against libels which attack private persons, or the private actions of men in public employments'; then added further prohibitions against 'invitations to disturb the peace of society by force, and the execution of laws'. 'Liberty of the press is the greatest bulwark of public liberty' was Mounier's not untypical proposal, and 'the laws must uphold it', as his draft went on to explain laboriously, 'by reconciling it with the appropriate means to ensure the punishment of those who could abuse it to spread seditious speeches or calumnies against individuals'.

By the time the delegates debated the declaration's free-speech clause, they had already agreed to Article 4, which expressed the overriding principle that 'Liberty consists in doing whatever does not injure another', and that those limits would be determined by law. That understanding provided the basic framework for their deliberations. Ultimately, on 24 August, it was the terms proposed by a leading *américain*, the Duc de la Rochefoucauld, that settled the wording of what became Article 11:

> The free communication of ideas and opinions is one of the most precious rights of man. Every citizen may therefore speak, write, and print freely, under condition of being responsible for the abuse of that liberty in cases provided for by the law.

Three days later, the declaration as a whole was adopted by the National Assembly. The king disliked its pretensions but finally, under extreme political pressure, assented to it on 5 October 1789; eventually, in 1791, it was to become the preamble to France's first written constitution. But even before it came into force, its approach to freedom of expression was to have a far-reaching effect on American minds.

In mid August 1789, Jefferson had received by letter from Madison in New York (sent in early June) the text of the constitutional amendments that he'd just submitted to Congress – including the Bill of Rights that Jefferson had long urged him to champion, with its clause guaranteeing the liberty of speech and press. Just hours after the French Assembly finalized its declaration, Jefferson sat down in Paris to reply to his friend. 'Their declaration of rights is finished,' he wrote, and then: 'I must say a word on the declaration of rights you have been so good as to send me. I like it as far as it goes; but I should have been for going further.' Here is how he urged Madison to expand his article on the right to free expression:

> The people shall not be deprived or abridged of their right to speak to write or *otherwise* to publish any thing but false facts affecting injuriously the life, liberty, property, or reputation of others or affecting the peace of the confederacy with foreign nations.

In other words, he rejected the absolutist approach, in favour of a balanced one: freedom of speech should not extend to falsehoods that injured any person, or jeopardized national security. By the time this letter reached Madison, Congress had already finalized the text of what became the First Amendment. But if Jefferson had had his way, its shape would have been completely different.

His views on this subject were not new. In the spring of 1776, attending the Continental Congress in Philadelphia, Jefferson had remained in close touch with his colleagues back in Williamsburg, who were busy drafting Virginia's revolutionary declaration of rights. In the proposals he sent them, he urged, among other things, the inclusion of a clause that 'Printing presses shall be free [to print what they like], except where by commission of private injury they shall give cause of private action.' The convention adopted several of his suggestions, but not that one.

Among America's earliest constitution-makers, Jefferson was essentially alone in favouring a balanced articulation of the liberty of the press. On another, later occasion, he proposed that 'Printing presses shall be subject to no other restraint than liableness for falsehoods'. That, Madison noted in 1788, was 'an innovation and as such ought to be well considered': it also prompted Madison to reflect again on his own persistent worry that perhaps government power was *not* in fact the main danger to press freedom. A few months later, nonetheless, ignoring such scruples, his own draft of the First Amendment fell back on a conventional, absolutist formulation. But in the autumn of 1789, when the text of the French Declaration of the Rights of Man reached the shores of the United States, all this changed: its alternative model of how to express the right to free speech had an immediate and profound influence on American thinking.

FRENCH INFLUENCES

We can trace that impact in detail through events in Philadelphia, the largest and most politically sophisticated city of the new United States. In the final months of 1789, three developments coincided there. The first was the state Assembly's ratification of Congress's proposed amendments to the national constitution. The second was a special state convention, summoned to revise Pennsylvania's own 1776 constitution and Bill of Rights. And the third was the arrival on American soil of the Declaration of the Rights of Man.

For months, the progress of the French Revolution, and the drafting of that declaration, had been front-page news across the Eastern seaboard. It was, after all, a business close to American hearts. As one Boston writer boasted: 'the first Declaration of Rights ever published in France, was almost verbatim a copy of parts of the American constitutions' – 'the spark from the altar of liberty of America ... has communicated its fire to France'. Many American papers carried translations of the Parisian proposals and debates. By the middle of November, the declaration's final text had been printed in English by journals up and down the coast.

Soon after that, Pennsylvania's legislators ratified the new federal Bill of Rights. As in virtually every other state, it didn't take them long. On a single day, 27 November 1789, and without much debate, the state Assembly approved what eventually became the first ten amendments. Its delegates had been in session since the beginning of the month, and adjourned shortly afterwards. But no one in Pennsylvania was paying much attention to them, nor had some of its leading politicians even sought a seat in the Assembly that autumn. Instead, they were focused on a different legislative body: the special convention to amend their state's own constitution. Its sixty-odd delegates had begun meeting two days earlier, on 25 November, in the same building, Philadelphia's State House. They soon took over its main Assembly Room, the hallowed space where both the Declaration of Independence and the national constitution had previously been drawn up. They worked hard throughout the winter, convening almost every day except on Sundays, until the end of February 1790. At that point they published the draft text they had agreed on, and adjourned to mid August to allow for public responses. In early September, after further weeks of formal discussion and amendment, Pennsylvania's new constitution and declaration of rights were finally adopted.

One of the issues this convention debated most vehemently was how to amend the state's famous 1776 formulation of the right to free speech. No other element of the declaration of rights provoked anything like as much discussion. The revised article went through half a dozen different drafts, and many more proposed amendments. Its evolution was also widely publicized. All the convention's sessions were open to the public; its proceedings were reported in the papers, their minutes published contemporaneously. Though they have been almost entirely overlooked, the detailed records of these intense, months-long debates are the fullest surviving evidence we have of the drafting of any early American free-speech law. And they conclusively prove something else that, as far as I know, has gone completely unnoticed. Even before the First Amendment had been ratified, Americans had begun to reject its traditional, absolutist formulation, in favour of the new, balancing approach articulated in the French Declaration of the Rights of Man.

That foreign text was fresh in everyone's mind. In the weeks leading up to the convention, most of Philadelphia's many papers had published it, alongside discussions of the state's own forthcoming constitutional revisions. Several of them also printed Robespierre's stirring speech of 22 August, extolling press freedom as the essence of liberty, but affirming that it should not transgress 'the laws which ought to be established for the sake of peace and tranquillity', and specifically recommending the treatment of the press under the British constitution.

The need to revise the state constitution's free-speech article was already being discussed. Just before the declaration arrived in America, no less than Benjamin Franklin, Pennsylvania's revered elder statesman, publicly complained about the 'abuse' of press liberty, and urged the state's legislators to make 'an explicit law' defining its 'extent and limits':

> It is said to be founded on an article in the state-constitution, which establishes the liberty of the press. A liberty which every Pennsylvanian would fight and die for: Though few of us, I believe, have distinct [i.e. clear] ideas of its nature and extent . . . If by the liberty of the press were understood merely the liberty of discussing the propriety of public measures and political opinions, let us have as much of it as you please: But if it means the liberty of affronting, calumniating and defaming one another, I, for my part, own myself willing to part with my share of it, whenever our legislators shall please so to alter the law; and shall cheerfully consent to exchange my liberty of abusing others for the privilege of not being abused myself.

How might lawmakers achieve this desired alteration? The French Declaration seemed to provide the answer. 'I confess the liberty of the press should be very sacred,' a correspondent of Philadelphia's *Federal Gazette* announced, within forty-eight hours of the text's arrival in the city, but plainly there needed to be 'bounds even to the liberty of the press', otherwise it degenerated into 'licentiousness'. And lo:

> while I am writing, I have just received the copy of the Declaration of Rights by the National Assembly of France, and am happy to find that I am in unison with the sentiments therein expressed . . . Art. 4th begins thus, 'Liberty consists in doing whatever does not injure another', and in art. 11th, 'the free communication of thoughts and opinions is one of the most precious rights of man; every citizen therefore may freely speak, write and print under condition of being responsible for the abuse of that liberty in cases provided for by the law'. And what does all this amount to but just the spontaneous dictates of reason and common sense . . . I hope our convention who is soon to meet will be able to secure to every virtuous printer, the most perfect liberty that is consistent with the good of society, and set bounds to such as have nothing to value themselves upon but their malignant inclination, and abilities to do mischief.

That is exactly what came to pass. Pennsylvania's 1776 declaration had included two separate clauses about free speech. First, 'That the people have a right to freedom of speech, and of writing and publishing their sentiments; therefore the freedom of the press ought not to be restrained', and secondly that 'The printing presses shall be free to every person, who undertakes to examine the proceedings of the legislature, or any part of government'. In 1789, everyone agreed that it made sense to combine these two sentiments into a single article. The second clause, about using the press to examine the proceedings of government, remained uncontentious, and its text reappeared, unchanged, in the new constitution.

But the first clause, whose wording had appeared self-evident in 1776, and had been copied by many other states, now seemed to most delegates clearly inferior to the French approach of balancing rights with responsibilities. The convention's drafting committee duly adopted the declaration's exact words. On 23 December 1789, it proposed the following formula:

> That the printing presses shall be free to every person who undertakes to examine the proceedings of the legislature or any branch of government, and no law shall ever be made restraining the right thereof. The free communication of thoughts and opinions is one of the most invaluable rights of man, and every citizen may freely speak, write and print, being responsible for the abuse of that liberty.

This text repudiated the absolutist free-speech model of all existing state constitutions – and of the national Bill of Rights ratified only weeks earlier by the Pennsylvania Assembly. When it came to be debated, some delegates in fact proposed that the state's clause should simply match the wording of the new First Amendment, and stipulate only 'That no law shall ever be made abridging the freedom of speech or the press'. But this motion was quickly defeated. Instead, the members agreed to follow a balancing approach to free speech, and accepted the drafting committee's model text without further debate. Then, they went further. All their energies over the ensuing months were focused on hammering out the wording of an additional, concluding sentence, to specify the exact scope of the right to free expression.

The key issue in these discussions was how far the freedom of speech and the press should extend to critical or abusive 'libels' of individuals. Initially, the delegates divided into three main positions. The most liberal stance was that the right to free speech justified publishing anything that was true. The middle view was that it should extend only to truths about people holding office or seeking election – that is, not to the conduct of private citizens. The most restrictive position was that only the publication of truths about the *public* actions of public persons was justified – free speech should not extend to scrutiny of their private lives. Beyond these differing views on the scope of legitimate free speech, the critical question was how to define 'truth', and who should do so – judges (as the letter of English law stipulated), or juries alone (as had come to be a popular American opinion ever since the Zenger trial), or some judicious combination of the two.

In late February, after debating many different proposals on these matters, the convention reached agreement on how to formulate the new final sentence of its free-speech article:

> In prosecutions for libels, their truth or design may be given in evidence on the general issue, and their nature and tendency, whether proper for public information, or only for private ridicule or malice, be determined by the jury, under the direction of the court, as in other cases.

In other words, 'public information' was a legitimate free-speech defence, and not just in respect of public officials; in trials for libel, juries should follow the instructions of the judge, and take into account not just the truth of a publication, but also its intent, 'nature' and 'tendency'.

Though this formulation was the outcome of a series of closely contested votes, it proved not to be the final word. When the convention reconvened in August, its members poured renewed energy into refining the clause's exact wording. They again refused to restrict free speech only to criticism of 'individuals in their public capacity'. But the compromise that was finally agreed did make clear that the main purpose of a free press was to scrutinize 'men in a public capacity' and to reveal truths 'for public information'. From 1790 onwards, Pennsylvania's new constitution accordingly defined the right to free speech as follows:

That the printing presses shall be free to every person, who undertakes to examine the proceedings of the legislature or any branch of government: and no law shall ever be made restraining the right thereof. The free communication of thoughts and opinions is one of the invaluable rights of man; and every citizen may freely speak, write and print on any subject, being responsible for the abuse of that liberty. In prosecutions for the publication of papers, investigating the official conduct of officers, or men in a public capacity, or where the matter published is necessary or proper for public information, the truth thereof may be given in evidence; and, in all indictments for libels, the jury shall have a right to determine the law and the facts, under the direction of the court, as in other cases.

AMERICAN ATTITUDES

The bloated, ungainly wording of Pennsylvania's 1790 free-speech article was a far cry from the elegant, categorical formulations that had characterized earlier American declarations, from 1776 all the way up to the First Amendment. Yet there was good reason for this new verbosity. For the first time in American constitution-making, Pennsylvania's legislators went beyond merely extolling the liberty of the press, to tackle the real, practical problem of how to distinguish between justified 'free speech' and unjustified abuse. Their adoption of the model of the French Declaration allowed them to specify, as the wording of no previous American law had done, that press liberty should advance truth but avoid harm. As one of their leaders, the law professor and Supreme Court justice James Wilson, publicly summed up American doctrine shortly afterwards: 'The citizen under a free government has a right to think, to speak, to write, to print, and to publish freely, *but with decency and truth, concerning public men, public bodies, and public measures.*'

The redrafting of Pennsylvania's state constitution was part of long-running political struggles between local radicals and conservatives, and over federal versus state power. But these divisions did not concern the state's declaration of rights, which was universally agreed to be in need of improvement. Still less did it affect the general enthusiasm for adopting the French free-speech model. Philadelphia's Federalist and anti-Federalist newspapers alike approvingly publicized the French example, and the convention's votes on the free-speech clause followed no obvious party division. In the end, its final wording was approved almost unanimously, by 62 votes to 2.

It proved to be the beginning of a sea change. Already, in 1780, several of Massachusetts's town meetings had complained that the state constitution's article on press freedom was too absolute, and about a quarter of the state's voters had rejected its proposed text. 'There being no restraint thereon,' the citizens of Dunstable observed, 'it may be made use of to the dishonour of God by printing heresy and so forth and likewise injurious to private characters.' Press freedom should not apply 'where it is extended to the abuse, or injury of private characters', agreed the freeholders of Berwick, Ware and Yarmouth. Chelsea's meeting voted to add the stipulation that 'its freedom is not such as to exempt any printer or printers from being answerable for false, defamatory and abusive publications.' The citizens of Boston wanted it specified that the freedoms of speech and print only applied 'with respect to public men and their public conduct and public measures'. In 1786, the legislators of Vermont came to a similar conclusion, and actually amended their state's free-speech clause to specify that it applied only to 'sentiments, concerning the transactions of government', not to other matters.

Pennsylvania was the first state to go further, and replace its old free-speech wording with a more modern, qualified formulation. Other territories soon did the same. In 1791, Delaware's legislators unanimously jettisoned its famous declaration 'That the liberty of the press ought to be inviolably preserved', and replaced it with a text fashioned after Pennsylvania's. So too did the newly minted states of Kentucky (1792), Tennessee (1796), Ohio (1802) and the short-lived Republic of West Florida (1810). In fact, between 1790 and 1959, every single territory joining the Union explicitly specified that their citizens' constitutional right to freedom of expression did not extend to its abuse. Most of the original thirteen colonies, too, eventually followed suit (only New Hampshire and Massachusetts did not). At their simplest, these state free-speech clauses just copied the central phrase of the French Declaration. 'Every citizen may freely speak, write, and publish his sentiments on all subjects, being responsible for the abuse of that liberty' became, in its entirety, the fundamental law of Alabama (1819), as (with minor tweaks) of Washington (1889), Idaho (1889), Arizona (1910) and Alaska (1956).

Other states, beginning with Mississippi in 1817, nodded to the First Amendment by asserting that 'No law shall ever be passed to curtail or restrain the liberty of speech, or of the press' – but inserted that clause alongside stipulations about prosecuting libel and being responsible for 'abuse'. In other words, like Blackstone, they commended laws against licentiousness, maintaining that these did not infringe the liberty of the press. 'No law abridging freedom of speech or of the press shall be passed,' begins the original constitution of West Virginia, a state created in 1863 in the midst of the Civil War:

> but the legislature may provide for the restraint and punishment of the publishing and vending of obscene books, papers, and pictures, and of libel and defamation of character, and for the recovery, in civil actions, by the aggrieved party, of suitable damages for such libel or defamation. Attempts to justify and uphold an armed invasion of the state, or an organized insurrection therein, during the continuance of such invasion or insurrection, by publicly speaking, writing, or printing, or by publishing or circulating such writing or printing, may be, by law, declared a misdemeanor, and be punished accordingly.

By the middle of the twentieth century, almost every state constitution defined free speech as a qualified right, rather than in the libertarian terms of the First Amendment. Indeed, they still do. Why should we notice that, or care about the hidden history revealed in this chapter? For several reasons.

First, the history of American free speech is always written as if it originated in an Anglo-American discourse of rights, which then branched off after 1776 into a self-contained national tradition, focused on the creation and interpretation of the First Amendment. That is only part of the story. Consciously and unconsciously, American free-speech ideals after 1789 were also deeply influenced by the alternative approach expressed in the French Declaration of the Rights of Man.

Perhaps even more so. Between the late eighteenth and early twentieth centuries, the accepted, orthodox meaning of the First Amendment was simply that the federal government had no power to regulate speech or the press – but that the states did. The brief controversy over the national Sedition Act of 1798 only strengthened this presumption. 'While we deny that Congress have a right to control the freedom of the press,' Jefferson explained afterwards, 'we have ever asserted the right of the states, and their exclusive right, to do so' – and certainly, he went on, such action was urgently needed, to address 'the overwhelming torrent of slander which is confounding all vice and virtue, all truth and falsehood in the US'.

Because most modern scholarship valorizes the First Amendment and its post-1919 interpretation, it tends to dismiss earlier American free-speech law and practice as misguided or irrelevant. But the history of state laws and declarations underlines the extent to which, from 1789 to the mid twentieth century, American attitudes were primarily derived from European models, not from the First Amendment. It was not until 1950 that Hawaii became the first (and thus far only) state to model its own free-speech article directly on the national constitution. Six years later, Alaska stuck with the conventional phrasing derived from the Declaration of the Rights of Man.

If James Madison had had his way in the 1780s, perhaps none of this would have happened. In 1789, having previously failed to give the national government a general veto power over all local laws, he had tried to get Congress to adopt a constitutional amendment banning any state from curbing press liberty, religious freedom and trial by jury – because 'I think there is more danger of those powers being abused by the state governments, than by the government of the United States.' Had it passed, that might have prevented states from deviating as they did from the absolutist free-speech model he had enshrined in the Bill of Rights.

In the event, there's a profound historical irony about the First Amendment's unique global status, and particular power, as the world's only free-speech law framed in unconditional terms. As we've seen, the reason for that phrasing was simply that it copied the state declarations of rights that had preceded it, from 1776 onwards. Yet within months of its passage in 1789, state legislators themselves had begun to shift towards a qualified approach to defining free speech, influenced by the French example. By 1919, when the Supreme Court at last started systematically applying the First Amendment, they thus reanimated an archaic textual relic that described free speech in a way that had been superseded more than a century earlier. In 1925, when the justices decreed that this text should henceforth be the paramount law of the land, not just at national but at every level of government, almost every local constitution had long since switched to a balancing definition.

If in 1789 the French Assembly had met just a few weeks earlier, or Congress a few weeks later, or the transatlantic post had been faster, it seems possible that the wording of the First Amendment itself, too, might have been rather different. That would not necessarily have changed its creators' desire primarily to limit the powers of the federal government ('*Congress* shall make no law . . .'). But it could well have affected the implicitly absolutist language in which the people's underlying right to press freedom was conceived. Given the choice, most American legislators after 1789 preferred to define free speech in qualified rather than libertarian terms. As it is, modern American free-speech jurisprudence is based on a text whose progenitors had begun to abandon its rhetorically absolutist approach even before it was incorporated into law in 1791.*

LAWS AND LIBERTIES

It's not hard to see why generations of American state politicians preferred to define free speech in balanced rather than absolutist terms. After all, from the 1780s onwards the concerns of such legislators were closer to those of the French National Assembly than

---

* A final irony is that, soon after the free-speech formulation of the Declaration of the Rights of Man was taken up in the United States, it became defunct in France itself. A new constitution adopted there in 1793 (but never implemented) would have replaced it with a clause modelled on the First Amendment ('The right to express one's thoughts and opinions by means of the press or in any other manner, the right to assemble peaceably, the free pursuit of religion, cannot be forbidden'). From 1795 until 1814, France's constitutions did not define the right to free expression at all, and thereafter pre-publication press licensing was reintroduced. Only since 1946 has the Declaration of the Rights of Man been reintegrated into the national constitution.

to the creators of the US Bill of Rights. State lawmakers, too, were mainly focused on establishing their own liberties, as sovereigns and citizens of their own localities, rather than on warding off governmental tyranny. That's one reason why the French example appealed to the legislators of Pennsylvania in 1789, and was so widely followed thereafter.

It was also doubtless because this balanced approach avoided both of the First Amendment's obvious blind spots. Instead of guaranteeing citizens' liberty of expression only vis-à-vis government, state constitutions do so more generally – which means, for example, that they can apply even in public spaces that are technically private property. Secondly, unlike the value-free, libertarian language of the First Amendment, they specify the importance of truth, decree that publications should be judged according to their 'good motives' and 'justifiable ends', and explicitly warn against the abuse of free speech. Until the later twentieth century, that outlook supported an American jurisprudence that attended more closely to questions of harm, truth and collective injury than it has subsequently, in the Supreme Court's increasingly expansive, individual-centred interpretations of the First Amendment. For better or for worse, the shape of free-speech jurisprudence is affected by the terms in which constitutional rights are defined.

Exactly how is never, of course, predetermined: it depends on the meaning invested in constitutional words by those with power. Most of the American founders appreciated that. As Hamilton scornfully put it in 1788: 'It would be quite as significant to declare that government ought to be free, that taxes ought not to be excessive, etc., as that the liberty of the press ought not to be restrained' – the declaration itself was but a meaningless slogan. Legally, freedom of speech never applied to slaves; nor much to free Black men and women; nor even, in many states until after the Civil War, to white people who argued against white supremacy. Louisiana's 1812 constitution upheld the freedom of the press and citizens' right to free speech 'on any subject', saving only 'the abuse of that liberty'. Its statutes clarified what this meant. To teach a slave to read or write was a crime. Next, 'free people of color ought never to insult or strike white people, nor presume to conceive themselves equal to the whites; but on the contrary that they ought to yield to them on every occasion, and never speak or answer to them but with respect, under the penalty of imprisonment.' And any person who dared to write, print, publish, read or even just privately speak about 'anything having a tendency to produce discontent among the free colored population of the state, or insubordination among the slaves', was to be imprisoned at hard labour, or executed.

Yet ultimately, constitutional formulas matter not just as the basis of law, but as shapers of popular attitudes. Bills of Rights were always in danger of being ignored or violated, Madison wrote to Jefferson, also in 1788, but their prime value was that 'the political truths declared in that solemn manner acquire by degrees the character of fundamental maxims ... [and] become incorporated with the national sentiment'. Sometimes this sentiment can run counter to, or ahead of, how lawyers and judges interpret the text. As we'll explore in later chapters, the notion that the First Amendment guaranteed citizens' free-speech rights not just against the federal government but also against local and state laws was popularized by successive groups of nineteenth- and twentieth-century social activists, long before it was accepted as orthodox judicial doctrine. But since the middle of the twentieth century in America, the increasing omnipotence of the First Amendment's modern doctrine has gradually crowded out alternative legal and popular presumptions. Over the past few decades, its clumsy formulation has bolstered an increasingly libertarian popular attitude to personal expression. This used to be just a national phenomenon; but more recently the rise of the internet has made it into a global problem.

Legally, private entities like Facebook, YouTube, X and other social media companies are not bound by the terms of the First Amendment. Yet nonetheless, as American businesses, their own policies, around the world, instinctively replicate the popular understanding of its principles. That is partly why they happily censor 'obscenity' (traditionally not protected by the First Amendment), yet have been much less concerned about their amplification of dangerous scientific and medical misinformation. It is also why they have been particularly reluctant to moderate any kind of 'political' speech, irrespective of falsehood or harm. After all, the Supreme Court has long held that political opinion is sacrosanct, and that 'under the First Amendment, there is no such thing as a false idea'.

As we'll see in Chapter 10, it likewise helps explain why the treatment of hate speech by American social media companies has been so lax and erratic – for, again, unlike in other countries, to express violently racist, antisemitic or equivalent views is in the United States treated presumptively as legally protected free speech. In other words, it is not just the immense greed of internet giants that explains such failings, nor the intrinsic difficulty of judging these matters at scale, but the fact that their policymakers intuitively conceive of 'free speech' in a particular, libertarian, modern American way. Now imagine if, instead, the United States' constitution explicitly warned against the abuse of speech, upheld the paramount importance of truth, and treated free expression as a balance between rights and responsibilities. That is the final reason it matters that its exceptionalism is, in fact, a historical accident. Not unlike the dinosaurs of Jurassic Park, the First Amendment was brought to life long after its bloodline had died out. But now we're stuck with it.

7

Legitimate and Illegitimate Expressions

In the course of the eighteenth and nineteenth centuries, the new ideals of speech and press freedom gradually spread across the globe. In different places they took different forms. But everywhere the enthusiasm for these novel ideologies came up against problems, both old and new. What exactly did press liberty encompass? How should abusive and dangerous speech be defined and dealt with? Which voices had the right to speak, and who deserved to hear them? Who was included in 'the public'? When was speech truly free? What was this liberty *for*? In their detail, the historical answers to these questions differed from our own – yet in outline we still approach them in the same general way. No matter how laws define it, the shape of free speech is never just about the content of utterances, but also always about their speakers, audiences and context.

LICENCE AND LIBERTY

Everywhere that press liberty was debated and written into law in the decades around 1800 – across North and South America, Europe, parts of Asia, Africa and Oceania – the new principle that freedom of expression should be the norm boosted political discussion, spurred the foundation of newspapers, and increased the power of print. Its codification in the much-publicized American and French constitutions helped enshrine it as a global political ideal. By 1790, it was possible even in St Petersburg to quote American state constitutions while arguing that 'the freedom of the press is the greatest bulwark of liberty', as the German-educated civil servant Alexander Radishchev did in his best-selling *Journey from St Petersburg to Moscow*. (Though not for long – within a few weeks, on Catherine the Great's orders, he was arrested, tried and sentenced to death for this seditious libel, while copies of his book were banned, rounded up and destroyed.)

Similarly, barely a dozen years after printing had been introduced in Brazil, its constitution of 1824 echoed the French Declaration of the Rights of Man in specifying that, though 'abuses' would be punished, 'All persons may communicate their thoughts by words and writings and may publish them in the press without censorship.' By then it was common for this new genre, the written constitution, to include such stipulations about press liberty: similar formulations had already appeared, for example, in the foundational documents of the Dutch Batavian Republic (1798 and 1801), newly independent Venezuela (1811), Spain and its American colonies (1812), Norway (1814) and the Netherlands (1815).

On the other hand, what these changed circumstances couldn't and didn't affect, despite the optimism of those who brought them about, were precisely the age-old problems of misinformation, slander and abuse that had given rise to the now increasingly curtailed regimes of speech control. In fact, far from diminishing these problems, the shift to a more permissive free-speech culture usually made them worse. More information meant more misinformation. More freedom also meant more abuse.

By the end of the eighteenth century, this realization had led even some of the most prominent early champions of press liberty to revise their views. In the Dutch Republic in the 1780s, during a disastrous war against Britain, a radical new political movement of 'Patriots' began to agitate for popular sovereignty and constitutional reform. Inspired by the American revolution, and echoing the oppositional Anglo-American rhetoric invented by Cato's Letters, their incendiary manifesto (anonymously distributed across the nation one night in 1781, and immediately banned – then repeatedly reprinted, and translated into French, German and English) described freedom of the press as the people's most fundamental right, 'the only support of your national liberty':

If we cannot speak freely to our fellow citizens, nor warn them in time, the oppressors of the people will have free rein. That is why those whose conduct cannot survive examination always strive against the liberty of writing and printing, and would love it if nothing could be printed or sold without permission.

The rise of the Patriots inspired a flood of new and increasingly strident political publications, attacks on William V, prince of Orange, and duelling attempts at censorship by local Patriot or Orangist authorities. In 1782, a Patriot propagandist published a Dutch translation of Elie Luzac's anonymous 1749 treatise on press freedom, helpfully explaining that its arguments justified his party's actions in the present. This must have infuriated Luzac himself, a fervent Orangist and frequent target of Patriot polemic, who was appalled by what he viewed as his opponents' dangerous demagoguery, and their poisonous spreading of libel and sedition. 'Newspaper writers', he complained in one of his many anti-Patriot diatribes, 'who turn their liberty to relate the news into the impertinence of publishing everything that surfaces in their raging and sick brains are a disgrace to nature and the pests of society. They may with justice be regarded as the scum of the earth.' It was entirely appropriate, he argued, to punish writings 'that have no other purpose than to dishonour one's fellow man . . . [and] to inflame the people, and incite them to murder, arson, and robbery'.

In France, Mercier had a similar epiphany. By 1798, he had come to blame the failings of the French Revolution squarely on the doctrine of 'the unlimited liberty of the press', which had unleashed a poisonous flood of slanderous, inflammatory populist print. No educated writer or seeker after truth, he claimed, had ever supported such unrestrained freedom: 'they always preserved a sort of decency; they never brutalized either their language, their opinions, or their persons'. This new ideal was, rather, the invention of those who 'seduced and deluded the multitude. Every mob-writer might push his lies and impudence as far as he thought proper; he was sure to meet with encouragement.' Reversing his earlier optimism, he now declared that there was no such thing as 'public opinion', let alone the wisdom of the general will: 'there is not an hundredth part of the people who know how to read, and not a thousandth who can distinguish truth from falsehood ... I have always seen an error, a danger, a snare, in the association of these words, *unlimited liberty of the press*.'

As the Swedish and Danish examples also illustrate, the intellectual movement towards treating freedom of speech as a basic right was thus mainly a change of rhetoric. It shifted the grounds of debate, and the presumed balance between liberty and restraint, but not the basic fact that, both in theory and in practice, press liberty was always constrained by pre- or post-publication regulations. Its shape and interpretation were never settled, but, on the contrary, unceasingly contested. Soon after the French National Assembly enshrined freedom of speech and print in its 1789 Declaration of the Rights of Man, a bishop in Brittany denounced that idea in a pastoral letter: 'Through a deplorable abuse of freedom [they] want all citizens to be allowed to think and write whatever they want.' For this, the Assembly ordered him to be prosecuted for slandering national honour.

Before long, it went much further. In July 1790, all 'seditious' writings were outlawed; a year later, so was speech or writing that insulted a public official, or was intended to 'degrade' or provoke resistance to any law or authority. After the collapse of the monarchy in 1792, successive Acts imposed the death penalty on anyone who proposed its re-establishment, and for 'disparaging the National Convention and the republican government', 'calumniating patriotism', 'spreading false news' or 'misleading public opinion'. Up to half of the 8,000 people imprisoned in Paris during 1793–4 were in jail for prohibited speech; more than a third of the 2,747 men and women executed by the city's Revolutionary Tribunal died for uttering 'seditious' or 'counter-revolutionary' words. In the Dutch Republic, the Patriots took power in 1795 with the help of a French army, and proceeded to impose severe penalties on hundreds, possibly thousands, of men and women for similar forms of 'sedition' – even as they also drafted constitutional protections for every citizen's right to express 'his thoughts and feelings in speech, by writing or by means of the press'.

Supporters of such punishments invariably saw them as perfectly compatible with the freedom of the press, which, they maintained, 'no law would dare circumscribe'. Among them was none other than Thomas Paine. In 1792 he had been found guilty of political libel and sedition in England, in one of the most famous press-liberty trials of the eighteenth century. A few months later, he nonetheless urged the French to criminalize slander against *their* politicians:

> If every individual is to indulge his private malignancy or his private ambition, to denounce at random and without any kind of proof, all confidence will be undermined and all authority be destroyed ... Calumny is a species of treachery that ought to be punished as well as any other kind of treachery.

He took the same view, a few years later, about the intolerable 'licentiousness' of the American press.

When the French constitution was revised in 1795, it declared in the same breath that there was 'no limitation to the liberty of the press', but that it could be curtailed 'when circumstances make it necessary'. As well as banning newspapers and punishing their editors, French governments increasingly heightened surveillance and pre-publication censorship, even as they continued to extol press freedom. They also put huge efforts into the correct education of the citizenry and the publication of 'useful' patriotic writings. 'Today we can hazard unlimited freedom without great risk,' opined the liberal French writer and statesman François Guizot on taking office in 1814, and yet 'if morality and reason are perverted, if passions abound without restraint ... licence will have to be restrained.' He then reintroduced pre-publication censorship across France. Only in 1881 would it be finally removed. Across Europe, the Americas and colonial territories during this era, most governments embraced a similar approach. As well as creating right-thinking citizens through programmes of national education, the reintroduction of prior censorship was almost everywhere periodically mooted or implemented – alongside laws enshrining liberty of the press and the freedom of speech.

ANGLOPHONE ATTITUDES

The English-speaking world was slightly different. Immediately after the haphazard English abandonment of licensing in 1695, various forms of governmental control over print had remained entirely conceivable. A 1698 law targeted blasphemous and doctrinally controversial publications. Into the 1710s, conservative authors urged the reintroduction of pre-publication licensing, as did repeated bills in parliament. No British statute was ever passed explicitly guaranteeing any form of press freedom. Across the Atlantic in January 1723, the Massachusetts House of Representatives decreed that James Franklin, the troublesome printer of the *New-England Courant*, was henceforth 'strictly forbidden by this court to print or publish the *New-England Courant*, or any other pamphlet or paper of the like nature, except it be first supervised, by the secretary of this province' – the kind of oversight, they noted, that had 'been usual' in the past. In 1737, to suppress political criticism, the British government introduced strict prior censorship over all stage plays.

To most natives and foreigners alike, it was nonetheless obvious that the English had by far the freest press in the world. Voltaire, who lived in London in the later 1720s, was transformed by the experience. That in England 'every man has the liberty of publishing his thoughts with regard to public affairs' epitomized for him its intellectual superiority. Not all foreign champions of press liberty were as admiring. Justus van Effen, a brilliant Dutch essayist who spent more than a decade in London around the same time as Voltaire, and translated Defoe, Swift, Mandeville, Addison and Steele, was appalled by the savagery of the capital's political press. The English tendency to conceive of print liberty as an unbridled, absolute right, he argued in 1733, didn't advance truth: instead, it destroyed reputations, sharpened partisan divisions and incited dangerous popular passions. It undermined rather than bolstered personal liberty. Two decades later, the German translator of Cato's *Letters*, Johann Gottfried Gellius, explained to his readers that the English had a tendency to spout wild general claims and unsubstantiated exaggerations. In countries where people weren't so obsessed with 'liberty', he observed, their attitudes tended to be more reasonable and nuanced. Later visitors to America often felt the same way. In the 1780s, the learned liberal scholar Valentín de Foronda was one of the earliest advocates of religious and political free speech in Spain. But on arriving in the United States a few years later, he was aghast at what he found:

freedom of the press as it is enjoyed here is not freedom, but rather an unlimited licence, a frenzy. Nobody is respected: France, England, Spain and their governments are endlessly insulted and mocked. Their own president, Mr Jefferson, is continually knocked down, trampled upon, vilified.

Yet, other than the peculiarly Anglo-American premise that press liberty meant the absence of 'prior restraint', anglophone free-speech debates and practices throughout the eighteenth and nineteenth centuries followed the same pattern as those elsewhere: what counted as 'free speech', and what didn't, was simply a contingent political question. As Niclas von Oelreich pointed out to his Swedish colleagues in 1766, the lack of prior censorship in England didn't provide its writers and printers with greater legal security, but quite the opposite. Many knowledgeable English observers agreed with him. That the law provided no clear definition of what could be safely published left authors at the mercy of hostile lawsuits, Defoe complained in 1704. A century later, the great legal reformer Jeremy Bentham took the same view. 'The liberty which *you* want, *we* have,' he explained to a French critic of pre-publication censorship: but it was only an arbitrary freedom, subject to the whims of hostile judges, juries and the huge expenses of any lawsuit, irrespective of the outcome. That was why the possibility of litigation was so fearsome to writers and publishers: they could easily be ruined, even if they won in court. British and Irish governments also retained many other forms of control over print: they taxed newspapers, controlled their distribution through the post office, and bribed and bullied journalists, as well as judicially harassing authors and publishers who were critical of them. Across the British Isles and America, as everywhere else, there was a continuous struggle – polemical, literary, legal and political – to define press liberty and to expand or constrain its limits.

Up to the 1760s, the argument that press liberty should include the right to criticize and ridicule government officials and policies had steadily gained ground. During that decade, the sensational governmental prosecutions of the populist English politician and writer John Wilkes, and the brilliant press-freedom polemics that he and his supporters produced in response, permanently influenced all subsequent anglophone discussions of press liberty. From the 1770s onwards, parliamentary proceedings were allowed to be freely printed. In 1792 a new Libel Act finally gave English juries, not judges, the right to determine whether a text was libellous, as had already become the practice in America since the Zenger trial of 1735.

Yet ministerial harassment of writers and printers and prosecutions for seditious libel nonetheless continued throughout the second half of the century, abetted by sympathetic judges, parliamentarians and citizens. In the anxious wartime decades following the American and French revolutions, when British governments were terrified of the spread of reformist and revolutionary ideas, they passed draconian new statutes against political dissent, in order to suppress working-class and progressive debating societies and organizations and demands for political and economic reform. The 1792 Libel Act was introduced just a few weeks after a new royal proclamation against 'wicked and seditious writings', and was used to launch an unprecedented number of prosecutions against radical writers, printers and organizers. Across the country, loyalist political societies went after 'disloyal' and 'licentious' writers and newspapers (while championing, of course, 'the true, genuine Liberty of the press').

Three years later, the Treasonable and Seditious Practices Act, directed against 'the multitude of seditious pamphlets and speeches, daily printed, published, and dispersed', made it a crime to speak, write, or print 'any words or sentences to incite or stir up the people to hatred' of the monarchy, laws or constitution. Even satirical cartoons of the king, for which there had previously been a flourishing market, now became illegal. From 1799, under the Seditious Societies Act, all printing presses, makers of presses, and type-founders had to register with the authorities, and printers were obliged to include their name and address on anything they produced. Following the so-called Peterloo Massacre of unarmed political protestors by the British army in 1819, further laws tightened restrictions on public meetings, 'blasphemous and seditious libels', and newspapers. That the liberty of the press was being destroyed was a long-standing oppositional trope, and by the early nineteenth century it had become a central theme of progressive English writing and image-making. When there were no clear rules, complained William Cobbett, and 'all is left to the opinions and the taste of others', such as government lawyers, conservative clergy-men and vigilante political groups, 'can any man be said to be *free* to write?'.

In the United States, whose newspapers closely followed these transatlantic developments, the Sedition Act of 1798 was a similar, partisan attempt by the governing Federalist party and president, John Adams, to clamp down on domestic dissent in a time of inter-national crisis and war. This law, which expired at the end of Adams's term in 1801, criminalized any intentionally defamatory 'false, scan-dalous and malicious writing ... against the government of the United States', its Congress or president. The controversy it created, and its opponents' argument that the statute was incompatible with the First Amendment, did not prevent the passage of other American laws during the nineteenth and into the later twentieth century that similarly criminalized 'disloyal', 'seditious' and otherwise unaccept-able political speech.

SPEECH AND SLAVERY

For many decades, criticism of slavery was commonly included in the category of unacceptable speech. From the earliest years of the United States, in fact, national debates about free speech were closely bound up with controversies over slavery. By the turn of the century, there were close to a million enslaved Black people in the United States, and only about one hundred thousand free Blacks (out of a total population of around five million). The new national constitution drawn up in 1787 affirmed and protected slavery; in addition, an Act of 1793, fur-ther strengthened in 1850, required the governments and citizens of Northern states to capture and return anyone who had escaped from enslavement, anywhere in the country. Under the cover of these 'fugi-tive slave' laws, not only escapees but free Black people, too, were regularly kidnapped, transported South and sold into slavery. (In a similar spirit, in the southern state of North Carolina during and after the American revolution, hundreds of Black men and women who had been living for years in freedom were arrested, re-enslaved and sold into renewed bondage, by authority of the state legislature, county

courts and local officials.) In the South, slaveowners could be prohibited from freeing their own slaves, and even the voicing of anti-slavery
sentiments was legally punishable. In fact, the more prominently such
ideas were debated in the North, the more tightly they were repressed
in the South. By 1854, North Carolina's laws explicitly prohibited
the circulation of any text that would 'cause slaves to become discontented', or 'free negroes to be dissatisfied with their social condition
and the denial to them of political privileges'.

This national struggle about whether slavery was an unspeakable
or a legitimate subject of public discourse also played out at the highest level of federal politics. In the later 1790s, groups of formerly
enslaved and free Blacks living in Philadelphia repeatedly petitioned
the United States' Congress, which met in their city. They were ordinary people – mariners, labourers, dockworkers, sawyers, waiters.
Many of them could not write. But they were part of the large, confident population of free Black Philadelphians, organized in the city's
Free African Society (founded in 1787) and its associated school and
churches. They had energetic and charismatic leaders, such as the
preachers and freedmen Absalom Jones and Richard Allen. They also
had close ties to white anti-slavery activists, especially Quakers, who
were experienced at lobbying local and national governments against
slavery, and continued to do so through the 1790s. The two free Black
petitions that these groups submitted in January 1797 and December
1799 thus built on many years of multiracial planning and activism.

Their demands were both bold and carefully calibrated to the
political circumstances of the moment. Though they were careful
to disavow 'immediate emancipation of the whole', their ultimate
demand was 'the adoption of such measures as shall in due course
emancipate the whole of their brethren'. Meanwhile, they drew attention to the injustices perpetrated in the name of the Fugitive Slave Law,
asked for legal protection against seizure by slave catchers, and decried
violations of the 1794 Slave Trade Act (which had banned US vessels
from taking part in the international trade in slaves). Fundamentally,
they contended, the enslavement of Black people was itself an 'unconstitutional bondage . . . a governmental defect, if not a direct violation
of the declared fundamental principles of the Constitution'. In consequence, they asked Congress to 'exert every means in your power to

undo the heavy burdens, and prepare the way for the oppressed to go free'. As early as 1793, they had drafted an abortive petition for the 'gradual emancipation' of all 700,000 Black people that they computed were held in bondage across the United States.

These petitions had the support of several Northern members of the House of Representatives, and may have had a modest legislative impact. In 1800, the Slave Trade Act was tightened; the following year, a slaveholder-supported bill that would have further weakened the position of free Blacks was narrowly defeated. But the Congressional discussion of Black demands also helped to harden the majority view among both Northern and Southern lawmakers. This was that even the amelioration of slavery was a matter 'very improper and unconstitutional', 'extremely injurious' and too 'dangerous and unpleasant' even to be discussed by Congress – not only because doing so was bound to have 'very serious, nay, dreadful effects' (that is, encouraging Black hopes and agitation), but because abolition was in any case an impossible and unwanted prospect. In 1797, the House refused even to receive the first petition, as the majority of members agreed that the status of Black people was solely a matter for individual states. In 1800, upon the submission of the second petition, it agreed almost unanimously that, though abuses of the Fugitive Slave Law and Slave Trade Act ought to be investigated, the petition's more general appeal for Congressional action against slavery was unconstitutional, had 'a tendency to create disquiet and jealousy, and ought therefore to receive no encouragement or countenance from this House'. Only a single congressman opposed this formal rebuff, the fearless George Thatcher, who presciently declared to his colleagues that slavery 'was a cancer of immense magnitude, that would some time destroy the body politic'. 'If gentlemen saw so great evil rise out of the debate on this subject,' he needled his colleagues, 'why did they introduce the evil practice?'

In 1800, his was a lone voice. His fellow Massachusetts delegate, Harrison Gray Otis, though not a slaveowner himself, agreed with the majority that anti-slavery speech was unconstitutional and deeply dangerous to public safety. Decades later, in 1835, when agitation and petitions to Congress on the subject had become much more numerous, and abolitionists appealed regularly to their rights of free speech, Otis continued to hold forth to appreciative Boston audiences on why abolitionist views were 'most dangerous', and 'ought never to be entertained' in public discourse, even in the North: 'The right of thought, and of speech, and of the freedom of the press, is one thing – that of combining to spread disaffection in other states, and poison the sweet fountains of domestic safety and comfort, is a different thing.' His sentiments were widely shared by other white politicians and writers, as well as by the violent mobs who assaulted anti-slavery groups across the North. 'We are told of the freedom of speech and of the press, liberty of conscience, etc.,' editorialized an anti-abolitionist Delaware newspaper. 'This is all very plausible and we are the last individuals who would in the slightest degree abridge these invaluable and sacred rights. But moral treason or the aiding and abetting of domestic insurrection is quite a different thing.'

The federal government agreed. In 1835 the Postmaster General and the president of the United States supported the efforts of postal officials in both North and South to suppress abolitionist papers sent through the mail, in spite of their legal obligation to transmit them. The following year, on identical grounds, the House of Representatives passed what became known as its 'gag rule', refusing consideration to 'all petitions, memorials, resolutions, propositions, or papers, relating in any way, or to any extent whatsoever, to the subject of slavery, or the abolition of slavery'. This was necessary, its members agreed, because it was 'extremely important and desirable that the agitation of this subject should be finally arrested, for the purpose of restoring tranquillity to the public mind'. The First Amendment's protections of petitioning, speech and the press clearly did not apply to criticism of slavery.

SPEAKERS AND LISTENERS

Ever since the principle of freedom of expression was first legally established, conflicts about free speech have usually been described in terms of their subject matter – as disagreements over *what* people should or shouldn't be allowed to say. That is how laws, judges and free-speech warriors tend to frame them. Free speech allows them to tell the truth about sex, religion or politics. Or, their opponents reason, it's not a matter of free speech but of protecting people against the dangers of obscenity, blasphemy or other kinds of poisonous ideas – the abolition of slavery, the promotion of communism, critical race theory, gender and LGBTQ+ equality, racist or antisemitic creeds, pornography, slanders against God, falsehoods about elections, medical misinformation, or whatever.

Focusing on content is also an obvious way of comparing speech restrictions between cultures and over time. Swedes in 1766 were not permitted to publicly debate Christian doctrine, advocate religious toleration or question the constitution. In the Spanish South American colony of New Grenada, Antonio Nariño, a leader of the movement for Columbian independence, was in 1793 imprisoned for secretly translating and printing the Declaration of the Rights of Man and of the Citizen – yet his own interpretation of press freedom was that it could extend neither to 'truths confined to matters of our holy religion, which admit no discussion' nor to 'the decisions of government, deserving of our silence and respect'.

Britons and Americans were freer to do those things – but only up to a different point. In 1797, for instance, Thomas Paine's *Age of Reason* was deemed blasphemous by a London court. Liberty of the press was a great and precious thing which should always be defended, the prosecutor, Thomas Erskine, told the jury, 'but this freedom, like every other, must be limited to be enjoyed, and, like every human advantage, may be defeated by its abuse'. That was the same Erskine who a few years earlier had fiercely defended Paine at his trial for seditious libel, quoting Hume, Burke, Locke and Milton in a stirring, much-republished defence of press liberty as the uninfringeable, 'dearest privilege of the people of Great Britain'.

In short, what's encompassed by free speech has always been contingent, changeable and defined primarily in the negative, by demarcating categories of morally, ethically or politically impermissible expression. Even in our age of limitless, globally available online pornography, for example, 'obscenity' is everywhere differently defined, but nowhere legally protected. (That is, the depiction of sexual acts may be permitted – but not if the law characterizes them as 'obscene', as pornography involving children, for example, always is.) The basic model of how we conceive of free speech, as the inverse of prohibited content, remains essentially the same today as it was in 1750.

Yet because the legal definition of the 'obscene', the 'blasphemous' and the 'seditious' has in most western cultures shrunk over time, histories of censorship and free speech tend to tell a story of irrational taboos gradually being replaced by the more reasonable attitudes of the present. In the same way, people today routinely rank entities – nations, organizations, university campuses – according to their supposed 'freedom' or 'censorship' of speech. In doing so, they valorize permissiveness of expression as the highest good, inherently more important than questions of truth, equity or harm. What all these scholarly and popular approaches to free speech also have in common is that they focus on content: which words and ideas are policed, or not.

But free-speech conflicts were, and are, never just about the content of words. They are also about *who* should be allowed to speak, who is permitted to listen, and whose voices are heard most loudly – in other words, about defining who gets to shape public discourse. Nowadays, the core definition of having a political voice is being able to participate freely and equally in the governmental process, especially through voting. It's notable that in modern America the First Amendment's injunction against laws 'abridging the freedom of speech' has come to legitimate shady and often anonymous entities spending unlimited amounts of money to influence the political process, yet has never been applied to gerrymandering or other forms of voter suppression.

In its most basic sense, political free speech is the right to discuss public affairs. In the eighteenth and nineteenth centuries, though the right to vote typically remained restricted to a small minority of free, white, propertied men, the new ideal of political free speech, together with the spread of print, nonetheless elevated the opinions of a broader public and their right to discuss them freely. In every system of even nominally representative government, that made more acute the question of who exactly was included in 'the people', irrespective of the scope of the franchise. Whose voices should help shape public policy, and whose should not?

This was never just a matter of who should be allowed to speak publicly, but also of who was included in the audience – and, there-fore, about the tone of public discourse. Ever since classical times, it had been a commonplace that uneducated people were susceptible to demagoguery. Before the eighteenth century, that had been a major reason for excluding them from political debate, and for restricting the circulation of controversial texts. But from the mid eighteenth century onwards, in an era of increasingly egalitarian rhetoric, mass political communication and press liberty, that was no longer feasible, esp-ecially in supposedly progressive republics and monarchies. Instead, the theory and practice of free speech everywhere came to rely on an unstable, constantly contested division between two types of com-munication, whose categorization depended on subjective judgements about a writer's intentions and supposed audience. On the one hand there was legitimate, 'reasoned', free speech and print. On the other hand were unreasonable, dangerous appeals to mob passions, which could not be safely permitted.

Thus, in 1792, England's attorney general explained that he had not prosecuted the first part of Paine's *Rights of Man* because he believed that its readership 'would be confined to the judicious reader', intelligent enough to see through the book's fallacies. But when the second volume was issued, he was compelled to take action – not because its content differed, but because, he claimed, it was now being 'thrust' and 'force[d]' into the hands of 'that part of the public whose minds cannot be supposed to be conversant with subjects of this sort, and who cannot therefore correct as they go along'. It was a calculated appeal 'to the ignorant, to the credulous, to the desperate' – 'dangerous in the extreme to those whose minds perhaps are not sufficiently cultivated and habituated to reading'. In 1797, Erskine attacked Paine's religious arguments on similar grounds. 'An intellectual book,' he explained, 'however erroneous, addressed to the intellectual world upon so profound and com-plicated a subject', would have been unobjectionable. But Paine's text was, instead, 'shocking and insulting invective', like 'the most shameless obscenity, manifestly [intended] to debauch innocence, and to blast and poison the morals of the rising generation'. Such calculated spreading of poison went beyond the bounds of reasoned, legitimate debate.

RACE AND REASON

Whenever the question of legitimate free speech intersected with prejudices about race or sex, it became particularly fraught. In March 1791,
during the early stages of the Haitian revolution and slave uprisings
across the Caribbean, including on Dominica, a white journalist there,
Thomas Anketell, published an alarmed editorial in his paper about the
local disorders. When the governor responded by suing him for libel,
Anketell's supporters, deprecating this attack on 'the rights of British
freemen', reminded everyone that 'the liberty of the press is regarded
by the most enlightened of mankind, as essential to the nature of a free
government'. Anketell himself immediately shifted the blame on to the
editor of a rival, francophone weekly, *L'Ami de la Liberté et l'Ennemi
de la Licence* ('The Friend of Liberty and Enemy of Licentiousness'),
who was, he sneered, 'a mulatto fellow of no character or principle'.
That was the paper, he warned the readers of his own *Charibbean
Register*, that was stirring up the local dark-skinned population: 'It
was not only read with avidity by free people of colour, but Negro
slaves were subscribers to it.' Dominica's House of Assembly concurred that Black and brown speech and print were the real danger:
both 'the example of several ill-disposed free people of colour', and the
weekly poison of *L'Ami de la Liberté*, 'in which such encouragement is
given to slaves and opinions promulga[ted in] their favour so dangerous to the lives and properties of their masters'. That was not a matter
of press liberty, but a simple 'evil' that should be forcibly suppressed.

In the same way, the American debates over slavery in the 1790s
and 1830s were not just struggles about the content of public political
discourse but over who should be allowed to participate in it. How far
should a government of whites attend to non-white people, whether
free or subjugated? In 1797, the first four Black men ever to petition
the United States' legislature cautiously disclaimed 'the privilege of
representation in your councils', and addressed its members only as
'fellow-men'. At this point, George Thatcher was unusual in referring
to Black freemen as 'dark-complexioned citizens', and in asserting
'that every man is born equally free, and that each have an equal right
to petition if aggrieved'. But by 1799, the second free Black petition,

too, referred to its subscribers as 'a class of citizens', spoke of 'us and the rest of the citizens of the United States', and argued that enslaved Black people were 'equal objects of representation and attention with themselves or others under the Constitution'.

These were contentious statements, for in fact the question of whether a non-white person could *be* a citizen was itself far from settled, even in Philadelphia itself, home of the largest free Black community in the country. Pennsylvania's 1790 constitution spoke only in general terms of citizens and freemen, but by the early nineteenth century free Blacks there were being openly and violently denied their civil liberties. 'The Negroes have an undisputed right of voting,' a local told the visiting Alexis de Tocqueville in 1831, but they never actually took part in elections, for 'the majority entertains very strong prejudices against the Blacks, and the magistrates are unable to protect them in the exercise of their legal privileges.' When the state's constitution was revised in 1838, it deliberately restricted citizenship to 'white freemen'.

Black men and women, and their allies, had been publicly contesting such racial discrimination ever since the revolutionary war in the 1770s, especially in places like Massachusetts with sizeable populations of free, literate Black people and rich newspaper cultures. Yet everywhere in the new republic in the years after its foundation, the already fragile rights of free Blacks were further whittled away. The Naturalization Act of 1790 specified that only 'a free white person' could become an American citizen; two years later, Congress allowed only 'white male citizens' to join state militias. 'The free negroes in our country,' a Virginia congressman explained in 1820, 'may be denizens, but none of them, it is apprehended, are citizens.' 'Denizens' were instead people 'admitted to some portion of the rights and privileges of citizens, but not all those rights'. On such grounds, southern and western states severely limited the liberties of free Black people; in northern states, too, their status was variable and almost never equal to that of the white inhabitants. Across the United States, the overwhelming majority of free Black men were not considered to be citizens, or to have constitutional rights, let alone the right to vote. Eventually, in 1857, the Supreme Court affirmed that no person 'of the African race' could ever be a citizen.

The Congressional debates of this era illustrate the same tendency to dismiss the claims of Black voices on governmental attention, and to stigmatize them as inherently irrational, dangerous and unworthy of participation in public discourse. In 1797, several members ridiculed Thatcher's claim of 'an equal right to petition'. 'If they are slaves, the Constitution gives them no hopes of being heard here,' James Madison flatly pointed out, and whether they were free or enslaved was not Congress's business to ascertain. Three years later, faced with the petition of over seventy Black freemen of Philadelphia, John Rutledge of South Carolina sneeringly referred to them as 'black *gentlemen*', uttering the word with such contempt that the short-hand writers taking down his speech italicized it. 'They now tell the House these people are in slavery,' he went on:

> I thank God they are! ... Already had too much of this new-fangled French philosophy of Liberty and Equality, found its way and was too apparent among these *gentlemen* in the Southern states.

It was dangerous for Congress even to discuss slavery, he reminded his colleagues, because this would encourage Black agitation:

> Because many of those people can read and write, and will be informed of what I am now saying ... They now will see that the argument has been agitated in the legislature; that the subject of emancipation has been discussed.

Another Southern congressman took umbrage at the Black petitioners' reference to '*us* and the rest of the citizens of the United States'. 'With all their philanthropy', he asked his anti-slavery colleagues, would they 'wish to see those people sitting by their sides deliberating in the councils of the nation? He presumed not.' Harrison Gray Otis summed up the prevailing, uneasy combination of white attitudes: on the one hand, disdain for Black people as intellectually inferior and inherently unworthy of citizenship; on the other, alarm at the prospect that 'those people' might nonetheless become literate and express political demands. The 1799 petitioners, Otis agreed, were but the stooges of experienced white activists: Black people could never have organized such a thing themselves. It was nonetheless vital not to give them a hearing. For that would be 'mischievous to America very soon ... It would teach them the art of assembling together, debating, and the like, and would soon, if encouraged, extend from one end of the Union to the other.'

Northern anti-abolitionists in the 1830s justified their actions in similar terms, even while routinely deprecating the 'evil' of slavery itself. Soon after the House of Representatives passed its gag rule, it also decreed for good measure that, whatever their grievance, 'slaves do not possess the right of petition secured to the People of the United States by the Constitution'. 'While we would maintain inviolate the liberty of speech, and the freedom of the press,' the leading citizens of New York state resolved at a public meeting in September 1835, 'discussions, which, from their nature, inflame the public mind', were a different matter. Abolitionists were engaged in 'unconstitutional and incendiary proceedings'; they were 'disturbers of the public peace', motivated by either 'delusion or sinister design', whose arguments were not covered by the right to free speech. 'It has, indeed, been said that nothing is to be feared from discussion, when reason is left free to combat error,' noted John Adams Dix, New York's Secretary of State and future governor. 'But . . . Is it not, under the peculiar circumstances of this case, unsafe in practice, so far as it is carried on by the circulation of abolition publications in the south?'

The problem, he explained, was not 'arguments addressed to the master, to convince him of the propriety of liberating his slaves, [which] would be harmless and might be useful', but that 'the arguments, and the representations with which they are accompanied, find their way to the slave'. Because of this theoretical possibility, such texts could not be defended as free speech. First, because of their tone: 'much of the matter contained in their publications is of the most inflammatory character . . . Addressed to the slave, it is an incentive to, and in some cases doubtless a justification, in his own sight, of insurrection and bloodshed.' Secondly, because the enslaved were in any case not governed by reason but by violent 'passions'. That meant they were incapable of rational debate:

> In communities of freemen, unrestrained discussion is indispensable as a safeguard against error and abuse. But who does not see that in dealing with an unenlightened population, placed by the force of circumstances in a peculiar relation to others, the effect of discussion may be to awaken

them to a knowledge of their condition without enlightening them as to the necessity which has produced it, and which has taken forever out of their control the ability of providing for their own relief consistently with the safety of the general society?

The attempt to place anti-slavery voices beyond the pale of free speech was highly successful in the South, but in the North eventually produced a counter-reaction. For years, Northern abolitionists were abused, attacked, prosecuted, jailed and sometimes even assassinated. Yet from the later 1830s, their argument that anti-slavery views were legitimate expressions of political opinion, and that it was rather their Southern critics who were the enemies of free speech, had begun to be widely accepted across the North, even by those who didn't much care for their aims. In turn, this inspired a new idea – that the freedoms of speech and press mentioned in the First Amendment were in fact national rights, which belonged to all citizens. In 1844, Congress voted to rescind its gag rule. In 1856, the Republican Party's presidential candidate John C. Frémont ran on the platform 'Free Speech, Free Press, Free Men, Free Labor, Free Territory, and Frémont'.

'Slavery cannot tolerate free speech,' the great Black abolitionist Frederick Douglass urged in 1860, in the midst of mob violence against abolitionist meetings in Boston, and that included 'the right to hear': together 'the right to speak and hear' were the most 'sacred' of all constitutional rights. The Civil War would never have broken out, he observed in 1863, if the federal government had but upheld the First Amendment as readily as it had supported the constitutional rights of slaveowners. Following the war, many politicians and citizens accordingly seem to have interpreted the Fourteenth Amendment of 1868, the cornerstone of America's new constitutional guarantee of racial equality, as enshrining this broad, national interpretation of the First Amendment – long before the Supreme Court began to weigh in on the topic.

SEX AND STATUS

Defining public discourse in ways that delegitimize certain voices or audiences, not just particular ideas, has always been intrinsic to the politics of speech – the rise of free speech didn't change that. But, as the abolitionist example illustrates, it did make it riskier, and liable to backfire. Telling people that their voices were not welcome in public debate might now more easily provoke them to push back, and demand the right to speak.

That was exactly what fuelled the nineteenth-century campaign for women's rights, which partly evolved out of the abolitionist movement. That men treated women as slaves was an age-old rhetorical trope. But in the decades around 1800, the widespread adoption of languages of universal rights, together with the rise of abolitionist sentiments, made it possible for some radical thinkers actually to join the cause of anti-slavery to that of women's rights. For was it not evident, the pioneering American feminist Margaret Fuller asked in 1843, that white men, in denying equal rights to both groups, harboured exactly the same irrational prejudices 'towards women as towards slaves'?

The first theorist of free speech to publicly take up both causes, albeit without explicitly connecting them, was probably the fearless eighteenth-century Parisian dramatist, pamphleteer and single mother Olympe de Gouges. Throughout the 1780s, she agitated against the enslavement of Black people; soon afterwards she took up the cause of women's political rights. On 14 September 1791, Louis XVI ratified France's new revolutionary constitution and Declaration of the Rights of Man, drafted two years earlier by the National Assembly. As we saw in the last chapter, this included two central clauses defining religious, intellectual and political freedom of speech:

> X. No one shall be disquieted on account of his opinions, including his religious views, provided their manifestation does not disturb the public order established by law.

> XI. The free communication of ideas and opinions is one of the most precious rights of man. Every citizen may therefore speak, write, and print freely, under condition of being responsible for the abuse of that liberty in cases provided for by the law.

That very day, as a protest against the document's innate chauvinism, de Gouges published her own counterblast, the *Declaration of the*

Rights of Woman and of the Female Citizen, whose wording cleverly reworked the original declaration's seventeen clauses. In doing so, it asserted first of all that women had an equal right to public, political speech:

> X. No one shall be disquieted for their opinions however fundamental; women have the right to mount the scaffold; they must equally be entitled to step up to the rostrum, provided their expressions do not disturb the public order according to the law.

But it also went further. Like most other feminists of the period, de Gouges saw the seduction and abandonment of women by men, and the social prejudices against illegitimacy and unwed motherhood, as foundational inequities of the patriarchal system. And so her riff on Article 11 explicitly linked the suppression of female speech to women's sexual oppression – and the right to free speech to the overthrow of the sexual double standard:

> XI. The free communication of ideas and opinions is one of the most precious rights of woman, because this liberty ensures the legitimacy of fathers towards their children. Every female citizen may therefore freely declare: 'I am the mother of a child that belongs to you', without a barbarous prejudice forcing her to hide the truth; except that she be answerable for the abuse of that liberty in cases provided for by the law.

This brilliant early feminist engagement with the new concept of free speech as a citizen's right went largely unremarked in its own time. But a few decades later, in North America, the same questions arose in a more sustained and consequential way: how far should women have a right to a public voice? Why should they be excluded from religious and political debate? In the 1830s and 1840s, as it was engaged in its national struggle over free speech and slavery, the American abolitionist movement came to be bitterly divided over these matters. As so often in the history of patriarchy, the attempt to restrict female speech was something of a rearguard action. For, ever since the beginnings of organized anti-slavery campaigns in the later eighteenth century, women on both sides of the Atlantic had played a major role in leading them. They spoke, wrote, petitioned and agitated alongside men.

In the early nineteenth century, however, their increasing public visibility provoked a chauvinist backlash.

Opponents of the anti-slavery movement routinely attacked women's participation in it as illegitimate, because politics was a male affair. In 1838, Congress was flooded with appeals against admitting to the Union the slaveholding rebel white and Hispanic colonists of Texas, who had recently seceded from Mexico after it abolished slavery. Among the signatories were tens of thousands of women. 'Many of these petitions were signed by women,' sneered a powerful Maryland congressman, dismissing them. 'He always felt regret when petitions thus signed were presented to the House relating to political matters' – females should stick to 'their proper sphere' of domestic duties, 'instead of rushing into the fierce struggles of political life'. A few years earlier, in 1830–31, the first large-scale women's petitions to Congress, protesting against the government's new genocidal policy of 'Indian removal', had attracted no such gendered opprobrium. The anti-slavery petitions were signed by many of the same women. But this time the response was markedly different.

That was because it seemed to herald much larger and more threatening changes. Opposing the mainstream policy of 'colonization', which aimed to decrease slaveholding through the gradual, voluntary emancipation and deportation of Black people to Africa, increasing numbers of anti-slavery activists agitated instead for the immediate abolition of all slavery across the country. This 'abolitionist' movement had originally been organized along gendered lines, with separate male and female meetings, societies and conventions. But towards the end of the 1830s, when prominent female activists like the Grimké sisters of South Carolina and the Massachusetts teacher Abby Kelley began to attract large mixed audiences and to join men in local meetings, their actions provoked anguished debate. In some associations, steps were taken to bar women from voting and prevent their election to committees; in others, they were given equal rights.

In 1829, the Connecticut schoolteacher and pro-colonization activist Catharine Beecher had been the chief instigator of the national women's protests against Indian removal, arguing that 'female petitioners can lawfully be heard, even by the highest rulers of our land'. But by 1837 she publicly decried abolitionist calls for equivalent action as essentially unfeminine. 'In this country,' she chided Angelica Grimké, 'petitions to congress, in reference to the official duties of legislators, seem, IN ALL CASES, to fall entirely without the sphere of female duty. Men are the proper persons to make appeals to the rulers whom they appoint.'

To feminist abolitionists, by contrast, the parallels between how slaves and women were treated appeared increasingly telling. 'The investigation of the rights of the slave has led me to a better understanding of my own,' Angelina Grimké replied to Beecher, and in consequence, 'I recognize no rights but human rights': everything that men did, including voting, petitioning and governing, women had an equal, inalienable right to. A few months later, in Congress, John Quincy Adams, the Massachusetts congressman and former president, explicitly connected the political speech-rights of slaves with those of women. Under the gag rule, the Speaker refused to let him argue on the floor of the House 'that slaves were not excluded by the Constitution of the United States from exercising the right of petition', or to have his words entered into the written record. Undaunted, Adams argued that not only slaves were included in 'the People of the United States', but also women, who surely had the right to a political voice: 'are women to have no opinions or action on subjects relating to the general welfare?' If it was contended that women had no right to petition 'because they have no right to vote', then, he responded provocatively, 'is it so clear that they have no such right as this last? And if not, who shall say that this argument . . . is not adding one injustice to another?'

Matters came to a head when in 1839 the national convention of the Anti-Slavery Association narrowly voted to give women equal rights in its proceedings, and the following year made Kelley a member of its business committee. This split the movement: the traditionalist delegates walked out to found a separate 'American and Foreign Anti-Slavery Society'. The following month, the presence of a handful of female American delegates precipitated a similar crisis at the World Anti-Slavery Convention in London, whose British organizing committee had presumed that only 'gentlemen' would attend. Indignantly, they seated the women delegates 'fenced off behind a bar and curtain', prohibited them from taking part in the formal discussion of their own status, and finally, by an overwhelming majority, excluded them from the convention. That night, Lucretia Mott and Elizabeth Cady Stanton, two of the rejected delegates, resolved 'to hold a woman's rights convention on their return to America', which they eventually did in 1848 at Seneca Falls in New York. This became the founding moment of the organized women's rights movement, which went on to win women the right to vote and hold public office. From the outset, its leaders conceived of their struggle not primarily as one for the franchise, but for the most basic political right of all – to speak freely to the public on matters of communal concern. 'In advocating liberty for the black race,' Stanton and her colleagues later recalled, they had been 'compelled to defend the right of free speech for themselves'.

MEANS AND ENDS

What conclusions can we draw from the history of free speech in the first century and a half of its existence as a legal and popular principle? And how do they relate to our own predicaments? The two questions are connected – because the underlying model of how free speech is constituted has remained the same ever since. Freedom of speech and liberty of the press have always been conceptualized primarily in terms of 'public' utterances, and defined mainly in terms of what was *not* to be so discussed. Less visible but equally important has also always been the definition of the public: who could listen, or speak, and on what terms. Whatever the particular public arena – streets, legislatures, the stage, the press, television channels, social media – those conditions always apply.

This simple model allows us to contrast what liberty of expression meant, and means, in different cultures, whether in the eighteenth and nineteenth centuries or in the present. It also points to important changes over time. Generally speaking, and especially since the social revolutions of the 1960s, the limits of impermissible content have in western countries been steadily eroded. Nowadays we also take a different approach to defining the public. Even as they deployed a new rhetoric of political equality, eighteenth-century observers perpetuated a model of the social order that was naturally unequal. To some extent, western laws about censorship, publication, obscenity and related matters retained some of those hierarchical principles into the 1960s. In the twenty-first century, by contrast, theories of free speech tend to presume the inherently equal status of all public voices and auditors, irrespective of whether they are, say, Catholic, Black, working class or female (the practice is, of course, a different matter).

So the domain of free speech has expanded in significant ways since the eighteenth century, especially in terms of its legal protection. And yet any ideology of free speech that invokes a distinct sphere of politics or 'public' activity is still bound to do so in gendered and otherwise normative ways. For example, one of the most widely celebrated legal and cultural developments of the twentieth century was the gradual collapse of censorship over sexual texts and images. By the 1970s, pornography had become much more widely and freely available across the western world than ever before. This was overwhelmingly theorized as a victory for freedom of expression, but also as relating to a particular realm of 'low value', non-political speech. Even as its rulings allowed for ever greater permissiveness, the American Supreme Court thus repeatedly affirmed that 'obscenity' was not protected by the First Amendment – erotic images were different from political discourse, the supposed 'core' of free speech. When, from the 1970s onwards, some feminist theorists such as Catharine A. MacKinnon and Andrea Dworkin began to argue that, actually, speech about sex *was* always political, and that pornography was a pervasive form of public language and action, which had deeply misogynist effects in the world, they received a chilly response from leading liberal philosophers – rather than a series of propositions open to debate, their claims were often dismissed as 'dangerous confusion' and 'an attack on freedom of speech'.

As well as some striking changes over time in the accepted realm of free speech, it's therefore hard not to notice, as well, a set of fundamental continuities. New content taboos and clashes over speech pop up all the time in different parts of our cultures. Despite the principle of equality of voice, the speech of women, trans persons, people of colour, the poor, the disabled and other relatively disempowered groups is still routinely marginalized. That is not a problem produced by our ideals of free speech – but any theory of free speech that ignores it is going to be very insufficient. Who can speak, who gets heard and who makes the rules about what one can say is always about power and authority, as much as about judgements of harm and danger. And that's even before we've begun to take into account (as we'll do in Chapter 10) the massive inequities of speech created and perpetuated by the shape and priorities of the media, whether eighteenth- and nineteenth-century newspapers, twentieth-century broadcasting or twenty-first-century social media platforms. The classic paradigm of free speech presumes that society consists of equally autonomous individuals, whose beliefs are made up of abstract notions they rationally assemble – choosing and discarding freely from a universal, neutral marketplace of ideas, in which all propositions are always given a fair and equal hearing, and people naturally discern and embrace the truth. Nothing could be further from the reality in which we actually live.

More fundamentally, to conceive of free speech only in terms of more or less permissiveness about what one can say, or in terms of the expansion of access to the public sphere, tends to a reductionist focus only on whether liberty of speech is 'advancing' or 'retreating'. The ultimate implication is that we should aspire to some kind of theoretical state of perfect freedom of expression for everybody. And that distracts us from grappling with the inherent contradictions and complexities of the free-speech model that we have inherited from the past.

Above all, it ignores the central question that so engaged eighteenth- and nineteenth-century observers – what is freedom of speech *for*? Their answers were multiple: its purpose was to advance truth, to spread enlightenment, to discuss political questions, to pursue justice, and so on. Each of those purposes required a different set of speech rules and conditions – for example, the prohibition of slander, the avoidance of obscenity or the exclusion of lies. Without those conditions, the discussion wouldn't be able to achieve its desired aim. The same holds true in our own time. Proper rules are constitutive of free expression: they give it meaning, they channel it towards its intended aim.

This is a fundamental reason why conflict over free speech is inevitable. Different aims require different constraints. If its purpose is to establish truth, it requires one set of conditions; if justice, a different set; if political legitimacy, yet another; if to create art or generate amusement, still others, and so on. It is an inherently unstable, contradictory ideal, even before we get to our own differences. And if, more simplistically, you think of freedom of expression not as a means to an end, but simply as an end in itself, then the result is that you elevate speech for its own sake to the supreme ideal: more important than truth, justice, equity, democracy or any other value. That is not only logically problematic, it also implies that any constraint is wrong. The practical effect of such an outlook is to worsen exactly the serious problems that most early theorists of free speech were so acutely concerned to avoid: a public sphere full of hatred and slander, the poison of untruth and the politics of demagoguery.

At a deeper level, too, the perennial free-speech questions of content and voice are not soluble by simply asserting that everyone should have an equal right to say everything. The purpose of speech is communication – but all communication requires shared rules, merely to be intelligible. Some of those are basic (you can read this because we both know English), but most are contextual (how you interact with your intimidating new boss is different from the way you address your children). So the significance of any utterance is closely dependent on context: who is speaking, what their intention is, who the audience is. The same words can have very different significance depending on these things – is it the president of the United States pronouncing them in a global broadcast, an academic interrogating them in a scholarly article, or a tipsy youth slurring them in a deserted bar?

This is why it is so hard to legislate in any hard and fast way about even the use of a single, freighted word, like 'nigger'. It is also why many free-speech conflagrations, whether in person, online or anywhere else, can be understood as miscommunication – that's to say, a misalignment between the intentions of the speaker, the nature of the audience and/ or the context of the utterance. And it also explains, more generally, why rules about free speech cannot simply be based on content. That is especially the case with humour and other forms of artistic expression – because those are the most complex, nuanced, context-dependent communications of all. What is funny, what is appropriate, what is in good taste – these are all relevant criteria when it comes to judging the free-speech boundaries of comedy. They all have different answers (and collectively we will invariably disagree about those), and they are all exquisitely reliant on context. In each case, the tone matters. The intention matters. The audience matters. The medium matters. The time and place matter. The occasion matters. The history matters. Everything does. Can jokes be told about the Holocaust? Of course. No subject is off limits. But that's not the hard question: whether it works as a joke, and whether we think it permissible, depends on who is doing the telling, why and where and when and to whom. A joke about rape told by a rapist is a completely different speech act from a joke about rape told by a survivor. A Jewish comedian in the Catskills in the 1930s poking fun at stingy Jews is one thing; a satire of grasping Jewish bankers uploaded to YouTube by a non-Jewish troublemaker in the twenty-first century is quite another – even if this person claims it's 'just comedy', and others, whether conscious of its antisemitism or not, find it funny.

It's right to draw such distinctions between permissible and impermissible speech. Informally we all do so all the time. Yet our free-speech principles, with their obsessive focus on content, aren't really sophisticated enough to help us articulate why – or even to acknowledge the basic truth that the meaning of all speech depends upon its context. The real questions are never 'Should people be allowed to say that?', let alone 'Do you support free speech?' They are, rather – what should 'freedom' mean? What is free speech for? And, whose speech are we talking about, where and to whom? Starting from those propositions probably won't make it easier for us to agree with one another: but it would surely produce a more honest and constructive conversation.

8

Imperial Entanglements

The modern ideal of speech and press liberty emerged in the eighteenth century, across Europe and its empires, out of several interrelated developments: the spread of print and a rising appreciation of its power; Enlightenment enthusiasm for the cross-border exchange of knowledge about every aspect of the world; and a growing belief that the workings of governments, too, would be improved by public discussion in newspapers, pamphlets and other forms of print.

It also coincided with new heights of European imperialism. What shape should press liberty take in colonial contexts, with their racialized gradations of citizenship, freedom and power? How did settlers and subalterns understand and manipulate notions of free speech? These questions were to arise everywhere across the globe in due course. But they pressed most urgently in the anglophone world, with its precociously assertive ideals of press freedom and its uniquely developed print sphere. By 1828, it has been estimated, nearly half of all the newspapers in the world were printed in English.

In the English-speaking settler colonies of the Americas, as we've seen, liberty of speech was a mark of racial hegemony, and the free press a tool of enslavement, long before they became associated with political revolution. Yet even in these circumstances, free speech could never be completely confined to ruling-class voices and arguments. Women, servants, foreigners, the religiously heterodox, the darker skinned and the enslaved – inferior people of all kinds – constantly asserted and appropriated the right to speak, to listen and to be heard.

Free speech took a still different shape in India, which in the second half of the eighteenth century unexpectedly became Britain's newest, largest and most prized colony. At the time, printed texts were largely unknown there, let alone ideals of press freedom. Its European population was tiny, dwarfed by the vast size, wealth and sophistication of the local cultures. Yet, beginning in 1757, a private British trading corporation with its own mercenary army, the East India Company, suddenly managed to expand its reach beyond a few coastal enclaves, and within a few decades gained power over Bengal and other valuable territories. So began almost two hundred years of British conquest and occupation of the subcontinent.

Tracing the story of how free-speech ideals and practices evolved in this context helps to illuminate the character of colonial rule and indigenous responses during the zenith of European imperialism. Just as importantly, the colonial experience profoundly infiltrated western ideas about free speech. Nowhere is this reverse impact clearer than in the life and thought of John Stuart Mill, the most influential Anglo-American theorist of personal liberty and freedom of expression. Mill was a great progressive philosopher, whose work remains foundational to anglophone theories of individual rights. Yet he also happened to be a dedicated, lifelong agent of the East India Company. The opinions about free speech that he put forward in his writings, including *On Liberty* (1859), the urtext of modern western liberal thought, are usually treated as neutral, universally applicable, inspiring arguments. But they were, in fact, profoundly imperialist and intellectually flawed claims.

JUSTIFYING EMPIRE

To understand how speech and press freedom developed in colonial India, we need first to grasp how imperial rule was justified. From around 1800, the British vindicated their overseas actions through an ideology of historical necessity. This had several ingredients: the old Protestant idea of God's providence; the more recent valorization of personal conscience, making intent rather than outcome the ultimate ethical criterion; and a new belief that human societies passed through stages of development, from the 'primitive' to the 'civilized', measurable by such criteria as their systems of agriculture, forms of government, and treatment of women. The upshot was that national fates were determined by divine destiny and immutable laws of social development. Compared with these inexorable forces, well-intentioned human agents could hardly bear much culpability for misfortune. What's more, because the arc of history was supposed always to bend toward progress, even destructive or immoral actions could be exculpated as likely to be eventually 'vindicated by history'. In the ethics of imperialism, then as now, final judgement is always deferred to the future.

This general outlook came to be deeply pervasive. Even some of the severest western critics of colonialism in the nineteenth and twentieth centuries shared its presumption that human history moved unstoppably forward along a single path, and that mere individuals could only enact what was predetermined. The effects of British rule in India were a 'devastating' chronicle of naked extortion, theft and murder, Karl Marx informed the readers of the *New-York Daily Tribune* in 1853. Despite all their high-minded cant, he noted, British imperialists were obviously motivated primarily by greed. Yet this 'dragging ... people through blood and dirt, through misery and degradation' was also a historical necessity, for 'England has to fulfil a double mission in India: one destructive, the other regenerating – the annihilation of Asiatic society, and the laying of the material foundations of Western society in Asia.' 'Whatever may have been the crimes of England,' he concluded, 'she was the unconscious tool of history in bringing about that revolution.' To occidental eyes, as the historian Priya Satia has wryly observed, the suffering of subjugated Indians was invariably good for them: 'merely birthing pain in the cause of some greater epochal labour'.

Yet, ironically enough, this attitude had itself originated in a deep sense of British guilt. In the later eighteenth century, faced with mounting evidence of imperial corruption, bloodshed and misrule, and the devastating loss of their thirteen North American colonies, Britons faced a crisis of conscience about the effects of their overseas endeavours. The origins of European empires were shameful, Adam Smith observed in 1776: mere 'folly and injustice' towards 'harmless natives' who had been brutally exploited, massacred and enslaved. Across Europe, other prominent Enlightenment thinkers, too, were highly critical of imperialism. That Britain's wealth and power in the Americas depended on the brutal exploitation of millions of kidnapped and enslaved Africans was by the later eighteenth century a particularly unavoidable, uncomfortable truth.

There was also mounting disquiet about British actions in India. For a century and a half after its foundation in 1600, the British East India Company, like other European merchant corporations, had been creating small coastal bases there, negotiating alliances with powerful local rulers, and profiting from the region's great wealth. Gradually the company and its small army of Indian soldiers ('sepoys') acquired more and more political power, aided by the decline of the Mughal Empire and the fracturing of its alliances. Then, from the mid 1750s onwards, capitalizing on local power struggles in Bengal, this trading enterprise had precipitously evolved into the military conquest, plunder and taxation of vast territories. The result was not just a massive and ongoing transfer of looted Indian wealth to the British Isles, and the fabulous enrichment of the company's own officers, but great public anxiety in Britain about all the private corruption and mismanagement that accompanied this unplanned imperial expansion.

'We have murdered, deposed, plundered, usurped,' one former MP wrote in horror to a confidant in 1772 – millions of Bengalis had recently perished in a famine caused by the East India Company's greed. By this point, the company was struggling with massive debts, and had to be bailed out by the Bank of England and the government. By the 1780s, despite several parliamentary attempts to fix it, the apparent misgovernment of India by a corrupt private corporation had become a major political scandal. When the first British governor of Bengal, the company officer Warren Hastings, returned to England in 1785, he was impeached and put on trial. At the same time, successive parliamentary acts and inquiries steadily diminished the East India Company's powers, and there were growing calls for it to be taken over completely by the government, as eventually happened in 1858.

It was to overcome this great crisis of confidence that the British after 1800 gradually developed the idea that their global imperial efforts were, in fact, driven by a high moral purpose. To redeem the past sins of slavery and misgovernment, Britain would henceforth strive everywhere to eradicate slavery and to free lesser peoples from mental and physical bondage – spreading liberty, Christianity and free trade, and replacing corrupt local manners with British civilization. This deeply racialized, hierarchical vision was embraced not just by conservative thinkers but also by most progressives: indeed, many of its principles were first developed by campaigners against the slave trade. For British observers of all stripes, freedom was something to be benevolently bestowed by whites; Black and brown peoples could only gradually become fully worthy of it.

As far as India was concerned, the most influential early proponent of this view was one of the most radical democratic reformers of the early nineteenth century, the tireless Scottish utilitarian James Mill. His huge, multi-volume *History of British India* (1817) took him twelve years to write and was an immediate, best-selling success. In it, he pronounced – without ever having set foot there or learned any of its languages – that the subcontinent was plainly a stagnant, ignorant place, where time had stood still for centuries. Indians were a 'rude and uninstructed', 'ignorant', 'barbarous', 'irrational', 'superstitious', 'uncivilized', 'listless and indolent', unpleasantly avaricious and physically filthy people. They exhibited 'a general disposition to deceit and perfidy', as well as 'habitual contempt . . . for their women' (a classic 'proof of barbarity' for thinkers like Mill). Their dominant religion's 'many gloomy and malignant principles' had fostered 'that disposition to revenge, that insensibility to the sufferings of others, and that often active cruelty, which lurks under the smiling exterior of the Hindu'. Their culture had never amounted to much, even in centuries past. Assertions to the contrary were just fables and misunderstandings: thus far, in fact, they had only 'made but a few of the earliest steps in the progress to civilization'. European peoples had through all ages shown 'superior character', 'manliness and courage'. By contrast, Indians had always been 'greatly inferior' in most things: they were 'an effeminate people', innately 'slavish and dastardly'.

True, Mill acknowledged, India's past government by the East India Company had been a tragedy of stupidity and greed – but now, going forward, the British had a great opportunity to replace its primitive culture with modern norms and laws. The best policy towards the few remaining independent Indian rulers, he later declared, was 'to make war on those states and subdue them', which would be easy as the

English were 'so far beyond the native in civilization': only European rule could bring progress to backward peoples. Mill's text became the leading handbook for British imperial officials ruling India. He himself, as well as all three of his adult sons, duly became senior officials at the London headquarters of the East India Company.

British administrators who actually went out to India were often more appreciative of its culture. Yet they invariably carried with them similarly paternalist views. George Campbell, the son of an East India Company medical officer, joined the Bengal civil service while still in his teens. Over the course of a long career, he became one of India's pre-eminent administrators, rising to lieutenant-general of Bengal, endlessly pushing new reforms, always concerned for 'the happiness and welfare' of the native population. All his life, he took for granted that, everywhere in the world, the civilization of 'whites' was superior to that of all the different kinds of 'blacks' and 'coloured races' over which they ruled. But he also sincerely believed that the latter could be improved, 'elevated' and 'assimilated to the white man's standard'. In 1853, he reported back enthusiastically to the British public that Indians seemed fully capable of receiving the 'benefits' of 'colonization, conversion, and the introduction of European morals, manners, and arts'. Evidently they just were still stuck at an earlier stage of development, like that of the Europeans of ancient times. But it was now Britain's divine destiny to lead them forward:

> Whether we go historically back or geographically east, we travel very much in the same direction, and most of the manners and customs which now seem peculiar to the East have had their parallels in the earlier days of the West. Then why should not the East be also capable of progress? Why, commencing from a similar level, should it not be raised as the West has been raised? ... I believe that we might and should do so ... and that Heaven has imposed on us a task which we may not neglect.

At the root of this outlook lay the dogma that British imperial rule was not self-interested, let alone profitable, but, on the contrary, a heavy, God-given responsibility to protect and tutor lesser peoples – 'the White Man's Burden', as the poet Rudyard Kipling would later famously term it. 'English government in India,' Mill argued in 1810, is for the sake of the natives, not of England. India has never been anything but a burden; and anything but a burden, we are afraid, it cannot be rendered. But this English government in India, with all its vices, is a blessing of unspeakable magnitude to the population of Hindustan.

That most Britons by the early nineteenth century had come to believe this myth, ignoring their nation's vast and increasing accrual of wealth from India, was an extraordinary feat of national self-deception. Like Marx, the French liberal thinker Alexis de Tocqueville was struck by the depth of British 'duplicity and hypocrisy' on the subject. 'The English did nothing in India but what all the other European nations would have done,' he wrote in 1843, yet 'what I cannot get over is their perpetual attempts to prove that they act in the interest of a principle, or for the good of the natives.'

The great Indian uprising against British rule in 1857, led by its own sepoys, together with other mid-nineteenth-century indigenous rebellions across the empire, forced some rethinking of this optimistic script – though not much. What had caused such horrendous violence? Was it evidence of British misrule? In the later nineteenth century, most Britons settled on the most convenient answer. History, it appeared, proved not just that certain societies were superior to others, but also that 'native' cultures were inherently primitive, violent and resistant to progress. The march of history had passed them by. That not only justified their subordination but made it historically inevitable.

This outlook was buttressed by the rise of Social Darwinist and more explicitly racist theories of social development. As Home Secretary in 1910, Winston Churchill, who had long believed that 'the Aryan stock is bound to triumph', proposed the mass sterilization and incarceration of 'degenerate' Britons, to strengthen the British 'race'. In a similar vein, he told an imperial committee in 1937:

I do not admit ... that a great wrong has been done to the Red Indians of America or the black people of Australia. I do not admit that a wrong has been done to these people by the fact that a stronger race, a higher-grade race, a more worldly-wise race to put it that way, has come in and taken their place.

As prime minister in 1943, while millions of Bengalis were dying in a famine caused by British grain policies, he explained his refusal to send aid by invoking the vision of 'Indians breeding like rabbits'.

The presumption that indigenous societies were irredeemably static and backward gave imperialism a different but deeper ethical justification. The moral basis for colonial rule now became that it was the best way of preventing anarchy. Rather than trying to civilize them against their nature, the British after 1857 switched from 'direct' to 'indirect' forms of governance, preserving rather than replacing the seemingly atavistic religions, customs and enmities of their colonial subjects. As well as subordinating them as a whole, they also increasingly subdivided indigenous populations into different castes, tribes, religions and races. Each of these groups' supposedly unchanging 'native' traditions was now codified into a separate system of customary law and authority, through which it was to be governed.

Meanwhile, because the British both benefited from indigenous disunity and presumed its timeless character, their imperial policies often exacerbated social conflict. By ordering fluid communal relations into fixed caste, tribal and religious identities, and giving such sectarian labels increasing legal and territorial significance, they politicized them in disastrous new ways. When violence subsequently erupted, it was blamed on ancient hatreds, not on colonial interventions. And as ethnic homogeneity became central to European notions of nationhood, it also justified the designation and displacement of 'minority' populations in the colonies, and the wholesale division of their territories: hence the partitions, for example, of Ireland in 1921 and India in 1947. Once again, the moral responsibility for any resulting bloodshed lay not with the benevolent colonial custodians but with the hot-headed, irrepressibly antagonistic natives.

PRINT COMES TO INDIA

In these distinctive circumstances, how did the British and their colonial subjects conceive of the liberties of speech and press? The first thing to notice is that print itself began as a colonial import. Precolonial India was a profoundly literate society, where reading and writing were highly valued and widely disseminated. Its trade, state-craft, legal systems and religions all sustained sophisticated scribal cultures. So did its vibrant public sphere of political debate, conducted not just in constant oral discussion but through the continual circulation of personal letters, private messages, public newsletters and written placards.

Print played no part in any of this. Nor did it in the communication systems of the East India Company and other European settlers, which also depended almost entirely on scriveners, messengers and handwritten documents. Though printed books were imported from abroad, there was until the end of the seventeenth century only a single press in India, a machine belonging to the Portuguese Jesuit mission in Goa. This arrived in 1556 and was used until 1674 to produce religious texts. Thereafter we know only of scattered experiments in printing in Bombay in the 1670s, among Danish missionaries in Tranquebar from the 1710s, and in French Pondicherry and English Madras from the 1750s and 1760s. It wasn't until 1778, several years after taking over the governance of Bengal, that the East India Company in that province acquired a press. This was the point at which printed discourse entered the Indian public sphere in a sustained fashion – followed almost immediately by the first conflicts over press liberty.

The introduction of this European technology at the company's Hooghly base, north of Calcutta, was part of a campaign by the inaugural governor-general, Warren Hastings, to impress on the British public the importance and cultural richness of their vast new colonial possession. His other great ambition was to master local laws and customs, so as better to rule the natives. To this end, he encouraged his subordinates to study Indian languages and texts. Under his patronage, one of them, Nathaniel Brassey Halhed, a brilliant young Oxford-educated linguist, wrote the first text printed at Hooghly, in the summer of 1778. He'd already produced for Hastings a digest of Hindu laws, compiled by a committee of Brahmin lawyers and sent to London for publication. Now, another polyglot company officer, Charles Wilkins, put together a press, taught a local blacksmith to cast types of the local script, and printed the hundreds of pages of Halhed's *Grammar of the Bengal Language*.

The book's purpose was to explain to the British that Bengal had a dialect that was not only worthy of study but a vital tool for their hegemony. For the British to master the Bengali tongue, Halhed urged, would provide 'a general medium of intercourse between the Government and its Subjects; between the Natives of Europe who are to rule, and the Inhabitants of India who are to obey'. The new rulers of Bengal should 'add its Language to their acquisitions . . . that they may convince while they command'. Along the way the British would be able to instruct 'the illiterate and careless race of modern Bengalese' in the proper use of their own language – for 'their forms of letters, their modes of spelling, and their choice of words are all equally erroneous and absurd'. Halhed was all of twenty-seven years old, and had spent barely six years in Bengal; yet with typical imperial hubris he had no doubt that his understanding of their vernacular already far surpassed that of the natives themselves. From the outset, as modern historians have noted, 'the conquest of India was the conquest of knowledge', and the command of language was part of the language of command.

More generally, Halhed confidently predicted, the introduction of printing would surely advance Indian society in many ways. Giving natives access to print, the great engine of progress, would enable

> Great Britain to introduce all the more solid advantages of European literature among a people whom she has already rescued from Asiatic slavery: to promote the circulation of wealth, by giving new vigour and dispatch to business, and to forward the progress of civil society by facilitating the means of intercourse.

This was a conception of printing as the noble tool of benevolent rulers, spreading enlightenment. But even as Halhed wrote this passage, its vision was already being challenged by the existence of another, rival operation, a few miles downriver, whose outlook was very different. Just a few months earlier, an impoverished, hot-headed Irish adventurer called James Hicky, imprisoned for debt in Calcutta's jail, had built himself the region's first printing press, on which he had begun to produce cheap handbills, advertisements, calendars, almanacs and other ephemera.

Hicky was a typical imperial entrepreneur, whose peripatetic life and opportunities had been shaped by the contours of Britain's expanding global reach. Born in Ireland in the 1730s, he had first trained with an attorney in Dublin, then apprenticed to a printer in London, served on a British warship, clerked for a barrister and finally worked as a surgeon's assistant on slave ships, helping to treat and subdue African captives on several transatlantic voyages to the Americas. Seeking greater fortune, he decided to try his luck in the East Indies. After landing in Calcutta in 1773, he had practised as a physician and tried to launch himself as a trader, but had gone bankrupt. Setting up a print shop was only his latest venture.

From his prison hut, Hicky had printed thousands of forms for the East India Company's army. But after he was released in 1778 and set up a printing office in the Calcutta bazaar, his attempt to win more lucrative government contracts was stymied by Wilkins's new press, which monopolized them. So Hicky did exactly what other British printers had done before him when entering new colonial markets in the Americas. To drum up trade, he started a paper. Proudly advertising himself as the East India Company's '*First*, and late printer', he obtained Hastings's permission 'to print a newspaper weekly, for the entertainment of the settlement'. In January 1780, *Hicky's Bengal Gazette: or Calcutta General Advertiser* became the first printed newspaper in the whole of Asia. It was an immediate hit. Within a few weeks, its columns were filled with paid advertisements, as well as news and comment, and Hicky had to attach a special box to the gate of his house 'for the more speedy and convenient reception of all useful and entertaining Intelligence, Poetry, etc.'.

For almost a year, he kept to the simple plan he'd originally conceived. His 'chief intention', he announced, was simply to supplant the multitude of native messengers messily hawking and posting handwritten adverts around town. Instead, his paper would provide a regular printed forum for circulating information 'useful or entertaining, and tending to promote the trading concerns of industrious individuals'. His prospectus specified twenty-two different types of useful information it would carry, from births, marriages and deaths, to the current prices of goods. To underline its uncontroversial, purely commercial intent, he promised that nothing 'that can possibly convey the smallest offence to any single individual shall ever be inserted' and, after the paper was launched, refused submissions that were political, 'being determined not to be the incendiary slave of any party'. In the first eleven months of its operation, while it had the field to itself, *Hicky's Bengal Gazette* printed very few opinion pieces, and made no reference to press liberty or related topics.

But the paper's success, which proved there was a lucrative market for newsprint among Bengal's thousands of European colonists, soon attracted better-capitalized rivals. Before long, a pair of well-connected English entrepreneurs started poaching Hicky's customers, acquired a press of their own and launched the *India Gazette; or, Calcutta Public Advertiser*, which was promoted and subsidized by leading Company officers. It was a more polished production, which soon became the unofficial journal of Bengal's government, luring away Hicky's subscribers and advertisers. This blow to his fortunes, just as he had finally struck gold, turned him from the proprietor of a bland commercial news-sheet into an embittered political crusader.

Though his rivals' motives seem to have been mainly commercial, Hicky interpreted the appearance of the *India Gazette* as a malign conspiracy. When it launched, his own paper accused a powerful local official of corruptly scheming to destroy him. After the Bengal Council condemned this public defamation, and banned the *Gazette* from the postal service, Hicky transformed its columns into a harsh, non-stop polemic against the 'tyranny' and corruption of the company, its government, officers, army, judiciary and clergy – attacking its leaders personally, in increasingly virulent terms, justifying himself with extracts from Cato's Letters, and casting himself as an unjustly oppressed champion of English liberty and freedom of the press.

After six months of this, Hastings and another local notable charged him with criminal libel. Hicky was arrested, jailed, convicted and sentenced to a further year's imprisonment. Throughout it all, from within the jail, he continued to print his paper – blasting Hastings, 'the Great Mogul', as a greedy, cowardly despot whose army was close to mutiny, and even justifying the rebellion of native rulers against him. In the end, after several further convictions for libel, Hicky's press was seized to pay his debts. His last *Gazette* appeared at the end of March 1782, with a final denunciation of Hastings's tyranny, oppression and persecution, and a desperate appeal for new advertisers. A few days later, his great rival, the *India Gazette*, announced the public auction of his press and types. His other competitor, the company's printer, Wilkins, snapped them up for a song.

GLOBAL ARGUMENTS AND IMPERIAL CIRCUMSTANCES

The rise and fall of *Hicky's Bengal Gazette* was an international event. From beginning to end, the paper was enmeshed in a global network of British, European and American print. When Hicky was a printer's apprentice in London, his own master, William Faden, had started up a successful daily paper, the *Public Ledger: Or, Daily Register of Commerce and Intelligence*, in 1760. Hicky's own project was modelled on that, and on other British and American examples. He was especially inspired by the success of newspapers in the West Indies, which he had noticed after landing there several times with his shiploads of enslaved, diseased and dying Africans. (As a printer in Calcutta, he too carried adverts for local slaves, and acted as a middleman for their sale and recapture.) The motto of his *Bengal Gazette* ('open to all parties, but influenced by none') adopted the famous slogan coined by Faden's *Public Ledger* – just as many American papers had already done. The *Gazette* partly relied on reprinting articles from overseas papers; soon enough it was absorbed into the same worldwide channels of circulating newsprint – its columns quoted and republished not just in the British, but also the French, German and North American press.

This international context explains how Hicky was able to transform his paper so quickly into a fully fledged medium of political opposition and free-speech ideology. By 1780 the East India Company's government of Bengal, and the apparent corruption and self-dealing of its officers, were hot political subjects, both in Britain and among local settlers. (Just as *Hicky's Bengal Gazette* was being shut down, in fact, the House of Commons was about to vote to recall Hastings, and his lifelong friend and client Sir Elijah Impey, the judge who had presided over Hicky's trials, to face charges of corruption.) As soon as Hicky opened his columns to political criticism, they were therefore inundated with anonymous correspondents venting their own complaints. Hastings's bitter rival on the Bengal Council, Philip Francis, a brilliant polemicist and experienced manipulator of public opinion, was among those who delighted in Hicky's new political stance and sought to exploit it, even after he returned to England during 1781 to lobby for Hastings's and Impey's impeachment. The rhetoric of corruption, tyranny and liberty that Hicky and his allies adopted was not local or novel, but international and well established. They compared themselves to English radicals, Irish patriots and American colonists – using a language of rights and injustice that by 1780 resonated across the war-torn anglophone empire, from Britain to North America, the Caribbean and India.

The many invocations and examples of press liberty that suddenly appeared in *Hicky's Bengal Gazette* after November 1780 were part of this familiar discourse. Like countless other radicals, Hicky cast himself and his supporters as 'Cato'. He cited the famous case of the London printer Henry Sampson Woodfall, who in 1770 had been acquitted of seditious libel, despite publishing in his paper a spectacular series of anonymous newspaper columns (signed 'Junius') that savaged the ministry of the day. And he appealed to the example and protection of John Wilkes, the great recent champion of English political liberty and press freedom, arguing that his own case was essentially the same.

Philip Francis was another master of such rhetoric. A decade earlier, at the outset of his political career in Britain, he had almost certainly been the secret author of the Junius letters, and Wilkes's great defender in the London press. Now, in Calcutta in November 1780, as soon as Hicky began to complain about oppression, he received an anonymous letter, quite possibly from Francis himself, comparing him to those two earlier guardians of liberty. It affirmed the printer's self-perception as a brave martyr resisting tyranny – and urged him, in the name of press freedom, to continue his attacks on Hastings and the East India Company:

> The case of Mr HICKY is exactly similar to that of Mr Wilkes. – The one standing up for the liberty of the press. The other for that of the subject. Junius makes the following just and elegant remark on the

oppression of Mr Wilkes – That the rays of royal indignation tended 'rather to illumine than to destroy the persecuted object of it etc.'

The author of these lines hopes the generosity of the settlement will verify this position of Junius, in the case of Mr Hicky, who I dare venture to say will never disgrace the name of an Englishman, or relinquish his birth right, by tamely submitting to arbitrary and illegal oppression.

Against such polemics, Hicky's opponents ranged not only their legal and political power but also their own alternative arguments about press freedom. On the one hand, they dismissed his writings as mere licentiousness. He had produced 'a weekly paper containing the most scurrilous abuse' and 'the most inflammatory libels', Chief Justice Impey explained to his friends back in England. On the other hand, they scorned the self-proclaimed champion of 'press freedom' as nothing more than a hypocritical, oppressive bully. When Hicky vociferously attacked his accusers, judges and juries, Impey pronounced from the bench: 'This is the boasted liberty of the press, the produce of a real slavery. Mr Hicky threatens those who prosecute him!' 'Freedom of the press is often converted into a destructive engine of public oppression and private wrong,' the *India Gazette* concurred. The mere deployment of the phrase, Hicky's critics urged, was no proof of the justice of a cause.

Such arguments, too, were familiar by 1782 to English-speaking consumers of print all over the globe – in Bengal as in North America, the West Indies and Britain itself. But in the controversy over *Hicky's Bengal Gazette* we can also faintly glimpse something novel: a specific concern about the danger of *colonial* free speech. 'I really wonder at your patience in suffering such a scoundrel as Hicky to publish loads of abuse every Saturday,' a senior army officer wrote to Hastings in the spring of 1781, having been personally subjected for weeks to public ridicule of his military command, greed for loot and adulterous liaisons with Indian women. 'Such a thing as that Gazette in such a place as this is not allowable.' *In such a place as this* – that is, where a few thousand Europeans ruled precariously over millions of potentially hostile natives.

On such grounds, local officials in all three British territories in

India (Bengal, Bombay and Madras), as in other embattled British possessions with small settler populations, like the South African Cape and Australia, largely dismissed appeals to press liberty as irrelevant to colonial circumstances, and regulated printers and newspapers much more strictly than was the case in Britain itself. In the 1790s, in the midst of war and panic about the global spread of the doctrines of the French Revolution, pre-publication censorship of newspapers was formally introduced in India, including a blanket prohibition against discussing 'the conduct of government or any of its officers', or anything that 'may tend to affect the influence and credit of the British power with the native states'. Colonial territories were always exceptional spaces, where different standards applied.

During these early decades, print in India remained an overwhelmingly European medium, mainly used for missionary and commercial activity, government paperwork and to circulate information among the settler population. The occasional inclusion of advertisements in Bengali, Persian and Gujarati in English newspapers proves that elite Indians were among their readers; and the East India Company presses also regularly produced texts in those languages – indeed, until 1835 Persian remained the official administrative language in British India. The actual work of printing, too, relied heavily on Indian employees. Yet every one of the thirty-plus periodicals published in India between 1780 and 1817 was owned and edited by white men and written in English. So, too, the controversies about press freedom that these papers were periodically embroiled in focused only on the rights of British settlers and their treatment by the East India Company – never on native Indian liberties, voices or audiences. Beneath the surface, nonetheless, as a Commons debate back in London in March 1811 revealed, the shape of press freedom in India was also already being profoundly determined by anxieties about the effects of print on the indigenous population.

Every speaker in parliament that spring agreed that British rule in India was tyrannical. A few parliamentarians deplored this and attacked the company. But most blamed the Indians themselves, a backward people wholly unsuited to liberty, who could only be governed dictatorially. And this meant that it would be very dangerous to allow them access to print. As one MP put it:

despotism had not been established there by England, but that it had been found there, where it had existed for many ages. The introduction of the liberty of the press might lead to the most fatal consequences, and in the present state of things, would unhinge the whole frame of Indian society.

In Calcutta alone, Sir John Anstruther would have his colleagues believe, 'there were at least 100,000 natives, capable of reading English' (this was a vast exaggeration: in reality there were probably only a few hundred). Printed discussion of the weaknesses and inequities of British rule would surely incite them to massacre the British, he warned, for it would 'prove, with how much ease and safety, by a judicious combination of the natives, the whole European population of Bengal might be exterminated'. The recent bloody slave insurrection that had overthrown white rule in Haiti had been sparked by an attempt to extend press freedom, the MP for Oxford asserted, even more wildly: the same could happen in India. 'Could anything be considered more perilous than to spread opinions of all kinds whatever throughout the whole of Hindustan?' asked Henry Dundas, an influential defender of the East India Company: nothing should be printed there that might 'excite irritation and hostility' or 'tumultuous proceedings'. 'The liberty of the press was not withheld merely from the principles of the government,' the prime minister himself concluded, 'but from the dispositions of the natives themselves. They were in that state that it might do them much harm, though if they were less ignorant it might be expected to be productive of the greatest good.'

Soon enough, the issue of native access to print could no longer be so easily swept aside. In 1813, the East India Company's power in India was greatly reduced by a parliamentary Act which decreed a new national 'Duty of this country to promote the interest and happiness of the native inhabitants ... [and] the introduction among them of useful knowledge, and of religious and moral improvement'. The governor-general, Lord Hastings (no relation of Warren Hastings), exhorted his officers that it was now their 'God-like bounty to bestow expansion of intellect' and 'the consciousness of human rights' upon the ignorant natives. Promoting freedom of discussion and publication would help them rise to British standards of intellect. In 1818, he duly ended pre-publication censorship in Bengal – after Britain's final victories in its long global wars against the French, and in those against the Maratha Empire, the last remaining indigenous power to resist it.

That same year, the first newspapers in Bengali were established, and Indian-owned presses began to proliferate in British territories. Throughout the early decades of British rule, Indians had maintained their own long-standing and sophisticated networks of oral and manuscript communication, instruction and political debate. Even without any knowledge of English, Indians were remarkably highly informed about the latest developments in European politics, a newly arrived settler observed in 1824, which 'implies other means of communication besides those which we supply and respecting which I have been able to obtain as yet very little information'. They soon took advantage of the freer availability of print as well – often to critique and challenge British hegemony. Large numbers of printed books, pamphlets and papers began to be locally produced as well as imported. By the 1820s, Calcutta had become a thriving centre of Indian-language as well as anglophone printing. At the end of the decade, its newspapers had grown more numerous and widely circulated than those of any other city in the British Empire, save London. In addition to those in Bengali, Persian, Urdu and Hindi, several of the English titles were now also owned and edited by Indians. The city's Hindu College, established in 1817, was educating Bengali children in English on a western curriculum, including Paine's *Rights of Man* and Mill's *History of India*. In 1828, the college's prize pupil, Kasiprasad Ghosh, who went on to become a noted poet in English, wrote a critique of Mill that was published in the *Calcutta Gazette*, and thence in the *Asiatic Journal*, the leading London periodical of Indian affairs.

The following decade, the governor of Bombay pithily summarized the revised British political calculus about Indian access to print. In his territory, too, native Indians had been agitating since the 1810s for press liberty. 'We are here in India, in a very extraordinary position,' he noted, as 'a small band of aliens ... [who] have established their despotic rule over a vast people':

This supremacy can only be maintained by arms, or by opinion. The natives of India must either be kept down by a sense of our power, or they must willingly submit from a conviction that we are more wise, more just, more humane, and more anxious to improve their condition than any other rulers they could have.

It was obvious that the latter was the only realistic option. But that raised an increasingly fraught question: exactly how far should the rights of Indians to freedom of speech and print extend?

INDIANS AND PRINT

One official who repeatedly wrestled with this problem was the experienced British administrator Mountstuart Elphinstone, who as governor of Bombay in the 1820s was a keen proponent of native education as an aid to British hegemony. At the start of his tenure in 1819, he too abolished pre-publication censorship, following the lead of his counterpart in Bengal. Of course, an 'uncontrolled press' was out of the question, he minuted in 1821: establishing 'a medium through which [an Indian] . . . might inveigh at discretion . . . against the disgrace of foreign rule, would be entirely unsuited to our situation in India'. But introducing print 'under the complete control of Government', with safeguards against 'publishing anything of dangerous tendency', was a different matter:

> I look on that art as too great a blessing to be withheld without the clearest and most incontrovertible reasons, and I see no such reasons in the case of India. That the press may in a long succession of ages cause the natives to throw off our yoke is possible and even probable, but it will in the first place destroy the superstitions and the prejudices of the natives and remove the pressing dangers created by the entire and marked separation between them and their conquerors, and this effect is certain while the other is problematical.

In other words, the spread of print under British control was certain to bring the natives closer to their white overlords. That it might ever do the opposite was only a very distant, theoretical concern.

Elphinstone's model presumed that India's British rulers were themselves unified in their outlook. But even as he wrote, events on the other side of the subcontinent were proving him wrong. In the capital of British India, the editor of the new *Calcutta Journal*, James Silk Buckingham, had repeatedly run into trouble with the authorities. In many ways his trajectory echoed that of his distant predecessor, James Hicky. Buckingham, too, was a self-made imperial adventurer; he had ended up in Calcutta after years travelling around the Mediterranean, the Atlantic, the Middle East and India. Like Hicky's, his paper began as a largely apolitical, commercial news-sheet, the brainchild of a local English merchant who admired Buckingham's prose and set him up as editor. As the first daily paper in India, it was supposed to make money for them both – and it did.

But then, the *Calcutta Journal* began to publish letters and columns criticizing aspects of the East India Company's rule. It also took up the cause of press freedom, drawing attention to the fervent discussions on the subject that were raging in Britain itself, and arguing for their relevance to India. It eulogized the struggles of British reformers, criticized the severe new laws against sedition, libel and blasphemy that the government had passed in Britain, and condemned its persecution of radical newspapers and journalists like Richard Carlile and William Cobbett. In response, the local administration withdrew the *Calcutta Journal*'s free postage and prosecuted Buckingham (urged on by his rival newspapers, which were run by Company loyalists and placemen). Finally, the governor-general expelled him from India – and reintroduced strict licensing of all presses and publications, to prevent public discussion of any governmental or 'political events or transactions whatsoever'.

There was nothing novel about this reaction. It was how the authorities in India had been dealing with troublesome print ever since its introduction. Even under the supposedly progressive regulations of 1818, newspapers had remained prohibited from commenting on the governance of India, the actions of local administrators or anything that might 'affect the British power or reputation in India' (as well as from any 'personal remarks on individuals, tending to excite dissension in society').

Yet behind the scenes, officials in Calcutta and London increasingly disagreed about how far to go in enforcing these rules. In the end, Buckingham was only deported after the liberal-minded governor-general Lord Hastings was briefly succeeded in 1823 by John Adam, the administration's chief censor and the *Calcutta Journal*'s long-time antagonist. The underlying difficulty was that, compared to Hicky's day, two things were now crucially different.

In the first place, the causes of British and Indian press liberty had come to be closely linked. Any action taken against the press in India, the leaders of the Tory government in London noted nervously in 1820, 'will rebound hither: and it therefore cannot be considered as a purely India question'. Their Whig and radical opponents in Britain took up Buckingham's cause, linking it to their own struggles against censorship. In the 1780s, Hicky's *Bengal Gazette*, too, had adopted the transnational rhetoric of press freedom, yet no one outside India had paid its travails any attention. Forty years later, by contrast, Buckingham's treatment became a prominent, long-running issue in Britain – a stick with which to beat the Conservative government, attack the East India Company's autocracy and critique colonial policy. Buckingham himself, a peerless self-promoter, kept up a constant, decade-long campaign of litigation and publicity that tied his own case to the great cause of press liberty. Within a few months of his return to London, with donations from his many supporters, he launched a new monthly, the *Oriental Herald and Colonial Review* (1824–9), as a counterblast to the East India Company's unofficial mouthpiece, the *Asiatic Journal*, and as a forum for keeping his own mistreatment, and the ideal of press freedom across the empire, before the public eye. Through tireless campaigning, publishing and public speaking, he became one of Britain's most prominent voices on Indian colonial policy. In 1832, he was elected to the new, reformed British parliament. Taking advantage of his power as an MP, he soon engineered the creation of a Commons select committee to investigate the suppression of the *Calcutta Journal* – and to compensate him for the huge capital losses he claimed to have suffered by it.

The second great change was that press liberty was now championed by Indians themselves. Soon after arriving in Calcutta in 1818, Buckingham had struck up a close friendship with a learned older Indian, Rammohun Roy, a rich Brahmin landowner who campaigned against various aspects of Hindu 'superstition' and 'idolatry', and was equally critical of orthodox Christianity. The charismatic, polyglot Roy worked with leading British officials for many years, taught himself fluent English, French, Latin, Hebrew and classical Greek, to go with his Persian, Arabic, Bengali and Hindi, helped found the Hindu College and an English-language school of his own, corresponded with intellectuals in Britain and Europe, and gathered around him a coterie of like-minded Indians and Britons. When he visited England and France in the early 1830s, at the end of his life, he was feted as a great progressive celebrity by everyone, including the kings of both nations. He was also the most prominent early Indian advocate for freedom of the press.

As a writer, Roy's earliest works had been composed as manuscripts, as was the Indian tradition. But he soon became an enthusiastic adopter of the new European technology of print, as well as of western ideas about freedom of thought (quoting Locke and Bacon 'on all occasions', as one early English acquaintance noted). His earliest printed work, in Persian and Arabic, appeared in 1804. By the time Buckingham met him, Roy was already an adept, transnational manipulator of western as well as Indian public opinion. He avidly read and interacted with India's various English-language newspapers, and was completely up to date on English and European politics. He published his religious pamphlets in English, as well as in Bengali and Sanskrit, and then sent them to London to be reprinted and publicized there. In due course, his ideas came to be published and discussed by leading intellectuals in France, Germany and North America, too.

When Buckingham launched the *Calcutta Journal*, Roy became a frequent contributor to its pages. Roy himself founded two weeklies for Indian readers, in Bengali (*Sambad Kaumudi*, 1821–36) and Persian (*Mirat al-Akhbar*, 1822–3), as well as an intermittent *Brahmanical Magazine* in English (1821–3). These publications reprinted news and comment from European papers and Indian manuscript newsletters, promoted Roy's causes of religious reform and social improvement, addressed appeals to the government, and repeatedly lauded press freedom – as a means of informing British officials about native grievances, and of spreading knowledge and enlightenment. The very first issue of the *Sambad* opened with an essay on 'the

Liberty of the Native Press'; later ones praised the *Calcutta Journal* and its editor. In turn, Buckingham, a great proselytizer for 'the benefits to be expected from the perfect freedom of the native press in India', enthusiastically promoted his friend's publications in his own journal, and printed English translations and summaries of their contents. When Roy's Christian printers turned down his controversial pamphlets, Buckingham helped him set up his own press. 'If it be true,' he explained, 'as is constantly asserted, that the ignorance of the natives is the greatest barrier to their political, civil, and religious happiness, everything that hastens the removal of this obstacle must be deemed a benefit.' The native press would be a 'powerful engine for spreading light and civilisation'.

In 1823, Roy criticized Buckingham's deportation in the *Mirat*, then closed down his own paper in protest at the new press laws. Together with other prominent Bengalis, including his friend Dwarkanath Tagore, the richest merchant of Calcutta, who invested in several Indian and English-language papers, he also mounted a public campaign for the freedom of the native press. Whatever Buckingham's offence, they argued, 'to punish millions for the fault imputed to one individual' was absurd. First they petitioned the Supreme Court in Calcutta, and then the ultimate imperial authorities – King George IV, his Council and his cabinet, in London. Though they could not stop the reintroduction of licensing (which was to remain in place until 1835), their arguments, which they also publicized in print, broke new ground in their confident assertion of indigenous rights. Meanwhile, other Indians bypassed what they deprecated as the 'shackled' and 'enslaved' Indian press by using London's newspapers to publicize 'the sentiments of the people of India'.

To make their case, Roy and his compatriots echoed the progressive British hope that press freedom bolstered native loyalty. Keeping people in ignorance, they argued, was despotic, dangerous and un-English – indeed, 'Asiatic'. In contrast, people 'placed under a good Government, from which they experience just and liberal treatment, must become the more attached to it, in proportion as they become enlightened and the great body of the people are taught to appreciate the value of the blessings they enjoy under its Rule'. This was in fact what had been happening: 'the natives of India being more and more attached to the British rule in proportion as they experience from it the blessings of just and liberal treatment'. They regarded the British not as 'conquerors, but rather as deliverers' from Mughal tyranny. The spread of print, especially of native newspapers, had 'already served greatly to improve their minds and ameliorate their condition'. The Indian population was now unshakably loyal, and had 'unlimited confidence in the British Government of India'.

They also mounted two more original arguments. The first was to assert that native press freedom had been unquestioned since the earliest days of British rule – it was 'the most precious of their rights, which has been freely allowed them since the establishment of the British power'. That was not true, but it cleverly deployed the trope of ancient liberties being 'suddenly' and illegally 'invaded'. Their second, related assertion was that hitherto Indians had been 'assured of the possession of the same civil and religious liberty which is enjoyed in England'. This too was a polemically savvy claim. British officials in India had in fact always considered the native press in a different light from European print, though by 1823 they had begun to realize that it was legally difficult to differentiate between the two. By arguing that all 'Inhabitants of Calcutta' deserved 'the same civil and religious privileges that every Briton is entitled to in England', the Bengalis silently elided this racial distinction, and put forth a simpler, bolder proposition. Indians in India, they claimed, had exactly the same free-speech rights as Britons in Britain.

Roy, Tagore and their fellow petitioners were entirely sincere when they described themselves as loyal subjects of British rule. Each of them had flourished through collaboration with the British, and they all admired European culture, technology and political principles. Though by the 1820s they were largely aligned with colonists who advocated free trade, unrestricted European settlement and other policies opposed by the East India Company, more generally they were exactly the kind of faithful, westernized, intellectual vanguard that British policy in India since 1813 had been intended to create. They even conceded that, 'to preserve the union existing between England and this country', press freedom in India should probably not extend to attempts 'to excite hatred in the minds of the natives of India against the English nation'. On the other hand, their attachment to British rule was always only a prudential accommodation to political realities. As a younger man, Roy had 'great aversion to the establishment of the British power in India'; now, despite the incessant racist humiliations that he and his compatriots suffered from its imposition, he sought to leverage it for himself and his people's advantage. As one of his English admirers noted, Roy was 'greatly attached to us and our *régime* . . . because he considers the contact of our superior race with *his* degraded and inferior countrymen as the only means and chance they have of improving themselves in knowledge and energy' – yet he also 'greatly disapproves of many acts' of the British government in India.

This was why press freedom was of paramount importance to him. To draw attention to native grievances, and inevitable instances of British 'error in managing the affairs of a vast empire', Roy argued that 'the unrestrained liberty of publication is the only effectual means that can be employed'. Indians had never yet abused this freedom, he claimed, and never would; existing laws against slander and sedition were in any case sufficient guarantee against that. When the *Mirat* condemned British policy in Ireland, or proposed restraints on the powers of British magistrates in Bengal, or criticized one of them by name for acting 'rashly and under the influence of passion', this was, in Roy's view, not abusing the press but fulfilling its central purpose.

A century after Cato's Letters codified a new model of political free speech, Roy's arguments echoed its well-known basic tenets: the central purpose of press liberty was 'public remark on the conduct of the public officers of government'; 'government can only be brought into hatred and contempt by its own acts'; only self-interested men in power feared 'a free press'; its suppression was despotic, and the result would be unchecked tyranny. But he also drove home an additional, sharply colonial warning – at one point explicitly comparing Indians to 'slaves'. Under the Mughals, Roy noted, Indians had enjoyed great 'political rank and power' in their own land. If the British, who had already stripped them of all this status and authority, were now also to argue that 'a colony . . . can never safely be entrusted with liberty of the press, and that therefore natives of Bengal cannot be allowed' it, 'this would be in other words to tell them that they are condemned to perpetual oppression and degradation, from which they can have no hope of being raised during the existence of the British power'. Such an attitude, he warned, would destroy loyalty to British rule.

BRITISH PRINCIPLES AND COLONIAL SUBJECTS

Was press freedom indeed compatible with, even beneficial to, colonial rule? Should Indians have the same free-speech rights as Britons? By the mid 1820s, there had come to be two poles of opinion on these questions. At one extreme was the position of Roy, Buckingham, the internationally influential legal reformer Jeremy Bentham, and other progressive thinkers in Britain and India. They argued that liberty of the press should be a universal right, because it always produced social enlightenment and better government, and that there was no fundamental reason why it should not extend equally to Indians.

'The cause is noble and of paramount importance to the[ir] immediate interests,' one aristocratic Benthamite army officer with long experience of India pointed out in 1823, quoting Roy alongside Aristotle, Milton, Locke, Bacon, Burke, Hume and Montesquieu. The subcontinent's indigenous rulers, he claimed, had never practised censorship: until recently, 'the people of India had the same liberty to write as to breathe or to live. No law forbad it.' Now, by contrast, they, a hundred million people, 'our fellow-subjects, who pay us, in yearly tribute, about twenty millions sterling', were being deprived of their ancient and natural rights of free expression, and, together with Europeans in India, subjected to 'mental despotism', like slaves. This in turn was bound to encourage misgovernment, native resentment, superstition and rebellion. 'Do not treat India as a colony,' he urged, 'and clap a padlock on her mind and stifle her reason.' Instead, 'treat her with the justice and humanity that is due to the subjects of the mother country, and she will be to you equally attached'. A few months later, the indefatigable author, Leicester Stanhope, travelled to Greece on a mission to support its people's movement for independence from Ottoman rule. During his short time there, he was so obsessed with establishing a free press that he acquired the nickname 'the Typographical Colonel'.

Stanhope's passing assertion about pre-colonial Indian freedoms appears to have been the only contemporary attempt to connect European ideals of speech and press freedom directly to a pre-existing indigenous doctrine, though without any very solid basis. Certainly, the rich oral and scriptural traditions of Mughal India had included practices of frank and irreverent speech. Other writers, too, sometimes evoked the idea that pre-colonial rulers, for all their despotism, had encouraged greater openness of discussion than the British. Stanhope also had in mind India's centuries-old, dynamic and sophisticated culture of individual and collective petitioning, which continued in the colonial era – sometimes even intruding into British politics. When Roy and his colleagues appealed to the imperial authorities in London, they were following in a long tradition of elite Indians who had done the same. Nonetheless, the specific ideal of press freedom as it developed in India from the later eighteenth century was a self-consciously western import, and understood as such even by anti-colonial thinkers who adopted its rhetoric. Though on other points they extolled the virtues of pre-colonial society, Roy and other Indian writers never made an equivalently direct claim about any earlier, indigenous tradition of free speech.

The idea was also quickly dismissed by those on the other side of the debate, who maintained that Indians had no history of free expression, and that colonial rule, whether in Ireland or India, was incompatible with press freedom. The public reason for this, endlessly rehearsed by supporters of the East India Company, was that the natives were still too simple-minded, not yet ready to be entrusted with such a powerful right. 'Political discussion is not suited to the prejudices or the capacities of an *uneducated* people,' the *Calcutta Monthly Journal* cautioned in 1821, when Roy launched the *Sambad*. British authority in India, the *Asiatic Journal* explained the following year, 'depends not on physical force, but on intellectual superiority', which was why native newspapers were a dangerous proposition. The native Indian had no commonality of interest 'with the stranger under whose sceptre he lives', nor sufficient 'understanding that can enable him to draw the line between the honest and open expression of opinion, and the badly disguised treason that lurks under the sulky remonstrance'. Roy himself was dismissed as no more than 'a presumptuous "Black Man"'. In such circumstances it was folly to permit a free European press, let alone to countenance his new journals for Indians – they seemed to have been founded mainly 'for the purpose of fomenting their accidental discontents, of opening their eyes to the defects of their rulers, of encouraging and giving utterance, not to their complaints, but to their remonstrances'. It would be 'like permitting the approach of a man with a lighted match in his hand to a barrel of gunpowder'.

In their private communications, British officials spoke more bluntly still. Given 'our peculiar situation in this country', warned the governor of Madras, Sir Thomas Munro, in 1822, control of the press would determine 'whether our dominion in India is to stand or fall'. 'In place of spreading useful knowledge among the people and tending to their better government', allowing the natives to print freely 'would generate insubordination, insurrection, and anarchy'. 'For what is the first duty of a free press? It is to deliver the country from a foreign yoke ... and if we make the press really free to the natives as well to Europeans it must inevitably lead to this result.' It would 'spread among the people the principle of liberty, and stimulate them to expel the strangers who rule over them, and to establish a national government'. The natives were already circulating calls for resistance, and attempting to foment mutiny among the company's sepoys: press freedom would allow them to publicize all the ways in which Europeans were exploiting their country, and inevitably inspire them to 'the overthrow of the government and the recovery of their national independence'. Maintaining 'the most absolute control' over print, on the other hand, was the 'natural' course of action. It would allow the benefits of printing to be slowly and gradually diffused among the natives, while fulfilling the main aim of British policy – to perpetuate their hegemony for as long as possible.

The ultimate foundation of British rule 'must be force', other influential officials secretly advised the new governor-general before he sailed to the subcontinent in 1823, though it was prudent to 'disguise [this] as much as possible'. Press freedom and political debate were the right and privilege of free peoples, like the British, 'but in no sense of the terms can the Government of India be called a free, a representative or a popular Government; the people had no voice in its establishment, nor have they any control over its acts' – nor should they. Because 'public opinion cannot be said to exist' in India, only *English* public opinion could discuss its governance. Because the native mind was still so intellectually immature, Elphinstone's successor in Bombay explained, press freedom could only be granted to this 'conquered people' in a very distant future: it would be 'one of the last boons which is given to a people whom . . . we have gradually matured into a state of society in which they are fit to receive it'. To bestow it any sooner would only 'hasten our own destruction'.

It was therefore worrisome that both 'black' Indians and 'half-castes' were now imbibing from print European ideas about 'freedom' and 'independence', together with 'notions of their own importance'. Most dangerous of all was the recent diffusion of native printing in indigenous languages, which might foment political discussions, or even the spread of 'the rights of man and other democratic doctrines'. That would be disastrous to British authority, 'and that vast Empire probably lost to us for ever'. From this perspective, Roy's and other Indian papers were not channels for education and loyal communication, but dangerous vehicles of insubordination. Instead of cementing native loyalty, British officials warned each other, press freedom for Indians would do the opposite, and 'lower the European character in the estimation of the natives'. Behind the scenes in 1822 and 1823, it was therefore not only Buckingham's *Calcutta Journal* that was targeted by the government crackdown, but also, as Adam later publicly acknowledged, 'the evils of an ill-regulated and licentious native press' – and the very idea that Indians might behave as Britons, and use print as a check against misgovernment.

NATIVE CHARACTER

On 20 May 1823, in the midst of this unfolding crisis, a young man called John Stuart Mill entered the service of the East India Company at its London headquarters. It was his seventeenth birthday. As part of his duties in learning to draft official dispatches, he read the various internal memoranda being circulating about press freedom in India. They left a lasting impression on his teenage mind: almost thirty years later, he could still instantly recall their central anxiety, 'that if full licence were allowed to the press, it would drive us out of India altogether'.

What the adult Mill himself thought about the rights of Indians to free speech and press liberty is a significant question, for two reasons. In the first place, he came to consider himself a great expert on India, and became a leading administrator of British rule over it (despite, like his father, never actually venturing anywhere near the country). For many decades he worked at the highest echelons of the East India Company in London. In the aftermath of the Indian rebellions of 1857, he was the company's staunchest public propagandist. The following year, after parliament liquidated the corporation, the British government offered him a seat on its new Council for India, which thenceforth ruled the territory from London. Britain's 'enlightened' governance of India, Mill wrote in an anonymous pamphlet around this time, had been 'not only one of the purest in intention, but one of the most beneficent in act, ever known among mankind'. He was sure that 'the verdict of history' would vindicate that.

On the other hand, at exactly the same time as he was engaged in this career, Mill also became the English-speaking world's leading theorist of personal liberty. His book *On Liberty* (1859), written at the high point of his involvement with Indian affairs, revolutionized western ideas about freedom of expression. The general connection between Mill's work as colonial administrator and as liberal philosopher has been the subject of much illuminating recent work. Here, I shall focus on his theory of free speech, which remains the most influential modern treatment of the subject – not least because it is invariably read as a statement about universally applicable individual rights. Yet in fact, as we shall see, Mill's arguments about freedom of expression were deeply coloured by his colonial attitudes. His example epitomizes how far, throughout the nineteenth century, even the most innovative western ideals of free speech continued to be profoundly affected by imperialist presumptions. That is significant in itself, and also raises further questions. What enduring effects did these formulations have in the postcolonial world – and what might be the implications for our own continued reliance on them?

The reason that John Stuart Mill entered the service of the East India Company as a teenager was that he was the brilliant, precocious, eldest son of James Mill. His father got him the job; John was being trained up to assist and in due course succeed him (as he eventually did, when James died in 1836).

The publication of James Mill's *History of British India*, early in 1818, after its dozen years of laborious gestation, had transformed his family's fortunes: on the strength of it, the East India Company appointed him to a high administrative position at its headquarters. From a precarious, impoverished hack writer and speculative philosopher, he now suddenly became a well-paid and immensely powerful imperial agent, who revelled in his newfound importance. By 1827 his influence as the chief writer of official dispatches was so pronounced that a new governor-general setting off for India quipped to him that 'I am going to British India; but I shall not be Governor-General. It is you that will be Governor-General.' It is possible that, in 1823, James Mill himself drafted the company's policy statements on the dangers of allowing press liberty in India.

He was also the dominant influence on his son's intellectual outlook, having subjected him since infancy to an extraordinarily demanding regime of home schooling, beginning with ancient Greek from the age of three. For the next eleven years of his life, young John spent his days studying at the same table with his overbearing, irascible father – learning classics, history, French, philosophy, mathematics and science under his tutelage, while James researched and wrote his magnum opus about India. He read the manuscript as his father composed it; at the age of four or five, he tried to emulate him by penning his own history of India. In early 1817, when he was ten, John read through every line of the finished work, out loud, to help his father with the final corrections. That *The History of British India* was a great masterpiece, as well as one of the foundations of his own education, was a certainty that he grew up with, and never doubted for the rest of his life.

From his earliest years, in consequence, John inherited his father's presumptions that all of the world's peoples could be measured against a single, uniform index of civilization, and that on that scale all non-European societies were still in their 'infancy' – their cultures 'savage' and 'barbarous', and their inhabitants, like children, irrational and mentally undeveloped, with 'unenlightened and perverted intellects'.

All this was, in fact, a crude oversimplification of the earlier think-ers from whom James Mill had derived his ideas, such as his mentor Bentham and Scottish theorists like Adam Smith, Adam Ferguson and James Millar, none of whom had suggested that stages of social development proceeded uniformly or correlated with differences in mental capacity. Over the decades, plenty of commentators crit-icized James Mill's writings about India. On other subjects, like the rights of women, John Stuart Mill famously repudiated his father's views, sometimes drawing on his own knowledge of Indian politics to do so. But about the character of India itself, he never changed his mind very much. In 1853, sitting down to pen his autobiography, he proudly began by describing himself as 'the eldest son of James Mill, the author of *The History of British India*' – proceeding to eulogize the book as 'one of the most instructive histories ever written', and his father as the greatest-ever force for 'the improvement of India', 'the originator of all sound statesmanship' in Indian affairs.

This intellectual inheritance created what seems to our eyes a glar-ing paradox at the heart of John Stuart Mill's mature philosophy. On the one hand, he was a lifelong crusader against group-think and group-based prejudice. As a teenager, he publicly defended the 'in-dependent negro commonwealth' of Haiti against white aggression; towards the end of his life, in the later 1860s, he spoke out against the overt racial bigotry of other British intellectuals, like Thomas Carlyle and John Ruskin, and led a public campaign on behalf of hundreds of Black Jamaicans who had been killed, injured and dispossessed by that colony's white British governors.

Yet on the other hand, despite consistently deploring racism, and always celebrating intellectual diversity, Mill also took for granted, like most of his British contemporaries, that all non-European cul-tures were primitive and intellectually backward. This was not, for him, correlated with skin colour – he also included the colonized Irish among such inferior peoples. Yet, though rejecting racial and biological essentialism, he embraced the idea of 'national charac-ter', which led him, like most Victorian intellectuals, to quite similar conclusions. We can glimpse these in his repeated references to 'the passive and slavish character of the people of many parts of India', or his belief that 'the Hindoos are a more ignorant and more passive people than the French Canadians', or his contrast between the active citizenship of 'Englishmen like ourselves' and the supposed passivity of Indian 'Musselmans and Hindoos'.

In his own mind, moreover, this combination of views was no paradox. On the contrary, it explained precisely why India had to be ruled despotically. The English settlers there were 'the more powerful race', but also given to 'oppression and injustice', and 'naturally inclined to despise the natives'. Left to their own devices, they would trample 'the interests and rights of the natives', for Indians themselves were of an intrinsically 'passive character'. It followed 'that the natives of India need protection against the English, and that to afford them that protection is one of the first duties of the British government in India'. English imperial rule was therefore necessary, benign, just and beneficial to its subjects – even though English colonists tended to be racist bullies. The problem of colour prejudice was never, for Mill, connected to the system of colonial rule itself.

Mill's views about Indian intellect, public opinion and the press essentially mirrored those of the East India Company – indeed, he rehearsed them for decades in private and public statements on their behalf. These days, he reported to the British parliament in 1852, there were certainly 'intelligent natives' to be found in India. But though there was no legal bar against Indians holding high office in their own land, they were not yet 'trustworthy' – 'there is a practical exclusion, and so there must be, until the natives are very much improved in character'. They remained 'a people most difficult to be understood, and still more difficult to be governed' – 'not capable of administering its own affairs'. ('I myself have always been for a good stout Despotism,' he explained to a correspondent in 1837.)

Because of this native backwardness, there was in Mill's view also no such thing as public opinion in India:

> the public of India afford no assistance in their own government. They are not ripe for doing so by means of representative government; they are not even in a condition to make effectual appeals to the people of this country; they cannot even make their circumstances and interests and grievances known ... therefore, the great security for good government – public discussion – does not exist for India, as it exists

for this country and its other dependencies [i.e. Britain's white settler colonies, like Canada and Australia].

Perversely, this meant for Mill that the opinions of intelligent and articulate Indians who *did* make themselves heard were to be dismissed as intrinsically suspect, self-interested and 'malcontent'. And that included the whole of the Indian periodical press. Though in Britain newspapers were a critical means of public debate, he argued, that was not true of the native Indian press – which was 'an organ exclusively of individual interests', the mouthpiece of 'rich individuals and societies representing class interests', not of 'the people of India'. The Indian people had no voice; they constituted no public; they had no means of making their views known. To Mill, Indians who did speak out were irrelevant exceptions that only proved this immutable rule.

Thus, he argued in a pamphlet in the aftermath of the 1857 rebellion, native critiques of British actions were invariably the work of 'some Indian malcontent, generally with objects opposed to good government', rather than true expressions of Indian opinion. Whereas in advanced civilizations, political debate and criticism were vital checks against misgovernment, he explained elsewhere, the opposite was true in India. If the natives were allowed to debate British rule, or even to read about internal British disagreements, that would only encourage 'Indian malcontents' and send entirely the wrong message:

> for, that there may be firm action notwithstanding divided councils, or that a government can be really formidable which allows itself to be bearded [i.e. mocked] and its acts railed at to its face, is a truth which it requires a much higher civilization than that of Orientals to understand or credit.

LIBERTY AND HUMANITY

Mill's views about freedom of debate in India contrasted sharply with his presumptions about what was appropriate for his own, 'much higher civilization'. Soon afterwards, he published *On Liberty*, which remains the best-known and most influential modern work on freedom of expression. The book was about personal liberty in general – but, within that, 'liberty of thought and discussion' was the central theme.

To understand how revolutionary Mill's arguments on this score were, one has but to compare them with his father's. All his life, James Mill had obsessed about press liberty. Like every British political radical of the early nineteenth century, he deplored the restrictions on seditious, libellous and religiously heterodox print that had always existed in Britain, and had been further tightened since the 1790s. Like progressive thinkers everywhere across the globe in the years around 1800, he yearned for 'a society in which freedom of the press had full scope; how virtue, how public spirit would flourish – what happiness, what peace would flow'! For decades, Mill read widely on the subject of press freedom; in the 1810s and 1820s, he published authoritative essays on it. It was central to his entire political philosophy – with the important and telling caveat that, in his mind, as later in his son's, it remained entirely separate from questions of *colonial* government. (A parliamentary committee, presumably aware of his frequently rehearsed arguments in favour of democracy, representative institutions and universal male suffrage, once asked the elder Mill if representative government might be practicable in India, too. 'Utterly out of the question,' was his reply.)

James Mill's fascination with press liberty was part of a more general tide of contemporary agitation against Britain's unreformed and unwritten constitution, which eventually culminated in the great modernizing Reform Act of 1832. He also analysed press liberty in transnational terms, tracing its recent evolution in France, Holland, Germany, Switzerland, Italy, Spain, Austria and the United States. Yet despite all this topical, up-to-date positioning, his basic theory rested on the same libertarian platitudes that had first been put forward by Cato's Letters, a century earlier, and had since been ceaselessly recycled.

Thus for James Mill the essential purpose of print liberty, 'this best bulwark of our liberties', remained that of holding rulers to account, critiquing 'the institutions and functionaries of government' and publicizing misrule. In practice, he complained, English laws hardly safeguarded this liberty; it existed only on sufferance. But ideally, the press should be completely free to opine on all political and religious matters, so that 'it would be impossible for the public to be deceived' about any important subject. In his most thoroughgoing analysis, Mill could conceive of only two appropriate restrictions. Press freedom should not extend to any 'direct exhortation' to forcibly oppose some *specific* governmental act – for example, it would be wrong to publish a handbill that 'may excite a mob to disturb the proceedings of a court of justice, to obstruct the officers of the law, police, or government'. And secondly, like Thomas Jefferson before him, he would also penalize 'false facts' – that is, malicious or baseless accusations about the public actions of public officials.

Mill's overall framing of the subject, too, was not much changed from Cato's original template. Above all, it sharply distinguished public from private affairs, and public from private persons. Mill's liberty of the press, in fact, concerned only the public actions of public officers. (So did that of Bentham.) It didn't extend to criticism of any other kind – especially not to the injury of any person's good name. Insults to the reputation of 'private men' were not free speech but violations of their 'private rights' – and so too were aspersions of the private actions or character of public officials. All these kinds of mischief required laws 'for protecting the *rights of individuals* against violations committed by the press'.

So, too, Mill, like most of his eighteenth-century predecessors, never actually conceived of press freedom itself as an individual right. It was rather something that benefited 'the people' collectively, an aid in their struggle against self-interested rulers. Its ultimate end was general 'human improvement' – 'the real point of importance is to establish correct opinions in the minds of the people'. The freer the press, the more enlightened the whole population would be.

At the heart of Mill's model were the dogmas first popularized by Milton and Cato, and endlessly repeated thereafter by their successors: that truth was singular, would always triumph in open debate and was intellectually irresistible. On every subject, he presumed, one could rationally arrive at uniform, 'correct opinions'. Once these had been established, the majority of people would always naturally 'embrace the truth'. It followed that 'freedom of discussion is the only security which the people can have for the prevalence of true opinions', because 'there is no possible means of obtaining truth, but through permission of error'. What's more, 'it is a fact, confirmed by the experience of all ages, that when truth combats with error on even ground, it is sure of victory'.

James Mill's views on press freedom reveal both how entrenched such platitudes had become in progressive circles by the early nineteenth century, and how little their underlying conceptions had changed over the previous century. His son grew up taking this orthodoxy for granted – at the age of eighteen, he published an almost forty-page article on the subject in the *Westminster Review*, liberally quoting his father's writings, reiterating their main tenets and inveighing in a similar vein against the 'abominations' of English press law. But in the 1850s, after three decades of further thought, John Stuart Mill came up with a radically novel way of thinking about freedom of expression, which still provides the basis for our own approach.

Happily, he announced in *On Liberty*, it was now no longer necessary to argue for '"liberty of the press" as one of the securities against corrupt or tyrannical government', because that point had already been proved 'so often and so triumphantly'. True, English law remained repressive, but in practice nowadays 'there is little danger of its being actually put in force against political discussion, except during some temporary panic, when fear of insurrection drives ministers and judges from their propriety' (in a footnote, he brushed aside the inconvenient truth that such an episode of panicked governmental repression had, in fact, just taken place).

Instead, the younger Mill conceived of the right to freedom of expression in much larger terms. It was not just a question of press liberty, but of all human 'thought and discussion'. It applied not merely to the debate of 'public' affairs, but encompassed all subjects. And crucially, he defined it as the right of every *individual*, to think and speak as they chose, not just of 'the people' in general. The rhetoric of free speech as an individual right was not new. It had been central to earlier notions of religious and scholarly free speech; Cato's Letters had adopted it too. But in Cato's and later discussions of political free speech, the language of individual rights had always sat uneasily with, and been subordinated to, the overriding focus on how press freedom would allow 'the people' collectively to ascertain self-evident truths. James Mill's account had epitomized this awkward balancing act. His son was the first modern anglophone theorist to abandon it, and to conceive of free speech *only* in terms of individual rights.

This was, in turn, because his conception of the purpose of free expression no longer prioritized political liberty, but something completely different: the 'mental development' of individuals. In John Stuart Mill's redefinition, free speech was not just the indispensable means to truth, wisdom or liberty – it was also, more importantly, an intrinsic good, part of every person's right to live a fulfilling life. What's more, he argued, it was not governmental restrictions that constituted the main threat to such freedom of expression, but the stifling effects of social norms – 'social intolerance' towards unorthodox ideas, and the 'tyranny of the majority'. That people could be coerced by the pressure of public opinion into mental conformity was, he urged, 'a social tyranny more formidable than many kinds of political oppression'. In short, freedom of expression was a vital 'necessity to the mental well-being of mankind (on which all their other well-being depends)'.

This wholesale reconceptualization of the scope and function of free speech led Mill to an equally far-reaching conclusion about its practice – no opinion should ever be silenced, even if plainly wrong. That was for several reasons: because truth was never certain, let alone self-evident; because a constant clash of opinions was the best way of maintaining mental acuity, as well as testing and advancing truth; and because even if something *was* wholly true, 'if it is not fully, frequently, and fearlessly discussed, it will be held as a dead dogma, not a living truth'. That way lay, in Mill's hyperbole, the horror of unthinking, 'ape-like' passivity and 'mental slavery'. For him, even truth itself was thus ultimately less important than the constant exercise of free expression for its own sake: 'to enable average human beings to attain the mental stature which they are capable of', and to produce 'an intellectually active people'. Indeed, he was careful also to stipulate that freedom of expression, as he conceived of it, was *not* a natural or 'abstract right ... independent of utility', but only the means to the noble end of intellectual self-development, and that his main focus was not political but rather 'moral, social and intellectual liberty, asserted against the despotism of society whether exercised by governments or by public opinion'.

Despite this radical rethinking of the terms and purpose of free speech, Mill could not escape the twin difficulties that had confounded all previous theorists of the subject, and that bedevil us still – the question of truth, and the problem of harm. Nor did he manage to solve them. The result was a deeply inconsistent argument: throughout *On Liberty*, Mill was continually forced to qualify his loud libertarian headlines with quieter caveats and concessions.

Previous anglophone theorists of secular free speech, from Cato to James Mill, had asserted that truth always won out over falsehood, and was irresistible to the human mind. John Stuart Mill rejected this premise out of hand: 'the dictum that truth always triumphs over persecution is one of those pleasant falsehoods which men repeat after one another till they pass into commonplaces, but which all experience refutes.' But despite this, and all his assertions about the benefits of allowing erroneous views and diversity of opinion, he also took for granted that, over time, truths did advance and become established, and that this was a mark of progress – 'as mankind improve, the number of doctrines which are no longer disputed or doubted will be constantly on the increase ... this gradual narrowing of the bounds of opinion is necessary in both senses of the term, being at once inevitable and indispensable'. Such settled consensus was 'salutary in the case of true opinions, as it is dangerous and noxious when the opinions are erroneous'. In Mill's text there's thus a constant, unresolved tension between his fear of accepted but false 'dogma' and his embrace of 'real', settled truths; between his view of erroneous opinions as helpful in sharpening the truth, and his apprehension that their spread might damage it.

Mill's reframing of the scope and purpose of free expression also led him to a radical dismissal of harms caused by speech. This was an even greater departure from all existing theories of free speech, whether religious, scholarly or political, which had always at the very least paid lip service to the real dangers of libel and falsehood.

On the surface, Mill's rhetoric about the necessary benefits of permitting fallacious views, and the closeness between truth and error, was not dissimilar to Milton's. But Milton, like all theorists of religious free speech, had been very clear that he was only talking about spiritual opinions, matters which ultimately only God could judge, and *not* about slanders or other speech with real-world effects. Cato and his many epigones had gone further, but still confined their free speech claims to truthful speech about 'public' matters, and always at least nominally deprecated libel and other speech 'injuries'. John Stuart Mill, by contrast, jettisoned all these traditional guardrails: the word 'libel' does not even appear in his text. Instead, he proclaimed, all speech should always be allowed, including 'the propagation of doctrines which we regard as false and pernicious', and 'dangerous to the welfare of mankind'. His implication was that such speech never really was injurious: or at least, that the greater harm always arose from the tyranny of conformity and the chilling of speech, rather than from expression itself.

To sustain this dubious line of argument, he was forced into another questionable but extremely consequential claim: that there was a sharp distinction between speech and 'action'. Earlier theories had distinguished between free speech and harmful speech: liberty versus licence. Now, Mill asserted instead that all speech should be free – because speech was never an act, and only acts could cause harm. This was a difficult line for him to tread, as his own most fundamental principle was that, though everyone should have liberty over their own physical and moral well-being, this didn't extend to conduct 'which concerns others' or would 'produce evil to someone else', or 'harm to others'. And, as he also acknowledged in passing, speech was pre-eminently *not* 'self-regarding conduct': it was 'a social act'.

Mill's solution – or, rather, his obfuscation – of this problem took two contradictory forms. Most importantly, he yoked together 'liberty of thought and discussion' as being essentially the same thing, and requiring 'absolute freedom of opinion and sentiment on all subjects, practical or speculative, scientific, moral, or theological'. Waving away the obvious objection that thoughts were wholly internal, but expression affects others, he continued:

> The liberty of expressing and publishing opinions may seem to fall under a different principle, since it belongs to that part of the conduct of an individual which concerns other people; but, being almost of as much importance as the liberty of thought itself, and resting in great part on the same reasons, is practically inseparable from it.

That was all. It was, and is, a notably weak assertion on which to ground such a far-reaching argument, and one that is easily refuted – our thoughts do not affect other people, but our expressions of them often do.

Towards the end of his book, while grappling with the same issue, Mill took a different tack, suggesting that in some circumstances speech did cross the line into conduct: 'even opinions lose their immunity, when the circumstances in which they are expressed are such as to constitute their expression a positive instigation to some mischievous act'. The sole example he gave was strikingly similar to the one his father had put forward almost forty years earlier: 'An opinion that corn-dealers are starvers of the poor ... may justly incur punishment when delivered orally to an excited mob assembled before the house of a corn-dealer, or when handed about among the same mob in the form of a placard.' But note that Mill's phrasing of the principle still implies that words themselves do not constitute action, but only 'instigate' it (the same dubious distinction lives on in our modern theory that speech is not an action but can be an 'incitement' to it). In the same passage, Mill also vaguely repeated his general caveat that personal liberty could never extend to being 'a nuisance to other people' or 'injury to others'. Yet because it would have wrecked the boldness of his overall philosophical scheme, he never stooped to consider how such restrictions were to be reconciled with 'absolute freedom of opinion and sentiment on all subjects', let alone how they should apply to the age-old problems of malicious lies, conspiracy theories, personal libels and other forms of expressive injury to others.

COLONIZATION AND CIVILIZATION

How did Mill come to develop this unprecedentedly radical set of views? It's not hard to see that he was led to it by his personal experiences of England as 'not a place of mental freedom'. For all the acclaim, power and celebrity that he had accumulated by the 1850s, he had also throughout his life faced mockery, antagonism and social ostracism, even from members of his own family, for his heterodox stances on hot-button topics – religious belief, contraception, relations between the sexes, the rights of women, political reform, and more. He had stood firm. 'No one can be a great thinker who does not recognise, that as a thinker it is his first duty to follow his intellect to whatever conclusions it may lead,' he wrote proudly in *On Liberty*. That others should be mentally cowed, socially victimized or legally punished for expressing heterodox opinions seemed to him both unjust and detrimental to social progress.

Yet his argument was also rooted in a deeply colonialist presumption: that Europeans alone stood in the vanguard of history, actively progressing, while other cultures remained static, degenerate and stuck in the past. Many other influential European thinkers held similar views. 'World history travels from east to west,' the great German philosopher and theorist of liberty G. W. F. Hegel had instructed his students in the 1820s – 'for Europe is the absolute end of history, just as Asia is the beginning'. (As for Africa, 'it is an unhistorical continent, with no movement or development of its own'.) From the 1840s, another grand theorist of the stadial development of human minds and societies, Mill's friend and associate Auguste Comte, together with his disciples, popularized a new sociopolitical concept, 'the west', as a unitary term for the shared civilizations of western Europe, the Americas, Australia and New Zealand.

Though Mill himself didn't adopt that particular neologism, he too had always taken for granted that civilization was more advanced, and was progressing more rapidly 'in modern Europe, and especially in Great Britain . . . than at any other place or time' – and especially compared to 'the East'. For all that they might once have had 'magnificent palaces and gorgeous temples', he explained, the rest 'of the world has, properly speaking, no history, because the despotism of custom is complete. This is the case over the whole East.' Europeans, by contrast, had developed beyond 'barbarism'. They had shaken off a similar 'mental despotism' in three historical stages: at the Reformation, during the Enlightenment, and most recently 'in the intellectual fermentation of Germany during the Goethian and Fichtean period' (that is, around 1800). The effect was that they were more 'well-developed human beings', with greater 'individuality' and 'originality', who travelled a 'plurality of paths'. The more intellectually and socially diverse its members, he believed, the more advanced a society was bound to be. The motto of his *On Liberty*, borrowed from

Wilhelm von Humboldt, was 'the absolute and essential importance of human development in its richest diversity'.

But, Mill warned, this evolution was not irreversible. In fact, he was writing precisely because, in his view, European progress had stalled. In its modern societies, 'public opinion now rules the world ... that is to say, collective mediocrity'. People no longer thought for themselves, but imbibed their opinions 'through the newspapers', which had led to intellectual enfeeblement, and a new 'despotism of custom' and mental conformity. 'We have a warning example in China,' he announced. That was the most advanced of all the non-European nations, and it had a great past; yet now 'they have become stationary – have remained so for thousands of years; and if they are ever to be farther improved, it must be by foreigners'. Just so, in Europe, 'the modern *regime* of public opinion ... is decidedly advancing towards the Chinese ideal of making all people alike.' In other words, because of their sheeplike addiction to modern media, Europeans were losing their intellectual individuality, the source of their forward momentum as a society. *On Liberty*, composed in the pessimism of late middle age, as he contemplated his own mortality, was Mill's clarion call against the danger of such enfeebling, Oriental regression.

His allusion to China itself being 'improved' by 'foreigners' was fleeting but extremely telling. As his readers would have known, this process had begun with the East India Company's hugely lucrative and socially destructive smuggling of vast quantities of opium from India to China, against the laws and wishes of the Chinese government. From 1839 onwards, this state-sponsored drug-running on a massive scale by Mill's employer had, in turn, led to the British army and navy's invasion of the country, the seizure of Hong Kong and other territories, years of bloody warfare, and the forcible imposition of ever more punitive trading terms by European powers on the defeated nation. As *On Liberty* was first being read in London and Calcutta, thousands of British and French troops were looting and destroying Beijing's Imperial Summer Palace. Before long, the British high commissioner in charge of this murderous campaign was promoted to governor-general of India.

At a fundamental level, therefore, Mill's argument about freedom of expression was saturated with imperialist presumptions about history, 'progress' and a sharp perceived division between 'civilized' Europeans and 'barbarian' others. Non-European cultures and peoples were intellectually inferior. They could not be treated as 'human beings in the maturity of their faculties', for whom liberty was a fundamental right, but only as unfledged children, in need of strict, adult governance. It's tempting to speculate about the psychological purchase of this metaphor for Mill, whose own childhood had been so unforgivingly strict, and who never actually parented any children of his own. But in any case, his intellectual application of it was brutal. In a single paragraph of his introduction, he explained that non-European human beings were so mentally immature that his theory of personal liberty could not, of course, apply to them – and, moreover, that such nations' only chance of progress lay in being despotically ruled by Europeans. Though the text never explicitly mentioned India, that was obviously the example uppermost in his mind:

> we may leave out of consideration those backward states of society in which the race itself may be considered as in its nonage. The early difficulties in the way of spontaneous progress are so great that there is seldom any choice of means for overcoming them: and a ruler full of the spirit of improvement is warranted in the use of any expedients that will attain an end, perhaps otherwise unattainable. Despotism is a legitimate mode of government in dealing with barbarians, provided the end be their improvement, and the means justified by actually effecting that end. Liberty, as a principle, has no application to any state of things anterior to the time when mankind have become capable of being improved by free and equal discussion. Until then, there is nothing for them but implicit obedience to an Akbar or a Charlemagne, if they are so fortunate as to find one.

This was the grandest exception of all to his radical thesis about freedom of speech as the necessary essence of personal liberty. He was only concerned with advanced nations, Mill announced in the opening lines of *On Liberty* – that is, 'the stage of progress into which the more civilized portions of the species have now entered'. He never categorically spelled out whom he included in this, but his examples and later writings made it clear: the British above all, other Europeans (especially the Germans and the French), Americans and presumably also other European settler-colonies around the world. Such people had 'long since' reached the stage of needing and benefiting from freedom of discussion; the nations of 'the East' decidedly had not. 'India (for example) is not fit to govern itself.'

'I am not aware that any community has a right to force another to be civilized,' Mill argued at one point, summing up his theory of liberty as it applied within western nations. But when it came to European imperial rule over 'backward' people, that was precisely what he himself repeatedly urged – and placed at the very heart of his theory of free speech. His British readers in India were quick to celebrate Mill's argument as justifying all the *limits* on liberty 'with which an intelligent but foreign despotism ought to content itself in ruling Asiatics'.

The next chapter will explore the peculiar effects of such imperial perspectives on how expression was regulated in colonial contexts – and the pernicious legacies of this into the postcolonial present. Though Mill's theory of liberty was hardly the only or even the most important source of imperial practice, that intellectual connection is one major reason to re-evaluate our conventional respect for *On Liberty* as a particularly inspiring exposition of modern free-speech doctrine.

You might protest that the text's colonial outlook is separable from its essential argument. Surely, the latter is salvageable if we just agree that there are no 'backward states of society', and that its precepts apply to all cultures? As we shall see, that's what nineteenth-century Indians themselves did, when appropriating Mill's arguments. But it's not that simple. For the reasons that Mill presumed that freedom of speech wouldn't work in 'backward' individuals and societies (that is, the reasons why in such circumstances it couldn't have progressive effects) are related to all the socially harmful kinds of expression that his broader argument repeatedly reveals but tries to cover up – people expressing themselves in unreasonable, injurious ways, instigating 'mischievous acts' in dangerous situations, and so on. In other words, the deeper problem is simply that his whole theory of expression rests on insecure foundations.

Mill's great contribution to the history of free speech was to try to theorize it, for the first time, wholly as an individual right – whose purpose was the development of individual identity and intellectual maturity. But it's startling to realize quite how flawed the resulting doctrine really is, because it never manages to overcome the basic problem that expression is not a private and self-centred, but a pre-eminently social, other-regarding act. Speech is not separate from action, as Mill would have us believe. At best, it is a particular kind of action, which deserves a degree of special latitude – though that is not Mill's argument. Nor, most fundamentally, are thought and expression essentially the same thing. That extraordinary assertion, which Mill tries to smuggle past his readers as furtively as possible, epitomizes the problem of conceiving of free speech only in terms of the rights of the individual – instinctively appealing though that is to our modern, individualist, rights-based sensibilities. It's a conundrum we are all still wrestling with.

9
Colonial and Postcolonial Unfreedoms

Everywhere across the globe during the nineteenth and twentieth centuries, imperial rulers keenly monitored their native populations for signs of unrest. In India, as in other colonial territories, this affected the shape of free speech in two main ways, even as the British continually congratulated themselves on being the greatest champions of free expression the world had ever seen. First, colonial definitions of press and speech liberty were always shadowed by the spectre of 'disloyal' or 'seditious' expression – and were continually contested by indigenous perspectives. Secondly, the native population was treated as presumptively irrational and hot-headed, resulting in distinctive laws about defamation and religious insult. Both of these pernicious colonial impositions, though often denounced by anti-colonial activists, were in due course inherited by the new nations of India, Pakistan and Bangladesh – with enduring effects to this day. Meanwhile, the approach to what we now call 'hate speech' took a revealingly different course in Britain, the United States and other nations.

HUMAN NATURE AND HUMAN PROGRESS

Towards the end of 1869, a brilliant, swashbuckling English lawyer and journalist called James Fitzjames Stephen arrived in Calcutta. Having just turned forty, he was sent out to the capital of British India to succeed his old Cambridge mentor, Sir Henry Maine, as the 'law member' of the governor-general's small ruling Council. In that capacity he set energetically to work, drafting new laws to regularize civil and criminal justice across the subcontinent. Like many dedicated imperialists, Stephen regarded himself as an enlightened reformer. His grandfather had been a leading anti-slavery campaigner, and his father was the powerful chief civil servant of the Colonial Office in London, who regarded the British Empire as an instrument of divine providence. Stephen himself was a religious progressive, an admirer of Bentham and a recent collaborator and self-proclaimed disciple of John Stuart Mill. Reviewing *On Liberty* in 1859, he had enthusiastically proclaimed himself in general agreement with its arguments. Yet since then, he had grown steadily more critical of the older man's views. His two years in India crystallized in his mind a profound rejection of Mill's influential theory of liberty and free expression. On his return home, just a few months before Mill's death, Stephen published his counterblast, *Liberty, Equality, Fraternity* (1873). From 'my Indian experience', he told his readers, he drew very different conclusions about the relationship between free speech, personal liberty and colonial rule.

Stephen's argument was ponderously obsessed with religious politics, and not particularly concerned to put forward its own theory of expression. But it did successfully identify several of the difficulties with Mill's argument. The most obvious was its overambitious scope. 'If Mr. Mill had limited himself to the proposition that in our own time and country it is highly important that the great questions of morals and theology should be discussed openly and with complete freedom from all legal restraints,' Stephen explained, 'I should agree with him' – he was all for intellectual liberty among the English (note his telling restriction to 'our own . . . country'). The problem with Mill's approach was that, 'for the sake of establishing this limited practical consequence', and carried away by his 'characteristic point and brevity', he had ended up putting forward a theory of wholesale liberty for all speech and action, which was full of holes.

Stephen didn't dwell much on Mill's assertion that speech and other forms of expression were akin to thoughts, rather than actions, except to dismiss it as bizarre. Of course speech always affected others. 'To publish opinions upon morals, politics, and religion is an act as important as any which any man can possibly do,' he pointed out, and a 'writer who makes a mistake in his speculations may mislead multitudes whom he has never seen'. In place of Mill's 'irrational' view that liberty was intrinsically good, and his 'worship' of differences of opinion for their own sake, he countered that one always needed to consider 'the object aimed at' by any speech or action, and the proportionality of any restriction upon it.

Above all, the younger man targeted what he regarded as Mill's wrong-headed views of human nature, and the supposed superiority of western intellect. On the one hand, despite noticing that, as things stood, 'the minority are wise and the majority foolish', Mill had presumed that greater liberty of expression would automatically improve everyone's mental powers. On the other hand, he had asserted that this was conceivable only in currently 'civilized' nations, whose populations were intellectually able to benefit from such freedom – as opposed to the supposedly mentally immature inhabitants of India, China and other non-western societies. Both these central assertions, Stephen countered, were verifiably false.

As far as human nature was concerned, in every society 'the wise minority are the rightful masters of the foolish majority' – and for their own good, in Stephen's view, because the latter were never swayed by rational argument. Greater freedom of speech, whatever its other merits, would do nothing to change that. And in this regard, he argued, there was no difference at all between cultures. To Mill's assertion that the inhabitants of modern western nations 'have become capable of being improved by free and equal discussion', Stephen retorted that, no, they hadn't – and never would be. It was simply not true that they generally acted rationally and in their own best interests, let alone on the basis of reasoned public deliberation: 'The minority gives way not because it is convinced that it is wrong, but because it is convinced that it is a minority.'

For Stephen, the essential difference was not between western and non-western cultures, but rather, in every time and place, between the 'very small minority of the human race' who were truly guided by reason and inner conviction, and 'the great mass of men', who could be bribed or cajoled into believing anything. Certainly, one might distinguish between more or less 'rough' and 'civilized' peoples, but this was merely a relative, ever-changing index. And in any case, the difference between them was not 'that force is used in the one case, and persuasion in the other', but simply the degree of power they could command.

In short, Stephen argued, coercion, not liberty, was in all cases the main engine of human progress. Throughout history, all the great political, religious and social advances 'were brought about by force, and in many instances by the force of a minority numerically small, applied to the conduct of an ignorant or very partially informed and for the most part indifferent majority'. As he proudly recounted, British rule over India, including its bloody suppression of the rebellion of 1857, was the supreme example of this. Its policies were 'forced upon the people, utterly against the will of many of them', and were deliberately destroying the authority and customs of the native religions. In doing so, the British were acting towards the Indians as the Romans had, with equal right, towards the Jews – violently exterminating their 'terrible' false religions and 'the last vestiges of [their] national independence'. To suppress the Indians' own opinions and resistance was, after all, to bring them 'in the direction of . . . what we understand by civilisation'.

IMPERIAL CONSTRAINTS

Most nineteenth-century white theorists of free speech supported the silencing of non-European voices. Though their premises and arguments were otherwise completely at odds, both John Stuart Mill and James Fitzjames Stephen agreed that colonized peoples had no right to freedom of expression – especially not to criticize British rule. The same attitude permeated the ranks of British administrators on the ground. As one critic of colonial justice, the Madras lawyer John Bruce Norton, put it in 1853, his colleagues' essential outlook remained that 'the subjects are only "niggers," ' and could be treated arbitrarily, as there was 'no press to give voice to grievances; no public to care for them, were they ever declaimed against, and especially inasmuch as the mild Hindu [i.e. Indian] is by nature long suffering, and not a little inclined to lick the hand that smites him'. (After the rebellion, Norton championed the freedom of the Indian press and criticized Mill's 'sophistry' in defending the East India Company; his son, Eardley Norton, in the 1880s became a prominent early member of the Indian National Congress, the first organized nationalist movement to emerge in the British Empire.)

As the technology of print came to be ever more widely diffused across the subcontinent, however, Indians themselves increasingly contemplated the question of press freedom. From a few dozen titles published in the 1820s, the number of works issued in India each year had by 1900 swelled to well over five thousand. In the 1820s, perhaps ten thousand Bengalis had been directly exposed to print in any language; by the 1850s that had exploded to about six million people in Bengal alone. Many Indians also devoured the latest publications from England. As an English businessman observed in 1853, the 'townsmen of Bombay' read John Stuart Mill and all the other latest English writings on India 'almost as soon as we do; they read them with far greater interest; they discuss them with an ability ... and with advantages to which we cannot pretend'.

To such indigenous eyes it remained a glaring injustice that, despite the huge expansion of printing, Indians, unlike Britons, were still not permitted a free press that could shape and publicly articulate their collective opinion. After *On Liberty* appeared in 1859, many Indian intellectuals therefore eagerly adopted its theory of free speech, strategically choosing to ignore Mill's exclusion of Indians and other 'backward' peoples from his argument. 'John Stuart Mill is the greatest [name] in recent British philosophy,' the Calcutta lawyer Ashutosh Mookerjea reminded his compatriots in 1873, throwing in a comparison with Milton's *Areopagitica* for good measure, and 'all those who have imbibed the true spirit of Mill's own impassioned pleading in behalf of free and equal discussion' would surely join him in rejecting Stephen's poorly reasoned criticisms of it. His own reading of Mill combined an agreement with its basic principles ('all men ... profit, more or less, by free discussion') with a canny recasting of its civilizational schema – including Indians among the 'people who have become capable of being guided to their good by free and equal discussion', and interpreting *On Liberty* as 'in one sense, a protest against European History'. Just as Cato's Letters had hijacked the theory of religious speech by ignoring its critical distinction between spiritual and political speech, so too Indian readers appropriated Mill for their own purposes, silently repositioning its original terms of reference. As so often in the history of free-speech arguments, it was a logically dubious but politically effective strategy.

Such intellectual debates were, though, but a sideshow. In practice, the contours of Indian press freedom, all the way up to the subcontinent's eventual independence in 1947, continued to be shaped by the two most basic presumptions of British imperial rule. The first of these was that, though liberty of the press was an indispensable tool of enlightenment, Indians should not be allowed to use it to undermine British hegemony. The result was a series of laws and practices that maintained government control of all printed materials, while simultaneously denying the existence of censorship – 'in the British colonies the press is as free as it is in England', the *Encyclopaedia Britannica* reassured its Victorian readers.

In fact, even after the 1820s regulations were repealed in India, which happened in 1835, only newspapers and printing presses licensed by the government were allowed to operate there. From the 1850s onwards, the new Indian Civil Service also instituted a vast network of surveillance – tracking, reading and confidentially reporting on every single work published in the country, with particular attention to veiled criticisms of British rule. As historians have pointed out, the great uprising of 1857 was itself 'a modern war of propaganda', in which native print played a key role and rebels routinely destroyed British presses; over the following decades, the propaganda battle continued. In 1870, an amendment to the new Indian penal code of 1860 instituted harsh penalties for any spoken, written or pictorial attempt 'to excite feelings of disaffection to the Government'. As Indian nationalist sentiment surged in the decades around 1900, and was channelled into increasingly prominent organizations and publications, both the police repression of critical voices and the national laws against 'disloyal' print grew ever sharper. During the unpopular Second Anglo-Afghan War of 1878–80, a Vernacular Press Act singled out the flourishing universe of Indian-language newspapers that were 'read by and disseminated amongst large numbers of ignorant and unintelligent' natives, imposing prior censorship and summary police suppression of any 'matter likely to excite disaffection to the government'. An 1898 amendment to the penal code subsequently expanded the meaning of 'disaffection to the government' to include 'disloyalty and all feelings of enmity'.

After the disastrous partition of Bengal in 1905 (by which British administrators had intended 'to split up and thereby weaken a solid body of opponents to our rule'), the gloves really came off. As nationalist agitation mounted, new laws empowered magistrates to dispense with jury trials in some sedition cases and to seize printing presses implicated in spreading disaffection, 'both by openly seditious writing and by suggestion and veiled incitement to inculcate hostility to British rule'. Writers and publishers across India were harassed, convicted and jailed for expressing purportedly anti-British sentiments. Of course, 'nothing can be further from our intentions or more opposed to the spirit of our general policy than to interfere in any way with the legitimate functions of the press,' the governor-general in India smoothly informed his Secretary of State in London in 1907, in the midst of this onslaught. 'But when the public safety is in danger [we have] the right to intervene ... Here is no question of the liberty of the press. The object is simply to stir up disaffection.' His subordinates put matters more simply. 'We must take whatever is absolutely the most effective measure for controlling sedition in the press,' one district commissioner urged, 'without regard to any Western theories or sentiments, which are not applicable to this country.' Small wonder that, when Indian nationalists in the 1920s came to draft their first proposed constitutions, they made sure to include 'free expression of opinion' among the basic rights of all Indians.

This pattern – of laws against 'sedition' and 'disaffection' being sharpened and wielded against anti-colonial activists, especially at times of political crisis – persisted for the remainder of British rule. Indeed, as we shall see, the same mindset underpinned the laws and practices of Independent India vis-à-vis internal dissent after 1947 – it still does. That is also true of the other basic British presumption: the notion that Indian natives differed profoundly from Europeans in their mental make-up. Because their feelings were easily hurt, especially by religious insults, they needed greater protection against abusive speech. For this reason, too, freedom of expression in India had to be strictly limited.

The originator of this idea is usually held to be the lawyer Thomas

Babington Macaulay, the first law member of the governor-general's Council, who in 1837 incorporated it into his proposed uniform penal code for India – an attempt to replace the mass of divergent local laws and jurisdictions. In addition to its restrictions on political speech and print, there were two main ways in which Macaulay's code defined freedom of expression in India in much narrower terms than existed in England, or indeed anywhere in the western world. The first was that it made no difference between speech and writing – in India, spoken words to 'harm the reputation' of a person were criminalized, and so too were verbal insults, even if not defamatory (in England, only defamatory public writing was punishable). The second was a sweeping prohibition on intentionally 'wounding the religious feelings of any person', even by a single word or gesture.

These definitions were not completely at odds with English law. The clauses on defamation, for example, treated truth as an absolute defence, which Macaulay believed improved on English legal doctrine (though none other than John Stuart Mill, reviewing Macaulay's text in 1838, was unconvinced). So too, in England at this time blasphemy remained a crime, though this was a much narrower and seldom prosecuted kind of religious insult. Finally, the code's repeated descriptions of the 'pain' inflicted by slander and religious offence employed that word as a standard term of British utilitarian jurisprudence, rather than in any literal or peculiarly Indian sense.

The overall effect was nonetheless to portray Indians as completely unlike Europeans. Especially in its treatment of Indian religious sensibilities, the text was shot through with condescension towards the 'monstrous superstition', 'most absurd ceremonies' and religious 'fanaticism' of the indigenous population. It described the population of India as a dangerously volatile mass of thin-skinned Hindu and Muslim zealots, liable to receive 'real ... and ... acute ... pain' from being exposed to each other's contempt – a situation 'pregnant with dangers' for the tiny minority of calm, reasonable British Christians who ruled over them. In 'the peculiar circumstances of this country', Macaulay explained, speech laws must be drawn as widely as possible, in order 'to prevent pain arising from opinion'. 'Religious discussion' was fine, but insult was not: 'wounding ... the religious feelings' of others had to be punished as a crime, for there was 'no country in which more cruel suffering is inflicted, and more deadly resentment called forth, by injuries which affect only the mental feelings'.

As Macaulay made clear, the overriding purpose of these restrictions was to prevent native unrest that would undermine British control: 'there is probably no country in which the Government has so much to apprehend from religious excitement among the people'. Yet he was not in fact the first to worry about these things: British anxiety about offending Indian religious sensibilities went back several decades. Ironically enough, it had originated in the East India Company's opposition to European, Christian proselytizing. For decades the company sought to exclude missionary activity from their territories, fearing that evangelical contempt towards the local religions would anger the native population. After 1813, when parliament nonetheless encouraged evangelization, they tried to control it as tightly as possible. That was why in 1818 and 1823 the governor-general's press regulations had prohibited only 'discussions having a tendency to create alarm or suspicion among the native population, of any intended interference with their religious opinions or observances'. Their concern was with British zealots stirring up trouble, not with strife between the natives. That remained an important motive after 1833, when the government lifted restrictions on European immigration into India – it was a recurrent theme in John Stuart Mill's early dispatches on behalf of the company.

Indians themselves ridiculed the idea that they needed any kind of special protection against 'irritating and insulting remarks'. For twenty-five years, English missionaries had been doing their utmost to discredit the local religions, Rammohun Roy and his fellow Calcuttans pointed out in 1823, preaching and publishing attacks on them in all the native languages. Yet

> no alarm whatever prevails, because [Indians] possess the power of defending their Religion by the same means ... many of them have exercised the freedom of the Press to combat the writings of English missionaries, and think no other protection necessary.

Indians were no different from enlightened Europeans in their attitude to religious toleration and expression, Roy urged: they, too, were convinced 'that true religion needs not the aid of the sword or of legal penalties for its protection'. This argument cleverly threw back at the British all their own most treasured arguments for religious toleration and press freedom. But it was also grounded in experience. Hindus, Muslims and people of intermediate and other faiths had after all lived alongside each other across India for centuries. As Leicester Stanhope observed, the principles of religious liberty had a far longer tradition in India than in England itself.

What's more, it was not just anglophile reformers like Roy who were early adopters of print. Many of his conservative Hindu critics, too, embraced it. To the publicity that Roy's vernacular newspapers gave his heterodox, and in their view abhorrent, religious views, they responded not with violence, or claims of unbearable insult, but by starting up their own weekly publications. 'To assert that discussion on religious topics will excite religious rancour among the natives of Indostan, is to be unmindful of their history' and their present outlook, Stanhope urged, having spent almost a decade living among them. 'They are a tolerant people, and exceedingly fond of discussion, especially on religious subjects.'

By the 1830s, however, such facts were increasingly being swept aside by British prejudices about the inherent inferiority and unreasonableness of Indian attitudes – as is epitomized not least by the massive popularity among English policymakers of James Mill's *History of British India*. The young Tom Macaulay was among those in England who were deeply influenced by that work, and by similar accounts of Indian cultural depravity. Born in 1800, he was an intellectual prodigy who grew up surrounded by leading Company figures – many of them zealous evangelists who viewed the Christianizing of India, and the suppression of its depraved heathen customs, as Britain's divine national mission. In London in 1831, as he was beginning to be involved in high-level policymaking about India, Macaulay tried to meet with the visiting Rammohun Roy, who seemed to be 'a very remarkable man'. But the more he read about the country, and the higher he climbed in its administration, the less he esteemed its backward culture and false religions. Ruling over Black and brown people in distant colonies was exhausting, the youthful MP and government minister complained in the spring of 1833, as he was drafting a groundbreaking new law on the governance of India, and others (including his father, the leading abolitionist Zachary Macaulay) were promoting the bill that would abolish slavery in the

West Indies. 'I am plagued out of my life between the Mogul and the Methodists, Ram[m]ohun Roy and the Antislavery Agency Society,' he wrote to his younger sister:

> The Niggers in one hemisphere
> The Brahmins in the other
> Disturb my dinner and my sleep
> With 'An't I a man and a brother?'

A few weeks later, in a major speech in parliament, he laid out his vision of India and its government. It was a country of stupendous wealth, the richest in the world, and a huge future market for British trade. Yet it was also 'a decomposed society', a politically 'unclean', unreadable place, where European rules about freedom and historical progress did not apply – 'the light of political science and of history are withdrawn: we are walking in darkness: we do not distinctly see whither we are going'. The British must therefore proceed very cautiously. Their 'enlightened and paternal despotism' was beginning to improve the country, much as the Romans had brought civilization to their subjugated peoples – yet it was obvious that Indians ('differing from them physically, differing from them morally') could not be trusted with European political rights and freedoms. Perhaps 'in some future age' they could be, or would even 'demand European institutions'. But for now, even though 'the higher classes of the natives' were improving mentally, 'the superiority of the European race' remained obvious – they were 'a people far advanced beyond [Indians] in intellectual cultivation'.

The following year, with James Mill's support, Macaulay was appointed to the newly created Supreme Council of India. He welcomed the challenge of 'legislating for a conquered race, to whom the blessings of our constitution cannot as yet be safely extended', and eagerly eyed the large salary, which would set him up for life. Yet his four years on the subcontinent did nothing to change his view of the 'absolutely immeasurable' chasm between the intrinsically superior, 'sound and useful knowledge' of Europeans, and the wholesale 'error' and 'falsehood' of past and present Indian erudition. Though he never bothered to learn their languages for himself, he therefore advised the Indian government in 1835 that 'a single shelf of a good

European library was worth the whole native literature of India and Arabia' – 'there are no books on any subject which deserve to be compared to our own.' When, around this time, he also pushed his colleagues to advance 'freedom of the press' in India, he completely ignored indigenous reading, writing and printing, and conceived of such liberty as applying only to the few hundred white settlers. The mind of 'the Bengalee', he later wrote, was 'weak even to helplessness'. The same derisive attitude towards Indians and their essentially alien mental outlook permeated the law code upon which he began work shortly afterwards.

COLONIAL PRACTICES

On completion of his draft code in 1837, Macaulay left India, never to return. For years, successive administrations variously ignored or tinkered with his text. Then, in the aftermath of the great rebellion of 1857, as the panicked British government took over control of the subcontinent from the East India Company, and the British frantically sought to bolster their self-image as just governors, ruling under equitable laws, the penal code was in 1860 finally put into statute. When Macaulay's proposal had first been circulated among local lawyers and judges, its prohibition of speech 'wounding the religious feelings of any person' had come in for particular criticism. But in the end, this clause survived unaltered (as section 298 of the new code), as did the essential form of his laws against verbal defamation (section 499) and 'disaffection to the government' (section 124A).

In the late 1830s, the experienced Madras judge John Fryer Thomas had warned that simply criminalizing any 'gesture or sound ... offensive to the religious feelings or prejudices of another' would be 'a dangerous novelty liable to extensive abuse': if it were enacted, there would be 'no limit to criminal prosecutions'. Not only was it an unjustifiable restriction on the honest and natural expression of opinion, it was bound to be seized upon as a new weapon by religious groups who already 'had ready recourse to the Courts of Law as a means of mutual annoyance'. Instead of pacifying sectarian hatreds, criminalizing religious offence would therefore worsen matters: 'if the Criminal Courts are to be at all times open to the zealots of different sects, on every trifling occasion, the result must be to foster bigotry, and to keep the religious animosity of sects at its height.' That is exactly what happened.

The British liked to think of their law and judges as rational, neutral arbiters above the fray, keeping the peace among their excitable, irrational Indian subjects – imposing order in place of strife. But in reality, the enactment and jurisdiction of their penal code itself created more religious conflict than it resolved. Because the new law presumed and rewarded the demonstration of religious emotionality, Indians increasingly internalized the notion that their religious feelings were fragile and easily hurt – and that they could co-opt the power of the state to punish those who inflicted such injury.

In particular, together with other later nineteenth-century British policies that grouped Indians into fixed religious categories, and played them off against each other, the code's new laws against religious insult helped to sharpen Hindu–Muslim divisions. In the 1830s, these had not loomed large. Judge Thomas noticed no such antagonism, only the prevalence of insults between the different sects within each religion: Sunni Muslims agitating versus Shias; Hindu adherents of Shiva abusing those of Vishnu; Vishnu-ites in turn split between opposed Vadakalai and Tenkalai denominations. But Macaulay, with characteristic obtuseness, conceived only of conflict between 'Hindoos' and 'Mahomedans', and by the end of the century this seems to have become the main way in which the law was actually deployed. It was, as Macaulay's successor James Fitzjames Stephen complained (though only after he, too, had returned to England), a really terrible statute: completely unjustified, wide open to abuse, 'and which might lead to horrible cruelty and persecution if the government of the country ever got into Hindoo or Mohammedan hands'.

Over time, however, its provisions were only expanded. From 1898 onwards, it became a crime not just to insult the religious feelings of any person, but also to attempt 'to promote feelings of enmity or hatred between different classes' of people (section 153A). In 1927, after a series of written denunciations of the prophet Mohammed by Hindus raised fresh questions about the exact scope of the law, an additional new clause sweepingly criminalized any deliberate attempt 'to insult the religion or the religious beliefs' of 'any class of citizens of India' (section 295A). Not only individuals, but entire religious groups, were henceforth to be protected from *any* kind of offence.

The orchestrated Muslim pressure campaign that led up to the enactment of the latter law epitomized the way in which, by this time, the battle over legal procedures and powers to punish 'insult' had become a powerful source of collective identity for the faithful of different sects and religions. But against this increasing trend towards weaponizing the laws against religious insult, and of the ham-fisted British propensity to see their further expansion as the best route towards maintaining colonial control, we can set the evidence of Indian leaders who took a different, less escalatory, view of religious speech, insult and jurisprudence.

In 1898, the British had added section 153A to the penal code because, the law member of the day explained at a meeting of the Legislative Council, 'sectarian animosity' threatened not only the well-being of any affected group, but was 'very dangerous ... [because] any accidental event may cause an explosion', even 'a general attack on the European community' – to the British, their own security was always the paramount concern. Similarly, they were sharpening up sections 124A ('disaffection') and 505 (circulating rumours likely to cause unrest – henceforth punishable if likely to incite communal enmity, even if true), because 'language may be tolerated in England which it is unsafe to tolerate in India, because in India it is apt to be transformed into action instead of passing off as harmless gas'. Indians were dangerously prone to violence, he asserted, and spoken disloyalty was 'even more dangerous than written sedition, because it operates more directly on the ignorant, and therefore the dangerous, classes'. All of his British colleagues agreed that these were necessary safeguards, faced with 'over 250 millions of Asiatics, mostly ignorant and credulous', and a 'vernacular press ... pouring forth a continual stream of calumny and abuse of the British Government in India'.

Moreover, the other British councillors argued, to restrict punishment only to direct incitement to disorder, as was the law in England, or to consider the *intention* of writers or speakers, would be wholly inadequate in colonial circumstances: it was 'the *tendency* of the writings or speeches which has to be regarded, and the cumulative effect of depreciatory declamation [i.e. criticisms of British rule] on the minds of an ignorant and excitable population'. In response to a huge outpouring of public criticism of the new clauses, some British officials protested as usual that press liberty would be completely untouched ('we want simply a free press that will not transgress the law of the land'), while others grumbled that 'philosophic treatises on the liberty of the subject or on freedom of discussion' were wholly unsuited to the savage realities of India. Indian criticism of British rule was growing, year by year, the lieutenant-governor of Bengal bluntly concluded, and there were now far too many 'semi-educated' natives – therefore the laws needed to be tightened. 'No government such as ours in India can afford to allow the minds of an ignorant and credulous Oriental population to be gradually poisoned and embittered by persistent calumny of the government and all its measures.'

By this time, however, a small number of loyal, hand-picked Indian members had been added to the Legislative Council. A majority of them in 1898 staunchly condemned the proposals, as violations of free speech and offensive in their presumptions about the native population. For eight long hours, throughout the Council's final discussion, they fought a principled rearguard action: voting against the new laws, referring to their previous written statements of dissent, introducing amendment after failed amendment. The sedition clause's wording was absurdly vague, Gangadhar Rao Chitnavis of Nagpur pointed out; 'disaffection' was nowhere defined, and impossible to measure; and in any case the changes were completely unnecessary – 'the educated Indian community' rejected British assertions that their compatriots were provoked to violence simply by reading things in a newspaper. As for section 153A, Hindus and Muslims largely lived in peace alongside each other, but this new law was bound to endanger that. Any 'over-zealous police-official, Hindu or Muhammadan' might abuse it, and 'mischief-loving people will be only too ready to use the law as a weapon against their antagonists, and social hatred may thus be perpetuated and intensified instead of being quenched'.

It was shameful that the government had refused to translate its proposals into vernacular languages, warned Panapakkam Anandacharlu, a leading south Indian barrister, journalist and member of the Indian National Congress. Yet even though only its English-speaking population had been notified, every organ of Indian public opinion unequivocally opposed the new sedition law. It was also ridiculous for the government to argue that educated Indians couldn't speak for the masses: 'who else are fit and on what credentials?' The law was being promoted on 'faulty and unfounded' principles; its passage would signal contempt for 'the whole of the people in this land'. These rushed-through proposals were 'obnoxious' assaults on the freedoms of speech and press, the lawyer Bishambar Nath agreed, which would imperil 'all open and honest criticism of public measures', and cause endless trouble by criminalizing religious disagreements. The Legislative Council, dominated by British government officials, was a rubber stamp for colonial rule, noted the Bombay Muslim lawyer and leader of the Indian National Congress, Ramhimtulla Mohamed Sayani, but the unanimous opposition of the vernacular press made crystal clear what 'the general native public' thought: these new laws were poorly conceived, completely unnecessary and downright dangerous in their muzzling of ordinary political and religious speech.

Thirty years later, in the 1927 debates over the proposed new section 295A, a minority of the Indian members in the recently created Legislative Assembly denounced it along similar lines. Criminalizing insults of 'religious beliefs' would not deter 'scurrilous attacks' but only 'increase fanaticism because it creates a new offence', they warned. To punish the mere expression of 'insulting' views, rather than any personal defamation or actual breach of order, would be a wholly unwarranted measure. 'Many of the greatest patriots of this country have been sent to jail' already under the unjust provisions of sections 124A and 153A, complained the Madras lawyer and nationalist journalist A. Rangaswami Iyengar, one of the editors of *The Hindu* newspaper. Indian 'rights of legitimate criticism, of freedom of speech and writing' were already 'very severely restricted', and this would only make things worse. His allies agreed it was 'most dangerous', rushed and 'panicky legislation', which would encourage 'intolerance and bigotry'. Religious strife between Indians was not intrinsic, several speakers observed, but in fact had been largely created by the ill-advised laws and misgovernance of their 'alien' British rulers; this latest disastrous measure 'will only lead to further agitation by the followers of the various sects, by the followers of Gurus, bogus Gurus, of bogus Avatars scattered all over India'. Yet once again, though there was some compromise on its exact wording, the dissenting voices could not stop the legislation.

For decades afterwards, and with growing intensity, Indian nationalists denounced British justice as a sham – especially its laws against 'disaffection' and 'sedition'. He proudly pleaded guilty to the latter charge, the London-trained lawyer Mohandas K. Gandhi told a court in 1922, for 'to preach disaffection towards the existing system of government has become almost a passion with me'. In his paper *Young India*, he repeatedly broadcast the same contempt for section 124A and its associated statutes:

> I do not know any Indian who has actually affection for the government as it is today established. It is a rape of the word 'law' to say that it is a government established by 'law'. It is established by the naked sword, kept ready to descend upon us at the will of the arbitrary rulers in whose appointment the people have no say.

Yet by 1947, ironically enough, a century of British speech laws that repressed political criticism and criminalized insults to religion had created not just a distinctive legal regime, but a widespread acceptance of its underlying prejudices. As a result, the dawn of independence brought almost no difference to the theory or practice of press and speech freedom in India: the colonial inheritance had become too deeply embedded in the national outlook. The horrific mass violence that accompanied the rushed British withdrawal and bloody partition of the subcontinent in 1946–8 seemed only to confirm that Indians *were* particularly 'excitable' and that religiously 'hurtful' language could not be safely permitted among them.

Throughout his life, Gandhi had been accustomed to include readings from the Quran at his public prayer meetings, drawing on a long tradition of inter-religious Indian spirituality, and as part of his efforts towards ecumenical harmony in the present. During partition, this practice increasingly enraged anti-Muslim Hindu nationalists against the Mahatma; in January 1948 it provided the pretext for their assassination of him. Gandhi thought that, by making

Hindus listen to the Quran, he 'could safely trample over the feelings of the tolerant Hindu', his killer proudly explained in court. 'To belie this belief I determined to prove to Gandhiji that the Hindu too could be intolerant when his honour was insulted.'

In this climate, it is hardly surprising that India's new constitution maintained the imperial status quo. At the outset of its framing, its greatest architect, Dr B. R. Ambedkar, who as a young man had studied in the United States, proposed a simple formulation, loosely based on that country's First Amendment: 'No law shall be made abridging the freedom of speech, of the press, of association and of assembly except for consideration of public order and morality.' But it was soon agreed that the constitution should not undermine the existing penal code, so that in the end its ringing guarantee of the fundamental 'right to freedom of speech and expression' was immediately followed by the lengthy qualification that this did not affect any existing or future law relating to 'libel, slander, defamation, contempt of court or any matter which offends against decency or morality or which undermines the security of, or tends to overthrow, the State'.

Sections 124A, 153A, 295A, 298 and 505 of the penal code are still in force in India, and further laws have been added to them. Though their text has remained fixed, the shape of their interpretation has shifted considerably. During the first forty years of the nation's independence, serious efforts were made by the courts and government to use this judicial inheritance to uphold the secular character of the state, and to guarantee the protection of minorities (especially Muslims) against slander and vilification. Over the past two decades, by contrast, right-wing Hindu nationalist governments have increasingly manipulated this legal framework to persecute and silence their critics and opponents – on the one hand deploying it against any perceived 'defamation' of Hindu sensibilities or officials, on the other hand ignoring (indeed, encouraging) virulent hate speech and violence against Muslim and other purportedly 'disloyal' citizens. In Pakistan and Bangladesh, too, in various often murderous ways, imperial laws and modes of thinking about speech, sedition and religious insult have become more and more deeply and destructively entrenched since independence, leading to countless cases of judicial and extra-judicial persecution, violence and killing.

SPEECH, IDENTITY AND HARM

This was the first tragedy of the Indian penal code's prejudices about excitable natives and their inability to tolerate hurt feelings: it created a pernicious set of speech laws and presumptions that has persisted across the subcontinent ever since. Its approach also spread further afield. The governors of the Dutch East Indies, for example, were strongly influenced by British policies in India. In 1914, to suppress nationalist agitation in their own colony, the Dutch imported sections 124A and 153A of the Indian penal code into its laws. Meanwhile, the British themselves imposed versions of the code (including its provisions against religious hurt) on many of their other Asian and African territories – including Burma, Ceylon (now Sri Lanka), the Straits Settlements (now Malaysia and Singapore), Zanzibar, East Africa (now Kenya), Tanganyika (now Tanzania), Uganda and Somaliland. In some of those places this framework was later abandoned; in others (such as Sri Lanka, Malaysia, Singapore, Kenya, Uganda, Tanzania and Indonesia) it took root and remains part of postcolonial practice.

The second tragedy was that other paradigms, which did not treat colonial subjects as essentially alien in character, were readily available. In 1870, the Colonial Office in London commissioned a talented young left-wing barrister, Robert Wright, to produce a model criminal code for all of Britain's imperial territories. His text, which James Fitzjames Stephen helped finalize on his return from India, took a completely different approach to the freedom of speech and print, essentially based on existing English law. Apart from insulting the Queen herself, the only form of prohibited expression was to publish a 'libel' – that is, a text or image that intentionally defamed a person, or that encouraged the unlawful overthrow of the government or the commission of a crime. Nothing was criminal if true and published for public benefit, or written in good faith, or expressed 'solely by gestures, spoken words, or other sounds'; nor were there any provisions against religious insult or anything like that.

The penal code for England that Stephen himself tried but failed to get through parliament in 1878 retained a wider definition of sedition, as including spoken words as well as writing intended to produce 'discontent or disaffection', or 'feelings of ill will and hostility between different classes'. It also punished the publication of a written 'blasphemous libel'. But otherwise it, too, left free the expressing of 'any opinion whatever upon any religious subject', as well as taking the same approach as Wright to personal defamation. A revised version of this code, produced in 1879, was subsequently adopted by many British colonies, including in Africa, Canada, New Zealand and Australia. As scholars of these various texts have established, the acceptance of one or other set of laws was invariably the product of personal prejudices, contingent circumstances, political shifts and other unpredictable factors – so that even though the substance and effects of each code were very different, it was fairly random which one ended up shaping the lives of particular colonial subjects and their postcolonial descendants.

The Indian model of criminalizing injured religious feelings is bad for many reasons. It originated in faulty early nineteenth-century British prejudices about irrational 'native' sensibilities and antagonisms. It allows subjective personal sentiments to hijack state power and drive criminal prosecutions. It grants a special, untouchable status to religious myths and beliefs. And, as we have seen, for all these reasons it is also wide open to abuse: it incentivizes the display of wounded emotions, can be easily deployed against political and religious opponents, and tends to aggravate rather than pacify sectarian antagonisms. Laws are not just neutral mechanisms for preserving order, or outgrowths of existing social norms: they also help to shape those norms, and their formulation and execution affect people's actions and presumptions.

Yet for the same reason it would be wrong to dismiss completely the utility of policing insults against 'classes' of people. After all, it's been obvious throughout history that the unchecked spread of hateful speech about racial, ethnic, religious or other groups can cause serious harm. A deep consciousness of that fact was one reason why early European theorists of religious toleration in the sixteenth and seventeenth centuries were so concerned to uphold 'civility' of speech and so acutely sensitive to the dangers of religious insult. They knew what horrible bloodshed could ensue when minority groups were allowed to be demonized and dehumanized. There are likewise plenty of examples in our own time of horrific violence prepared and fomented by the unimpeded dispersal of group hatred, whether by antisemites, Islamophobes or white supremacists in notionally Christian nations, or against Muslims, Rohingya or Tutsis, in India, Myanmar or Rwanda. Hateful speech about minorities encourages discrimination and violence towards them. But it's not enough to deprecate it on those grounds alone (let alone, as modern American jurisprudence does, to take legal action only when it spills over into such actions). The more basic, prior harm is that deliberately abusive speech damages the social reputation and standing of such groups as equal members of the community – in the same way that the reputation of individuals is harmed by defamation and lies. To argue about racial differences or religious truth or gay marriage is not hate speech; to deliberately abuse people in a way that proclaims their collective inferiority is a different matter.

This is the traditional western approach to what is traditionally called 'group libel'. It's different from the Indian model because it's not based on an injury to personal feelings, but on the principle of equal treatment and protection under the law. Similarly, it targets not fleeting speech but only deliberately insulting published words and images, according to the seriousness of their reach and effect. Group libel degrades people's individual and collective dignity: it attacks them as contemptible, unequal citizens, or as lesser, even subhuman, beings. That, in turn, harms the public good, because it undermines the very basis of the democratic political order. Laws against hateful speech therefore uphold the principle of equal status. In other words, they are political statements. Their primary value is symbolic, rather than practical, for it's obvious that their formulation and application must involve many difficult and essentially contextual judgements – the boundary between immutable 'identity' and mutable 'beliefs', questions of intent and effect, the character of 'truth', 'honest belief', 'fair comment', and so on. Yet even if their wording is never watertight, or their application difficult and infrequent, or those prosecuted portray themselves as martyrs to free speech, the existence of such laws asserts the polity's collective view that it is unacceptable for its vulnerable minorities to be publicly bullied and denigrated. (Which particular identities require such legal protection is likewise a political judgement that differs by culture – though nowadays it invariably includes minority racial and ethnic identities, which in modern western democracies are held to be the most immutable, the most likely to be demeaned, and therefore the most in need of the state's assurances of equality.)

In English law, as in that of most other western countries, these principles emerged fairly haphazardly in the nineteenth and twentieth centuries out of the jurisprudence of religious toleration, personal libel and public order. Their precise shape differed according to the priorities of the local political elite. Often, as in Stephen's imperial law codes of the 1870s, the prohibition against insulting 'different classes' of the population sat alongside continued special protections for the status of Christianity. In England and America, the legal prohibition of blasphemy likewise only covered insults to the Christian faith; in some Southern US states, for similar reasons, public schools and universities were prohibited from teaching the theory of evolution. In Germany, on the other hand, under the penal code of 1871, all religious communities were protected against 'public insults', and regular attempts were made to punish antisemitic writings until the Nazi seizure of power in 1933. In France, too, group defamation was criminalized, by a press law of 1881.

From the 1930s onwards, the global political climate gave fresh impetus to laws against group libel (as well as statutes proscribing the expression of anti-democratic political ideologies). The rise of fascism and organized antisemitism, a growing awareness that democracy was easily undermined by hate-mongering propaganda, the profound trauma of the Holocaust, and an increasing abhorrence of racial discrimination – between the 1930s and 1970s, all these sharpened the desire to defend the fabric of democratic citizenship against the poison of unchecked ethnic slanders. As soon as the Nazis took power, the British and South African governors of the formerly German colony of South West Africa brought in a law prohibiting the encouragement of 'hostility between the different races of the community'; in 1939 this was used to punish the anti-British Afrikaner nationalist Manie Maritz for his viciously antisemitic writings. Similar laws were passed in South America. In England itself, at the height of anti-Jewish violence and polemic, the fanatical antisemite and Nazi sympathizer Arnold Leese, whose writings and journal, *The Fascist*, spread endless conspiracy theories about Jewish bloodlust and world domination, was in 1936 put on trial, together with his printer, for anti-Jewish libel 'with intent to create ill-will ... [and] promote feelings of hostility' towards Jews – despite Leese's protests that this was an 'attack on free speech' and that 'the maintenance of free speech demands that Jewish ritual murder shall be a subject for open discussion'. A jury convicted the two men of 'public mischief' for 'libellous statements concerning people of the Jewish faith ... to the endangerment of peaceful relations' between Jews and non-Jews.

This prosecution was brought under English common-law provisions against seditious libel and public disorder, whose exact scope had never been precisely defined. Even at the highest levels of the legal system, that left in dispute exactly what the threshold should be for prosecuting antisemitic or otherwise abusive speech against any group. Should it be the incitement of actual disorder, or the intention of producing such disorder, or simply the 'tendency' of the utterance to stir up trouble? But there was no great appetite for clarifying this question, because such prosecutions could only be brought by the government, not as civil actions – and to those in power the common law's indeterminate scope was only an advantage.

From the 1930s up until the early 1960s, the position of successive Conservative governments thus remained that no new laws were necessary to deal specifically with group libel. That 'would be biting into freedom of speech', Britain's Home Secretary in 1963–4 explained to his fellow MPs: 'a form of political censorship'. For defenders of the status quo, the underlying model remained that of rambunctious debate at a public political meeting. In discussing contentious issues, it presumed, verbal excess and offence were inevitable – rather than penalizing words, the emphasis should therefore be on whether they caused a breach of the peace. As an official parliamentary report of 1948 concluded, 'Group Defamation' could not be criminalized without 'curtailing free and frank – albeit hot and hasty – political discussion and criticism'.

Yet in the course of these decades others gradually came to the opposite view. Around the time of Leese's prosecution, a coalition of left-wing MPs tried to outlaw propaganda 'calculated to incite racial or religious prejudice whereby a breach of the peace is likely to be occasioned', while a new self-defence organization, the Jewish People's

Council Against Fascism and Anti-Semitism, proposed the prohibition of 'words calculated to bring any racial community into public hatred or contempt'. In 1946, Sir Oscar Dowson, the government's chief legal adviser (and, a few years later, a leading author of the European Convention on Human Rights), pointed out that hate speech could be socially harmful even without any immediate breach of the peace. In an age of mass media and propaganda, he noted,

> the fact that there is no violence or disorder does not mean that no disturbance to the State can result from the persistent persecution of a particular class of quiet and law-abiding citizens by a campaign of outrageous allegations. Such publications, if repeated over and over again, have (as in the case of advertisements) some effect on the minds of even perfectly rational people and this produces . . . the exciting of ill-will between one class and another.

By this point, the British Communist Party, the National Council for Civil Liberties (founded in 1934) and the Board of Deputies of British Jews had all come to support legislation against group libel.

In the 1950s and 1960s, as the rising numbers of Caribbean and other imperial immigrants to Britain were met with racist hostility, anti-racist activists took up the same cause. Among them were several Labour Party politicians whose outlook was informed by their personal experience of the antifascist struggles of the 1930s and 1940s, and the connection between fascism, antisemitism and the horrors of the Holocaust. 'In the light of what has happened since the early 1930s,' a senior MP argued in 1963, it was untenable to allow freedom of speech for essentially anti-democratic purposes, or to pretend that 'uttering words of race hatred' had no 'insidious influence' on public discourse and the fabric of society. In this case, breach of the peace was the wrong standard. After the Labour Party was elected in 1964, a clause prohibiting the deliberate public incitement of hatred 'on grounds of colour, race, or ethnic or national origins' was included in the new government's flagship Race Relations Act of 1965. Its purpose was, as one supporter put it, 'to prevent arising in this country in relation to the coloured immigrants the kind of situation which arose in relation to the Jews in this country in 1935 and 1936'. On comparable grounds, similar statutes were enacted across post-war western Europe, and in other democracies like Canada and New Zealand, and remain in force today. As the current Danish law expresses it, no one may publish statements 'by which a group of people are threatened, derided, or degraded because of their race, colour of skin, national or ethnic background, faith, or sexual orientation'. That is not what the right of free speech is for.

LIBEL AND POLITICS

For many decades, the United States was in the vanguard of such attempts to combat group libel, and to define it as beyond the bounds of free speech. Of course, as the Nazis themselves had admiringly observed, racist and white supremacist ideologies were deeply embedded in American life and laws, including those relating to speech. In the spring of 1920, the all-white legislators of Mississippi went so far as to criminalize the printing, publishing or circulation of 'arguments or suggestions in favor of social equality, or of intermarriage, between whites and negroes'. By this point, Americans were also in general much less prone than Europeans to seek legal redress for personal libel. Nonetheless, in some parts of the country around this time, the libel laws were interpreted to encompass religious and other groups, as well as individuals, and some new statutes against 'engendering race or class hatred' were also successfully formulated. One major reason for this was the activism of Jewish and African-American groups and their supporters. Prominent among them was the so-called Anti-Defamation League, founded in 1913 amid a frenzy of antisemitic publicity, following the framing for child murder of a Jewish citizen of Georgia, Leo Frank, who was later lynched by a mob. The league's purpose was to combat, 'if necessary by appeals to law, the defamation of the Jewish people'. In the 1920s it agitated for group libel laws, and persuaded several large cities to create ordinances against Henry Ford's antisemitic newspaper, the *Dearborn Independent*.

Meanwhile, in June 1917 in Illinois, where hundreds of Black workers had recently been murdered by white mobs, the state legislature passed a statute, introduced by Robert R. Jackson, one of its two Black members, forbidding the publication of materials denigrating or inciting contempt for 'a class of citizens of any race, color, creed or religion'.

They were particularly concerned to combat the poison of white supremacist propaganda, such as D. W. Griffith's recent film, *The Birth of a Nation* (1915), which celebrated the Ku Klux Klan and its lynch mobs. On the same day, they therefore also banned the manufacture, sale and exhibition of postcards, films and other visual representations of the 'hanging, lynching or burning of any human being'. That *The Birth of a Nation* set out 'deliberately to slander and vilify a race', as the pioneering sociologist and civil rights activist W. E. B. Du Bois put it, spurred popular and official measures against it in other places, too. A few years later, the spread of fascism provoked a further flurry of action: between the 1930s and 1950s, American experimentation with group libel laws paralleled that of other western democracies. Promoting hatred of 'any group ... by reason of race, religion, or manner of worship' was outlawed in New Jersey in 1935; similar laws were passed in Massachusetts (1943), West Virginia (1943), Indiana (1947), Connecticut (1949) and Minnesota (1963), and proposed in many other places, including New York, Michigan, Ohio, Rhode Island and, as national statutes, in Congress. Some remain in force today, including the state laws of Massachusetts, West Virginia, Connecticut and Minnesota.

As in other countries, these efforts have always been controversial. Between the 1910s and 1950s there were many alternative views about the proper use of the criminal law, the scope of the First Amendment, and the best ways of combating group hate. The Anti-Defamation League and its counterparts eventually changed their minds over the wisdom of group libel laws, and several of them were eventually struck down by the courts. But many others still stood when, in 1951, the Supreme Court took up the matter. The previous year in Chicago, where Black families moving into formerly all-white neighbourhoods were being subjected to a terrorist campaign of firebombing and mob riot, a leading white supremacist, Joseph Beauharnais, had been convicted under the 1917 state law, after a young Black clerk and member of the American Civil Liberties Union, Clifford McFarland, filed a complaint about one of his racist pamphlets. Beauharnais appealed, arguing that his rights to free expression were being infringed. 'This is a white man's country, and in order to keep it that way, we must fight. If we can't fight, we will have a totalitarian government, like

Russia,' his lawyer explained. The leadership of the ACLU, which had already assisted New Jersey's Nazis in overturning that state's group libel law, and helped an antisemitic Chicago preacher to win a recent free-speech case before the Supreme Court, now likewise supported Beauharnais's argument for protection under the First Amendment.

Two members of the Supreme Court agreed with this claim. To Justice Hugo Black of Alabama, a former Klan member himself, the conviction was a straightforward infringement of the First Amendment, and an affront to 'the Founders' who had composed it: no governmental institution ever had the right 'to decide what public issues Americans can discuss ... that is the individual's choice, not the state's'. Neither local nor national laws could ever 'punish people for having their say in matters of public concern', or make 'opinions punishable as crimes'. What's more, only individuals could be libelled, not 'huge groups': 'group libel' was but a new-fangled euphemism for 'expansive state censorship'. To make this argument, strikingly, Black's dissent never acknowledged the violent tone or context of Beauharnais's writings (though it did reproduce his leaflet as an appendix). If such language could be criminalized, Black grumbled, then surely segregationist states might equally jail people simply 'for advocating equality and nonsegregation': this was just a battle of ideas. In his judgement, the defendant had merely been 'expressing strong views', 'peacefully petitioning' on 'questions of wide public interest and importance'. His language was 'mild'; there was little or no danger 'in such public discussions'. In place of denigration, contempt or harm, Black saw only subjective judgements about what some person 'may find unduly offensive to any race, color, creed, or religion', and warned that 'it is now very dangerous indeed to say something critical of one of the groups'. Justice William Douglas, too, agreed that it was normal for political debate to provoke 'unseemly language' and 'intemperate speech'; that the First Amendment was absolute; and that if Beauharnais was punished today, then 'tomorrow a Negro will be hailed before a court for denouncing lynch law in heated terms'.

Yet all seven of the other justices took the opposite view. Robert H. Jackson had not long ago presided over the Nazi war crimes tribunal at Nuremberg, and in 1949 vociferously dissented from his Supreme Court colleagues' permissive stance towards the Chicago antisemite who had whipped up a mass audience against the supposed global conspiracy of bloodthirsty communist Jews who were out to murder Christians and destroy America. Now, though dissenting from the majority on procedural grounds, he agreed that Beauharnais had produced a 'reckless and vicious libel', and that, though the federal government could not, individual states had a perfect right to establish laws against group libel, in order to 'place decent bounds' on racial and sectarian disparagement. 'Abuses of our freedoms of expression', he warned, could harm minorities and tear apart societies, as recent history had proved: laws against such things were difficult to formulate, and might not work, but they were entirely constitutional. Justice Stanley Reed likewise agreed on 'the constitutional power of a state to pass group libel laws to protect the public peace'.

In their majority opinion, the five remaining justices stressed that libels and 'personal abuse' were not 'opinion' or protected political speech; that states had the power to penalize group defamation when it affected the 'peace and well-being' of the community; and that both 'the tragic experience of the last three decades' and the longer history of white supremacist violence in Illinois amply proved 'that the wilful purveyors of falsehood concerning racial and religious groups promote strife and tend powerfully to obstruct the manifold adjustments required for free, ordered life in a metropolitan, polyglot community'. Whether laws against group libel could combat 'the systematic avalanche of falsehoods' was an open question; but legislators could certainly try.*

Though this judgment has never been overruled, most observers now believe it to be obsolete, for it has come to be inconsistent with many subsequently established shibboleths of American First Amendment jurisprudence. Neither the federal nor local governments, we are now told, may ever restrict *any* 'viewpoint', however virulently

---

* A decade earlier, in a 1942 ruling which still stands, the Supreme Court also unanimously affirmed the basic doctrine that 'libelous' and 'insulting' words, 'which by their very utterance inflict injury or tend to incite an immediate breach of the peace' were not protected by the First Amendment – because 'such utterances are no essential part of any exposition of ideas, and are of such slight social value as a step to truth that any benefit that may be derived from them is clearly outweighed by the social interest in order and morality'.

expressed. Nowadays, it's all mere 'opinion'. By and large, as a consequence, twenty-first-century Americans have become as inured to the extraordinary levels of lying and slander in their public discourse as they have to the equally staggering incidence of mass murder by guns in their schools and streets, and for the same reason – the acceptance of a relatively recent and novel set of presumptions about the meaning and importance of constitutional clauses drawn up two hundred and fifty years ago.

America is now the only country in the world where even local ordinances against 'hate speech' are treated as presumptively unconstitutional. It would be one thing to give up on the possibility of legal action against group defamation for practical reasons – in acknowledgement that such discourse is simply too widespread and deeply rooted in American life to be amenable to legislative change. Yet instead this exceptionalism is usually celebrated as being a matter of principle, and held up as an example for other cultures to emulate. It is true that even non-Americans are inclined to agree that group libel laws are clumsy mechanisms – difficult to enforce, unlikely to eradicate racism and bigotry, and potentially counterproductive in their enforcement. But it is not true that, as is also sometimes argued, their effect of driving harmful abuse underground, and causing it to be circulated more furtively, is a drawback: on the contrary, that is the central purpose of such laws. For in this case, sunlight and exposure are not disinfectants but rather the opposite: especially in the era of social media, the oxygen of publicity tends to boost the circulation and normalization of hatred and bigotry.

What's more, the idea that the government must remain 'neutral' towards group libel because ultimately even racist abuse is a form of political expression, and to curb it would infringe the rights of the speaker, is hardly conclusive. For what does it mean for a society to permit such abuse, let alone to view it as 'protected speech'? It signifies that the views expressed have more value than the harm that they perpetrate. That is not, in fact, a neutral position. Of course, racist and hateful speech is harmful, those who take this stance invariably concede, but 'we' just have to tolerate that, because laws curbing expression would be more damaging to our society. Or, they object, it's not the hateful views themselves that are accorded greater value – only the principle that they should be allowed to be expressed. That, too, seems, at best, a hypocritical distinction to make. We're back at that most basic question of all – what is free speech *for*?

As in 1952, when the Beauharnais case was decided, reasonable people can still disagree on whether criminalizing group libel is a good idea, and on the difficulties of implementing such laws: it's a hard social and legal problem. But the fact that the dominant legal tendency in the United States is now no longer to grapple with the difficulty, but simply to dismiss it as irrelevant, has had a further, more problematic, cultural consequence. Over the past several decades this dismissive, laissez-faire presumption has inevitably come to dominate the outlook of American citizens, and thence the leaders of the American corporations whose decisions, in practice, now most consequentially determine the tone and content of most of our national and global public discourse – publishers, broadcasters, media companies, internet service providers, YouTube, X, Facebook, and the rest. How these private conglomerates handle hate speech ultimately determines most powerfully of all how far it is amplified or restricted everywhere – yet because American law no longer bothers to consider such matters, our overlords of communication too feel increasingly free to ignore, downplay and generally botch their own treatment of it. After all, their ultimate concern is with profit and market share, not with the public interest. So how did Americans, and thus all of us, end up in this peculiar situation? That is one of the central questions we shall pursue in the final chapter of this book.

10

The Marketplace of Ideas

Our modern western theories of speech and press freedom, especially in the United States, focus largely on limiting governmental power over expression. That is partly because they were originally created in reaction to such control. Over time, especially in the anglophone world after 1800, the notion that freedom was intrinsically good, and 'censorship' always bad, also took on a certain logical momentum of its own. Once you accept the negative definition of liberty that John Stuart Mill so influentially championed (that it consists in the state and community leaving individuals to act as they please), rolling back constraints on expression becomes a positively virtuous pursuit, a mark of civilizational progress.

Yet, as we have seen, arguments about free speech also developed their anti-governmental shape for more banal reasons. The loudest and most innovative claims for press liberty have often come from venal journalists, attention-seeking printers, profiteering media owners, ambitious lawyers and self-interested corporations – in other words, from people using the rhetoric of rights and liberties to benefit themselves, under the guise of advancing the public good.

For all these reasons, it might seem perverse to talk of Marxist ideals of free speech. For surely totalitarianism is antithetical to individual freedom of utterance? What strikes us most forcibly about places like the Soviet Union and modern China is precisely the omnipresence of governmental censorship, the sinister echoes of Orwell's Big Brother. Those are cultures, we tend to agree, *without* liberty of expression – dystopian societies that confirm our own prejudices about the dangers of state regulation and forced intellectual conformity.

So it's curious to find that, in fact, the foundational documents of such countries, too, purport to value free speech. Both 'freedom of speech' and 'freedom of the press' have been guaranteed to citizens of the Soviet Union, Cuba, China, North Korea and every other communist nation that has ever existed. Partly, of course, these are but empty rhetorical gestures. Their inclusion (like the equally ubiquitous constitutional guarantee of freedom of religion) must to some degree be an attempt to ward off outside accusations that these governments don't actually protect their citizens' rights. That itself is significant – for more than a century now, it seems, press and speech freedoms have established themselves as such powerful global ideals that every nation has had to endorse them publicly. But there's more to it than that.

For, as the detailed text of their laws and constitutions makes clear, these societies define press and speech liberty in significantly different ways than western nations do. The communist approach to free speech has its own lengthy history, which is closely intertwined with that of liberal democracies. Marx himself was an accomplished journalist, as was Lenin. Partly because of their own experience as propagandists and publishers, socialists and communists from the nineteenth century onwards produced the most penetrating critiques of western liberal theories of print liberty. Exploring these helps us understand how and why they came up with their own conceptions and practices – and highlights, as well, the most serious and continuing blind spots in our own ideology.

The anti-capitalist challenge also had a direct impact on western free-speech principles. For over a century now, it has been especially influential on the changing shape of American First Amendment law. To understand how this came about, we'll need to start by tracing how, after 1700, speech, previously the most important medium of communication, gradually came to be regarded as less potent than print – which in turn had far-reaching consequences for attitudes to the press.

By the early nineteenth century, as a result, two things were becoming abundantly clear to intelligent observers across the western world. First, that the explosion and increasing deregulation of print had created an unprecedented new media landscape. But secondly, that this was a deeply rigged, mercenary marketplace, in which private money and capitalist prejudices, not just governmental power, determined whose voices were heard, and whose were not. These twin problems, so pressing in our own age of communications revolutions and the billionaire ownership of media platforms, and so commonly regarded as unprecedented, are in fact not new at all.

THE IMPACT OF NEW MEDIA

The history of free speech is also the history of new media. As in the present, so in the past: ideas about freedom of expression have always been stimulated by revolutions in communication. Milton's early arguments for press liberty were provoked by such a moment – because of the collapse of censorship, more works were published in England during the 1640s and 1650s than had been produced in the whole of the previous century, since the invention of printing. After 1700, the permanent abandonment of licensing produced an even more dramatic and lasting explosion in the number of printing presses, books and pamphlets, in new forms of distribution (circulating libraries, book clubs, coffee houses, the expansion of the national postal network) and new genres of cheap communication, especially newsprint. This practical transformation explains why it was in the English-speaking world that 'liberty of the press' first became such a hot-button issue.

In addition, this media revolution helped provoke a remarkable shift in English attitudes towards speech. As we saw at the start of this book, from the beginning of recorded history through to the seventeenth century, spoken words had been regarded as the pre-eminent type of communication: bad speech of every kind was routinely policed and punished.

In the course of the eighteenth century, this changed. The new ubiquity and importance of printed communication seems to have had a major impact on people's attitude towards the potency of spoken words. Of course, by this point print itself had been around for centuries. But consider that the great communications revolution of our own time, which has likewise transformed the world with remarkable speed over the past few decades, also came about long after computers had first been put to use by specialists in various fields. In the eighteenth century, too, it was not the invention of a new technology, but its application on a far greater scale than ever before that was decisive, producing an unprecedented shift in how English-speaking people conceived of the relative power of spoken and printed words.

As a result, across England and its American colonies, people stopped suing each other for verbal insults. Ever since the middle ages, this had been an extremely common form of litigation; yet in the early eighteenth century, it almost completely disappeared. The same thing happened to insubordinate speech. For hundreds of years, noblemen had prosecuted their inferiors for the crime of so-called *scandalum magnatum* (that is, speaking ill of a noble). During the sixteenth and seventeenth centuries, such suits had become increasingly frequent and successful. But in the eighteenth century they pretty much vanished. There was a similar sharp decline in prosecutions for seditious words, which before 1700 had been very common. Even during the revolutionary panic of the 1790s, very few people were actually punished for spoken sedition, compared with earlier periods. Instead of treating verbal utterances as dangerous, capable of destroying personal reputations and governmental order, the English had begun to regard them as relatively innocuous.

This was not just because of the increasing power of print: it was also bound up with changing conceptions of the spoken word. Eighteenth-century observers treated speech less as a danger to interpersonal relations than as one of the great pleasures of sociable life. This attitude fitted many new, enlightened presumptions – for example, that God was essentially benign, that human beings tended naturally to virtue, and that refined intercourse between the sexes was an index of civilization. It was also advanced by new physiological, materialist understandings of the body, and how language was produced – not by the heart or the soul, but by the vocal cords.

Before 1700, anglophone moralists had devoted hundreds of pages to best-selling, frequently reprinted discussions of 'the government of the tongue', that most unruly part of the body. But in the eighteenth century this popular genre essentially died out, and was replaced by a fascination with the art of conversation – benign, friendly and sociable speech. 'Upon the Government of the Tongue', the last text published in English on the topic, appeared in 1726. Like his sixteenth- and seventeenth-century forerunners, the author, Joseph Butler, was a serious theologian, a popular writer and an influential ethicist. But his approach was essentially the opposite of his predecessors' – people were naturally good, and God had created language for their 'enjoyment'. Gone was any mention of the depravity of human nature, the wickedness of the tongue or the difficulty of restraining it. When the apostle James referred to 'bridling the tongue', Butler assured his readers, he was not referring to bad words, but merely to the fault of excessive 'talkativeness'. His concern was not the avoidance of sin, but the rules of polite conversation.

It also became increasingly common around 1700 to distinguish speech from other kinds of action. Even in defamation litigation, for example, less weight came to be placed on insulting words than on other abusive acts. Judges, legal authorities and even witnesses in such cases increasingly doubted that words themselves could cause any real harm. As Trenchard and Gordon asserted in 1721, 'speaking falsely' surely always did less 'hurt to human society and the peace of the world' than 'acting wickedly'.

This distinction helped create a new sense that written words were weightier than spoken ones. This had not been the case before – traditional presumptions about the potency of speech had been forged in a largely oral world. Before about 1600, even lawyers did not distinguish between spoken slander and written libel. In 1644, Milton's *Areopagitica* still took for granted that the verbal spread of ideas, 'from house to house' was 'more dangerous' than their publication in print. Only in the decades that followed was this presumption gradually reversed. Towards the end of the seventeenth century, English lawyers began to argue that there was an essential difference between offensive spoken words, on the one hand, and writings on the other – 'because such are public, but words are private offences'.

We can trace the same evolution in the language of legislation. Medieval and early modern statutes hadn't much differentiated between the spoken and written word. A 1275 English Act against sedition, for example, made it criminal simply 'to tell or publish any false news or tales'. The Statute of Gloucester (1378), against slander, 'false news', and so on, forbad anyone to 'speak or to tell' any falsehood. These laws don't mention script at all. The equivalent late sixteenth-century statutes were primarily concerned with speech, and only secondarily with anything written or printed. In the seventeenth century, they began to treat speech and writing as fairly equal. Thus some of James I's declarations referred only to 'pen or speech', or seditious 'speaking or writing', ignoring print, while the Treason Acts of the 1640s and 1650s applied equally to 'openly declaring', preaching, writing and printing. As late as 1686, a royal proclamation in Scotland reissued ancient prohibitions against disloyal public and private speaking of all kinds, without any mention of written or printed communications.

It's telling that this was a Scottish proclamation, not an English one. In places where writing and printing were less prevalent, or in circumstances where governors felt their authority was uncertain, as in colonial contexts, the policing of speech remained very important, as we've seen. During the United States' Revolutionary War, most of the rebellious states enacted laws criminalizing Loyalist speech, as well as writing. In 1792, likewise, the state of Virginia passed an Act against 'false news', modelled on ancient English statutes. This was an attempt to suppress the oral circulation among enslaved and free Black people of news about the revolution that had recently broken out in the nearby French slave colony of Saint-Domingue.

The laws of eighteenth-century European nations, too, sometimes evoke a world in which print remained a marginal and tightly controlled medium, and the main concern was with policing speech and script. In early eighteenth-century Russia, for example, any unauthorized verbal discussion of the tsar's person or policies could be treated as a capital offence; while in 1718 Peter the Great made it a crime for anyone to write anything 'behind locked doors'. In mid-eighteenth-century Sweden, unsanctioned discussion of sensitive subjects was forbidden even in private, manuscript writings. That was why the Swedish Ordinance of 1766 was concerned throughout with 'the freedom of writing and of the press', permission to *write* as well as print: both had been previously restricted, and both were important. Print was still far from dominant. In France the policing of spoken words also continued for much longer. A whole series of laws of the Ancien Régime and revolutionary France criminalized verbal expression; during the 1790s, as we saw in Chapter 7, thousands of men and women were imprisoned and executed for voicing 'seditious' views.

In England, by contrast, eighteenth-century laws treated printed and written words as more serious than spoken ones. Even public preaching gradually came to be regarded as categorically different from print. Already in 1710 that was evident in the trial of Henry Sacheverell, a firebrand Tory clergyman, scourge of religious toleration, and later Jacobite, the most notoriously seditious preacher of his age. It wasn't primarily his public sermons that got him into trouble, but his printing and publishing of them – the former were listened to by a few hundred men and women, but their best-selling print versions reached as many as a quarter of a million people. By the end of the century, this distinction had hardened. Apart from the tiny trickle of prosecutions for verbal sedition, law enforcement had come to be overwhelmingly concerned only with written, printed and published documents. After 1800 very few people were ever put on trial in England for speech, and juries seem to have become increasingly unlikely to convict anyone just for uttering words – even if they praised Napoleon, damned the king or wished for 'the cutting off the head of the Prince Regent'.

The language of the law confirmed this shift. In the United States, too, the Sedition Act of 1798 criminalized 'writing, printing, uttering, or publishing any false, scandalous and malicious *writing or writings* against the government'. Before 1700, 'uttering' and 'publishing' had often referred to spoken words. But now, although a few people were prosecuted for speech, the terms of the Act itself only mentioned written or printed texts. On the whole, spoken 'words vanish in air', a legal authority explained in 1801, 'but words written ... may do a lasting injury'. In Britain, likewise, the 1792 Proclamation against sedition ignored speech altogether, and was only concerned with 'writings ... printed, published, and industriously dispersed'. The Treasonous and Seditious Practices Act of 1795 did cover seditious 'writing, printing, preaching, or other speaking': but the more serious offence of 'treasonous words' could only be committed by 'printing or writing'. Later Treason and Sedition Acts, in 1817 and 1819, did not mention speech at all.

This was a momentous change. Previously it had always been presumed that the speaking of seditious words was itself a disorderly act, a breach of the peace. Yet since the early eighteenth century the potency of speech has come to be increasingly discounted, compared with other kinds of communication – whether script, print, newspaper publication, film, broadcasting or the internet. Already by the time of the Victorians it had become largely accepted that, as we still presume today, spoken words were only culpable if they provoked a separate action – an 'actual' 'breach of the peace'. By itself, it seems, speech was no longer considered capable of seriously disturbing anything.

Of course, it's possible to think of many caveats to this general trend. Throughout the eighteenth century, and beyond, there were plenty of ways and contexts in which spoken words remained powerful, potentially dangerous or subject to restraint, even in a print-saturated culture. We might think of oaths, promises, verbal commands, the word of a merchant or a gentleman, 'fighting words', and so on. From 1737, all the way to 1968, the text of all plays publicly performed in Britain had to be approved in advance by a government censor: public speech from the stage was held to be especially potent. Fresh laws against profane swearing were also passed in England in 1694 and 1746. And beyond the legal and governmental regulation of speech, private and social norms of behaviour obviously remained (and remain) very important in shaping how people speak.

Yet the overall result was nonetheless a radically new and different attitude to speech – a recognition that writing, and especially print, was a more powerful medium of expression than verbal utterance. This outlook did not devalue words compared with other actions – it stressed rather that different media of communication had a differing range, reach and potency in the world, and that rules of expression should take that into account. That is an important insight. By contrast, the more recent notion that all 'speech', irrespective of its medium, can be lumped together as essentially harmless, compared with 'actions', is a much clumsier and evidently questionable presumption.

Whatever the exact intellectual genealogy of these ideas, it was only in the nineteenth century that English-speaking people started to presume that 'sticks and stones may break my bones, but words will never harm me'. That adage was first recorded in 1862. Nowadays, it is the attitude we like to take. Our modern conception is that words, especially spoken ones, are different from physical actions, and far less potent. But that is exactly the opposite of the traditional, pre-modern view – that 'the stroke of the tongue breaketh the bones'.

PRINT, MONEY AND CLASS

The fact that print had become a far more powerful medium than script or speech was by the nineteenth century also widely acknow-ledged in discussions of press freedom. And yet it had only a minimal impact on most theories of the subject. On the one hand, the par-ticular power of the press was implicit in every practical curb and complaint of its 'licence': its critics invariably singled out this medium as a particular engine for evil. Yet on the other hand, positive argu-ments *for* free speech continued to lump together talk, script and print, sometimes noticing but never worrying about the differences between them. This outlook was epitomized by John Stuart Mill's enthusiasm for 'the press – and of late, above all, the periodical press' as the most powerful and progressive force in society. 'The real political unions of England are the newspapers,' he gushed in an essay of 1840. 'It is these which tell every person what all other persons are feeling, and in what manner they are ready to act: it is by these that the people learn, it may truly be said, their own wishes.' Despite his later pessim-ism about how public opinion in fact stifled intellectual originality, he never developed this into a critique of the media, preferring simply to praise the press, in conventional terms, as the conduit of 'public opinion . . . the supreme power' and a bulwark against governmental tyranny.

Mill cannot have been oblivious to the fact that, in reality, the marketplace of print was a cut-throat, mercenary arena. He grew up in the shadow of a father who made his fortune by writing for the public. He himself was a seasoned book reviewer and anonymous propagand-ist for the East India Company, as well as a canny, audience-aware author in his own right ('The more I think of the plan of a volume on Liberty, the more likely it seems to me that it will be read and make a sensation,' he wrote to his wife Harriet in 1855, excitedly anticipating the huge sales of *On Liberty*). But because he and other nineteenth-century liberal thinkers couched their arguments about freedom of expression mainly in terms of an opposition between collective and individual rights, the government and the people, their models tended to ignore the crucial intermediary role of the media in shaping public debate.* The result was an increasing mismatch between the theory of free speech and the realities of the commercial marketplace.

This was hardly a new problem. The commercialization of news pre-dated the printing press; and, as we saw in Chapter 3, Trenchard and Gordon's pioneering free-speech theory of the 1720s was already pro-foundly shaped by the corrupt conditions of political print. But since then, as the market for news had continued to grow, so too had its overtly commercial character. Across England and Wales in 1781, there were 76 local and national papers and periodicals; by 1851, the number of newspapers alone had increased to 561. The rate of failure remained high (250 new ventures were started up in 1832, most of which soon went under), but meanwhile the costs involved in publishing skyrock-eted. Around 1800 it was still possible to start or take over a London daily for around £1,000; by 1846 the launch of one such paper, the *Daily News*, was said to have cost £100,000. Such vastly larger sums partly reflected the expense of the increasingly industrial technolo-gies of printing, but also the soaring profits to be made from sales and advertising. In the 1780s, a popular paper might have hoped to provide annual returns of around £1,000 to its investors; in 1845, *The Times* was able to pay its shareholders a dividend of almost £30,000.

Most English papers also accepted subsidies from the government of the day, or from opposition parties – or simply adjusted their pol-itics in pursuit of profit and market share. In addition, until the mid nineteenth century, government taxes on paper and advertisements, partly intended to make newspapers too expensive for poor people, were a further way in which the world of print was strongly moulded by financial as well as political forces. The repeal of those taxes in the 1850s was, in turn, designed to rig the market so as to destroy the cheap underground newspapers of the radical working-class move-ment, which had flourished on a completely different, more egalitarian economic basis. In all these ways, despite its increasing diversity of

---

* Though it's notable that, as we saw in Chapter 8, Mill's critiques of the native Indian press did precisely centre on its domination by rich individuals and 'class interests'.

outlets, the marketplace of printed news and opinion, instead of being transparent, neutral or equally accessible to all, was dominated by hidden, money-grubbing and partisan concerns.

This was true not just in England but across all the different press regimes of the western world. By the early nineteenth century, it had therefore become commonplace for knowledgeable observers to stress not only the increasing power of print, especially the periodical press, but also its corruptible and duplicitous character. 'The corruption and baseness of the press', complained William Cobbett in 1807, made it an enemy to real freedom: the rich and the powerful controlled everything, while the poor and oppressed had 'no means whatever of appealing to the justice of the public'. In this new 'mechanical age', Thomas Carlyle wrote in 1829, newspaper editors were the new overlords, but both their motives and ends were pernicious. The misguided protagonist of his novel *Sartor Resartus* (1834–5) exults that 'Journalists are now the true Kings and Clergy'; yet the effects of their output are plainly satanic. The great French writer Honoré de Balzac projected similar arguments in his early novels of the 1830s, informed by his painful recent experiences as a printer, publisher and journalist. 'Journalism, you see, is the religion of modern society,' one of his characters explains – by which he means that its devilish practitioners have immense power, yet use it to purvey fables that they themselves don't believe. It was not just government censorship that obstructed the truth, was the moral, but the incentives of the marketplace. Print was but a commodity; its success depended on capital, not skill; newspapers routinely misled their readers for money.

This analysis was taken a step further by the writers and readers of the politically radical, 'unstamped' English press – so called because it proudly evaded the Stamp Duty on paper, as well as other attempts to suppress working-class print. These cheap popular papers, whose overall circulation rivalled that of the legal press, explicitly connected the unfreedom and venality of print to the oppression of the labouring classes. Unceasingly attacking their stamped competitors as corrupt, they called out the hypocrisy of so-called champions of the 'free press', who in fact continually manipulated the law and the marketplace 'to perpetuate the slavery and degradation of the working classes'. In their view, the legal press spoke only for 'capitalists, idlers, and plunderers' who got rich off the backs of the workers who actually produced national wealth. The printing press was the most powerful tool ever invented, 'either for good or evil', the *Poor Man's Guardian* warned in 1835 – but in England, France and the United States alike, it was now largely in the clutches of 'profit-men', rather than voices 'which support the rights of labour'. As the paper's much-persecuted publisher Henry Hetherington explained, radical journals were thus engaged in a twofold project of political justice: 'accelerating the establishment of the Liberty of the Press, and clearing the way for the not-far-distant emancipation of the working classes'. In the following decade, drawing on similar insights, a talented young European journalist would begin to rethink the conventional theory of press freedom. His name was Karl Marx.

Throughout the first half of his adult life, Marx was a busy writer for progressive papers – not just in Germany, Belgium and France, but also for British and American journals. Pretty much every continental paper he was involved with during the 1840s was heavily censored, harassed and eventually shut down by the authorities. The first major political essay he ever published was a free-spirited attack on censorship, provoked by a Prussian proclamation of December 1841. A few months later, on his twenty-fourth birthday, he began his career on the Cologne *Rheinische Zeitung* with a widely noticed series of articles on the same subject; the following year, after continual battles with the censors, he resigned its editorship in protest at their actions. At this point, before Marx had developed a systematic political philosophy of his own, his views were fairly conventional. His main arguments were that the Prussian system of prior censorship should be replaced by a modern press law, as in other countries, and that a free press embodied 'the voice of the people' (or, as he put it elsewhere, 'the fearless speech of free men') – it both 'is the product of public opinion, [and] also produces public opinion'.

In 1844, Marx moved to Paris, embraced communism, embarked on his lifelong collaboration with Friedrich Engels, and began with him to set out the theoretical framework of a new, materialist approach to history, politics and the liberation of the exploited working peoples of the world. Upon the outbreak of the 1848 revolutions across Europe, the two of them rushed back to Prussia to found a new paper in support of the cause. By now, they had developed a more sharp-edged, combative belief in the power of the press to effect change. Before its suppression and Marx's exile to London in the spring of 1849, their *Neue Rheinische Zeitung* openly advocated 'revolutionary terrorism' and 'social-republican revolution'. When Marx was prosecuted for its attacks on government officials, he defiantly replied in court that 'the first duty of the press ... is *to undermine all the foundations of the existing political system*'.

Alongside this growing belief in the revolutionary agency of print, Marx and Engels also developed a more throughgoing critique of liberal notions of press freedom. Their central concern was with the pernicious power of money. The vastly unequal distribution of wealth systematically distorted the operation of the media, overamplifying some voices while suppressing others; what's more, the pursuit of profit was incompatible with the pursuit of truth. Already in his earliest writings about censorship, in 1842, Marx had been interested in how press liberty was affected by financial constraints. '*The first freedom of the press consists in not being a trade*,' he mused; and yet, 'Of course the press is also a trade, but this is not the business of the writer, but of the printers and book dealers.' In France, he noted, newspapers were 'not subject to intellectual censorship, to be sure, but subject to a material censorship, the high security deposit [required for a licence to print]. This affects the press materially, because it pulls the press out of its true sphere into the sphere of big business speculations.'

In 1846, in an article for an English Chartist weekly, the Leeds *Northern Star*, Engels explained the causal connection between class oppression and faulty, liberal ideas of press freedom – or, as he put it, 'the difference between liberty of *money* and liberty of *man*'. The middle classes, he argued, appeared progressive in their liberal ideals – 'to recognize equality in principle, to free the press from the shackles of monarchical censorship', and so on. The problem was that

> thereby all former individual and hereditary privileges are replaced by the privilege of *money* ... which means, in short, nothing else but giving *inequality* the name of equality. Thus the liberty of the press is, of itself, a middle-class privilege, because printing requires *money*, and

buyers for the printed productions, which buyers must have money again.

This was not free speech but an inherently unfree, unfair and undemocratic state of affairs. The result, as the brilliant founder of German Social Democracy, Ferdinand Lassalle, explained in 1862, was that 'the possibility of appealing to the *thought of the people*, of enlightening and leading them, has become the privilege of the possessors of capital' – 'public opinion' was the creation of '*capital*, and . . . the privileged wealthy bourgeoisie'.

ADDRESSING MEDIA DISTORTION

In the later nineteenth and early twentieth centuries, it was not only socialists and communists who highlighted these problems. Many other leading European and American scholars took a similarly critical approach to the conventional liberal theory of press freedom. In Germany in particular, with its less libertarian intellectual and political tradition, several leading writers from the 1850s onwards pushed back against the tendency of Anglo-American and French free-speech theorists to ignore the role of the media, presume the superiority of free markets in all spheres of life, and theorize liberty of expression only as an abstract personal right. Instead, they prioritized the public interest, focused on the material conditions that shaped public opinion, and grappled with the relationship between freedom of expression and the distorting structures of the communicative marketplace.

One such thinker was the influential political scientist Karl Knies, whose many publications included a pioneering 1857 monograph, *The Telegraph as a Means of Communication, with Discussions of News Media in General*. In it, he laid out the far-reaching social and intellectual implications of the 'world-historical revolution in the means of communication' that he was living through, and compared the media landscape of his age with that of previous historical eras. Communication, Knies argued, was a basic human necessity, and modern technologies (the press, the railway, telegraphy) exponentially assisted and expanded it. Yet it was crucial to regulate these so that they benefited society as a whole, rather than only the rich and the highly literate, and for journalists to take seriously their 'heavy moral responsibility' as moulders of public information and opinion.

Like Knies, the journalist, politician and professor Albert Schäffle was a sharp critic of socialism. Yet he, too, agreed that the shape of the media landscape was largely determined by commercial pressures, and that these were essentially at odds with the public good. It was clear that modern democratic societies required a properly function-ing public sphere, and that newspapers were by far 'the most powerful means of influencing public opinion'. But at the same time, the con-temporary press was plainly corrupt and degenerate, in thrall to a variety of special interests. Above all, its ownership by large corpo-rations, banks and stockholders, and its pursuit of profits through advertising, created only a manipulated, artificial public discourse. (It also, he noted, exploited and degraded journalists themselves, turn-ing them into mere disposable, proletarian slaves of their capitalist owners.) To ameliorate these problems – and to do so without re-introducing government control over the press, or restricting freedom of expression – Schäffle proposed a variety of structural reforms: placing newspapers in the hands of publicly owned corporations; establishing co-operative printing plants open to any individual or organization; profit-sharing with the writers and journalists respon-sible for press content; the separation of advertising from newsprint. In the 1910s and 1920s, his protégé Karl Bücher and the leading soci-ologists Ferdinand Tönnies and Max Weber were among those who put forward similar analyses and proposals to address the basic prob-lem that, under a capitalist media system, 'newspapers only address the "public interest" insofar as this does not hinder their publishers' profit motives'.

All these theorists were acutely aware that they were battling against two much simpler views of the relationship between mass media and freedom of expression. In one corner, Knies explained in 1857, were the proponents of laissez-faire, especially dominant in North America, whose single guiding principle was individual liberty and the minimiz-ing of governmental intervention. This led them naïvely to presume that 'the uninhibited pursuit of private interests automatically and necessarily and always leads to the realization of the common good'.

At the other extreme were the socialists, obsessed only with achieving 'equality of life for all individuals', who therefore argued that 'state authority has to order everything and that there was no place for free private enterprise'. Knies was right that nineteenth-century socialist theories ignored individual liberty of expression. But in other respects their proposals for redressing the distortions of the commercial marketplace paralleled his own.

Like Marx, later socialists saw liberty of the press as an indispensable tool of mass agitation and working-class liberation. In the face of capitalist power and anti-socialist laws, press freedom for the labouring classes was an absolute necessity, wrote the great European socialist leader Karl Kautsky in an influential 1891 manifesto, which remained the dominant interpretation of Marxist theory until the First World War. So important was the struggle to obtain press freedom that anyone who obstructed it, even inadvertently, 'must be fought as much as the recognized opponents of the proletariat'. On the other hand, socialists also continued to grapple with the question of how to rescue the marketplace of ideas from the perverse distortions of capitalist greed. As well as publishing dozens of local and national papers, Kautsky's own German Social Democratic Party repeatedly considered plans to nationalize or 'socialize' parts of the commercial mass media, in order to create a less corrupt and fairer playing field for intellectual exchange. But in the end it was the Bolsheviks in Russia who, upon seizing power in the revolution of 1917, took the most radical steps to reconfigure the public sphere and the meaning of press freedom.

Their leader, Vladimir Ilyich Ulyanov, a prolific journalist for the underground press who went by the pen name Lenin, had spent many years pondering this critical issue. In exile at the turn of the century, and inspired by Kautsky's party and manifesto, he had published a pamphlet of his own, *What Is to Be Done?* (1902), which considered how a similar mass social-democratic workers' movement might be organized in Russia, despite his country's complete absence of political and press freedom. Even though everything had to be done clandestinely, Lenin was optimistic that a workers' uprising against autocracy was imminent: and that, even more than in western Europe, 'the revolutionary newspaper' was key to organizing it.

By the time the revolution eventually came, a decade and a half later, circumstances in Russia had changed dramatically. In the autumn of 1917, after tsarist censorship had been abolished, the Bolshevik press was engaged in fierce struggles against its political rivals in the capital, Petrograd (formerly St Petersburg). For Lenin, ending the supremacy of the deceitful bourgeois press and reshaping the media landscape for good nonetheless remained a core political aim. Press freedom as it was currently constituted, he wrote in late September, meant only 'freedom for the *rich* systematically, unremittingly, daily, in millions of copies, to deceive, corrupt, and fool the exploited and oppressed mass of the people'.

Within hours of the Bolsheviks' violent coup, on 27 October, having already shut down many rival papers, he issued a telling decree on the subject. Their actions against 'the counter-revolutionary press' had drawn accusations of hypocrisy, it began, as if 'the new socialist power had violated a fundamental principle of its programme by encroaching upon the freedom of the press'. But this was untrue, because real press liberty had never yet existed:

> what this liberal facade actually conceals is freedom for the proper-tied classes, having taken hold of the lion's share of the entire press, to poison, unhindered, the minds and obscure the consciousness of the masses. Everyone knows that the bourgeois press is one of the most powerful weapons of the bourgeoisie. Especially at the crucial moment when the new power, the power of workers and peasants, is only affirming itself, it was impossible to leave this weapon wholly in the hands of the enemy, for in such moments it is no less dangerous than bombs and machine-guns. That is why temporary extraordinary measures were taken to stem the torrent of filth and slander in which the yellow and green press would be only too glad to drown the recent victory of the people.

All printed 'insubordination', 'sedition' and 'slanderous distortion of facts' was therefore now strictly prohibited.

Once the new regime was secure, Lenin promised, the press 'will be granted complete freedom within the bounds of legal responsibility': its future press laws would be 'the broadest and most progressive' ever. But within days the Bolshevik leaders, led by Lenin and Trotsky, clarified that their suppression of bourgeois papers and seizure of their plants was in fact not just an emergency action to stamp out 'attempted counter-revolution, but was an essential transitional measure in establishing a new press regime in which public opinion will not be fabricated autocratically by the capitalists who own the newsprint and printing-presses'. There was to be no going back:

> The restoration of so-called 'freedom of the press', i.e. the return of printing presses and newsprint to the capitalists, poisoners of the people's consciousness, would be an impermissible capitulation to the will of capital, a surrender of one of the most important strong points of the workers' and peasants' revolution.

Their alternative vision of true press freedom soon took practical shape. On the same day, 4 November, they resolved that all private printing presses and paper stocks should be confiscated and turned over to public use: 'so that parties and groups can use the technical means of printing in accordance with their actual ideological power, i.e. in proportion to the number of their supporters'. Instead of the rigged capitalist marketplace of ideas, they would create a fair and equal one.

Three days later, in the same spirit, they tackled another prominent source of capitalist power and media corruption, by nationalizing the production and sale of all advertising. Early in the new year, a 'Revolutionary Press Tribunal' with far-reaching powers was set up to punish 'crimes and misconduct against the people committed through the use of the press', such as the publication of 'false or perverse information about public matters'. At the same time, to sustain the many printers now struggling to find work, as well as to educate the masses, they established a State Publishing House, whose remit was to produce large quantities of textbooks, free 'popular editions of classics', and 'great works of literature, which, according to the present decree, are made the property of the people'. In July 1918, the first constitution of the new Soviet Republic enshrined this novel definition of free speech in its basic law:

> For the purpose of securing the freedom of expression to the toiling masses, the Russian Socialist Federated Soviet Republic abolishes all dependence of the press upon capital, and turns over to the working

people and the poorest peasantry all technical and material means of publication of newspapers, pamphlets, books, etc., and guarantees their free circulation throughout the country.

This radical restructuring of the marketplace of ideas aroused huge opposition, not just from those immediately targeted but also from other revolutionary groups with whom the Bolsheviks initially shared power, such as the Mensheviks and the Left and Right Socialist Revolutionaries – and even from a significant minority of leading Bolsheviks themselves, including Nikolai Ivanovich Derbyshev, their own recently installed press commissar. Throughout November and December 1917, as the country descended into civil war, these dissenting voices denounced the press and advertising decrees, tried to get them repealed, called for the restoration of press freedom, and finally resigned their positions in protest.

Their arguments were echoed by the revered socialist writer Maxim Gorky, a long-time supporter of the Bolsheviks, whose paper *New Life* was one of the few allowed to remain in circulation, until it, too, was suppressed in the summer of 1918. Previously he had critiqued capitalist newspapers as no more than 'a tangle of venomous snakes, poisoning and frightening the average citizen with their wicked hissing and teaching him "freedom of speech" or, to be more precise, freedom to distort the truth, freedom to slander'. But after the Bolshevik coup, Gorky repeatedly blasted Trotsky and Lenin for their despotic, outrageous, 'shameful attitude toward freedom of speech', which would do 'great harm to the cause of the revolution'. The Bolshevik redefinition of press freedom, Karl Kautsky himself warned in 1918, was not a socialist measure but simply a dictatorial power grab by a small faction of extremists who had been unable to win power through democratic means.

It was indeed. And yet it was also a principled attempt to address the central problems of media ownership, profit and the public good that socialists had by then been grappling with for almost a century. That was why already on 4 November 1917, barely a fortnight after the coup, when Bolshevik press policy came under bitter attack in the Central Executive Committee, several speakers stoutly supported it. Of course 'we defend press freedom', Varlam Avanesov explained, but this concept must be divorced from old petty-bourgeois or bourgeois notions of liberty. If the new government has had the strength to abolish private landed property, thereby infringing the rights of the landlords, it would be ridiculous for Soviet power to stand up for antiquated notions about liberty of the press. First the newspapers must be freed from capitalist oppression, just as we have freed the land from the landlords, and then we can promulgate new socialist laws and norms enshrining a liberty that will serve the whole toiling people, and not just capital.

To 'return to the capitalist way of doing things' was impossible, agreed Trotsky: why should those with money be allowed to flood the media landscape with lies, irrespective of their popular support? There were only two points of view on this question: 'either freedom for the bourgeois press or confiscation of paper and printing-presses for transfer to the hands of the workers and peasants'. 'We are moving full steam ahead toward socialism,' Lenin concluded confidently, and so 'of course we are introducing something new'. Henceforth, liberty of the press would no longer simply mean 'freedom to buy up quantities of newsprint and to hire a mass of scribblers'. We must 'prevent capitalists alone enjoying freedom of the press and flooding the villages with their cheap newspapers. We must get away from the notion that a press dependent on capital can be free. This is an important question of principle.'

TOTALITARIAN TRUTH

Reader, you know how this story ends. Not with the 'broadest and most progressive' freedom of speech in all of history, as Lenin had promised, but with the profoundly unfree, totalitarian dictatorship of the Communist Party and its equivalents – in the Soviet Union, its Eastern European vassal states, many postcolonial socialist experiments around the world, and nowadays above all in mainland China, the most elaborate censorship regime the world has ever seen. These are places where dissenting political speech is treated as a serious crime; where even holding up a blank piece of paper in public can lead to arrest and imprisonment.

'Citizens of the People's Republic of China', Article 35 of its current constitution proclaims, 'enjoy freedom of speech [and] of the press'. But later articles clarify that these rights are strictly limited: citizens have an overriding duty 'to safeguard the unity of the country', to 'respect social ethics' and to uphold the 'honour and interests of the motherland'. Above all, as Article 51 spells out, 'the exercise by citizens of the People's Republic of China of their freedoms and rights may not infringe upon the interests of the state, of society and of the collective'. The Communist Party decides what views individuals may or may not express. What this means in practice is that the state owns or controls all publishers, and that their editors carefully screen everything they put out. Users of the internet are largely cut off from non-Chinese sites, while their own traffic is heavily monitored and censored, both automatically (through the blocking of thousands of sensitive keywords and phrases, like, say, 'Tiananmen Square 1989') and by an army of millions of invisible human censors who constantly monitor and delete online speech. As in the case of the prior censorship carried out by print and online editors, these post-publication scrubbers take their direction from a national network of censorship offices under the ultimate control of the party's Propaganda Department.

So we're faced with a great historical irony. Marxists began by accurately critiquing the obvious flaws of the capitalist media system: real liberty of the press, in their view, would mean creating a marketplace of ideas free from the corrupting effects of money. Yet after overthrowing capitalism and completely reconfiguring the economics of publishing, they ended up justifying ever stricter censorship – mainly on the grounds that, even in a socialist dictatorship, bourgeois doctrines would otherwise return to corrupt and mislead the people. In 1921, when another Bolshevik leader urged him to re-establish press freedom, Lenin replied that the concept was intrinsically 'anti-proletarian'. 'The "freedom of the press" slogan became a great world slogan at the close of the Middle Ages and remained so up to the nineteenth century,' he explained, and that meaning still persisted outside Russia: 'All over the world, wherever there are capitalists, freedom of the press means freedom to buy up newspapers, to buy writers, to bribe, buy and fake "public opinion" *for the benefit of the bourgeoisie.*' Therefore, were it to be re-established in Russia, 'freedom of the press will be a weapon in the hands of *this world bourgeoisie*. It is not dead; it is alive. It is lurking nearby and watching,' waiting to pounce and crush the revolution. 'We have no wish to commit suicide, and therefore, we will not do this.'

A century later, the same paranoid mistrust of popular judgement continues to drive the media policy of the Chinese Communist Party – heightened by the terrible warning example of the Soviet Union's collapse after it loosened censorship during the 1980s. In April 2013, at the start of its most recent crackdown against freedom of expression, a secret 'Communiqué on the Current State of the Ideological Sphere' was sent out from the party's Central Committee to its local officials across the country, in order to combat 'Western anti-China forces and internal "dissidents" . . . actively trying to infiltrate China's ideological sphere and challenge our mainstream ideology'. Among the chief ideological dangers it warned against was the western concept of press freedom. It was critical to reject this and hold firm to 'the Marxist view of news . . . [and] freedom of the press', or else further subversive ideas would creep in:

> The ultimate goal of advocating the West's view of the media is to hawk the principle of abstract and absolute freedom of press, oppose the party's leadership in the media, and gouge an opening through which to infiltrate our ideology . . . In the face of these threats, we must not let down our guard or decrease our vigilance.

How do citizens in such societies conceive of free speech? In the early decades of the Soviet Union, even dissenters usually did so in terms of class. In 1921, one of the main demands of the rebellious sailors of the Kronstadt uprising was 'to give freedom of speech and press to workers and peasants, to anarchists and left socialist parties' – it was envisaged as a collective right rather than an individual one. Around the same time, Gavril Myasnikov, the first prominent Bolshevik to be permanently expelled from the party, also advocated freedom of expression in terms of particular social groups (initially he proposed it for everyone 'from monarchists to anarchists inclusive', later only for proletarians, not for the bourgeoisie). In 1936, Stalin's new constitution, as well as maintaining the guarantee of the people's access to printing presses, paper and other materials, added that all citizens had the right to freedom of speech and of the press, 'in conformity with the interests of the working people, and in order to strengthen the socialist system'. A few brave Russians used this promise to criticize the government, but many more wrote in to complain that the article smacked of a 'bourgeois' conception of universal, personal rather than class rights – a favourite suggestion was that only the peasant and worker classes deserved free speech.

By the 1960s and 1970s, this corporate understanding had become less dominant, but conventional Soviet understandings of rights continued to view them as capacities bestowed and materially enabled by the state, rather than inherent in individuals. Human rights could not be conceived of as 'natural' or separate from the state: they were embedded in social systems, and paralleled by duties towards the collective. Their dual purpose was 'the harmonious development of the personality and of society as a whole'.

In consequence, even communist dissenters of this period who argued against censorship and for greater freedom of expression usually did so in terms that differed significantly from western notions of rights. When the dissident physicist Andrei Sakharov surveyed the three main threats to freedom of thought in the Soviet Union in 1968, he ranked state repression of artistic and political expression alongside 'the deliberate opium of mass culture', and the influence of 'cowardly, egotistic, and philistine ideologies'. His central proposal was that 'irresponsible and irrational censorship' (that is, the existing system, whose terms were never publicly or legally fixed) be replaced by a new 'special law on press and information'. This would 'clearly and convincingly define what can and what cannot be printed and would place the responsibility on competent people who would be under public control'; promote social progress; and 'provide for the material resources of freedom of thought'. He and others also used underground publication to challenge the conventional logic of Soviet civil rights. Instead of demanding that the state provide the material resources for free expression, they took the means of production into their own hands, manufacturing and clandestinely distributing *samizdat* texts using typewriters and carbon paper. As well as arguing for free speech as a personal right, they thus articulated it as a collective social practice – but in a public sphere beyond the control of the state.

More generally, no matter how much they might chafe against the constraints of censorship, serious writers in communist states tended to share a commitment to literature as a moral and national force – as well as a deep disdain for the western concept of press freedom. 'Literature in the GDR has a special function, far more than in Western countries,' the brilliant East German dissident novelist Christa Wolf told a journalist in 1984. 'I do not know of any country in the world in which there is no ideological censorship or censorship of the market.' Writing was surely everywhere a matter of systemic constraints: 'press freedom' was only a euphemism for the economic censorship that oppressed western writers. After the fall of communism, the writer John Erpenbeck noted that under the East German regime he'd experienced every form of state repression – but the western system was worse: 'No form of censorship is so devastating, so damaging to personalities and to literature altogether, as the brutal censorship of the market.' Many of his compatriots agreed: market censorship not only ruined the quality of literature, but was 'stronger', more intrusive ('marked by the grossest interference and incompetence'), 'far more degrading', and destructive of 'human dignity'.

There are obvious parallels between the theory and practice of totalitarian censorship regimes in the twentieth and twenty-first centuries on the one hand, and the policing of speech and print in the pre-modern world on the other. Both restricted expression in order to benefit the public good; both were authoritarian but rooted in popular attitudes; both are antithetical to our modern western model of free expression. Yet both also pose a critical question for our own presumptions about free speech: what about the truth? How is it to be protected and advanced? It's easy to disagree with the totalitarian answer, which is that the party decides what is true, propagates this line to the people and suppresses challenges to it. But it remains an important question – especially in an increasingly fragmented western media marketplace whose incentives are geared overwhelmingly towards profit, short-term attention and partisan advantage. Who among us really believes that Rupert Murdoch, Elon Musk, Mark Zuckerberg or the hedge fund that owns your local newspaper, values the pursuit of truth more than their own financial and political interests? Yet these are the people who ultimately exercise the greatest sway over our western media landscape and diet.

The idea that journalists and the media should be neutral truth-tellers has a long history as a rhetorical claim, but as a matter of practice it's a much more recent and fragile creation. Only in the twentieth century did newspapers and broadcasters around the world begin to formalize their responsibilities to the public, and to institutionalize journalistic training, fact-checking, the separation of editorial from commercial decisions, and other protocols intended to bolster truthful, objective reporting. Even then, of course, there was always a tension between such aspirations and the media's dependence on advertisers, the social and political biases of its owners and employees, and the pressures of competition. Nowadays, even if its conventions live on, the heyday of that pre-internet ideal of neutral, objective authority is surely past.

The digital revolution, and the subsequent emergence of new corporate giants like Google and Facebook, wrecked the business model that sustained this era, by siphoning off advertisers and forcing the news press to more or less give away its products for free. Worse, by treating all news as interchangeable 'information', irrespective of its source, and facilitating a flood of cheap materials that competed with 'legacy' institutions for attention and authority, it destroyed the latter's standing as authoritative interpreters of current events and professional arbiters of truth. In a world where news and its interpretation have become democratized into an online free-for-all, and one whose main gatekeepers disdain to police lies and misinformation, how to discern and agree on the facts has become even more complicated than before.

As in previous eras, some journalism today produces truth-seeking, high-quality information about the world. Not all major news outlets are run primarily for profit. Most countries have publicly funded broadcasters, just as most also have laws regulating the private ownership of mass media, if only to prevent monopoly control. Some major media organizations, like the *Guardian* newspaper, are owned by non-profit trusts whose purpose is to safeguard their editorial independence and freedom from commercial or political interference. The *Financial Times* is now in the hands of a Japanese corporation that is itself an employee cooperative. Even the private ownership of media channels by pluto-crats is not always motivated solely by the pursuit of monetary gain or political sway. Some individuals and families also regard their stew-ardship of local or national news channels, at least in part, as a public service. The current billionaire proprietors of the *Los Angeles Times* and the *Washington Post*, for example, certainly meddle in their papers' cov-erage in ways that are at best awkward and at worst venal. But their initial acquisition of these titles, and their continued willingness to lose large amounts of money on supporting them, also reflect an appreci-ation of their value to the public.

Yet all this covers only an expensive, small and shrinking corner of the market; much more of what passes for printed, broadcast and online 'news' is low-value garbage and outright misinformation. 'The real opposition is the media,' Donald Trump's political adviser Steve Bannon revealed after the 2016 election – 'and the way to deal with them is to flood the zone with shit.' It proved to be a winning tactic, and it's been much emulated, before and since. So how, in such cir-cumstances, do our blanket avowals of free speech and freedom for 'the press', equally applicable to all actors, protect the truth – let alone advance it? Or do they, in reality, achieve the opposite? Current west-ern theories of free speech, with their focus on individual rights, and their relative neglect of the public good and the realities of the media landscape, are poorly equipped to address this vital problem.

FIRST AMENDMENT ARGUMENTS

It was not always so, even in the United States. The history of modern First Amendment doctrine is often told as a heroic story of All-American progress. From 1919 onwards, so it goes, a series of brilliant justices of the Supreme Court took up the question of free speech, debated and refined their ideas over time and progressively advanced towards an ever-better definition of what the First Amendment really means – centred on the right of individuals to express themselves, irre-spective of the content of their views.

Yet that modern interpretation's exclusion of collective rights, speech content and considerations of the public good is, in fact, a fairly recent development. For most of the twentieth century, American jurisprudence and public opinion moved in the opposite direction, concerned with the harms of particular kinds of speech, the rights of groups and the inequities of the media landscape. Until the 1960s, American attitudes on these topics remained broadly comparable to those of other western cultures (including, as we've already seen, on the prohibition of hate speech); only thereafter did they strongly diverge. One of the central reasons for this curious trajectory, and indeed the main reason why the Supreme Court first began to rethink the First Amendment in the later 1910s, was the free-speech thought and activism of socialist, communist and other left-wing groups in America and across the globe. In other words, the modern history of the First Amendment is an international, not just a national, story. Its initial innovations weren't created by judges so much as forced upon them by leftist lawyers and activists. And without the earth-shattering impact of the Bolshevik revolution, the shape of American free-speech doctrine would probably have looked very different.

In April 1917, the United States entered the First World War on the side of the Allied powers, including tsarist Russia. Six months later, following the revolution, civil war erupted in Russia. When the Bolsheviks unilaterally made peace with the Germans, the US, alongside the other Allies, invaded Russia to support its anti-communist forces. These successive developments were greeted with dismay by many Americans. In Philadelphia in August 1917, the local committee of the American Socialist Party mailed a flyer to thousands of newly drafted men, urging them not to serve if they were 'conscientiously opposed to war'. Its arguments invoked the language of the constitution and the religious free expression clause of the First Amendment, but its rhetoric was also distinctively socialist. 'Will you let cunning politicians and a mercenary capitalist press wrongly and untruthfully mould your thoughts?' it asked -- 'were you misled by the venal capitalist newspapers'? Within days, the party's outspoken local secretary, suffragist and recent Congressional candidate, Dr Elizabeth Baer, was arrested and put on trial, along with four of her senior party colleagues; she and Charles Schenck, who had mailed the leaflets, were found guilty and sentenced to several months in prison. A year later, a group of young Russian and Ukrainian Jewish immigrant anarchists in New York, among them Mollie Steimer and Jack Abrams, were jailed for between fifteen and twenty years for making handbills denouncing the invasion of Russia.

Thousands of other Americans were arrested and harshly punished for uttering similar views throughout 1917 and 1918, including the charismatic national leader of the Socialist Party, Eugene Debs, who was sentenced to ten years in jail. (Like hundreds of others, Debs was still in prison during the presidential election of 1920, when, as in his previous run in 1912, he received almost a million votes.) They were all convicted under the terms of an Espionage Act passed in the spring of 1917, which prohibited 'false reports' and the obstruction of recruitment, and a 1918 amendment to it that more broadly criminalized 'any disloyal, profane, scurrilous, or abusive language' about the United States, its form of government or its war aims. A few of these defendants managed to appeal their convictions all the way to the Supreme Court. By the time their cases were heard, at the very end of 1918 and throughout 1919, the European war was already over, but mass hysteria about the dangers posed by foreign-born socialists and other radical immigrants (the first 'Red Scare') was just beginning. Among the appealed cases were those of Baer and Schenck, Mollie Steimer and her comrades, Debs, Jacob Frohwerk of Missouri, who'd criticized the war in his local German-language paper, and a group of almost thirty German-American socialist farmers in South Dakota who had privately petitioned their governor about the draft and other wartime measures, and threatened to campaign against his re-election.

All of them argued that their utterances were protected by the First Amendment. For American socialists this was not at all a novel idea. On the contrary – that speech and press freedom were vital to the labour movement was as central a proposition for them as it was for their European counterparts. They also drew inspiration from a popular tradition of American activists, lawyers and public officials invoking the First Amendment's protection of controversial speech. As we noticed in Chapter 7, this constitutional argument had been pioneered by nineteenth-century abolitionists and campaigners for Black civil rights. In the second half of the century, it was also taken up by a variety of libertarian radicals, including campaigners for women's rights, free love, contraception, religious freethought and other topics whose public discussion was commonly suppressed as 'obscene' under laws such as the federal Comstock Act of 1873. One organization dedicated to supporting such legal and intellectual claims was the National Defense Association, founded in 1878. Another active and well-connected group was the Free Speech League (1902–19), whose concerns extended to the defence of anarchist and socialist views, as well as anti-colonial speech in the Philippines, Puerto Rico and Guam, territories which had been forcibly occupied by the US since 1898. Its secretary, Theodore Schroeder, produced a stream of publications defending 'constitutional free speech' for all viewpoints. As well as innumerable cases in lower courts, the league also sponsored appeals to the Supreme Court on First Amendment grounds in 1904 and 1912. One of its leaders, the New York attorney Gilbert Roe, was friendly with Louis Brandeis, and in 1916 helped to get him confirmed as the first Jewish justice of the court.

Labour organizers were in the vanguard of this popular free-speech movement. From 1906 onwards, with support from the Free Speech League, the Industrial Workers of the World, a newly founded radical socialist trade union, fought hundreds of widely publicized legal and physical battles across America, over the right to support strike action and disseminate their anti-capitalist views. These publicity-seeking 'free speech fights', as the IWW termed them, carried on into the war years, and deliberately invoked the First Amendment. Some of the union's members viewed the constitution with the same contempt in which they held the capitalist press – as a mere tool of the ruling class, which no more protected modern workers than it originally had 'the negro slaves whose slavery was confirmed and upheld by it'. But many others argued the opposite, claiming that the First Amendment's original meaning guaranteed their rights, even though the employer class and their judges were now trying to cover that up. On the streets, in court, in newspapers and other publications, they contended that 'it was we who were upholding constitutional law', and their opponents who were disregarding it. Debs, one of the founders of the IWW, took the same line, incessantly invoking his supposed First Amendment right to speak out.

The chief arguments for a constitutional right to free speech that would later be taken up by mainstream lawyers and judges were thus first advanced in court by members of the American labour movement and other mainly left-wing campaigners. The ideas themselves were not new, but this was the main way in which they came to be popularized at the highest levels of the legal system. The First Amendment was 'absolute and complete', the famous advocate Clarence Darrow urged the Supreme Court in 1903 on behalf of the Free Speech League and an anarchist defendant: 'the fundamental basis of free opinion demands that convictions shall be freely spoken to the end that the truth shall be known. Upon this freedom all progress depends.' The First Amendment, Debs's lawyer informed the Supreme Court in January 1919, was 'the vital issue of this case' – 'the millions in many countries who respond to the idealism of Eugene V. Debs will bluntly speak of the *Debs* case as a free speech fight'.

By this point, though government officials and judges largely maintained the position that the First Amendment could not invalidate existing laws, the contrary argument thus already had a long history and a prominent place in public and legal discourse. In 1912, following a bitter and violent free-speech fight in San Diego waged by the IWW and the Free Speech League, the governor of California asked a local businessman to conduct a public inquiry into the union's claims of 'denial of constitutional rights'. His report decried the IWW's 'unholy and reckless' aims and methods, and concluded that their mass defiance of local ordinances against public speaking deserved 'the most extreme punishment within the law'. But it reserved its harshest condemnation for the police and vigilantes who had otherwise infringed the campaigners' 'inviolable' and 'constitutional right of free speech'. State and federal judges, too, frequently dealt with First Amendment claims, not always unsympathetically, and with the related argument (which the Supreme Court was finally to accept in 1925) that its scope extended to state and local laws, not just national ones, because the post-Civil War Fourteenth Amendment of 1868 prohibited any local abridgement of national rights ('No State shall make or enforce any law which shall abridge the privileges or immunities of citizens of the United States'). The same issues were raised explicitly before the Supreme Court in 1877, 1882, 1892, 1904, 1907, 1913, 1915 and implicitly at other times.

In 1907, a majority of that court, led by Oliver Wendell Holmes, stuck with the conventional line – upholding the conviction of a Colorado Democratic politician and newspaperman, Thomas Patterson, who had printed a series of articles attacking a judgment by his state's Supreme Court, and claimed the truth as his defence. Holmes ruled that this was all a state matter, and that the First Amendment did not apply. And even if it had, he explained, the settled English and American law, going back to Blackstone, was that the 'liberty of the press' did not extend to its abuse. The First Amendment was meant only to prohibit '*previous restraints* upon publications', not punishment after the fact for speech 'deemed contrary to the public welfare' – which 'may extend as well to the true as to the false'. Yet by now, two of his colleagues had come to disagree with this traditional outlook. John Marshall Harlan, the longest-serving justice, issued a ringing dissent, holding that the First Amendment trumped all state laws and judgments about the common good:

> The public welfare cannot override constitutional privileges, and if the rights of free speech and of a free press are, in their essence, attributes of national citizenship, as I think they are, then neither Congress nor any State since the adoption of the Fourteenth Amendment can, by legislative enactments or by judicial action, impair or abridge them. In my judgment the action of the court below was in violation of the rights of free speech and a free press as guaranteed by the Constitution.

Harlan died in 1911. Less than a decade later, in the midst of the Red Scare, in response to mounting socialist free-speech agitation and the heated national controversy over the Espionage Act, the Supreme Court was forced once again to consider these long-simmering, rival points of view. It did not substantially change its mind. All the appeals on First Amendment grounds were dismissed. Setting out the court's unanimous judgement in Baer and Schenck's case, Holmes conceded that his ruling in the Patterson case had been too restrictive. The First Amendment, he now believed, didn't only prohibit 'previous restraints', it also precluded some post-publication checks. Yet its precise reach always depended on context: speech was an act, and 'the character of every act depends on the circumstances in which it is done . . . The most stringent protection of free speech would not protect a man in falsely shouting fire in a theatre and causing a panic.' The key question was, therefore, did the particular words in the particular context 'create a clear and present danger that they will bring about the substantive evils that Congress has a right to prevent'? That judgement would always be a matter of 'proximity and degree'. In this case, 'in ordinary times' the defendants 'would have been within their constitutional rights' to publish what they did: but not so in the special circumstances of war, to which the provisions of the Espionage Act referred. Elizabeth Baer and Charles Schenck were duly locked up. Jacob Frohwerk, like Eugene Debs, was jailed for ten years. Mollie Steimer got fifteen years, and Jake Abrams and two of his comrades twenty years each; a few years later, the government deported all four of them to the Soviet Union.

In the conventional hagiography of the First Amendment, the year 1919 is nonetheless held up as the great moment of creation. Textbooks, popular histories and serious legal scholars all agree that it marked the beginning of 'the Free Speech Century': these were 'the Supreme Court's first decisions interpreting the First Amendment's guarantee' of press and speech freedom. As we've already noticed, that's a pretty dubious oversimplification. But even if, as First Amendment lawyers commonly do, we restrict ourselves only to the judgments of the Supreme Court itself, and attempt to construct from them an intellectual lineage of current American free-speech ideology, it's a questionable place to start – though the personalities involved do make for a compelling narrative.

Of the justices on the bench at the end of the First World War, the most intellectually adventurous was the elderly Oliver Wendell Holmes. He was a voracious reader, always keen to keep up with the latest ideas in politics, economics and literature, as well as in law. As a young graduate of Harvard Law School in the 1860s, he'd got to know John Stuart Mill in London, and studied his writings. Now, in his late seventies, faced with the crop of Espionage Act cases and the free-speech arguments put forward by their socialist and anarchist defendants, he reread *On Liberty*, as well a recent volume, *The Decline of Liberty in England*, recommended to him by a precocious young English socialist lawyer at Harvard, Harold Laski, and Laski's own book *Authority in the Modern State* (1919) – which, like Mill, advocated absolute freedom of thought as the only 'safeguard of progress'. From 1918 onwards, in conversation and correspondence with Laski, his Harvard Law School colleagues Zechariah Chafee and Felix Frankfurter, the brilliant New York judge Learned Hand, his progressive new fellow justice Louis Brandeis, and others, Holmes gradually evolved from his earlier views towards a new conception of the scope of the First Amendment.

He first articulated this in 1918, when the rest of the bench looked set to uphold the conviction of the South Dakota socialist farmers who'd petitioned their governor. In the end, no judgment was ever issued, because at the last moment the government conceded the case on a technicality. That seems to have been because Holmes had drafted (and Brandeis proposed to join) a dissent arguing that the First Amendment should protect 'opinions and speech that could not be imagined to do harm, although opposed to our own'. On similar grounds, though Holmes himself wrote the unanimous opinions upholding the convictions of Baer, Schenck, Frohwerk and Debs (as did Brandeis in another case against a socialist anti-war speaker), the two of them a few months later dissented from the harsh punishment of Steimer, Abrams and their fellows. 'Only the present danger of immediate evil or an intent to bring it about' justified curtailing speech, they argued, and 'nobody can suppose that the surreptitious publishing of a silly leaflet by an unknown man, without more, would present any immediate danger' to the war effort. The constitution seemed instead to support 'free trade in ideas – that the best test of truth is the power of the thought to get itself accepted in the competition of the market, and that truth is the only ground' upon which one could safely proceed.

Until Holmes's retirement in 1932, the two of them authored several other notable free-speech opinions. In 1925, the Supreme Court upheld the conviction of the New York communist journalist Benjamin Gitlow, who had been arrested in 1919 and imprisoned in Sing Sing for publishing a revolutionary, anti-capitalist manifesto – even though, as the court noted, 'there was no evidence of any effect resulting from the publication and circulation of the Manifesto'. Though the majority in this ruling did finally accept the long-asserted progressive argument that, because of the Fourteenth Amendment, the

First Amendment applied not just to federal laws and actions, but to state and local ones too, the court also maintained the traditional view that free speech did not extend to 'utterances inimical to the public welfare', such as 'inciting' revolution. So Gitlow was returned to prison. 'Every idea is an incitement,' Holmes responded, in dissent: in this case, which concerned the pathetic views of a small minority, there was 'no present danger' and so no reason to suppress them. 'No danger flowing from speech can be deemed clear and present', Brandeis wrote two years later, in another case against a communist organizer,

> unless the incidence of the evil apprehended is so imminent that it may befall before there is opportunity for full discussion. If there be time to expose through discussion the falsehood and fallacies, to avert the evil by the processes of education, the remedy to be applied is more speech, not enforced silence.

It's easy to be distracted by such beautiful mantras. But in terms of American free-speech jurisprudence, the most important development of the inter-war years was simply that the pressure of socialist and communist agitation and arguments, together with a broader liberal reaction against the persecution of anti-war speech, finally forced the Supreme Court to engage with, and partially accept, a much more populist view of the scope of the First Amendment. By contrast, Holmes and Brandeis's new doctrine of 'present danger' was less of a watershed. Its main intellectual contribution was simply to import some of those popular assumptions into Supreme Court jurisprudence. In wonderfully quotable form, echoing the refrains of Milton, Cato, Mill and other earlier theorists, they reiterated the presumption that free and full discussion would always lead to truth, and introduced the related metaphor of the 'marketplace of ideas'. (That phrase, which pithily improved on Holmes's original formulation about 'the competition of the market', seems to have entered popular circulation in the 1920s.) As a substantive free-speech doctrine it was much less successful: only in the later 1950s did it briefly become the authoritative view. During Holmes's and Brandeis's lifetimes it was mainly articulated in dissent, and didn't sway the majority of the court, which, like

English and European judges of the period, continued to conceive of press and speech freedoms in more Blackstonian terms – liberty versus licence.

Nor did it underpin the more libertarian, 'content-neutral' free-speech doctrines that the court's majority began to adopt from the 1960s onwards – and still subscribes to. That was because it was based on different principles. Though Holmes and Brandeis's model decried as overly vague the Blackstonian approach, which prohibited speech with a bad 'tendency', their own theory was simply a sharper-edged version of it – a balancing act between liberty and licence that drew the line in a different place. Instead of a distant tendency, it looked for an immediate, identifiable danger – optimistically presuming that all otherwise anti-social and misleading utterances would simply, in time, be defeated by the truth-establishing properties of 'the market'. What remained the same was the presumption that speech was an act, capable of serious harm; and that the injuriousness of utterances should be judged according to their content and context. That was why they upheld many convictions for apparently dangerous anti-capitalist speech, but opposed those where the equivalent utterances seemed essentially harmless ('a silly leaflet', a sincere pacifist, a tiny powerless political group). His dissent in the Gitlow case, Holmes tellingly wrote to Laski in 1925, merely upheld 'the right of an ass to drool about proletarian dictatorship'. For him, as for his colleagues, harm remained the key criterion.

COLLECTIVE RIGHTS AND WRONGS

Holmes and Brandeis's heroic rhetoric, and the conventional focus on it, also obscures other crucial dimensions of American free-speech debates in the early and mid twentieth century. Because the two of them simply channelled the conventional anglophone model of press freedom as liberty from governmental constraint, their judgments took for granted that truth would automatically emerge in a free 'marketplace of ideas', and that free speech was an individual right. But that outlook ignored the concern of many contemporary

Americans – scholars, politicians and citizens alike – about the glaring inequities of the capitalist media landscape itself, and the relationship between individual and collective rights.

There are two intertwined stories here. The first is about how, in the aftermath of the First World War and the Red Scare, the traditional free-speech ideals of American socialists, which had always, as for their European counterparts, focused on press and speech liberty as tools for *collective* agitation – the rights to strike, picket, boycott and unionize – were gradually supplanted by a much less radical conception of free expression as only a personal, individual right.

In his 1891 manifesto, Karl Kautsky had highlighted the idea that press freedom was vital to collective anti-capitalist action: for organizing labour, communicating with the working classes, and aiding strikes and boycotts. That was the strategy that the IWW pursued in its pre-war speech fights. It was a battle focused on winning political power, rather than on influencing Supreme Court attitudes. Indeed, American socialists and communists were deeply sceptical of the judiciary's anti-labour and anti-democratic biases, and with good reason. From the later 1890s onwards, the Supreme Court regularly struck down state and national regulations on banks, insurers and other industries, as well as democratically passed laws enforcing minimum wages, maximum working hours, safe working conditions, restrictions on child labour, and so on – on the grounds that these infringed the supposedly constitutional right of private contract. Local courts likewise commonly sided with anti-labour forces. Socialist appeals to the First Amendment were therefore mainly an incidental polemical and judicial strategy – the larger aim was always to win votes, change laws and co-opt the power of the state to pursue policies that would curb capitalist exploitation and advance social welfare. Indeed, most leftists never believed that individual rights should trump the public good. As a leading progressive jurist explained, that was precisely the problem with the current economic and legal set-up, which 'exaggerates private right at the expense of public interest': in fact, 'the individual interest in free belief and opinion must always be balanced with the social interest'.

There had always been a tension between this collectivist outlook and the more individualistic principles of the Free Speech League and its nineteenth-century abolitionist, freethinking and anarchist fore-bears. In the interwar years this came to a head, forcing a striking shift in the aims and tactics of the league's most prominent successor, the American Civil Liberties Union.

The ACLU began in 1920 essentially as a propaganda branch of the labour movement, 'to serve the cause of freedom of expres-sion in the industrial struggle', as one of its founders, the lawyer Walter Nelles, put it in an internal memo. 'We are frankly partisans of labour,' he explained – but to win public support for strikes and industrial action, it was vital also to attract 'liberals not connected with the labour movement', and 'those who stand on general prin-ciple for freedom of expression'. In the face of continued anti-union action by government and courts during the 1920s (including a fur-ther series of Supreme Court curbs on strikes and boycotts), the ACLU's early free-speech literature described the United States as 'a class government – a government by and for business', aided by 'reactionary . . . federal and state supreme courts' and an American public 'drugged by propaganda and blinded by a press necessarily subservient to property interests'. Tellingly, it put the legal 'right' to free speech in inverted commas, and stressed that this was of sub-sidiary importance to achieving the natural rights of labour and 'progress to a new social order'.

Over time, however, the ACLU's strategy of appealing to a wider constituency by standing for 'the expression of all opinions, however radical' created a conundrum. By the mid 1920s, the national lead-ership no longer thought it wise to advertise that they stood for 'the overthrow of the capitalist system'. In 1921, the organization had singled out the Ku Klux Klan as one of its particularly violent and dan-gerous anti-labour enemies. Yet within a few years it was supporting the Klan's own legal campaigns to organize and march in public. By 1933, the ACLU had gravitated to defending the rights of antisemites to broadcast over the radio, and of American Nazis to hold public ral-lies. The following year, it issued a pamphlet, *Shall We Defend Free Speech for Nazis in America?*, posing a question to which its answer was a resounding yes: 'Is it not clear that free speech as a practical tactic, not only as an abstract principle, demands defence of the rights of *all* who are attacked in order to obtain the rights of *any*?'

Its long-time director, the former IWW organizer Roger Baldwin, reassured the readers of *Soviet Russia Today* that these were only temporary, tactical alliances: 'If I aid the reactionaries to get free speech now and then, if I go outside the class struggle to fight against censorship, it is only because those liberties help to create a more hospitable atmosphere for working-class liberties.' But in reality that was no longer true. The union's main purpose was evolving into something different and much more straightforward: judicial protection for all speech. 'To defend the rights of the Nazis is the best possible answer to those who accuse the ACLU of being exclusively Red,' one of its members wrote in, appreciatively – viewpoint neutrality increasingly became the organization's guiding mantra, and litigation its main weapon. And though the union stressed its abhorrence of the views of Nazis, antisemites, Klan members, and the like, it never conceded the obvious fact that, in actively defending the rights of such speakers, it was inevitably also always normalizing and amplifying their message – infusing it with the oxygen of publicity and bestowing upon it a greater aura of legitimacy than it would otherwise have. That remains the case today. The ACLU's theory asserts a distinction between the right to speak and the content of speech. Yet its actions proclaim that even the most hateful, untrue or otherwise toxic views are worthy of public dissemination – that these are ideas that *deserve* to be heard.

The ACLU's shift in principles partly reflected its increasing success in legal battles, which led its leaders to revise their initially dismissive attitude towards the courts. But it also resulted from changing political circumstances. The passage of a major new federal labour law in 1932, and the election of Franklin D. Roosevelt a few months later, set up a lengthy struggle between the new progressive president and the conservative Supreme Court over his ambitious social and economic policies. When in 1937 Roosevelt threatened to expand the bench unless it stopped blocking his New Deal legislation, labour leaders and many liberal intellectuals supported him. But after the court climbed down, dropping its 'liberty of contract' doctrine, and issuing a series of landmark pro-labour-speech rulings, permitting picketing and other forms of labour agitation, the ACLU increasingly allied itself with conservative, business-friendly groups. For in these new legal circumstances it was increasingly employers and plutocrats who cannily rallied to 'freedom of speech' and championed the independent power of the Supreme Court, in order to further their own interests. Through clever public relations, a business lobbying group proudly noted in 1939, they had successfully managed 'to link free enterprise in the public consciousness with free speech'. As corporations increasingly argued that they, too, had First Amendment rights, and that these were infringed by government regulation and pro-union rules, the ACLU placed itself firmly on their side.

This extraordinary realignment was controversial within the ACLU's ranks, and outraged many labour organizers. Baldwin and the ACLU leadership seem to have regarded it only as a necessary compromise: enlarging the realm of everybody's free speech would surely benefit unions too. Around 1940, when the Supreme Court issued a landmark judgment that mass picketing was protected by the First Amendment, this probably looked like a plausible strategy. But in the longer term it had the opposite effect. Though the ACLU never receded from its new, content-neutral position, and continues up to this day to support the anti-regulation, anti-union free-speech claims of businesses, the Supreme Court after 1940 rapidly abandoned its protection of the right to strike, picket and unionize. By the later 1950s these forms of labour agitation, which the ACLU had been founded to defend, were no longer linked to the First Amendment, and states and employers, supported by the courts, increasingly moved to curtail them. In subsequent decades this imbalance has grown ever starker. Nowadays, once more, American laws tightly restrict the ability of workers to picket, strike and unionize – while almost half of the Supreme Court's recent free-speech judgments have been in support of businesses and trade groups challenging regulatory constraints on First Amendment grounds. When money talks, American courts listen. As the numbers show, 'the corporate takeover of the First Amendment' is now complete.

By reconceiving freedom of speech in traditional terms – that is, solely as a question of individual liberty unconstrained by government control – the leaders of the ACLU in the 1930s reverted to a simple and consistent message. This allowed them to claim the moral high ground as defenders of the constitutional rights of every American.

But to do that, they had to jettison their original, much more radical conception of what free speech was *for*, and how its application might transform society for the better – as well as the insight that the much-vaunted 'marketplace of ideas' was in fact (as a labour leader complained in 1940) only 'a *monopoly* market', no more capable of automatically safeguarding true equality of speech than the capitalist system was of creating a fair distribution of wealth.

THE PROBLEM OF PRESS FREEDOM

Which brings us to the second crucial but underappreciated story: of how twentieth-century American commentators and policymakers perceived, and tried to rectify, the evident failings of the media marketplace and its dubious relationship to the production of truth.

Back in the 1830s, Alexis de Tocqueville had contrasted the American newspaper scene favourably with that of the French. Not because it was freer (he didn't anyway think that press liberty was an unequivocally good thing), but because it was so decentralized. In the United States, unlike in Europe, he said, there was no real money to be made from journalism. As a result, there were papers everywhere, instead of just 'a few powerful organs', as in France. That meant that, though the periodical press collectively wielded immense sway over American public opinion, it could not be centrally organized or manipulated. Whether or not that was a plausible interpretation in Tocqueville's time, it certainly was no longer true half a century later. As in 'most parts of the civilised world', so in America, a visiting British politician noted in 1879: 'the rich people rule the press, and the press rules the country'.

Over the decades that followed, despite the launch of some successful progressive and campaigning ('muckraking') new titles, the mass-market American news press became ever more heavily capitalized and industrialized, increasingly consolidated into smaller numbers of corporately owned titles and syndicates, and heavily dependent on advertising. As many observers complained in the late nineteenth and early twentieth centuries, this increasingly turned news itself into a manipulated commodity, whose content was primarily determined by the interests of its owners, rather than of the general public. After all, noted the pioneering sociologist Edward Ross in 1910, 'to expect a newspaper magnate to run his newspaper in the interests of truth and progress is about as reasonable as to exhort the mill-owner to work his property for the public good instead of for his private benefit'. This in turn undermined democracy, for 'the newspaper-owner manufactures the impressions that breed opinion and, if he controls a chain of important newspapers, may virtually make public opinion without the public knowing it!'*

What could be done to remedy this dangerous situation? Several early critics thought the solution might lie in establishing non-profit newspapers, funded by endowment or subscription. But others took aim at the conventional theory of press freedom itself. Instead of just focusing on the liberty of authors and publishers to express themselves, surely one should also consider the rights of the public to be properly informed? In a series of influential studies of public opinion, the brilliant journalist and presidential adviser Walter Lippmann argued that, given the complexity of modern news production and consumption, the simple free-speech doctrines of Milton and Mill (and, he implied, the recent Supreme Court opinions of Holmes and Brandeis) were simply 'misleading' – 'too feeble and unreal ... to protect the purpose of liberty, which is the furnishing of a healthy environment in which human judgment and inquiry can most successfully organize human life'. Because the critical issue was the formation of public opinion, 'the protection of the sources of its opinion is the basic problem of democracy. Everything else depends upon it.' The real question was therefore not how to define freedom of speech or opinion, but how best to guarantee citizens' access to accurate public information and knowledge.

In the 1930s, in the context of economic depression, New Deal government activism and the rise of dictatorial regimes across Europe, the exact relationship between American political liberty and press freedom became an urgent, widely debated, national question – 'the

---

* This was a very different view of the modern media than Justice Holmes's Olympian platitudes around this time about 'free trade in ideas' and 'the competition of the market' – but then Holmes was so lofty that he refused to read newspapers.

problem of the freedom of the press', as it was described. In Roosevelt's own words, the American people had a rightful 'interest in freedom of the news as well as in the preservation of a free press'. 'Do we have a free press?' his Secretary of the Interior, Harold Ickes, was asked on national radio in 1939. On the contrary, Ickes replied, highlighting recent examples of its rampant partiality. By and large, he argued, American newspapers were but the 'shackled' mouthpieces of business interests, deviously used to sway public opinion in their favour and pervert the political process – 'the lack of a free press is the most serious threat confronting our democratic government and our social order'. No one wanted to introduce government censorship, but newspapers were a major private industry with huge sway: why should its practices be exempt from regulation for the public good?

Most Americans agreed, according to opinion polls; so did journalists, and even some powerful publishers themselves. If the press was not regulated, the great magazine magnate Henry Luce told the former president Herbert Hoover in 1937, 'I can see nothing to rely on except private conscience. And if you will rely to some extent on the private conscience of editor-publishers . . . why not rely also on the private conscience of bankers, manufacturers, educators, etc.?' In this spirit, Congress and the administration between 1933 and 1942 tried to enact a variety of economic reforms – outlawing deceptive advertising, introducing price, trade and labour regulations for media companies, and bringing an anti-trust suit against the monopolistic practices of the Associated Press wire service.

Their efforts largely failed. Like other American businesspeople in the early twentieth century, most newspaper publishers and advertisers had grown keen on the idea that the constitution guaranteed their freedom from any form of public control. From the 1920s onwards, the Supreme Court's new interest in protecting free speech inspired them with additional confidence. When a virulently racist and antisemitic Minnesota paper was banned under a state law prohibiting 'malicious, scandalous and defamatory' publications, a coalition of rich, conservative publishers, aided by the ACLU, managed to convince a narrow majority of the court in 1931 that the statute contravened the First Amendment. Shortly afterwards, faced with New Deal attempts to regulate their business practices, they went on the legal and polemical offensive, trumpeting the dubious but simple message that the constitution exempted the press from *any* regulation, and attacking every proposed reform as an 'un-American', sinister harbinger of totalitarian censorship.

Following the 1933 passage of the National Industrial Recovery Act, which called for codes of practice be drawn up by trade groups in every industry, covering labour conditions, price regulations, and so on, the American Newspaper Publishers Association urged its members to boycott the law, because this might 'lead to or approximate censorship'. A decade later, its lead counsel warned that antitrust regulation of the Associated Press would make Americans as unfree as people in Nazi Germany: both would be suffering under a 'government-controlled press'. Newspapers, their owners, the advertising industry and its associated businesses all piled on such hyperbole, in the age-old tradition of self-interested anti-regulatory polemics about the 'liberty of the press'. The press, they claimed, was not an industry at all, but 'a public service institution' with 'a sacred duty to the public whom they serve'. The real threat to its freedom, they urged, came from the New Dealers themselves, who were expanding the scope of government 'propaganda', and plotting for 'unlimited power of suppression', 'censorship', 'betrayal of democracy' and 'dictatorship'. This was cynical and/or paranoid hogwash, but its endless repetition gradually redefined the popular understanding of what liberty of the press should mean.

Throughout the 1940s, progressive arguments continued to be influential in policymaking circles. The various federal and Supreme Court judgments in the 1943–5 Associated Press monopoly case invoked the idea that press freedom ought to encompass a collective, public right to truthful information and a diversity of opinions (Roosevelt's 'freedom of the news'), not just the right of publishers to do what they liked. They also agreed that the First Amendment permitted the government to impose economic regulations on the press. So did much of the analysis produced by a landmark Commission on Freedom of the Press, funded by Luce and composed of more than a dozen of the leading white, male minds of America, which between 1943 and 1947 considered 'the freedom, functions, and responsibilities of the major agencies of mass communication' in the modern world. In 1948, the legal philosopher Alexander Meiklejohn's influential *Free Speech and Its Relation to Self-Government* argued that there was a categorical difference between speech in pursuit of merely private aims and that of citizens 'planning for the general welfare'. Only the latter was covered by the First Amendment, not 'the most flagrant enslavements of our minds and wills' that were perpetrated by privately owned commercial media under the guise of free speech.

Yet despite the intellectual purchase of the idea, no authoritative consensus on how to define press freedom as a positive public right was ever firmly established. That proved to be a fatal weakness. Taking the District and Supreme Court judgments together, the Associated Press ruling resulted in no less than seven separate opinions – three dissenting from a more expansive interpretation of press freedom as including the rights of the public vis-à-vis private corporations, the others all upholding it but on different grounds. The Commission on Freedom of the Press likewise started from the proposition that the traditional conception of press freedom as an absence of governmental restraint was 'too simple', and out of date in the modern world, and that it ought now also to include 'the right of the citizen and the public interest' – it should mean 'freedom for' as well as 'freedom from'. The first draft of its recommendations accordingly proposed 'vigorous, continuous governmental intervention' to prevent monopolies and maintain competition; there was also enthusiasm for stronger action against the deliberate publishing of lies. But in the end the commissioners, fearful of government 'totalitarianism', found it impossible to agree on any substantive practical changes. After cataloguing all the ways in which the mass media had become a 'large-scale enterprise, closely interlocked with the system of finance and industry', whose interests were antithetical to those of the democratic public, and whose 'faults and errors ... have become public dangers', their final report fell back weakly on simply exhorting publishers to act more responsibly towards the public – as a 'moral', rather than a legal, duty.

In America, therefore, increasing awareness of the problems of the capitalist media system throughout the nineteenth and early twentieth centuries ultimately had a paradoxical effect. In the long term, the pressure of progressive criticisms ended up strengthening avowedly libertarian, anti-governmental free-speech theories and practices. By the 1950s, the essentially mercenary and partisan character of the mass media had come to be widely accepted, even by its critics, as the necessary result of press freedom, rather than an obstacle to it. With increasing success, newspaper owners' own propagandists reaffirmed the simple, traditional argument that liberty of the press, and the First Amendment, were only about autonomy from state intervention – and that the greater that autonomy, economically and otherwise, the freer the press. All that remained of arguments about the public good was the pious hope that journalists and their publishers, like other business-people, would exercise their power with 'social responsibility' – from the 1950s onwards that duly became the mantra of journalism schools and high-minded media barons.

'In the United States the battle for freedom of the press,' a scholar of journalism had explained in 1945,

> is no longer primarily a battle to wrest more such freedom from gov-ernment. It is to make freedom of the press more of a reality for the average citizen, who does not and cannot own a newspaper, by curbing the increasing monopoly of this right by an ever smaller number of corporations and individuals who, as owners, enjoy the only real free-dom of the press today.

Scarcely fifteen years later, by 1960, that intellectual battle had been largely lost. In the decades that followed, left-wing American think-ers, such as Herbert Marcuse and Noam Chomsky, continued to produce coruscating critiques of the biases and stultifying effects of their nation's mass media. But these no longer influenced conventional or judicial understandings of free speech. Instead, the mainstream swerved in a different direction: the American libertarian experiment was about to begin.

THE LIBERTARIAN REVOLUTION

It was not only because of domestic opposition that American courts, policymakers and intellectuals between 1940 and 1960 drifted away from their previous interest in regulating the media and redefining the meaning of press freedom in more egalitarian ways. This shift also resulted from the changing international context – the Second World War, and the Cold War that followed it. For almost a century, up to the 1940s, American attitudes towards liberty of the press had been seriously influenced by socialist ideas. After 1945, the communist challenge continued to have a major impact on American ideology – but now in the opposite way.

'At the present moment in world history,' President Truman told Congress in the spring of 1947, in one of the opening salvos of the Cold War, 'every nation must choose between alternative ways of life.' One was the American way, 'distinguished by ... guarantees of individual liberty, freedom of speech and religion, and freedom from political oppression'. The other, he warned, 'relies upon terror and oppression, a controlled press and radio ... and the suppression of personal freedoms'. In the decades that followed, this central Cold War concern – to support individual freedom of expression, and reject anything that smacked of the collectivist, 'controlled' media of communist societies – gave a huge new boost to narrowly libertarian ideologies of free speech, and to advocates of an unfettered capitalist media marketplace, for whom (as one industrialist put it) 'freedom of enterprise and personal freedom are but expressions of one and the same thing'. That meant giving up on any hope of reforming the commercial media system, and instead celebrating its independence from public constraint. From this vantage point, the capitalist press was the freest, and thus the best. 'Free people have a rugged sales resistance to propaganda,' the American attorney general assured his compatriots in 1941. The fact that Americans were overwhelmed by 'high-powered advertising propaganda of every kind' did not impair their judgement, merely sharpen it, he boasted. It was only 'the oppressed and the enslaved', in other countries, who were easy prey for misinformation.

To begin with, this new enthusiasm for unlimited freedom of expression didn't extend to communist doctrines themselves. In 1940, by which point the Communist Party of the United States had about 75,000 members, a new statute criminalized the 'advocacy ... of overthrowing or destroying the government of the United States by force', 'affiliation' with any group encouraging this, and even to 'conspire' (that is, talk) to another person about such advocacy. This became one of the legal foundations of the so-called Second Red Scare, between 1945 and 1958, during which tens of thousands of Americans were investigated, sacked, blacklisted, imprisoned and otherwise persecuted for suspected 'disloyalty' and 'un-American activities', such as membership of the CPUSA. Many of them invoked the First Amendment in their defence, but to no avail. In 1951, the Supreme Court ruled that the constitution had never protected 'those abuses of expression which a civilized society may forbid', and that communists were engaged in a 'conspiracy . . . [that] is a substantial danger to national order and security'. Six years later, however, by which time public anxiety about domestic subversion was beginning to wane, and four of the court's justices had been replaced, it changed its mind. In the earlier ruling, most justices had perceived an imminent threat from communist organizing, whereas two dissenters saw only the impotent 'talk' of a tiny, unsuccessful party that had been thoroughly rejected by American voters – no 'overt acts', no 'clear and present danger', no 'immediate injury to society'. By 1957, the majority had shifted to that view. The central criterion remained that of social harm.

In other respects, too, such as the legal treatment of lies, obscenity, libel and hate speech, American free-speech attitudes in the 1940s and 1950s remained broadly in line with those of other western nations, balancing individual freedom against judgements of harm and social order. But the post-war decades also opened up a new arena of international competition between different free-speech ideologies. What should freedom of expression mean in the new world order? In occupied Germany, the British instinctively fell back on the principles they had long employed in their colonies. In Japan, its American conquerors hurriedly foisted a version of the First Amendment on the defeated nation. And on the global stage, the formulation of international legal treaties exposed the differences between American, western European, communist and postcolonial conceptions of liberty of speech. The treatment of racial and religious hatred was a particular flashpoint, for various reasons – the horrific recent experience of the Nazi occupation and the Holocaust, the commitment of communist and postcolonial nations to combating fascist and racist ideologies, and the awkward problem (happily exploited by its ideological opponents) that the United States itself, the self-proclaimed standard-bearer of international freedom and equality, was in its domestic laws and practices profoundly racist.

Between 1946 and 1966, during the drafting of international conventions concerning genocide, racial discrimination, and civil and political rights, the Soviet Union and other nations thus consistently urged the prohibition of 'dissemination of ideas based on racial superiority or hatred' – against the narrower focus on 'incitement' and 'action' usually favoured by American diplomats. In June 1952, the Ukrainian delegate to the United Nations' Human Rights Commission noted acidly that 'a Mississippi State law prohibited propaganda in favour of racial equality; perhaps the United States delegation was opposed to prohibiting propaganda of racial hatred because it shared that view'? (He also slammed 'the monopolistic Press of the United States, operated by its owners entirely for profit and for the advancement of their own selfish interests'.) In reply, the American representative triumphantly pointed to the Supreme Court's *Beauharnais* ruling, just a few weeks earlier, upholding the state of Illinois's ban on 'any matter that exposed any group to hatred and contempt on the grounds of race or colour'. He agreed that 'such domestic legislation was highly desirable'. Throughout the 1950s and early 1960s, despite differences of approach, the United States' international position gradually became more accommodating of the regulation of hate speech.

But then American attitudes sharply diverged. In a series of judgments during the 1960s and 1970s, the Supreme Court fundamentally changed its interpretation of the First Amendment. This revolution upended the legal principles governing freedom of expression in the United States: it's the point at which American free-speech ideals really became exceptional, compared with those of the rest of the world. One of its main results was to end any constraint on hateful or otherwise discriminatory speech. Nowadays American Nazis, antisemites, racists and other spreaders of group hatred all shelter behind the First Amendment. American media companies proudly follow the same principles, and export them around the globe, with predictable results. Yet ironically enough, this legal revolution began, in the early 1960s, when the justices of the Supreme Court sought to aid the struggle against racial discrimination, and for Black civil rights.

Until this point, American law, like that of other countries, had treated defamation as an obvious harm. As the Supreme Court had noted in *Beauharnais*, and continued to affirm over the following decade, libel was never protected by the First Amendment. Its exact definition varied by locality, and it was usually treated as a civil injury rather than a public crime, but all Americans were free to sue if they believed their reputation had been injured by false reports. The new problem presented to the Supreme Court in 1962 was that racist Southern judges and juries had been successfully using their local libel laws, and the award of huge damages, to cripple civil rights activists and suppress national press coverage of their struggle.

In 1960, a group of prominent civil rights supporters, calling themselves 'the Committee to Defend Martin Luther King and the Struggle for Freedom in the South', placed a fund-raising advertisement in the *New York Times*, calling attention to the brutality of Southern police and officials. Its account of events included some factual errors. For this, the white supremacist police commissioner of Alabama's capital, L. B. Sullivan, won the gigantic award of $500,000 in damages against the *Times* and four local Black ministers, associates of Martin Luther King, whose names had appeared (without their knowledge) in the ad – a judgment unanimously upheld by the state's zealously white supremacist Supreme Court. Other Alabama segregationists also went on the attack against the paper, winning large sums: even its reporter was sued for criminal libel after he wrote about their campaign of terror. By the end of 1961, the *New York Times* faced potential judgments of over six million dollars, and had been forced to pull its staff out of Alabama to avoid further intimidation and potential bankruptcy. The following year the paper and the ministers appealed the Sullivan case to the Supreme Court. Alabama's weaponization of libel law, they argued, had national ramifications for the civil rights struggle, as well as 'the rights of free speech and press – roots of our democracy'. If left unchecked,

> Racist and segregationists will now have a new weapon in their arsenal of oppression. This form of racial oppression and terrorism, with its ominous parallels in the recent history of Nazi Germany, will take on a new and more terrible form through the façade of libel prosecutions.

Hitherto, the Supreme Court had always refused to hear appeals involving local libel laws. But throughout the 1950s it had issued a series of landmark decisions advancing civil rights. It's not surprising that it took this case; nor that it eventually ruled unanimously to reverse the judgment; nor that its ruling claimed only to be following age-old precedents. In fact, however, in seeking to advance the cause of civil rights, it radically altered American free-speech doctrine.

The new principle it conjured up in its 1964 judgment was that public officials could not claim defamation except if they could prove 'actual malice' (a legal term meaning completely intentional falsehood). Three of the justices would have gone further still, and proclaimed an unconditional right to defame public officials, even if 'deliberately and maliciously false'; but even 'actual malice' was an almost impossible standard to meet. 'Libel' was only a subjective label, the court declared – the more important principle was that 'debate on public issues should be uninhibited, robust, and wide-open, and that it may well include vehement, caustic, and sometimes unpleasantly sharp attacks on government and public officials'. In other words, abuse, falsehood and defamation came with the territory of public life: they were protected free speech, and could never be subject to criminal or civil restraint. Neither the cause of truth, nor irresponsible or negligent behaviour by a publisher, nor the real injury to public persons wronged by falsehood were relevant considerations – any law that 'dampens the vigor and limits the variety of public debate' must be unconstitutional.

This was only the start. Between 1964 and 1974, as well as raising the bar for libel actions by private citizens, the court steadily expanded the sphere of 'public' persons without legal protection against defamation, falsehood and abuse. From 'public officials' this gradually ballooned into the much larger and more amorphous category of 'public figures', including private citizens (such as singers or athletes) without any role in public policy, and even obscure people (like the traumatized victims of crime) who had become newsworthy through no desire or action of their own. It's an open question how far the class of unprotected 'public persons' might be held to reach nowadays, in the age of social media.

An additional feature of the court's libertarian revolution was its abandonment of concern about other kinds of harm, most notably those caused by different forms of what's usually termed hate speech – expressions of racial, ethnic or religious contempt, the circulation of destructive lies about minority groups, and encouragements to harm or discriminate against them. Though it has never explicitly reneged from its *Beauharnais* judgment, since 1969 the Supreme Court has repeatedly struck down local laws and ordinances against such hateful expression. On First Amendment grounds, it has allowed, among many other examples, the public speeches of an Ohio Ku Klux Klan leader who called for 'revengeance' against Jews and 'niggers', and their expulsion from America; the right of American Nazis to march in full regalia through an Illinois village heavily populated by Jewish Holocaust survivors; and the actions of a group of Minnesotans who placed a burning cross in the front yard of the only Black family in their neighbourhood. The last group had been convicted under a local ordinance prohibiting swastikas, burning crosses, and other incitements to 'anger, alarm, or resentment ... on the basis of race, colour, creed, religion or gender' – which the Supreme Court invalidated as unconstitutional.

In doing so, the majority of the court set itself against almost a century of American legal tradition that had first established the *Beauharnais* ruling and then, in the 1980s and 1990s, further extended protections against abusive speech in workplaces, on university campuses and in other settings. Rejecting the argument that 'protecting the community against bias-motivated threats to public safety and order' is a legitimate governmental interest justifying restrictions against hate speech (as Minnesota's Supreme Court had held in 1991), it has gradually come to base its interpretation of the First Amendment on a different pair of principles. The first is the dogma of 'content' and 'viewpoint' neutrality. In the United States, public bodies of all kinds must allow free and full expression of all ideas, no matter how evidently erroneous, foul or socially corrosive. Truth does not matter. The second, related conceit is that the likely or even the actual long- or short-term consequences of speech and other expression can never be taken into account. You may spend years publicly celebrating the murder of Jews, broadcasting the inferiority of African-Americans, or promoting the persecution of your Muslim neighbours. You probably couldn't do this in your workplace, if it could be defined as harassment or discrimination against other workers. But otherwise under American law these are not actions, only words, and therefore free. Only if you directly threatened a particular person with violence, or deliberately provoked others to some act of *immediate* lawlessness, would your utterance be culpable – anything short of that remains protected free speech.

We might call this the 'just suck it up and yell back' doctrine, for it also incorporates a third, attractively simple but empirically dubious principle. This is that the only feasible remedy for harmful, untruthful or otherwise bad speech is simply – more speech, of an opposing kind. The truth will surely win, is the underlying sentiment. ('Expose through discussion the falsehood and fallacies ... the remedy to be applied is more speech, not enforced silence,' as Brandeis put it in 1927.) Is this faith justified, especially given the practical realities of our wholly imperfect marketplace of ideas? Why should bad-faith spreaders of disinformation be treated as responsible or persuadable interlocutors? And meanwhile, what about the collateral damage – who ends up bearing the burden of the spread of poisonous lies and hatred? Which groups are most likely to suffer the practical effects? How are ordinary citizens meant to navigate and judge the veracity of an unregulated stream of dubious and untrustworthy information? What if all this undermines democracy itself? According to the current creed, these are simply not questions to be considered.

DEMOCRACY AND SPEECH

Since the 1960s, American free-speech jurisprudence has gradually abandoned any conception of the common good, beyond its abstract obeisance to 'free debate' as the highest ideal. Yet this is not because it has developed a coherent doctrine of equal democratic citizenship requiring an equal say in the marketplace of ideas, despite what its philosophical defenders have sometimes argued.

On the contrary. Arguments about popular sovereignty, participatory citizenship and the value of protecting unpopular, dissenting ideas have certainly always been especially prominent in American understandings of free speech. That began as an inheritance from the English tradition – but already by 1800, as many foreign observers noticed, it had taken on a distinctive, democratic character of its own. By the later nineteenth century, American legal scholars justified free speech largely in such terms, and so did the Supreme Court after 1919, when it began to reinterpret the First Amendment as it applied to political speech. These ideals, and the uplifting rhetoric associated with them, continue to animate both popular and legal understandings about free speech in America today. As a result, no other culture in the world is as permissive towards the public expression of its citizens' political views, broadly defined – even if hateful, untruthful, antidemocratic or genocidal. Yet whether one thinks that a matter of celebration or of concern, the product of clear-sighted doctrinal consistency or of blinkered disregard for true democratic values, it is only one strand of First Amendment jurisprudence.

The problem is that the freedoms of speech and of the press have never been defined only in such terms. Ever since the 1930s, and in accelerated fashion since the 1970s, the Supreme Court's practical jurisprudence has also continued to extend First Amendment rights to advertisers, corporations and moneyed partisan groups, not just to individual citizens and 'the press'. And that in turn is based on its increasing adoption of the simplistic and ahistorical view that 'the First Amendment's unequivocal command that there shall be no abridgement of the rights of free speech and assembly shows that the men who drafted our Bill of Rights did all the "balancing" that was to be done in this field.' Basically, this outlook presumptively forbids lawmakers and judges from imposing any further restrictions based on considerations of the public interest. The net result is a skewed relationship between free speech and democracy.

For example, the United States Congress has repeatedly tried to regulate the disproportionate influence of money in American politics – no other country in the world permits such vast sums to be spent on swaying elections. In 1971 and 1974, successive iterations of the Federal Election Campaign Act set limits on campaign fund-raising and spending, and created the Federal Election Commission; while in 2002 the Bipartisan Campaign Reform Act tackled the problem of wealthy individuals, unions and businesses spending unlimited amounts of 'soft' money to influence elections – especially the increasing and opaque funding by such outside parties of tendentious ads attacking or promoting particular policies and candidates. Yet the Supreme Court has, with increasing boldness, struck down most of these regulations as impermissible infringements of free speech. The proposition that there is a 'governmental interest in equalizing the relative ability of individuals and groups to influence the outcome of elections', it ruled in 1976, 'is wholly foreign to the First Amendment'. Since the 2010s, on similar grounds, it has allowed unlimited outside spending for political purposes by corporations, unions and partisan associations, as well as unrestricted direct spending on federal campaigns by rich individuals. ('The whole point of the First Amendment is to protect individual speech,' the chief justice ruled in 2014, 'not a collective conception of the public good.') In First Amendment doctrine, as in American politics, political speech and the spending of money are now essentially the same thing: more money, more voice.

Of course, the Supreme Court is neither a homogenous nor an unchanging entity, and in its details the trajectory of American First Amendment jurisprudence over the past half century has been far from linear or consensual. Legal scholars have for decades now been complaining that it has become 'striking chiefly for its superficiality, its internal incoherence, its distressing failure to facilitate constructive judicial engagement with significant contemporary social issues connected with freedom of speech'. More recently, many of them have taken aim at the court's narrow and abstract conception of expressive freedom, its use to reinforce the negative liberty of the already powerful, and its flat refusal to consider the realities of social and economic inequality, the interests of the less powerful or the positive rights of the democratic citizenry in general.

Nor is it hard to find dissents from the court's recent rulings that uphold older principles of free speech, and explicitly consider the public good. It had always previously been accepted, Justice Byron White noted in a 1992 concurrence, that nobody had a First Amendment right to say things that were dangerous, obscene, libellous or otherwise 'worthless or of *de minimis* value to society'. The extension of First Amendment protections to hate speech was therefore a simplistic and alarming departure from settled precedent. 'I see no First Amendment values that are compromised by a law that prohibits hoodlums from driving minorities out of their homes by burning crosses on their lawns,' his colleague Harry Blackmun agreed, 'but I see great harm in preventing the people of Saint Paul from specifically punishing the race-based fighting words that so prejudice their community.'

In 2010, likewise, four justices, led by the ninety-year-old John Paul Stevens, complained that the majority of their colleagues' newly radical, 'blinkered and aphoristic approach to the First Amendment' upended a century of consensus about regulating money in politics. It would 'promote corporate power at the cost of the individual and collective self-expression the Amendment was meant to serve . . . [and] cripple the ability of ordinary citizens, Congress, and the States to adopt even limited measures to protect against corporate domination of the electoral process'. In 2014, another minority of four justices, in a dissenting opinion authored by Stephen Breyer, maintained that the First Amendment was intended to advance 'not only the individual's right to engage in free speech, but also the public's interest in preserving a democratic order in which collective speech *matters*'. In 2018, defending the court's previous approach of balancing First Amendment rights in the workplace against other important public-interest considerations, Justice Elena Kagan argued that the majority's latest extreme, anti-union reinterpretation of the settled law 'goes wrong at every turn . . . by weaponizing the First Amendment, in a way that unleashes judges, now and in the future, to intervene in economic and regulatory policy'. 'The First Amendment,' she concluded, 'was meant for better things. It was meant not to undermine but to protect democratic governance.'

In addition, though American legal doctrine has evolved elaborate rules to adjudicate speech actions within the boundaries of the First Amendment, the location and shape of those boundaries themselves (that is, what 'speech' it is held to cover, and what not) is largely determined by extraneous political, economic, social and cultural factors. In consequence, many kinds of expressive action remain legally regulated or otherwise outside the scope of the First Amendment, including some forms of political utterance (conduct around polling stations, for example, or disclosure requirements on electioneering communications). Yet it's nonetheless undeniable that American free-speech doctrine as a whole now rests on different foundations than it used to before the 1960s, and that it has become globally exceptional. American observers tend to celebrate this as a sign that their free-speech approach is more intellectually advanced than that of the rest of the world. The Supreme Court itself, unlike its counterparts elsewhere, has since at least the 1960s smugly disdained to consider any foreign free-speech laws or opinions as relevant to its own deliberations. But the rest of the world begs to disagree. Despite the indisputable sophistication of modern First Amendment jurisprudence, even other English-speaking nations around the world, with similar legal systems and traditions, have overwhelmingly rejected its new principles, continuing instead to approach free speech as a question of harm, proportionality, unequal power relations, democracy and the common good – not just of individual and corporate rights against the state. So, how to explain the American revolution?

Historical approaches to this question usually focus on two kinds of contingent, short-term explanation. One is the changing personalities and ideological make-up of the judicial bench; the other, the domestic social and political context in which particular free-speech cases have arisen. Both of these are part of the answer. But the new trajectory was also made possible by some deeper, more fundamental differences between American jurisprudence and that practised in the rest of the world.

The most obvious of these is the peculiar structure of American law, as it evolved in the course of the twentieth century. All systems of government with judicial supremacy over the legislature tend to develop more consistent free-speech rules than those where the limits are left to lawmakers alone. That is because jurisprudence, more than ad hoc law-making by politicians, seeks to create seemingly coherent principles. It favours simplicity and consistency. Since the early twentieth century, the growing scope of the US Supreme Court's pretensions to review speech laws on constitutional grounds has made it internationally one of the most powerful such bodies. In 1925, the same year that the Supreme Court began to interpret the First Amendment as applying to all levels of government, and as overriding state and local laws, a new Judiciary Act, promoted by the justices themselves, radically transformed its jurisdiction and greatly strengthened its power.

In turn, as we've seen, the court's growing omnipotence has encouraged litigants to seek judicial review as a way to negate the political and law-making process – invariably in the direction of undoing regulations of expression. Finally, the complexities of the federal system and the sheer size of the United States further encourage the court to promulgate broad and simple rules: its national judgments have to cover wide variations in local outlook.

These structural features explain why in the United States the free-speech rulings of the Supreme Court have taken on such an outsized influence. They also help to explain why those rulings have tended to ever-greater apparent simplicity and abstraction. But to fully understand the latter trend, and its libertarian turn, we also need to bring back into focus its wildly eccentric intellectual foundation – the peculiar text of America's constitutional Bill of Rights. No other country in the world bases its rules about freedom of expression on an archaic document drawn up more than two hundred years ago by violent rebel settlers deeply distrustful of governmental power and obsessed with individual liberty for propertied white men. Compared with any modern democratic constitution, the United States' antiquated charter includes startlingly few rights, so those that *are* listed (especially those listed *first*) are presumed to be especially important. Equality, proportionality, privacy, bodily autonomy, social rights, the common good: none of these are given the same prominence in the text as freedom of speech and the press – most are not mentioned at all. And the key basis of the libertarian swerve is an even more exceptional textual oddity: the absolutist formulation of the First Amendment itself. After the failure of twentieth-century attempts to establish a broader, community-centred definition of its scope, the political triumph of simpler, anti-governmental interpretations of its meaning by the 1960s increasingly gave libertarian arguments the upper hand.

A key figure in bringing about this transition was the Supreme Court justice Hugo Black, who had been appointed in 1937 and served until 1971. Already in the 1940s, he had begun to advocate a literal approach to the constitution's text, especially the 'absolute and unqualified language' of the First Amendment. In 1952, he dissented from the *Beauharnais* ruling on hate speech, because in his reading 'the First Amendment, with the Fourteenth, "absolutely" forbids such laws without any "ifs" or "buts" or "whereases".' By 1960, he had become confident in his view that the constitution's purpose was 'to withdraw from the Government all power to act' in respect of speech or the press – no matter how far-reaching the implications, or how dangerously simplistic his fellow lawyers might deem this approach to be. He always carried a copy of the constitution with him. If ever a litigant disagreed with Black's approach to the First Amendment, they would be asked to read its text aloud. As soon as they uttered the phrase 'no law', Black would say 'thank you' and take back the booklet – as far as he was concerned, there was nothing more to discuss. It's notable that, in Black's view, the First Amendment did not protect the wearing of black armbands to school in political protest, nor attending court in a jacket that said 'Fuck the Draft', nor even public marching, picketing or flag-burning. Like every self-proclaimed free-speech 'absolutist', before and since, he had particular views on its scope. Nonetheless, slowly but surely, both during and after his tenure, the Supreme Court as a whole came to embrace his general approach to questions of speech.

The upshot is that, nowadays, to cry 'First Amendment' in an American courtroom is to invoke a card that trumps almost everything else, as long as you can define your actions (refusing business to gay customers, say, or circulating instructions for how to make untraceable 'ghost' guns, or practising polygamy, or attempting to undermine the results of an election) as a form of expression. It may not work. But because there is no equally clear countervailing principle to limit it, it's become an irresistible legal weapon – with a unique power not only to undo any form of governmental censorship, but equally to dissolve constraints, rules and laws that might otherwise serve to prevent harm, or to advance democracy, equality or collective well-being. Until the 1960s, American judges generally held such considerations – truth, harm, context, the public interest – to be central to the definition and purpose of free speech. These days, by contrast, American law students are largely taught to disdain that approach ('ad hoc balancing') as an imperfect previous stage in the evolution of First Amendment dogma, and to dismiss the rest of the world's continued application of similar principles as similarly woolly and out of date. The libertarian doctrines that Americans have now instead embraced certainly make for a philosophically simpler and more hard-edged set of rules. But to refuse to consider the actual functioning of the media, or the content of speech, or the fact that utterances are actions, or the perennial difficulty that their exact meaning and force is always context-dependent, is also to ignore the essence of how expression actually works in the world, and what the hardest problems of free speech really are.

THE ONLINE MARKETPLACE

A century ago, intellectuals, policymakers and ordinary citizens across the western world broadly agreed that they were living in an unprecedented era of mass-media revolution, and tried to determine the implications for freedom of speech. Too much government control was pernicious, for obvious reasons – but so was leaving everything to market forces, which inevitably favoured the rich and already powerful. Communists were obsessed with the latter predicament – which led them to embrace extreme forms of state regulation. Americans broadly followed the opposite trajectory: by coming to focus exclusively on the problem of governmental power, they ended up with the worst excesses of deregulated plutocracy.

Yet to suppose, as do the distinguished legal minds of the ACLU even today, that 'the alternative to private control of speech and the media is state control' is itself to set up a tired and misleading dichotomy. Around the world, and even in America itself, there are plenty of other models for how different media are regulated or operated in the public interest, without being under direct 'state control'. The *Guardian* newspaper, the second most widely read English-language paper around the world, is completely free to read online by everyone, because it is operated by a private, non-profit trust with a public mission. The BBC and its American equivalents, National Public Radio (NPR) and the Public Broadcasting Service (PBS), are not under 'state control'; nor are public broadcasters in most other advanced democracies; and nor, necessarily, are the national bodies that oversee radio, television and other channels of mass communication in many nations. The basic principle that systems of regulation can be set up to operate independently or at arm's length from the government of the day is surely undeniable, even if we can quibble about how best to implement it, or note that some such entities are more successful than others. (After all, the difference between nations whose public discourse is dominated by government propaganda and those with a genuine plurality of publicly regulated media is essentially that between would-be or actual autocracies and healthy democracies – it's related to their political and civic culture as a whole, not to their doctrines about free speech.)

Likewise, even though people are bound to disagree on the exact definition of the common good, a paramount purpose of laws and governments has always been to safeguard the public interest. As we've seen throughout this book, that has created difficulties for successive ideals of free speech – from the confusions inherent in the presumption by early theorists that the common good was, like the common will, simply singular, through to the problems that arose once influential thinkers like John Stuart Mill began to conceive of the right to free speech as pertaining exclusively to individuals. To define free speech without taking the public interest into account at all, as very recent libertarian theories prefer to do, hardly counts as a satisfactory solution.

It's also reverses a long historical trend. For most of the twentieth century, in America as elsewhere, the growth of powerful new media was met by the creation of public-interest laws and watchdogs. As we saw at the start of this book, when the novel technology of the printing press had first spread across Europe, it too had been regulated. By 1900, the new ideal of print liberty had everywhere broken down such state control, at least to some degree. But even in the United States, where the principle of press freedom was most fervently advanced, its terms were taken literally: the freedoms of speech and the press did not automatically extend to other media. They did not apply to films, the Supreme Court ruled in 1915, for

> the exhibition of moving pictures is a business, pure and simple, originated and conducted for profit like other spectacles, and not to be regarded as part of the press of the country or as organs of public opinion within the meaning of freedom of speech and publication guaranteed by the constitution.

Nor did the First Amendment extend to the radio, Meiklejohn explained in 1948, which 'is not engaged in the task of enlarging and enriching human communication. It is engaged in making money.' From their inception, these new forms of mass communication were treated as businesses and publicly regulated in various ways; so too, in due course, was television.

Long after the attempt to craft a broader, public-centred interpretation of the First Amendment had been abandoned with respect to print media, it therefore persisted in attitudes towards broadcasting. In 1934 the Communications Act created a Federal Communications Commission to license and regulate broadcasters 'in the public interest'. From 1949 onwards, among other rules, the 'fairness doctrine' of the FCC required all radio and television stations to devote airtime to matters of public importance, and to present a diversity of viewpoints about them. In 1969, on those grounds, it revoked the licence of a segregationist Mississippi television station. In the same year, the Supreme Court unanimously upheld the commission's broad regulatory authority, including the fairness doctrine, as entirely constitutional, because the 'First Amendment is relevant to public broadcasting, but it is the right of the viewing and listening public, and not the right of broadcasters, which is paramount'. That was exactly the opposite of its view, by then, of the rights and responsibilities of newspaper and magazine publishers. No matter the many failings and biases of print media, it explained in another unanimous ruling around this time, 'a responsible press is undoubtedly a desirable goal, but press responsibility is not mandated by the Constitution and like many other virtues it cannot be legislated'. Laws could be made to enforce public accountability upon broadcasters, but not on print publishers.

To its libertarian and right-wing detractors, then and now, this approach to broadcasting was no more than a concealed form of government censorship. In any case, during the 1970s and 1980s, in parallel with the Supreme Court's increasing free-speech permissiveness, the membership and rules of the FCC, too, moved steadily in a more libertarian direction. One important reason for this was a steady assault on its traditional principles by self-interested radio and cable TV broadcasters (a new medium that was, from its inception, more loosely regulated). The 'Moral Majority' mass political movement of evangelical Christians that would transform American politics in the 1980s, for example, began at a 1979 anti-fairness doctrine 'Freedom Rally' in Dallas, called by a popular televangelist who'd been dropped by his TV station for preaching against homosexuality. In 1987, finally, the commission itself, invoking all the libertarian buzzwords of the Supreme Court's recent jurisprudence, but going still further, ruled that there should be no First Amendment difference at all between broadcast and printed media – the fairness doctrine was abolished, for 'the First Amendment was adopted to protect the people *not from journalists, but from government*'. In turn, this development further fuelled the boom in right-wing talk radio and heavily partisan cable channels, like Fox News, from the 1990s onwards.

When the next great communications revolution, the internet, exploded upon the world in the 1990s, beginning in the United States, how American policymakers approached the question of its relationship to speech and press freedom was therefore influenced by three major considerations. The first was the long-established regulatory framework of the FCC, including the tradition of public-interest rules for broadcast media. In February 1996, the Telecommunications Act that established foundational rules for the internet accordingly included a whole section (Title V, also known as the 'Communications Decency Act') regulating various forms of obscenity and violence, including penalties for using computers to communicate sexual materials to minors. What became the law's most consequential clause, specifying the relationship between internet companies and online speech, was enacted as an amendment (Section 230) to the still in force Communications Act of 1934.

The second factor, which was the direct impetus for Section 230, was a question specific to the new medium: what responsibility did internet platforms have for materials posted online? Should they be treated as the publishers of other people's speech, like a broadcaster or newspaper editor – or only as a distributor, like a bookshop or mail carrier, which was not liable for the content of what it circulated? By mid 1995, the evolving case law was that companies that exercised editorial control over their online forums could be treated as publishers, liable for defamation. This was a logical finding, but it threatened to incentivize corporations not to moderate anything at all.

The final driving force behind the policy that emerged was a passion for free markets and free expression, and against governmental regulation. The principles of 'Internet Freedom' that gave rise to Section 230 didn't just encompass permissive attitudes towards free speech, they also reflected a profound new geopolitical moment: the 'end of history', as an influential American State Department official had famously proclaimed in 1989. This was the final, inverse contribution of communist doctrine to American free-speech ideology. In the 1990s the collapse of the Soviet Union and its satellites, and the worldwide advance of capitalism and liberal democracy, appeared to have proved, as a matter of historical fact, that laissez-faire policies were the naturally pre-eminent, culminating form of social and economic organization. This gave a tremendous additional boost to libertarian principles. By the end of the twentieth century, China was the only remaining communist world power, but to American observers it seemed clear which way the tides of history were flowing – and that the latest communications revolution, born in the US, was pushing them along. 'We know how much the Internet has changed America, and we are already an open society,' President Clinton marvelled. 'Imagine how much it could change China.' There, too, 'economic innovation and political empowerment, whether anyone likes it or not, will inevitably go hand in hand' – 'liberty will spread by cell phone and cable modem'.

This was the triumphalist free-trade outlook that American politicians in 1996 enthusiastically codified into law (helped by heavy lobbying for 'deregulation' by all the telecom businesses involved). Though the internet was based on infrastructure originally funded and created by the US government, the text of Section 230 thus pointedly sought 'to preserve the vibrant and competitive free market that presently exists for the Internet and other interactive computer service, unfettered by Federal or State regulation'. It also acknowledged that online speech could and should be subject to controls, for example if it 'be obscene, lewd, lascivious, filthy, excessively violent, harassing, or otherwise objectionable'. But its governing principle was that all such 'blocking and screening of offensive material' should be left to private individuals and internet companies. To encourage websites to weed out objectionable material, it gave them two kinds of legal immunity – they could not be treated as 'the publisher or speaker' of any content posted by a user, but they also had an absolute right to censor anything, 'whether or not such material is constitutionally protected' speech. (After all, as private actors, the First Amendment did not apply to them.) There wasn't actually much else specifically about computing in the 1996 Act. But, as would come to be endlessly celebrated by its boosters over the ensuing decades, Section 230's main immunity clause proved to be 'the twenty-six words that created the internet'. Meanwhile, within a few months of the passage of the Telecommunications Act, all of its Title V restrictions were struck down by the Supreme Court, as incompatible with the First Amendment.

FREE-SPEECH FUTURES

Thirty years later, we know how things have turned out. On the one hand, the Chinese Communist Party has successfully nailed Jell-O to the wall, and tamed the internet into a conduit of state indoctrination. Authoritarian regimes everywhere increasingly try to follow suit. On the other hand, granting American for-profit companies an absolute, unsupervised and legally untouchable power over online expression throughout the rest of the world has had some disastrous consequences. In 1995, the main type of obviously harmful speech that American legislators were concerned about was children being exposed to sexually explicit materials. Congress's approach to this issue – leaving everything to the wisdom of private enterprise – was soon overwhelmed by the explosion and profitability of online pornography. Nowadays, the problem of children's exposure to porn is vastly greater than it was thirty years ago. And it has been joined by many other kinds of harmful speech which have flourished online, especially since the early, decentralized, less profit-driven experiments of the pre-algorithmic internet were overtaken by its current, corporatized form – political and scientific misinformation, the systematic harassment of individuals and social groups, endless hate speech, extremist ideologies and celebrations of horrific violence.

Most elements of the modern internet, from algorithmic search engines to online consumer reviews, raise potential issues of free speech and harm. But they are most pressing in the case of the huge American platforms that now globally dominate online public discourse, such as Google and YouTube (owned by Alphabet), Facebook and its ancillary social media companies (owned by Meta), and Twitter (bought in 2022 by Elon Musk, the world's richest person and a self-proclaimed 'free-speech absolutist', and rebranded as 'X'). That is firstly because of their unprecedented size and power. Facebook has more than three billion active users globally. Most of the world's advertising now appears on its company's websites and those of Alphabet. Everyone on the planet who has access to these platforms interacts with them constantly. Never before in history have there been media channels with such an extraordinary grasp on human attention, or with such global reach and financial clout. Secondly, it's because, in different ways, they profoundly shape their users' perceptions of the world. Many people now consume and exchange news and information largely through these online portals. Finally, it's because all of them, practically even if not legally, act as publishers of content, not just as neutral conduits for it. They purposefully arrange the information on their websites, algorithmically targeted at each viewer, so as to boost certain communications and demote others. And they also all have standards about permissible and impermissible speech, which they enforce (or not) as they please, free from external oversight.

The profound failures of this system have been widely documented. In the United States, Twitter, Facebook and other social media sites were heavily implicated in the Russian government's successful efforts to influence the 2016 presidential election; later they became central to the dissemination of misinformation about Covid-19 and vaccines, among other matters of critical public importance. In Myanmar in the later 2010s, Facebook was systematically used to spread violent propaganda against the Rohingya, leading to genocidal atrocities against that Muslim minority. In India over the past decade, similarly false and bigoted anti-Muslim disinformation has flourished on social media, fuelling daily hatred and violence. The defenders of Section 230, and the internet companies themselves, say that they are doing their best. Content moderation 'at scale' is hard, they point out, and standards of acceptable speech differ widely across the different territories in which they operate. New laws could never be the answer to the problems of free speech on social media, Facebook's 'Head of Policy Management' warned in 2019. The only solution was voluntary actions by social media companies, so that 'the incentives of business, governments, and the public are aligned'.

Yet the basic problem with this attitude is precisely that, as any nineteenth- or early twentieth-century critic of the mass media could have told you, the incentives of private media companies are *never* aligned with the public good, however we might define that. On the contrary, they are largely in tension with it. The business model of online platforms is simple. It depends on attracting users, keeping them hooked to their sites for as long as possible, showing them advertisements and making money from that – all the while hoovering up their personal data, so as to better target them with further ads and content that will keep them 'engaged' and addicted, while also monetizing that private data in other ways (such as by selling it on to other companies). It has nothing to do with advancing free speech, democracy, truth, social cohesion or other public values – corporate gesturing to such concepts is at best naïve hope, at worst just cynical spin.* Of course, these companies provide services that people like to use, and their effects can be socially beneficial. In places around the world without many other avenues for free expression or independent reporting, their arrival might in principle even improve the health of the media landscape, rather than (as has proved the case in most democracies) degrading it – though even on that score, their overseas record is decidedly mixed, and often disastrous. But ultimately, what

---

* It is striking that American policymakers have been quickest to raise the alarm and take bipartisan action (in a law passed in April 2024) against the Chinese media giant TikTok, the only large and influential social media company in the US that is in non-western ownership, over its unwarranted data-gathering and surveillance of users, and its potential for exercising malign social and political influence over them. This despite the fact that, as one US senator pointed out in the course of the debates, 'American companies are doing the same thing, too.'

corporations care about most is turning a profit for their owners and shareholders. And this, in turn, is why their content-moderation practices fail so often and so badly.

The problem of online content moderation is only partly one of scale and intrinsic difficulty. More basically, it's one of money: of employing people to do the hard, unpleasant job of endlessly sifting through violent and offensive texts and images, and deciding about their meaning and effects. Some of this can be automated, but because the meaning of speech is so exquisitely context-dependent, much of it requires human judgement. It's not surprising that most online social media platforms are vastly more successful at excluding sexual imagery than hate speech. It's much easier to train your software to spot pictures of genitals than it is to interpret the nuances of potentially anti-semitic, Islamophobic or mendacious writings. Yet online corporations loathe spending money on this unprofitable human labour, and try their hardest to conceal the sordid reality of their moderation practices from public view. Every outside investigation reveals the same pattern – essentially, it's dirty work that is outsourced to a woefully inadequate number of underpaid and overwhelmed contractors, hired in places where labour is cheap, and usually overseen by executives without much linguistic competence or familiarity with the cultures in which their platform is operating. Compared with the corporate leaders' ambitions to move fast, break things and monetize human attention for profit, targeting harmful content is a low priority, especially when it comes to far-away foreign markets. It's also invariably the first thing to be cut when savings need to be made – after Musk acquired Twitter, its global content-moderation and harm-policy units were soon decimated.

The fact that these corporations are led by Americans makes the problem worse, for they invariably take for granted the shibboleths of their own culture's current free-speech doctrine: speech is not action; the answer to bad speech should be more speech, not 'censorship'; America's 'content-neutral' approach is the best; all ideas deserve an airing in the marketplace; truth will out; Section 230 absolves them of all responsibility; individual 'freedom' is the highest good. Those are not principles disposed to see editorial intervention in other people's online expression as desirable, let alone essential.

Yet the deepest issue is that, ultimately, the very aims of content moderation – preventing harm and misinformation – get in the way of the corporate priority to make money. When Facebook entered Myanmar in the 2010s, just as the country's internet use was exploding, it quickly gained a near-monopoly on online communication, and was soon co-opted by the country's military dictatorship and ultra-nationalist politicians to spread hatred and incite violence against its ethnic minorities. The company did virtually nothing to stop this. It had no office in the country; no knowledge of the language; almost no staff to oversee the uses to which its platform was being put, or to filter the violent, genocidal propaganda that it was soon transmitting to millions of Burmese. All it cared about was growing its market share.

In India, similarly, where it now has hundreds of millions of users who communicate in dozens of languages, Facebook has been notoriously unwilling to police the systematic spreading of hate and violent incitement by Hindu nationalists allied to the country's increasingly authoritarian government. Even when its own, vastly overwhelmed, content-moderating staff raise red flags, Facebook's local executives often overrule them, so as to remain in favour with nationalist politicians. Twitter (now called X) takes a similar approach to these problems. 'We had just promised [Wall] Street 3x user growth,' a former executive explained in 2023, off the record, 'and the only way that was going to be possible was with India.' In any case, as these corporations have also amply proved in their home territories, divisive and extreme content is actually good for business. It generates clicks and 'engagement'. It feeds on itself; it trains the algorithm to provide more, to go further; it keeps people hooked much more effectively than sane and boring stuff. And because this business model also rewards grass-roots creators of material who manage to attract sizeable audiences, plenty of people now also earn large incomes from spreading deliberate lies online. If you want to make serious money, trying to prevent harmful speech just gets in the way.

It does not seem likely that American policymakers will be able to address these problems effectively anytime soon. That's not just because its internet corporations are immensely rich, powerful and influential; nor because the question of their speech regulations has been politicized by right-wing politicians complaining about partisan 'censorship'. It's rather because their practice so thoroughly epit-omizes American free-speech attitudes in general. The libertarian revolution in First Amendment jurisprudence over the past few dec-ades has left Americans with a doctrine that is singularly ill-equipped to deal with the present moment. The mantra of strict content and viewpoint neutrality doesn't help when dealing with an avalanche of misinformation spread by bad actors and amplified by greedy cor-porate algorithms – nor does the presumption that truth will always emerge in open, unregulated discussion. Explicitly freeing corpora-tions from any responsibility for spreading and promoting poisonous ideas, and barring all 'public figures' from any redress against blatant defamatory lies, are also not ideal conditions for advancing truth and protecting democracy. Neither the principle that speech is separate from action, nor the dogma that hate speech is best countered by more speech, nor the belief that speech should never be 'chilled', are very persuasive when set against the daily, years-long reality of har-assment, violence and misinformation orchestrated and celebrated worldwide through online platforms.

The presumption that free-market economics and voluntary cor-porate action are enough to safeguard the rights of the public, let alone advance the common good, looks equally naïve when set against the actual effects of a public sphere largely monopolized for profit by giant businesses. The increasingly absolutist anti-governmental interpretation of the First Amendment, whereby (as a federal judge ruled in 2023) it is illegal for the government even to ask a private company to do something about the spread of egregious medical mis-information online, doesn't inspire confidence even in the possibility of legislation. Nor, in the final analysis, does a legal approach to free speech that increasingly cares only about the rights of individuals and of corporations, not the interests of the broader public, civil soci-ety or a functioning democracy. The more the marketplace of ideas shifts online, the less satisfactory becomes the principle of leaving its shape and substance entirely in the hands of an arbitrary group of profit-seeking capitalists. But for the time being, American free-speech jurisprudence has essentially backed itself into a corner.

Given that the problems of online speech have been so largely cre-ated by American companies following current American principles, it's ironic but perhaps not surprising that the different attitude to freedom of expression that has always been favoured by other cultures seems better equipped to tackle them – or at least to try. Back in the late 1940s, when US laws and attitudes still broadly shared that alternative, balancing approach to free speech, Eleanor Roosevelt, the tireless civil rights activist and widow of President Franklin D. Roosevelt, led the drawing up of an international Universal Declaration of Human Rights, which was adopted in 1948 by the newly formed United Nations. Article 19 of this brief document set out that 'everyone has the right to freedom of opinion and expression; this right includes freedom to hold opinions without interference and to seek, receive and impart information and ideas through any media and regardless of frontiers'. The two final articles specified the limits of this and all other individual rights. They could not extend to any act contrary to the principles of the United Nations, or intended to destroy rights. More specifically, every person had 'duties to the community'. All individual rights were thus subject to legal limits 'for the purpose of securing due recognition and respect for the rights and freedoms of others and of meeting the just requirements of morality, public order and the general welfare in a democratic society'. As well as its clear statement that individual liberties were always to be balanced against the rights of others and the principles of democracy, it's notable that this definition incorporated the cutting edge of American free-speech theory at this time – the presumption that free speech meant not just the right to *impart* information and ideas, but equally to *seek* and *receive* them. Throughout this era, definitions of press and speech freedom were commonly seen as encompassing a broader 'freedom of information' – 'the task of ensuring the free flow of truthful and honest information', as one UN delegate expressed it in 1946.

The Universal Declaration had no immediate legal force, but it soon inspired the creation of another document that did, and which now covers almost 700 million people in forty-six different nations – the 1950 European Convention on Human Rights. The laws and courts of every country in Europe are subject to this charter of fundamental rights, and to the supreme jurisdiction of the supra-national European Court of Justice, which exists to enforce it – from Albania to the United Kingdom, from Azerbaijan to Ukraine (only Russia, which was expelled in 2022 over its invasion of Ukraine, is now no longer part of this legal framework).

Adopting the Universal Declaration's approach, the European Convention's creators agreed that 'everyone has the right to freedom of expression', and that this meant the right to receive as well as to impart information and ideas. They also stressed that, because free speech 'carries with it duties and responsibilities', it was legitimately subject to legal restrictions that 'are necessary in a democratic society'. Beyond national security, those included public safety, the prevention of disorder, 'the protection of health or morals', 'the authority and impartiality of the judiciary' and 'the protection of the reputation or rights of others'. 'Broadcasting, television or cinema enterprises' could be subject to state licensing, and the rights of any speaker must always be balanced against their responsibilities to the public.

This general approach, which not only balances liberties against duties, but also foregrounds the rights of others, the difference between citizens and corporations, and the paramount duty of states to promote democratic values, creates a much more complicated situation than in the United States – and not just because there are plenty of differences of detail between the speech and press laws of different European nations. Attending carefully to the context, reach, intent and effect of expression, as well as its content, instead of simply maximizing the rights of speakers, can lead to seemingly inconsistent or divergent judgments and penalties. The stronger libel laws are, the more open to abuse, especially by deep-pocketed litigants. Strict injunctions against contempt of court can weaken public oversight of legal proceedings and of potential miscarriages of justice. All these are features of free-speech jurisprudence in Britain and other European countries. Legally, instead of ever-clearer and sharper rules, which the modern American system valorizes, the balancing approach is likely to produce only an endless sequence of cases where judges and courts muddle through to the best of their judgement, taking into account the changing values of their communities on particular subjects. But perhaps that's a reasonable price to pay for attending to the real-world purposes and effects of speech in plural, democratic societies.

More importantly, the balancing outlook also allows for a more cogent approach to the free-speech problems that have been so hugely amplified by the digital revolution – and to holding media corporations to account for their role in exacerbating them. In the European Union, as of 2024, the Digital Services Act and the Digital Markets Act oblige internet companies to protect their users and to safeguard the public interest – or else be fined billions of dollars, and be made to change their business practices. Those new obligations include: forcefully combating misinformation; mandatory transparency about a platform's amplification of divisive content; new procedures to flag and quickly remove illegal or dangerous material (including hostile state propaganda and medical misinformation); external as well as internal mechanisms for users to contest disputed content moderation; yearly public audits of the harmful content and the 'systemic risks' to the public interest of platform's operations; robust systems to prevent manipulation; access for researchers to a platform's data; and bans on advertising targeted at children, or on the basis of race, religion, political views and other characteristics, or at users who do not wish to share their personal data. The larger the platform and its profits, the more onerous its legal responsibilities.

In the United Kingdom, a less ambitious Online Safety Act of 2023, again backed by the threat of large fines and intervention by the national media regulator, imposes on online platforms a similar 'duty of care' towards the public, mandating them to take proactive steps to reduce risks to their users, especially children, to be fully transparent about their content-moderation procedures, and to limit the amplification of harmful content, such as that promoting eating disorders, self-harm, misogyny or antisemitism.

As critics of these statutes have noted, they are imperfect measures. As with any law, their effectiveness will depend on how well they are enforced. But whatever their outcome, they remind us of the complexities of free speech, and of a conception of it that has a much longer and richer history, even within the United States, than the arid reductionism of recent American presumptions. For these are not measures taken only in reaction to the recent practices of US corporations – they also develop further several principles that have been central to non-libertarian free-speech doctrine for the past three centuries. Their outlook balances the rights and profits of speakers, publishers and corporations against their responsibilities – towards their users, audiences and the public as a whole. It recognizes that publishers of speech and shapers of public discourse should be held accountable for their actions, and their effects on the world, proportionate to their power. It presumes that the marketplace of ideas ought to serve the public good, and that the truth can sometimes need protection from deliberate falsehood. It appreciates that the content of speech matters – yet also that its meaning is always dependent on the identity of the speaker, the audience and the context. Above all, it recognizes that speech is an *action*, and that it can sometimes cause harm, whether singly or cumulatively, to individuals, groups or the public more generally. How to judge all these things is difficult; to agree on rules about them, even more so; to enforce those consistently, hardest of all. But it's probably better than to ignore them altogether, and just hope for the best. And that is also why the history of free speech matters. The richer our collective understanding of how and why, over the past three hundred years, we've conceived of and come to stand for 'free speech', the better equipped we'll be to safeguard its future.

Afterword

From the Past to the Future

What use is history in thinking about free speech in the present?

People tend to answer that question in one of two ways. The first response comes from those who like to see a clear line from the past to the present. That includes civil liberties lawyers, the tech and media leaders whose decisions shape our modern communicative world, and most chroniclers of censorship. Their presumption is that, over the past three hundred years, western societies have progressed from repression to ever-greater freedom of expression. The American strand of this story is by far the most widely celebrated. Its basic narrative is that the principles of modern free speech were implicit in the words of the First Amendment, drafted in 1789; that the US Supreme Court has interpreted them with ever-greater sophistication over the past century; and that those ideals remain true in our own time – even if the rise of social media has complicated their practical application. In this view, freedom of expression is always simply 'advancing' or 'retreating' – it's either 'under threat' or being 'defended'.

The alternative answer, more recently proposed by some journalists and social scientists, is essentially that the internet has broken history. Our free-speech norms and laws, they argue, were created in a vastly different environment. They can no longer cope in the face of twenty-first-century information overload, trolling and online disinformation, and need to be reconceived. History is irrelevant.

As this book has shown, both of these approaches are fundamentally mistaken – or at least grossly insufficient. The crisis of truth and trust we face today is by no means unprecedented. Fake news, lies, slander and the destabilizing impact of revolutionary new media were equally prominent problems around 1700, when free speech was first theorized in its modern form – and continued to be throughout the nineteenth and twentieth centuries, as its principles evolved. Meanwhile, the first approach, with its faith in ever-greater 'freedom', captures only part of the story, which is the increasing western mistrust of public censorship. It misses the central point that who can speak, who gets heard and who makes the rules about what one can say, has always been more about power than about truth, fairness or rational debate. In fact, the marketplace of ideas has always been mercenary and partisan. People's views, and their expressions of them, are not the product of entirely autonomous and rational choices, driven by some intrinsic human capacity to identify and favour the truth. The liberty of some comes at a cost to others: freedom for the wolves means death for the sheep. What's more, like wealth, freedom is a relative concept: certain people have more of it than others, yet almost no one ever thinks they have enough. Since it was first coined, three hundred years ago, 'free speech' has therefore been a perennially weaponized slogan, wielded as often by the powerful against the weak as by the weak against the strong.

Throughout history, there are countless examples of public lies and deceptions metastasizing with alarming ease, speed and real-life consequences. This, too, is equally true of our own time. The demagogue who defeated Hillary Clinton in 2016 lost the next American presidential election, in 2020, fair and square. But then, characteristically, he concocted an unceasing stream of outrageous bullshit to pretend that he hadn't, and incited his supporters to violently stop the legitimate transfer of power to his successor. Because of his words, election officials across the country had their lives destroyed by his adherents; the United States Capitol building was invaded and ransacked; people were maimed and killed.

When faced with legal challenges to his ongoing behaviour, the demagogue's lawyers invariably invoked his and his supporters' First Amendment rights. The wide acceptance by tens of millions of Americans of his blatant untruths, and his party's craven and cynical amplification of them for partisan purposes, seriously destabilized popular trust in fair elections and the rule of law, and thus the foundation of the entire political system of the United States – as well as helping him and his acolytes to win re-election in 2024. The more libertarian our free-speech doctrines are, the less able they are to counter the toxic effects of blatant lying in public life – in fact, they only make it worse. ('Much that he has said has been patently false and has caused great harm to countless individuals, as well as to the Republic itself,' even the ACLU acknowledged in 2023 – before predictably pivoting to support, and thus amplify, the demagogue's overriding claims to 'a First Amendment right to speak'.)

Conversely, this book's charting of the evolution of our present world view has also, I hope, brought out how messy, fragile and contingent it is – the product of millions of constantly shifting choices and circumstances. At every stage, things could have developed otherwise. In different places, they did. That is why we've ended up with such varying ideas about free speech in our different societies. Our own presumptions are not the result of some naturally ordained progress towards perfection, but simply where we happen to be now. We could make other intellectual and practical choices in the future. Circumstances change. And doubtless we will, too. Free speech is always in flux.

For all these reasons, as I've tried to show, the real history of free speech has the potential to illuminate our current predicaments in surprisingly direct ways. For the reason why, over the course of three hundred years, it has proved impossible to turn the mottoes of press and speech liberty into coherent, watertight doctrines is not only because they have been interpreted in many different ways. It's also, more basically, because of the inherently fraught relationship between free-speech ideals and the reality of actual speech – that is, the ways in which human communication, whatever the medium and the scale, really works.

For example, it's obvious that two contradictory things are true. On the one hand, as we've seen, speech is always free. Even in the most oppressive circumstances it remains irrepressible and potentially subversive. It's not truly possible to stop people from communicating, any more than we can stop them from thinking.

On the other hand, as we've also noted, speech is never free. Because all communication requires rules, and therefore constraints. Even to speak to yourself requires following some basic laws of language – otherwise it is just unintelligible noise. And the moment you try to communicate with other people, many more requirements come into play. In fact, the effect of what you say – in person, in writing or in any other way – may be largely determined not by your own intentions, but by whatever presumptions your interlocutors bring to your words. The ultimate meaning of any utterance is created in the minds of its audience, not in that of the speaker.

So much for actual speech. Freedom of speech, by contrast, is an essentially artificial doctrine. It only works by minimizing or denying some basic facts about communication. The stronger its pretensions, the more forcefully it tries to do so. The first of its claims is that speech is separate from action. That is not true. Speech is itself an action. Most of the time, it's a fleeting, trivial, weak kind of act. But all communication has effects in the world: that is what it's for. And sometimes those effects, individually or cumulatively, are destructive in more than a trivial way, to other people or to the public as a whole. People in the past knew this only too well. Doctrines of free speech that balance rights with responsibilities grew out of this realization. Americans until fairly recently acknowledged it too – and still routinely do in different settings, for example when considering the problem of workplace harassment. Only modern First Amendment dogma, pretending that speech and action are essentially separate, tries to define away questions of libel, falsehood and civic harm.

The second inconvenient truth that theories of free speech are forced to minimize is that the effect of words always depends on their context, not just on the content. Who is speaking, to whom, where, when and why? What is the medium, the audience, the intent, the desired or actual effect? Is it a one-off statement, or part of a pattern? In short, how does this utterance fit into the world? No two speakers are alike; different expressions of the same words can have vastly different meanings and consequences, depending on the context. These are, again, basic truths about how words work in the real world. But they are problematic for conceptions of free speech as an individual right, precisely because they imply that different people might be treated differently for seemingly similar actions. After all, laws and rights are predicated on exactly the opposite principles: equality of status; equality of treatment; consistency; transparency. That is why it's simpler, and might seem fairer, just to strip away as much as you can of those potentially subjective, context-dependent judgements, and to move towards a more 'absolutist' approach to expression. But in doing so, you're simply widening the gap between your doctrine of 'free speech' and how speech really works.

A related problem with laws about expression is that, even leaving aside these fundamental difficulties of meaning, context and consistency, it is very hard to enforce them. In ordinary communication, expressive rules, which take in context as well as content, are constantly being refined and enforced, both face to face between individuals and in larger groups. That's what people describe when they refer to 'cancel culture'. There are two basic reasons why this has become such a prominent feature of our present communicative world, and why, as older people and free-speech libertarians like to complain, it feels as though there is 'less free speech' these days than there used to be. One reason is political: it's a result of the growing power and voice of previously marginalized groups, and the rise of identity politics. In liberal democracies, one cannot any longer unthinkingly or uncontroversially broadcast sexist jokes, homophobic slurs, racist and ethnic stereotypes, and many other kinds of previously normalized but now contentious speech. You can view this as a sad diminution of 'free speech' – or as a welcome and overdue denunciation of the automatic right to say hateful and ill-judged things. For are those now calling out that previous presumption as ill-founded not simply exercising their own liberty of expression? Is 'cancelling' a form of speech or of action? (It's both, of course.) Controversies over boycotting, which have raged ever since the origins of the practice in the nineteenth century, tend to take a similar form. Ultimately, such questions and divisions are at base always arguments about substantive issues (sexism, transgender policies, the politics of the Middle East, and so on), masquerading as clashes about speech rights.

These conflicts have in turn been turbocharged by the second reason for the rise of 'cancel culture'. The world of 24/7 news and social media has made the process of public judgement much more fast-paced, visible and brutal. Online speech can spin out of its creator's control even more quickly and massively than any other kind. Social conventions differ and change; misjudge your audience (even if *they* misinterpret *you*, or it turns into a completely different audience than you were actually addressing), and they will inevitably abandon, criticize or punish you. That kind of online judgement tends to involve vastly more people than any kind of real-life interaction, and is also much more likely to be vicious and abusive – people both are and feel much freer to abuse others in cyberspace than in person, especially as they can do so anonymously. What's more, despite the bottomless ephemerality of the online world, it's also in some respects the most permanent medium of personal shame. Every online exchange, no matter how casual or fleeting, is electronically recorded. Once they're out of your personal control, any embarrassing expressions, stories or details posted to the internet are liable to remain in the public domain indefinitely, for anyone to be able to retrieve in the blink of an eye.

Social and linguistic norms evolve largely organically, and their sanctions, online and off, are largely informal. To enforce such things by law, especially for a whole nation, is a much harder proposition. After all, the larger the group the more difficult it is to agree on the exact terms. Laws can't be updated as quickly and automatically as expressive norms. And legal mechanisms are in any case clumsy instruments to apply to speech, writing and images. They require resources to be spent on policing and prosecuting utterances; their procedures are cumbersome; their sanctions limited and blunt. (This is not just a problem for whole nations: university campuses struggle with the same difficulties.) As the history of legal regulation abundantly shows, it does work, both directly and as a way of inhibiting certain kinds of unwanted speech – but its exercise can also have the contrary effect, of giving publicity and moral authority (as martyrs for 'free speech') to the very ideas and practices that it tries to suppress.

This is one reason why it is a mistake, when grappling with freedom of expression, to focus too much on speakers. For often the critical issue is not speech per se but the responsibility for its amplification. Beyond the rights of individuals and the powers of governments, one needs therefore also to consider the crucial role of the people and mechanisms in the middle – the largely private media (whether printed, broadcast or online) through which most 'public' speech is actually boosted, circulated and consumed. Of course, 'the media' is made up of lots of different publishers, channels and other forms of amplification, with vastly different reach and power, who quite reasonably adopt a wide range of different standards and practices. But, allowing for all those differences, the key question remains – what are those media's responsibilities to the public good, however defined, and how should these duties be articulated and enforced? For example, do they claim to respect the truth, or the equal dignity of citizens, or the principles of democracy? Are they a forum for news, entertainment, personal interaction or some combination of these things? What norms do they purport to uphold, what resources do they devote to this, and how effectively and transparently do they do so? For the simple fact is that even the most libertarian, free-for-all website has to moderate its content, to ensure that people don't post anything wildly illegal. So it's reasonable to demand that moderation policies and practices be transparent, proportionate to a particular channel or medium's range and reach, and accountable to the society in which they operate.

It's not rational to presume that all these things will take care of themselves, especially where vast sums of money and other forms of power are involved. In every sphere of life – foods, medicines, financial services – it is generally understood that markets need guardrails, in order to protect their users against cheats and liars, as well as to benefit the common good. The same is true of the communicative marketplace. Instead of endlessly disagreeing about the limits of individual free speech, it's probably more productive to focus on how best to regulate or incentivize the practices of different forms of media so that they take into account the wider public interest. That means at a safe distance from direct or partisan governmental control, but it also means more than the fig leaf of 'self-regulation'. It's about making media entities take responsibility for their actions in the world, as many already do, and being able to hold them quickly and effectively accountable when they demonstrably fail to abide by their own standards. False advertising harms the public. So do quack medicines. We have developed mechanisms for dealing with both. We know that misinformation is a similar problem, especially online – and that there are other worrisome features of our new, fast-evolving media landscape. The mass public release of tools of Artificial Intelligence by companies greedy for attention and profit is already making all this more acute. Some societies are trying to address these things, others are largely failing. The more we allow the debate about them to degenerate into partisan claims about free speech or censorship, the more we'll fail.

Where does all this leave free speech? Setting aside the more technical question of its exact legal definition, we obviously can't jettison it as a concept – nor should we. The brilliant literary critic Stanley Fish once wrote a book entitled *There's No Such Thing as Free Speech: And It's a Good Thing, Too.* As well as the assertion encapsulated in its title, he also maintained that, though 'free speech' was a meaningless catchphrase, it nonetheless remained a supremely powerful rhetorical tool. For that reason, one should always claim to stand for it – if not, your political opponents will inevitably grab the rhetorical high ground and say 'we're for free speech and you are for censorship and ideological tyranny'. At which point whatever serious, worthy argument you're really trying to make will be almost impossible to salvage.

That's been true over the past three hundred years, and it's still true today. You might be reading this in China, Iran, Russia or some other country with an undemocratic, repressive regime. You might be gay or trans, or pro-choice, or pro-life, or pro-Palestinian, or pro-Israel, Christian, Muslim, Jewish or atheist, in a place where that is contentious. Or you might be none of these things – but whatever your personal outlook, you will surely know that people everywhere are always trying to restrict the expression of unwelcome ideas. At an individual level, whatever your truth, freedom of speech is an inspiring ideal – an encouragement to speak out and to fight for others to be heard, too. Throughout history, it's been an integral part of most political struggles, a valuable weapon for the weak as well as the strong.

But for the same reason, it has also often been deployed by the powerful to discredit others – as it still is. In the United States, grassroots efforts to track and call out the spread of disinformation online, including propaganda seeded by Russia, China and other hostile foreign entities, are now routinely attacked and legally challenged by right-wing politicians, as well as by the media organizations most prone to amplifying such garbage, as unwarranted 'censorship' – a threat to 'free speech', the First Amendment and democracy itself. It's only superficially an irony that exactly the same kinds of right-wing lawmakers and activists are simultaneously putting in place an ever more repressive system of governmental censorship in states they control, aimed at curtailing press criticism of their actions, making 'religious liberty' an excuse for discriminatory speech and action, and suppressing the discussion of racism, sexism, gender identity, sexual orientation and other unwelcome subjects in public schools, universities and other arenas. Nor is it surprising that they have seized on the language of 'fake news' and 'disinformation' to describe what they're supposedly battling against. As we've seen throughout this book, appropriating and weaponizing powerful catchphrases in a logically incoherent but politically effective way has been central to the history of free speech for three hundred years. We're still living in that moment, and we always will. There will never be a single answer to the question 'What is free speech?'.

That is why it is unhelpful to distil our disagreements into the simplistic query 'Are you in favour of free speech?' Nor does it make sense to elevate freedom of expression into an important end in itself, as is conventional – let alone to make it the highest ideal, as is also a popular position ('I'm an absolutist!'). Those are all just ways of not having to think too hard about the real problems of speech, while simultaneously feeling morally superior.

If you've read this book, you'll know that there are more meaningful questions to ask, namely 'What is free speech being invoked *for*, in this particular instance?' and 'How far do I agree with those aims?' – do I favour them, am I indifferent, or do I oppose them? It doesn't follow that one should only permit speech whose aims align with one's own, or to which one is indifferent. Tolerance of opposing views is a virtue, and a necessity in any democratic society. What's more, even if you disapprove of them, any flourishing culture is going to be full of lies, bullshit and offensive language. There are contexts in which each of these may be tolerable or even appropriate. But it is also perfectly reasonable to oppose utterances that you believe to be seriously harmful, and to argue that these shouldn't qualify as 'free speech'. That is, again, not to say that they should be automatically sanctioned. But it does mean looking beyond the complacent First Amendment platitude that the only possible response even to truly injurious utterances is simply to counter them with more speech.

And it certainly means denying such expressions the moral and legal authority of being treated as 'free speech'.

To take this alternative approach is, unfortunately, a far more tedious and tiring way of going through life than just to proclaim that you're a 'free speech absolutist' and be done with it. Because having to answer those two meaningful questions, over and over again, forces one to confront, in each different case, the real, underlying political stakes. It compels one to argue about where the limits of permissible expression should lie *with regard to those particular questions*, and then to consider the exact context and effect of every controversial utterance. Is it antisemitic to criticize Zionism, or to accuse the state of Israel of apartheid? Does it undermine the fabric of our democracy to spread lies about elections? Is it putting lives at risk to amplify misinformation about a deadly contagious disease? Do we want to live in a society in which children are invariably exposed to hardcore pornography? Does it demean a vulnerable immigrant minority to ridicule their holiest beliefs? Should any of this be allowed as a form of art, or satire, or academic enquiry, even if it would be objectionable in other settings? The questions are endless. Yet those are, in fact, precisely the kinds of issues that we *should* be focusing our debates on, rather than being continually short-circuited into abstract arguments about the 'right to free speech' or the dangers of 'censorship', 'indoctrination' or 'cancel culture'. The next time you hear someone invoke one of those slogans, try to look past it – which substantive issue are they're attempting to distract you from? In truth, talk about free speech can never be separated from the larger questions of how society ought to be organized: it can't be theorized in the abstract, without taking into account those substantive issues.

The ultimate argument for free speech as a personal right is that it is the counterpart of freedom of thought. It allows people to express their personal identity, and promotes their intellectual development. For only by trying out ideas on each other, so the argument goes, can we figure out what to believe, criticize what is wrong and progress towards the truth, individually and collectively. Advancing truth has always been a guiding principle, as well as a purported aim, of most forms of free speech.

Yet the curious reality is that, in every sphere of life actually devoted to the collective pursuit of truth, the greatest freedom of enquiry goes hand in hand with clear rules of expression. That is true, for example, of good investigative journalism, which depends not just on hiring the best reporters and pursuing hidden stories wherever they may lead, but also on producing solid evidence, endless fact- and source-checking, careful editorial oversight, and an openness to acknowledge and correct mistakes. This is one reason why quality journalism is so poorly appreciated by the masters of the internet, who hate 'friction', champion 'disruption' and disdain the inherited authority of 'legacy' or 'mainstream' media. After all, all those quality-control mechanisms slow things down, add expense and limit your freedom to just assert whatever you like. But that is precisely the cost of getting it right. Not all journalism is equal, even if it pretends to be telling you the truth. In fact, 'the press', in the sense of a truth-seeking fourth estate, has always been just as much of a weaponized catchphrase as 'free speech': anyone can claim its noble mantle, even for dubious ends.

Scholarship, whether produced in universities or outside them, is the arena of human life in which these principles have been most thoroughly institutionalized. It's obviously a deeply imperfect sphere: scholarly life is as rife with social biases as the wider cultures in which it is embedded, and its processes are not immune from fraud and abuse. But it remains the best example we have of a speech model that has as its overriding purpose the advancement of truth about hard questions – and that has been proven to work.

This model rests on three fundamental pillars. The first is complete freedom of thought and enquiry – a principle that evolved out of the long tradition of scholarly 'liberty of philosophizing' whose history we surveyed in Chapter 5. In modern universities this concept is usually defined as 'academic freedom'.* Its legal corollary is the prin-

---

* The exact definition and application of this term remains contentious, especially in the United States and to a lesser extent in the United Kingdom, where university campuses have in recent years been roiled by clashes over 'free speech'. One reason for this ongoing controversy is that it is often presumed that, if universities are dedicated to free enquiry, they should permit a maximal liberty of expression for their members and on their grounds (including for outside speakers) – otherwise they are supposedly failing in their mission. Both university administrators and their culture-war enemies (who are keen to foment or publicize clashes over controversial 'free

ciple of academic tenure – job security for academic staff, in order to insulate their activities from political and other external pressures. Its essence is that a scholar may freely pursue any question, wherever it leads, no matter how controversial or distasteful. But the second principle is that, for your ideas to be accepted, they have to pass a very highly regulated system of quality control – expert, double-blind peer reports, experimental replication, post-publication reviews and other forms of fact- and claim-checking by knowledgeable authorities. Your argument needs to rest on solid, verifiable evidence, and to meet disciplinary standards. Last of all, in disseminating it, you must follow norms of scholarly respect and civil expression. Even repellent ideas and fierce disagreements must be expressed in non-abusive language. None of this is easy or natural; all of these protocols have had to be laboriously invented, refined and upheld by generations of scientists and scholars. But that's the point. Trust and authority have to be earned and constantly revalidated. To establish facts and advance the truth requires not just individual effort but lots of collective rules and agreement. In other words, the closest approximation to our popular ideal of the marketplace of ideas as a generator of truth is scholarly freedom of enquiry and debate – but what that looks like up close is the opposite of the venal, free-for-all, click-bait gutter of the real-world public sphere. Instead of absolute liberty of expression, the real truth-seeking marketplace depends on all sorts of regulation.

That may seem like a paradox, but it isn't really. It's the logical outcome of considering what freedom of enquiry might be for, and how we collectively could best pursue that aim. Different ends require different means. Free speech, too, can have various different aims. Its history does not suggest that greater freedom of expression automatically leads to better outcomes, that liberty of speech should necessarily be allowed to trump other principles, or even that it is

---

speech' on campuses) tend to take this premise for granted. But it is not, in fact, a necessary corollary of the academic freedom of scholars pursuing knowledge. Speech in the classroom, speech by students, the speech of visitors to a campus, and any other form of expressive activity that may take place on a university's grounds, are all significantly different from the core business of scholarly freedom of enquiry and utterance as defined here. They should not all be lumped together as university 'freedom of speech'.

best conceived of only as an individual right, rather than as a public or collective good. In fact, that history always leads us back to harder and more fundamental questions. What should 'freedom' mean, and whose freedom are we talking about? What are our aims as a society, and how can we advance them? What do we do when those ends conflict with each other, or we ourselves cannot agree? What kinds of communication help or hinder us in resolving those problems? Just talking in the abstract about 'free speech' won't get us very far; nor will setting up legal doctrines that ignore how communication really works in the world. Only by pursuing those ever-evolving basic questions can we truly begin to grasp what free speech is, could be or should be – and hence, to arrive at a better understanding of ourselves, and each other.

Notes

The spelling and punctuation of quotations from older works has been generally modernized. Unless otherwise indicated, all translations into English are my own, and quoted italics are those of the original source. In order to save space, I have dispensed with a separate bibliography, shortened titles and not given places of publication except for works published outside London before 1900. Biblical quotations are from the King James translation of 1611. References to US state legislation, unless otherwise indicated, are taken from the original texts collected in the Hein Online database, 'State Constitutions Illustrated'; references to Cato's Letters are to the date and text of their original newspaper publication, followed in square brackets by the standard number (1–138) by which each essay has been identified since the collected edition of 1733.

ABBREVIATIONS

1834 CJ Report	*Report from the Select Committee on the Suppression of the Calcutta Journal,* House of Commons Papers 1834, 601
Applebee's	*Applebee's Original Weekly Journal*
BJ	*British Journal*
BL	British Library
CW	*The Collected Works of John Stuart Mill,* ed. John M. Robson et al., 33 vols (1963–91)
HBG	*Hicky's Bengal Gazette; or The Original Calcutta General Advertiser*
JA	Jamaica Archives, Spanish Town
KUL	University of Kansas, Spencer Research Library

LBS	Legacies of British Slave-ownership database (www.ucl. ac.uk/lbs)
LEF	*Selected Writings of James Fitzjames Stephen: Liberty, Equality, Fraternity*, ed. Julia Stapleton (2017)
LJ	*London Journal*
NRS	National Records of Scotland, Edinburgh
ODNB	*Oxford Dictionary of National Biography* (2004), online edition (www.oxforddnb.com)
PGM	*The Papers of George Mason*, ed. Robert A. Rutland, 3 vols (1970)
PJM	*The Papers of James Madison, Congressional Series*, ed. William T. Hutchinson et al., 17 vols (1962–91)
PTJ	*The Papers of Thomas Jefferson*, ed. Julian P. Boyd et al. (1950–)
TLA	The London Archives (formerly London Metropolitan Archives)
TNA	The National Archives, London

INTRODUCTION

2 *'Good luck!'*: speech by Bill Clinton at Johns Hopkins University, 8 Mar. 2000.

2 *'increasingly futile'*: Audra Ang, 'Hillary Clinton Memoir Altered by Chinese Publisher to Delete Sensitive Subjects', Associated Press, 23 Sept. 2003.

2 *official censors*: Robert Darnton, *Censors at Work* (2014), pt 1.

4 *global concept*: on the contemporary world, see esp. Timothy Garton Ash, *Free Speech* (2016).

8 *brilliant work*: see e.g. Catharine A. MacKinnon, *Only Words* (1993); Stanley Fish, *There's No Such Thing as Free Speech and It's a Good Thing, Too* (1994); Judith Butler, *Excitable Speech* (1997); Robert C. Post (ed.), *Censorship and Silencing* (1998); Frederick Schauer, 'The Boundaries of the First Amendment', *Harvard Law Review* 17 (2004); Rae Langton, *Sexual Solipsism* (2009); Jeremy Waldron, *The Harm in Hate Speech* (2012).

9 *'I write in order to act'*: Voltaire to Jacob Vernes, *c.*15 April 1767, Letter D14117 in *Les Œuvres complètes de Voltaire*, ed. Theodore Besterman et al., 205 vols (1968–2022), 116: 53.

1. THE POWER OF SPEECH

11 *'words are but wind'*: William Shakespeare, *The Comedy of Errors*, Act III, scene 1; see also John Spurr, 'A Profane History of Early Modern Oaths', *Transactions of the Royal Historical Society* (2001), 55–6.

11 *'A word is a bird'*: quoted in Nicholas Ostler, *Empires of the Word* (2005), 84.

11 *'All things are founded'*: *Manu's Code of Law*, ed. and trans. Patrick Olivelle (2005), 137.

11 *'Be a craftsman in speech'*: quoted in Ostler, *Empires*, 122.

12 *'Death and life'*: Proverbs 18:21.

12 *'The tongue is a fire'* etc.: James 3:6, 3:8.

12 *Other scriptural passages*: see Edward Reyner, *Rules for the Government of the Tongue* (1658 edn), esp. [A4v–A7v], 103–5.

12 *treated as crimes*: Martine Veldhuizen, *Sins of the Tongue in the Medieval West* (2017).

12 *'to tell or publish'*: Statute of Westminster, 3 Ed. I c. 34 (1275).

12 *'false news'* etc.: Statute of Gloucester, 2 Rich. II c. 5 (1378).

12 *defamation, 'scolding'*: see e.g. Richard Wunderli, *London Church Courts and Society on the Eve of the Reformation* (1981), 63–80; Marjorie McIntosh, *Controlling Misbehavior in England, 1370–1600* (2009), 58–65; Veldhuizen, *Sins of the Tongue*, ch. 5.

12 *medieval Iceland*: *Laws of Early Iceland*, trans. Andrew Dennis et al., 2 vols (1980–2006), 2: 195–200.

12 *heresy and blasphemy*: see e.g. Psalms 15:3, 34:13, 39:1, 50:19; 1 Peter 3:10.

13 *Alexander Champion*: Martin Ingram, *Church Courts, Sex, and Marriage in England, 1570–1640* (1987), 95.

13 *burnt at the stake*: William Monter, 'Heresy Executions in Reformation Europe, 1520–1565', in Ole Peter Grell and Bob Scribner (eds), *Tolerance and Intolerance in the European Reformation* (1996).

13 *new crime of 'sedition'*: see e.g. 26 Hen. 8 c. 13 (1534); 1&2 Phil. & Mary c. 3 (1554–5); 1 Eliz. c. 6 (1558); G. R. Elton, *The Tudor Constitution* (1982 edn), 59–80; Simon Walker, 'Rumour, Sedition and Popular Protest in the Reign of Henry IV', *Past and Present* 166 (2000).

13 *more than a hundred*: David Cressy, *Dangerous Talk* (2010), 50.

13 *'reproach, or slander'*: *The Acts of the Parliament of Scotland*, ed. Thomas Thomson, 11 vols (1814–75), 3: 375 (1585, c. 1); see also 3: 296 (1584, c. 8) and 4: 65 (1594, c. 15).

13 *John Stubbs dared write a pamphlet*: *John Stubbs's 'Gaping Gulf'*, ed. Lloyd E. Berry (1968), xxxiv–xxxvii.

14 *laws against insubordinate criticism*: see Wendell Bird, *Press and Speech Under Assault* (2016), 49–51.

14 *cursing and swearing*: Ashley Montagu, *The Anatomy of Swearing* (1967), 129–30, ch. 9; Thomas Waters, 'Irish Cursing and the Art of Magic, 1750–2018', *Past and Present* 247 (2020).

14 *'scolds' and 'barrators'*: on scolds, barrators and cucking-stools, see e.g. Laura Gowing, *Domestic Dangers* (1996), 115, 122; Keith Thomas, *In Pursuit of Civility* (2018), 91.

14 *'branks'*: Margo Todd, *The Culture of Protestantism in Early Modern Scotland* (2002), 141–2, 257 n. 116, 259 n. 125, plate 15; and more generally on speech and its regulation, 135, 143, 147, 157–9, 167, 235–51, 258–9, 261, 287–8, 298, 352–5, 360, 375–6, 382–3, 395–6.

14 *'he was as good a man'*: *The Life of Edward Earl of Clarendon*, 2 vols (Oxford, 1760), 1: 57; see also G. D. Squibb, *The High Court of Chivalry* (1959), 64.

14 *all reputable citizens*: see e.g. Ian Maclean, 'The Law of Defamation and the Theory of Meaning in Europe, 1500–1630', *Journal of the Institute of Romance Studies* 1 (1992); Donald Spaeth, 'Words and Deeds', *History Workshop Journal* (2014), 5–6.

15 *main preoccupation was to limit it*: see e.g. Arlette Farge, *Subversive Words*, trans. Rosemary Morris (1994); Jane Kamensky, *Governing the Tongue* (1997); Jonathan I. Israel, *Radical Enlightenment* (2001), ch. 5; Debora Shuger, *Censorship and Cultural Sensibility* (2006); Cressy, *Dangerous Talk*; *Censorship and the Press, 1580–1720*, ed. Geoff Kemp and Jason McElligott, 4 vols (2009).

15 *'The stroke of the whip'*: Ecclesiastes 28:17.

15 *'a bitter jest'*: Robert Burton, *The Anatomy of Melancholy* (1621), 198. For other examples, see Proverbs 25:15 ('By long forbearing is a prince persuaded, and a soft tongue breaketh the bone'); Bartlett Jere Whiting, *Early American Proverbs and Proverbial Phrases* (1977), 447 ('A soft Tongue breaks the bone': last recorded 1744); Cressy, *Dangerous Talk*, 5.

15 *'Many times a scorn'*: John Donne, *A Sermon of Commemoration* (1627), 11–12.

15 *'their good names'*: *The Use of the Law*, 1, in *The Lawyers Light* (1629). Cf. Dianne Hall, 'Words as Weapons', *Éire-Ireland* 41 (2006).

15 *'declare hatred'* etc.: Thomas Hobbes, *Leviathan* (1651), ch. 15; see also Teresa M. Bejan, 'Hobbes Against Hate Speech', *British Journal for the History of Philosophy* 32 (2024).

15 *'if a man calls another man'*: *Laws of Early Iceland*, trans. Andrew Dennis et al., 2 vols (1980–2006), 2: 354; see also 1: 258.

16 *the personal duel*: David Quint, 'Duelling and Civility in Sixteenth Century Italy', *I Tatti Studies in the Italian Renaissance* 7 (1997); Courtney Erin Thomas, *If I Lose Mine Honour I Lose Myself* (2017), ch. 1.

16 *quarrelling in a church*: 5&6 Edw. VI, c. 4.

16 *Defamation cases*: Spaeth, 'Words and Deeds', 10.

16 *any language that gave offence*: 'An Ordinance Against Challenges, Duels, and All Provocations Thereunto' (June 1654), in C. H. Firth and R. S. Raitt (eds), *Acts and Ordinances of the Interregnum, 1642–1660*, 3 vols (1911), 2: 937–9.

16 *the record makes clear*: Caroline Boswell, 'Provoking Disorder', *Journal of British Studies* 53 (2014), esp. 890, 893–4, 904–8. Cf. Steve Hindle, 'The Shaming of Margaret Knowsley', *Continuity and Change* 9 (1994), 406; Spaeth, 'Words and Deeds'.

16 *'offences against God'* etc.: Frame of Government of Pennsylvania, 5 May 1682.

16 *'shall abuse or deride'*: Great Law of Pennsylvania, 7 December 1682; see also Kamensky, *Governing the Tongue*; Kristin A. Olbertson, *The Dreadful Word* (2022).

16 *'subject to more errors'* etc.: Reyner, *Rules*, sig. [A7v], 69, 72, 105, 112–13; cf. William Perkins, *A Direction for the Government of the Tongue* (Cambridge, 1593), 11, 67.

17 *'Swearing, blaspheming'*: Perkins, *Direction*, sig. A2r.

17 *bad words* etc.: ibid., 26–7, 55, 68–73; Reyner, *Rules*, 22–3, 91ff.; John Ball, *The Power of Godlines* (1657), 327–9.

17 *'burning in the face'*: TNA, SP 12/118, fol. 72r.

18 *Speech is an action*: cf. J. L. Austin, *How to Do Things with Words* (2nd edn, 1975).

18 *'should never say anything'* etc.: *Manu's Code*, ed. Olivelle, 182, 216.

19 *set down his law code*: *The Laws of the Earliest English Kings*, ed. and trans. F. L. Attenborough (1922), 26–9.

19 *'If inferior persons'* etc.: *Wentworth Papers 1597–1628*, ed. J. P. Cooper (Camden Society, 4th series, vol. 12: 1973), 18; see also 22–3.

19 *'our elders and betters'* etc.: Perkins, *Direction*, 64.

19 *'good speech'*: Aysha Pollnitz, 'Old Words and the New World', *Transactions of the Royal Historical Society* 27 (2017), 146.

19 *'keep silence'* etc.: 1 Corinthians 14; 1 Timothy 2.

20 *female virtue*: Gowing, *Domestic Dangers*, 61 and *passim*.

20 *'Mother, go back up'* etc.: *Odyssey* 1.325–64.

20 *sexist presumptions*: Mary Beard, 'The Public Voice of Women', *London Review of Books*, 20 Mar. 2014.

20 *European feminist argument*: Hannah Dawson, *The Penguin Book of Feminist Writing* (2021).

20 *In fiction*: see e.g. Edith Joyce Benkov, 'Language and Women', in Julian N. Wasserman and Lois Roney (eds), *Sign, Sentence, Discourse* (1989).

20 *'and requested to have vote'* etc.: *Proceedings and Acts of the General Assembly of Maryland: January 1637/8–September 1664*, in *Archives of Maryland*, ed. William Hand Browne, 72 vols (Baltimore, 1883), 1: 215.

20 *strong political opinions*: see e.g. Andy Wood, 'The Queen is "a goggyll eyed hoore"', in Nicholas Tyacke (ed.), *The English Revolution* (2007).

20 *limits of female speech*: Gowing, *Domestic Dangers*.

20 *'It is objected against women'*: [Bathusa Makin], *An Essay to Revive the Antient Education of Gentlewomen* (1673), 11.

21 *spoke irreverently and out of turn*: Sara Mendelson and Patricia Crawford, *Women in Early Modern England* (1998), ch. 4.

21 *'enemies of common society'*: *The Oxford Francis Bacon*, vol. 1: *Early Writings 1584–1596*, ed. Alan Stewart (2012), 343.

21 *'have no voice'* etc.: Sir Thomas Smith, *De republica Anglorum* (1583), 33.

21 *'that no person whatsoever'*: quoted in Philip Hamburger, 'The Development of the Law of Seditious Libel', *Stanford Law Review* 37 (1985), 688.

21 *'matters of state'*: *The Works of Francis Bacon*, ed. James Spedding et al., 14 vols (1861–79), 14: 129.

21 *Among the core powers*: Hobbes, *Leviathan*, ch. 18.

22 *'for the example of others'*: *Acts of the Privy Council of England*, ed. John Roche Dasent et al., 46 vols (1890–1964), 14: 277.

22 *'malicious pamphlets'* etc.: 'An Advertisement Towching Seditious Wrytings' [after 1590], TNA, SP 12/235, fol. 178r; *The Oxford Francis Bacon*, 1: 305–12.

22 *'The ordinary precursors'* etc.: *Stuart Royal Proclamations*, ed. James F. Larkin and Paul L. Hughes, 2 vols (1973–83), vol. 1, nos 208, 218.

22 *'Not without good reason'* etc.: Niccolo Machiavelli, *Discourses* (1531), 1.8, 1.58; see also David Coast, 'Speaking for the People in Early Modern England', *Past and Present* 244 (2019).

23 *'truth for us nowadays'*: Michel de Montaigne, *The Complete Essays*, trans. M. A. Screech (1991), 756; see also Perez Zagorin, *Ways of Lying* (1990); idem, 'The Historical Significance of Lying and Dissimulation', *Social Research* 63 (1996); Dallas G. Denery II, *The Devil Wins* (2015),

ch. 3; Penny Roberts, '"Acceptable Truths" During the French Religious Wars', *Transactions of the Royal Historical Society* 30 (2020).

23 *'the infirmities and sins'* etc.: Perkins, *Direction*, 60, 63, 64.

23 *'Be rather silent'*: Elizabeth Jocelin, *The Mothers Legacie to Her Unborne Childe* (1624), 53 (published posthumously).

23 *Truth was not a sufficient defence*: Roger B. Manning, 'The Origins of the Doctrine of Sedition', *Albion* 12 (1980), 100–101; Cressy, *Dangerous Talk*, 30.

24 *'that great and immoderate'*: quoted in Shuger, *Censorship*, 13.

24 *Policing expression*: for this and the following paragraph in this chapter, see ibid.; Mark Kishlansky, 'A Whipper Whipped', *Historical Journal* 56 (2013); idem, 'Martyrs' Tales', *Journal of British Studies* 53 (2014).

24 *wild rumours and slanders*: see e.g. *The Voices of the People in Late Medieval Europe*, ed. Jan Dumolyn et al. (2014); Jan Dumolyn and Jelle Haemers, '"A bad chicken was brooding"', *Past and Present* 214 (2012); idem, '"A blabbermouth can barely control his tongue"', in Thomas Cohen and Lesley Twomey (eds), *Spoken Word and Social Practice* (2015); Adam Fox, *Oral and Literate Culture in England 1550–1700* (2000), ch. 7; Robert Darnton, *The Revolutionary Temper* (2023).

24 *'crying most fearfully'* etc.: quoted in Fox, *Oral and Literate Culture*, 360.

25 *Duke of Buckingham was a serial murderer*: Alastair Bellany and Thomas Cogswell, *The Murder of King James I* (2015).

25 *European popular political consciousness*: see e.g. Farge, *Subversive Words*; Lisa Jane Graham, *If the King Only Knew* (2000); David Zaret, *Origins of Democratic Culture* (2000); Tim Harris (ed.), *The Politics of the Excluded, c.1500–1850* (2001); Karin Bowie, *Public Opinion in Early Modern Scotland, c.1560–1707* (2020); and the literature cited in these works.

26 *hugely misinformed public*: for a brilliant contemporary illustration of this moment, see Wenceslaus Hollar, *The World is Ruled and Governed by Opinion* (engraving, 1642).

2. TOLERATING WORDS

27 *new ideas*: see e.g. Alexandra Walsham, *Charitable Hatred* (2006); Benjamin J. Kaplan, *Divided by Faith* (2007); Eliana Glaser (ed.), *Religious Tolerance in the Atlantic World* (2014).

28 *unwelcome messages*: see e.g. *John Stubbs's 'Gaping Gulf'*, ed. Lloyd E. Berry (1968).

28 *'backbite and slander'* etc.: quoted in Margo Todd, *The Culture of Protestantism in Early Modern Scotland* (2002), 372.

28 *parrhesia* etc.: outstanding treatments of these various earlier modes of free speech include Arnaldo Momigliano, 'Freedom of Speech in Antiquity', in Philip P. Wiener (ed.), *Dictionary of the History of Ideas* (1973); Ineke Sluiter and Ralph M. Rosen (eds), *Free Speech in Classical Antiquity* (2004); Arlene W. Saxonhouse, *Free Speech and Democracy in Ancient Athens* (2006); Michel Foucault, *Discourse and Truth and Parrēsia*, ed. Paul-Henri Fruchaud, Daniele Lorenzini and Nancy Luxon (2019); Irene van Renswoude, *The Rhetoric of Free Speech in Late Antiquity and the Early Middle Ages* (2019). For their later evolution, see esp. David Colclough, *Freedom of Speech in Early Stuart England* (2005); Robert G. Ingram et al. (eds), *Freedom of Speech, 1500–1850* (2020), chs 1–5.

28 *'gracious licence'* etc.: G. R. Elton, *The Tudor Constitution* (1982 edn), 270; see generally 265–74, 285–6, 289.

28 *'God's holy truth'* etc.: John Foxe, *The Ecclesiastical History* (1570 edn), bk 11, p. 1812 (quoted from the online edition at dhi.ac.uk/foxe/).

29 *'To kill a man'*: Sebastian Castellio, *Concerning Heretics*, ed. and trans. Ronald H. Bainton (1935), 271.

29 *Sebastian Franck*: Samme Zijlstra, '"Tgeloove is vrij"', in Marijke Gijswijt-Hofstra (ed.), *Een schijn van verdraagzaamheid* (1989), 44–5, 57–8.

29 *Transylvania*: E. M. Wilbur, *A History of Unitarianism in Transylvania, England and America* (1952), 38–40, 48.

29 *'faith is the gift of God'*: a reference to Ephesians 2:8–9.

29 *'great dissidence in the affairs'*: quoted in Norman Davies, *God's Playground* (1981), 160; see also Janusz Tazbir, *A State Without Stakes*, trans. A. T. Jordan (1973), ch. 6.

29 *more prudential than principled*: the protections of the Warsaw Confederation mainly applied only to the nobility: for their limited practical application to other classes, see Tazbir, *State Without Stakes*, chs 7–9.

29 *'the writing, publishing, printing'* etc.: Dirck Volkertszoon Coornhert, *Synod on the Freedom of Conscience*, ed. and trans. Gerrit Voogt (2008), 171, 176–8; see also Session 15, *passim*.

30 *novel liberty*: a useful survey is Benjamin Woodford, 'Developments and Debates in English Censorship During the Interregnum', *Early Modern Literary Studies* 17 (2014). New press laws were passed in 1643, 1647, 1649 and 1655.

30 *'I contend not for variety'* etc.: [Francis Rous], *The Ancient Bounds, or Liberty of Conscience Tenderly Stated* (1645; written in 1644), [A4v], 31, 64–5; see also Blair Worden, *God's Instruments* (2012), ch. 3. Cf.

John 8:31–2: 'Then said Jesus to those Jews which believed on him, If ye continue in my word, then are ye my disciples indeed / And ye shall know the truth, and the truth shall make you free.'

30 *there is but one truth* etc.: [Henry Vane], *Zeal Examined* (1652), 19–21.

31 *gentle exhortation*: Henry Robinson, *Liberty of Conscience* (1643), 17.

31 *Conscientious idolaters*: [Vane], *Zeal Examined*, 20.

31 *'teach or publish erroneous doctrines'* etc.: Robinson, *Liberty of Conscience*, 16–19.

31 *divorce his wife*: on Milton and divorce, see Joe Moshenska, *Making Darkness Light* (2021), 296–9.

32 *'Let her and Falsehood grapple'*: John Milton, *Areopagitica* (1644), 35.

32 *'may have more shapes'* etc.: ibid., 26, 31, 36.

32 *'the knowledge of good'* etc.: ibid., 12, 35.

32 *'there is no book so bad'*: Pliny the Younger, *Letters*, 3.5; see also Erasmus, *Adagia* (Basel, 1533 edn), preface; Cervantes, *Don Quixote*, pt 2, chs 3 and 59; Ann M. Blair, *Too Much to Know* (2010), 13.

32 *'free debate'* etc.: Milton, *A Treatise of Civil Power* (1659), 22–3.

32 *'fleshly wisdom'* etc.: [Vane], *Zeal Examined*, 23–4, 45.

33 *government licenser*: this career seems to have ended when Milton ran into trouble for having licensed a heterodox theological work in Latin. He was only following the principles he'd once set out in a pamphlet against banning books, he told the parliamentary committee that summoned him. See Leo Miller, 'New Milton Texts and Data from the Aitzema Mission, 1652', *Notes and Queries* 37 (1990), 281; Gordon Campbell and Thomas N. Corns, *John Milton* (2008), 245–8.

33 *it simply lapsed*: see Raymond Astbury, 'The Renewal of the Licensing Act in 1693 and Its Lapse in 1695', *The Library*, 5th series 33 (1978); Michael Treadwell, 'The Stationers and the Printing Acts at the End of the Seventeenth Century', in John Barnard et al. (eds), *The Cambridge History of the Book in Britain*, vol. 4: *1557–1695* (2002).

33 *tolerance of heterodox ideas as dangerous*: Mark Goldie, 'The Theory of Religious Intolerance in Restoration England', in Ole Peter Grell et al. (eds), *From Persecution to Toleration* (1991).

34 *fuelling irreligion*: see e.g. Lambeth Palace Library, MS 939/10 (1695); Francis Gregory, *A Modest Plea for the Due Regulation of the Press* (1698); G. C. Gibbs, 'Press and Public Opinion', in J. R. Jones (ed.), *Liberty Secured?* (1992), 238–9.

34 *rediscovered and popularized*: see e.g. 'Philopatris' [i.e. Charles Blount], *A Just Vindication of Learning* (1679); Charles Blount, *Reasons*

Humbly Offered for the Liberty of Unlicens'd Printing (1693); *A Complete Collection of the ... Works of John Milton*, ed. John Toland, 3 vols ('Amsterdam' [i.e. London], 1698); John Milton, *Areopagitica* (1738 edn).

34 *John Locke*: John Coffey, *Persecution and Toleration in Protestant England, 1558–1689* (2000), ch. 3.

34 *'She is not taught by Law'* etc.: [John Locke], *A Letter Concerning Toleration* (1689), 9, 40.

34 *'speculative opinions'* etc.: ibid., 39, 40, 55.

35 *religious uniformity remained central*: for example, despite Frederick the Great's personal disdain for Christianity ('an old metaphysical fiction, stuffed with contradictions and nonsense, born in the fevered imagination of the Orientals ... embraced by fanatics, exploited by opportunists, and believed by imbeciles'), and his embrace of Prussia's long history of religious toleration, the Lutheran state church played a vital role in government, and the regime's censorship laws were formulated accordingly: T. C. W. Blanning, *Frederick the Great* (2015), 194 (quoted); idem, *The Culture of Power and the Power of Culture* (2023), 202–5, 212, esp. 224–5; Franz Etzin, 'Die Freiheit der öffentlichen Meinung unter der Regierung Friedrichs des Großen', *Forschungen zur Brandenburgischen und Preußischen Geschichte* 33 (1921), 89–129; Henri Brunschwig, *Gesellschaft und Romantik in Preußen im 18. Jahrhundert* (1975), 46.

35 *allowed women to debate*: Keith Thomas, 'Women and the Civil War Sects', *Past and Present* 13 (1958).

35 *'It is not done well'*: Boswell's *Life of Johnson*, ed. G. Birkbeck Hill and L. F. Powell, 4 vols (1971), 1: 463.

35 *early campaigns for women's rights*: see e.g. [Eliza Sharples], *The Isis* (1832); 1848 Seneca Falls Declaration, in Elizabeth Cady Stanton et al., *History of Women Suffrage*, 6 vols (New York: 1881–1922), 1: 70–73.

35 *tone and content*: see Teresa M. Bejan, *Mere Civility* (2017).

35 *'Reproachful language'* etc.: *The Writings of William Walwyn*, ed. Jack R. McMichael and Barbara Taft (1989), 241.

36 *'public good'* or *'civil society'*: see e.g. [Rous], *Ancient Bounds*, 2; [Locke], *Letter Concerning Toleration*, 45.

36 *'slanderous'* etc.: Coornhert, *Synod*, 176.

36 *'manifest good of societies'* etc.: [Rous], *Ancient Bounds*, 2; [Vane], *Zeal Examined*, sig. [A3v]; 'Philopatris', *Just Vindication of Learning*, 15–18; Campbell and Corns, *John Milton*, 282–3.

36 *'opinions contrary'*: [Locke], *Letter Concerning Toleration*, 45.

36 *all of them would punish opinions*: this was equally true of the very few writers who advocated complete liberty of conscience, even for Catholics and heathens: see e.g. *Writings of William Walwyn*, 14, 112–13, 139–41, 239–41; [Robinson], *Liberty of Conscience*, sig. [A4v]; [Roger Williams], *The Bloody Tenent, of Persecution* (1644), 87; John Toland, 'The Life of John Milton', in *Works of John Milton*, ed. Toland, 1: 21; Bejan, *Mere Civility*, 76.

37 *James Nayler*: *Diary of Thomas Burton*, ed. John Towill Rutt, 4 vols (1828), 1: 24–184; Richard Bauman, *Let Your Words Be Few* (1983); Leo Damrosch, *The Sorrows of the Quaker Jesus* (1996).

37 *fears of Quaker anarchy*: Carla Gardina Pestana, 'The Quaker Executions as Myth and History', *Journal of American History* 80 (1993).

37 *prosecutions for atheism and blasphemy*: David Nash, *Blasphemy in the Christian World* (2007).

37 *several US state constitutions*: including Arkansas, Maryland, Mississippi, North Carolina, South Carolina, Texas and Tennessee.

37 *non-believing professor*: *Silverman v. Campbell, et al.*, South Carolina Supreme Court (1996).

37 *'8THEIST'*: *New York Times*, 16 Aug. 2016.

37 *religious liberty of speech*: *303 Creative LLC v. Elenis*, 600 US 570 (2023).

37 *arguments for sexual promiscuity*: Faramerz Dabhoiwala, *The Origins of Sex* (2012), ch. 2.

3. INVENTING FREE SPEECH

39 *Inventing Free Speech*: an earlier version of this chapter was published as Fara Dabhoiwala, 'Inventing Free Speech', *Past and Present* supplement 16 (2022).

40 *'Cato's Letters'*: the only modern edition – *Cato's Letters*, ed. Ronald Hamowy, 2 vols (1995) – simply reprints the 1755 book version.

41 *first widely discussed*: see e.g. Elizabeth Christine Cook, *Literary Influences in Colonial Newspapers* (1912); Clinton Rossiter, *Seedtime of the Republic* (1953); *The English Libertarian Heritage*, ed. David L. Jacobson (1965); Leonard W. Levy, *Emergence of a Free Press* (1985); Bernard Bailyn, *The Ideological Origins of the American Revolution* (1992); Heather E. Barry, *A 'Dress Rehearsal' for Revolution* (2007).

41 *'daring and well-developed'* etc.: Levy, *Emergence*, 109, 115.

41 *most important English-language text*: Wendell Bird, *The Revolution in Freedoms of Press and Speech* (2020), strongly critiques Levy's overall argument but entirely agrees on this point.

41 *scholarly analyses of their work*: in addition to works cited in the preceding notes to this chapter, see esp. J. M. Bulloch, *Thomas Gordon* (1918); Caroline Robbins, *The Eighteenth-Century Commonwealthman* (1959), 115–25; J. G. A. Pocock, *The Machiavellian Moment* (1975), 467–77; Jonathan Duke-Evans, 'The Political Theory and Practice of the English Commonwealthsmen, 1695–1725' (University of Oxford DPhil thesis, 1980); Marie P. McMahon, *The Radical Whigs* (1990); Shelley Burtt, *Virtue Transformed* (1992), chs 4–6; Annie Mitchell, 'The Character of an Independent Whig' (University College London PhD thesis, 2004); Lee Ward, *The Politics of Liberty in England and Revolutionary America* (2004); *ODNB*; Justin Champion, '"Anglia Libera"', in David Womersley (ed.), *Cultures of Whiggism* (2005); Giovanni Tarantino, *Republicanism, Sinophilia, and Historical Writing* (2012).

42 *free parliamentary debate*: cf. David Colclough, *Freedom of Speech in Early Stuart England* (2005).

43 *rational 'public', or a dangerously misinformed 'mob'*: Mark Knights, *Representation and Misrepresentation in Later Stuart Britain* (2005).

43 *press freedom*: John Barnard et al. (ed.), *The Cambridge History of the Book in Britain*, 7 vols (1999–2019), 4: ch. 25; Jason Peacey, *Print and Public Politics in the English Revolution* (2013).

43 *English political discourse*: see esp. Laurence Hanson, *Government and the Press 1695–1763* (1936); Karl Tilman Winkler, *Wörterkrieg: Politische Debattenkultur in England, 1689–1750* (1998); Ashley Marshall, *Political Journalism in London, 1695–1720* (2020). I leave aside here the earlier (and continuing) phenomenon of manuscript publication, for which see Harold Love, *Scribal Publication in Seventeenth-Century England* (1993); George L. Justice and Nathan Tinker (eds), *Women's Writing and the Circulation of Ideas* (2002); Noah Millstone, *Manuscript Circulation and the Invention of Politics in early Stuart England* (2016). For the importance of scribal news and comment until the mid eighteenth century, see [Joseph Addison?], *The Thoughts of a Tory Author Concerning the Press* (1712), 5; Henry L. Snyder, 'Newsletters in England, 1689–1715', in Donald H. Bond and W. Reynolds McLeod (eds), *Newsletters to Newspapers* (1977); Alex W. Barber, '"It is Not Easy What to Say of Our Condition, Much Less to Write It"', *Parliamentary History* 32

(2013); Rachael Scarborough King, 'The Manuscript Newsletter and the Rise of the Newspaper, 1665–1715', *Huntington Library Quarterly* 79 (2016).

43 *'here we dare speak'*: *Observator*, 6 Nov. 1706.

44 *'false news'* etc.: [Daniel Defoe], *Commentator*, 4 and 8 Jan. 1720.

44 *'Falsehood flies'*: Jonathan Swift, *Examiner*, 9 Nov. 1710; see also idem, *Gulliver's Travels* (1723), pt 2, ch. 3; David Womersley, 'Swift and Free Speech', in Robert Ingram et al. (eds), *Freedom of Speech, 1500–1850* (2020). Cf. [John Arbuthnot], *Proposals for . . . A Treatise of the Art of Political Lying* (1712); Winkler, *Wörterkrieg*, ch. 7.

44 [footnote] *'a Man may be allowed'*: *Gulliver's Travels*, pt 2, ch. 6.

44 *'the mischiefs that proceed'*: [Defoe], *Commentator*, 8 Jan. 1720.

44 *'spreading false news'*: *By the Queen, a Proclamation for Restraining the Spreading False News* (1702); see also Abel Boyer, *The History of the Reign of Queen Anne . . . Year the Fifth* (1707), 486–9; *Journal of the House of Lords* [London 1767–], 21 [=1718–21]: 229–32, 242.

44 *political criticism*: Hanson, *Government and the Press*, ch. 1; John Feather, 'The Book Trade in Politics', *Publishing History* 8 (1980); Philip Hamburger, 'The Development of the Law of Seditious Libel', *Stanford Law Review* 37 (1985); P. B. J. Hyland, 'Liberty and Libel', *English Historical Review* 101 (1986); Michael Harris, *London Newspapers in the Age of Walpole* (1987), esp. ch. 8; *Censorship and the Press, 1580–1720*, ed. Geoff Kemp and Jason McElligott, 4 vols (2009), vol. 4; Thomas Keymer, *Poetics of the Pillory* (2019).

45 *'liberty of the press'* etc.: [Daniel Defoe], *An Essay on the Regulation of the Press* (1704); BL, Add. MS 4295, fols 49–50 [*c*.1717].

45 *leaders of the so-called Leveller movement*: [Richard Overton], *A Remonstrance of Many Thousand Citizens* (1646), 13–14, 19; *To the Right Honourable, The Supreme Authority* [1649]; [John Lilburne], *Englands New Chains Discovered* [1649], sigs [A3v–A4r], [B2v]; William Walwyn, *Walwyns Just Defence* (1649), 25; see also David R. Como, *Radical Parliamentarians and the English Civil War* (2018), 96, 263–4, 281–2, 299–300, 345–7.

45 *paraphrases of Milton's Areopagitica*: 'Philopatris' [i.e. Charles Blount], *A Just Vindication of Learning* (1679), A2v, 2, 8–12 (cf. [Blount], *A Brief Answer to Mr L'Estrange* (1680), 5–7); William Denton, 'An Apology for the Liberty of the Press', 6–7, in his *Jus Caesaris* (1681); [Charles Blount], *Reasons Humbly Offered for the Liberty of Unlicens'd Printing* (1693), 8; *A Complete Collection of the . . . Works of John Milton*, ed. John Toland, 3 vols ('Amsterdam' [i.e. London], 1698), 1: 21–3,

423–42. See also William Lawrence, *Marriage by the Morall Law of God Vindicated* (1680), 164–7.

45 *passing remarks*: cf. Eckhart Hellmuth, '"The Press Ought to be Open to All"', in Gordon Pentland and Michael T. Davis (eds), *England and Scotland, 1688–1815* (2016); Alex W. Barber, *The Restraint of the Press in England 1660–1715* (2022).

45 *a 'civil' and 'natural right'*: [Matthew Tindal], *A Letter to a Member of Parliament* (1698), 7, 24–32 (abridged as *Reasons Against Restraining the Press* (1704)). Cf. *Censorship and the Press*, ed. Kemp and McElligott, 4: 11–12, 29–30; [John Asgill], *An Essay for the Press* (1712), 4; Ernest Sirluck, '*Areopagitica* and a Forgotten Licensing Controversy', *Review of English Studies* 11 (1960); Geoffrey Kemp, 'Ideas of Liberty of the Press, 1640–1700' (University of Cambridge PhD thesis, 2000), 241–51; Stephen Lalor, *Matthew Tindal, Freethinker* (2006), ch. 3; Barber, *Restraint of the Press*, 121–39.

45 *contemporary observers*: *A Letter to a Member of Parliament Shewing the Necessity of Regulating the Press* (Oxford, 1699), 58, 61; *Arguments Relating to a Restraint Upon the Press* (1712), 6, 18–22; J. A. W. Gunn, *Beyond Liberty and Property* (1983), 271–3.

45 *'plausible pretences'* etc.: quoted in *Censorship and the Press*, ed. Kemp and McElligott, 4: 103–17; see also Keymer, *Poetics of the Pillory*, 122–5; Bird, *Revolution in Freedoms*, 92–102, 107–12; Mark Knights, *Trust and Distrust* (2021), 266–8, 273–5.

46 *'Nothing could be'* etc.: Alex Barber, '"Why don't those lazy priests answer the book?": Matthew Tindal, Censorship, Freedom of the Press and Religious Debate in Early Eighteenth-Century England', *History* 333 (2013), 681, 706. Cf. [Addison?], *Thoughts of a Tory Author*, esp. 13; [Francis Atterbury], *English Advice to the Freeholders of England* (1714), 28, 31; *The Craftsman's Doctrine and Practice of the Liberty of the Press* (1732); Winkler, *Wörterkrieg*, 407–12.

46 *Cato's Letters*: Charles Bechdolt Realey, 'The London Journal and Its Authors, 1720–1723', *Bulletin of University of Kansas* 36 (1935); *English Short Title Catalogue* (estc.bl.uk); *English Libertarian Heritage*, ed. Jacobson, xxxi, lxiii; for translations, see e.g. *Brieven door een voornaam Lord . . . op den naam van Cato* (Delft, 1722); *Brieven over de Vryheid . . . van Cato*, 3 vols (Alkmaar and Amsterdam, 1752–4; 2nd edn, Utrecht, 1766); *Cato: oder Briefe von der Freyheit*, trans. Johann Gottfried Gellius, 4 vols (Göttingen, 1756–7); S. R. E. Klein, *Patriots Republikanisme* (1995), esp. 72–3; catalogue of the Bibliothèque Nationale de France.

47 *history of free speech*: cf. [Thomas Gordon], *Three Political Letters* (1719).

47 *journalistic style* etc.: Lawrence E. Klein, *Shaftesbury and the Culture of Politeness* (1994); Knights, *Representation and Misrepresentation*, 53–7, 151–2, 262–6, ch. 7.

47 *'general reasonings'*: *The Fourth Collection of Cato's Political Letters* ([1721]), iv; see also *The Sixth Collection of Cato's Political Letters* (1722), [i].

47 *'levelled only at guilty men'*: *A Continuation of the Political Letters in the London Journal, to Jan. 28. 1720–1* ([1721]), 'Advertisement'. Cf. *Cato's Letters*, 4 vols (3rd edn, 1733), 1: xix.

47 *'against all bad administrations'*: James Ralph, *A Critical History of the Administration of Sr Robert Walpole* (1743), 505. Cf. Winkler, *Wörterkrieg*, 230–34.

47 *'faction or cabal'*: *Cato's Letters* (3rd edn, 1733), 1: x. Cf. *The Correspondence of Jonathan Swift*, ed. Harold Williams, 5 vols (1963–5), 2: 380; Winkler, *Wörterkrieg*, 339–48.

48 *'defence of treason'* etc.: Edmund Massey, *The Signs of the Times* (1722), 34; *Applebee's*, 3 Feb. 1722; see also ibid., 2 Sept. 1721; *A Collection of . . . Mist's Weekly Journal*, 2 vols (1722), 2: 161–3, 172–91, 210–18, 221–6, 295–301, 320–24.

48 *'vilifying the administration'* etc.: [Daniel Defoe], *The Director*, 2–16 Jan. 1721; *The Censor Censur'd* (1722), 2–3, 13. For rhetorical overlap between Cato and Jacobite arguments, see the *Freeholder's Journal*, 5 Sept. 1722; Winkler, *Wörterkrieg*, 348–60, 369, 420; Ian Higgins, 'Remarks on *Cato's Letters*', in Womersley (ed.), *Cultures of Whiggism*, 128–32, 139–41.

48 *'sometimes silly'*: *Historical Manuscripts Commission: Report on Manuscripts in Various Collections*, 8 vols (1901–14), 8: 326. (Molesworth once unsuccessfully attempted to have his own writings inserted in the *London Journal* as those of Cato: KUL, MS G23, fols 30r, 34r–v.)

48 *'when he is painting'* etc.: [Matthew Tindal], *A Defence of our Present Happy Establishment . . . From the Falsehood and Malice of Several Late Treasonable Libels, viz. Cato's Letters* (1722), 26. Cf. [Jonathan Swift], *The Importance of the Guardian* (1713), 24–5.

48 *'uncorrupt heart'*: [Thomas Gordon], *The Conspirators* (1721), v.

48 *the same treatment*: [Gordon], *Conspirators*, pt 1, dedication, 29–31; [Gordon], *Three Political Letters*, esp. 34–8; [Thomas Gordon], *Francis, Lord Bacon* (1721); *LJ*, 25 March, 6 May 1721 [22, 28].

48 *'Defaming an Administration'* etc.: [Thomas Gordon], *The Art of Railing at Great Men* ('1723', i.e. November 1722; partially reprinted in *Pasquin*, 23 and 31 May 1723, and in [Thomas Gordon], *The Humourist* [vol. 2], ('3rd edn', 1724), 96–105). Walpole's propagandists later repeatedly reused this essay, concealing its authorship: *BJ*, 9 Nov. 1728; *The Free Briton*, 22 July 1731; 28 June 1733.

49 *'Never was there a writer'*: The *Historical Register ... Volume VI* (1721), 214.

49 *Cato's language was indeed incendiary*: on the assassination of Caesar, etc., see *LJ*, 12, 19 and 26 Nov., 3, 17, 24 and 31 Dec. 1720; 3, 7, 14 and 21 Jan., 11 and 18 Mar., 2 and 9 Dec. 1721 [2, 3, 4, 5, 7, 8, 9, 10, 11, 12, 13, 20, 21, 55, 56].

49 *'Mr Gordon, the reputed author'*: *Historical Register ... Volume VI*, 215; see generally 203–23.

49 *To escape arrest*: *Daily Journal*, 10, 12, 13, 15 and 17 June; 4 and 31 July 1721; *Evening Post*, 13 and 17 June 1721; *Weekly Journal or British Gazetteer*, 10 June 1721; *Applebee's*, 17 June 1721; TNA, SP 35/27, fols 56–7 (17 June 1721).

49 *explosive exposé* etc.: *LJ*, 12 Aug. 1721; TNA, SP 35/28, fols 10, 12–18, 20–4, 26; 35/30, fol. 113; 35/31, fol. 8; *Applebee's*, 22 July, 19 and 26 Aug. (quoted: 'the young Defoe' etc.) 1721; *Historical Manuscripts Commission ... Duke of Portland*, 10 vols (1891–1931), 5: 624; Realey, 'London Journal and Its Authors', 13–20, 33.

49 *Trenchard and Gordon continued*: cf. their boastful advert in *The Post-Boy*, 22 Aug. 1721.

49 *'malicious and scandalous libels'* etc.: TNA, SP 35/28, fol. 32.

51 *defences of toleration*: tellingly, their earliest treatment of free speech essentially plagiarized Tindal's arguments about religious liberty of expression – but only for fun: [John Trenchard], *A Short Vindication of the Ld Archbishop of Canterbury* (1719); cf. KUL, MS G23, fol. 15r-v; [Thomas Gordon], *A Letter to the Lord Archbishop* (1719).

51 *nonconformist backgrounds*: B. D. Henning (ed.), *The History of Parliament: The House of Commons 1660–1690* (1983), s.v. 'Trenchard, William'; Beinecke Library, Yale, MS Osborn c502, 31; BL, Add MS 70032, fols 49r–50v; KUL, MS G23, fols 15r, 46v, 50r; Duke-Evans, 'Political Theory and Practice of the English Commonwealthsmen', ch. 1; Lalor, *Matthew Tindal*, 29.

51 *'bold and dangerous falsehoods'*: [Thomas Gordon], *The Character of an Independent Whig* (1719), 27.

51 *'liberty of conscience'* etc.: *Independent Whig*, 17 Feb., 30 Mar., 8 June, 10 Aug. 1720.

51 *'freedom of [religious] opinion'* etc.: *Independent Whig*, vol. 4 (1747), no. XXVI; see also *English Libertarian Heritage*, ed. Jacobson, xxx–xxxii. As was conventional, Trenchard and Gordon's arguments for religious freedom were limited to Protestants: they took for granted that Catholic, Muslim and atheist beliefs were false and dangerous.

51 *'all opinions are equally indulged'* etc.: *BJ*, 20 Oct. 1722 [100].

52 *'the Right of every Man'*: *LJ*, 4 Feb. 1721; 20 Jan. 1722 [15, 62].

52 *'base and mean thing'* etc.: *LJ*, 10 June 1721 [32]; *BJ*, 20 Oct. 1722 [100].

53 *'abuse of words'* etc.: [Gordon], *Character of an Independent Whig*, 27; [Thomas Gordon], *Considerations Offered upon the Approaching Peace* (1720), 5–6; *Fourth Collection of Cato's Political Letters*, iv; *BJ*, 16 Mar. 1723 [120]; *Pasquin*, 15 Oct. 1723; [Gordon], *Humourist* (1724), 105–11. Cf. Winkler, *Wörterkrieg*, 340–41.

53 *'Misrepresentation of public measures'*: *LJ*, 4 Feb. 1721 [15].

53 *'they have no interest'* etc.: *LJ*, 8 Apr. 1721 [24].

53 *'external delusion'* etc.: *LJ*, 25 Mar. 1721 [22].

53 Trenchard and Gordon's solution: *LJ*, 4 Feb., 25 Mar., 8 Apr. 1721 [15, 22, 24]; *BJ*, 20 Oct. 1722 [100]; cf. *LJ*, 21 Jan., 4 Mar. 1721 [13, 19].

53 *'a crime to talk'*: [Tindal], *Letter*, 24–5.

53 *'trustees of the people'* etc.: *LJ*, 4 Feb. 1721 [15]; for the longer history of this central theme, see Knights, *Trust and Distrust*, ch. 9.

53 *'no other liberty'*: [Tindal], *Letter*, 24, 27; cf. [Tindal], *A Second Defence of the Rights of the Christian Church* (1708), 23; and [Tindal], *Reasons Against Restraining*, 14.

53 *'the great Bulwark of Liberty'*: *LJ*, 4 Feb. 1721 [15]: the title of the essay was added in *Cato's Letters* (3rd edn, 1733).

54 *'an evil arising'*: *LJ*, 10 June 1721 [32].

54 *'libelling'* as a serious evil: John Milton, *Areopagitica* (1644), 5–6, 39; Alison A. Chapman, *Courts, Jurisdictions, and Law in John Milton and his Contemporaries* (2020), chs 2–3.

54 *'this cruel practice'*: *Spectator*, 7 Aug. 1712; cf. 27 Mar. 1711; Pierre Bayle, 'A Dissertation Concerning Defamatory Libels', in his *An Historical and Critical Dictionary*, 4 vols (1710), 4: x–xxvii of appendix.

54 *'the judgement of the people'* etc.: *LJ*, 10 June 1721 [32]; *BJ*, 20 Oct. 1722 [100].

54 *'foment popular'* etc.: *BJ*, 20 Oct. 1722 [100].

55 *two lengthy manuscripts and a series of pamphlets*: both manuscripts are undated, hitherto unattributed, and in scribal hands (the first with corrections in Tindal's own hand). Their texts overlap, and Tindal also mined them for his many published pamphlets: BL, Add. MS 61705, 'The Criterion: Or Certain Tests to Judge of the Designs of Private Men in Censuring Publick Persons & Measures, With Remarks on the Character of the Independent Whig' [early 1720]; BL, Add. MS 61707, 'Anti-Cato: Or the Political Letters in the London Journal Examin'd, and Their False Reasonings and Fatal Tendency Expos'd' (evidently prepared for the Commons' committee investigating Cato's Letters in June 1721); For Tindal's pamphlets, see [Matthew Tindal], *The Judgment of Dr Prideaux* (1721 [i.e. 1722]), 26 (quoted: 'infinite absurdities'); [Tindal], *Defence of Our Present Happy Establishment*, title-page (quoted: 'Cato the Journalist'); [Tindal?], *Cato's Principles* (1722); [Tindal], *An Enquiry into the Causes of the Present Disaffection* (1723); [Tindal], *Corah and Moses* (1727). Cf. also [Tindal], *The Defection Consider'd* (1717), 12–14, 21–2; [Tindal], *An Account of a Manuscript* (1718), 23.

55 *'If the people are able'* etc.: [Tindal], *Enquiry*, 4–12; [Tindal], *Defence of Our Present Happy Establishment*, 3.

56 *'either he does not know'* etc.: [Tindal], 'Anti-Cato', fol. 3r; [Tindal], *Defence of Our Present Happy Establishment*, 4, 15, 29, 31; [Tindal], *Prideaux*, 95; [Tindal], *Enquiry*, esp. 3–6; cf. *Censor Censur'd*; Winkler, *Wörterkrieg*, 340–41.

56 *'highly criminal'* etc.: [Tindal], *Defence of Our Present Happy Establishment*, 31; [Tindal], *Enquiry*, 24–7.

56 *'the support of all our liberties'* etc.: [Tindal], 'Anti-Cato', fols 39r–48r; [Tindal], *Enquiry*, 23–7; cf. [Tindal], *Letter*, 25–7. The image of the press as a destructive 'engine' was not new: cf. Bodleian Library, Oxford, MS Tanner 25, fol. 362r [1693].

56 *'most countries'* etc.: [Tindal], *Letter*, 27; cf. [Tindal], *An Essay Concerning the Power of the Magistrate* (1697), 184–6.

57 *Francis Bacon*: *The Oxford Francis Bacon*, vol. 1: *Early Writings 1584–1596*, ed. Alan Stewart (2012), 305–425.

57 *'double the number of papers'*: TNA, SP 35/30, fol. 134. Cf. *An Historical View of the Principles, Characters, Persons, &c of the Political Writers* (1740), 12–14.

57 *'falsehood and scandal'* etc.: *Spectator*, 7 Aug. 1712; cf. [Addison?], *Thoughts of a Tory Author*, 5–6; *A Vindication of the Press* (1718), 8–9.

57 *the world's first 'free' press*: *New Cambridge Bibliography of English Literature*, ed. George Watson, 5 vols (1969–77), 2: 1269–1346; J. A.

Downie, *Robert Harley and the Press* (1979); Hanson, *Government and the Press*, ch. 4; Winkler, *Wörterkrieg*; Jeremy Black, *The English Press in the Eighteenth Century* (1987), ch. 6; Harris, *London News-papers*, chs 6–8; David Lemmings, 'The Dark Side of Enlightenment', in David Lemmings and Claire Walker (eds), *Moral Panics, the Media and the Law* (2009); Marshall, *Political Journalism*.

57 *Walpole*: *Correspondence of Jonathan Swift*, ed. Williams, 3: 207; *The Country Journal: or, the Craftsman*, 31 July 1731; *A Further Report from the Committee of Secrecy ... Delivered the 30th of June 1742* (1742), 25–9, appendix 13; Hanson, *Government and the Press*, 109–18; Simon Targett, '"The Premier Scribbler Himself"', *Studies in Newspaper and Periodical History* 2 (1994); idem, 'Government and Ideology During the Age of Whig Supremacy', *Historical Journal* 38 (1994), 2; Tone Sundt Urstad, *Sir Robert Walpole's Poets* (1999), ch. 4.

57 *Tindal's many anonymous critiques*: Tindal's manuscript tracts sur-vive among the papers of his patron, Lord Sunderland, and extolled his leadership. An April 1720 letter, apparently accompanying the first manuscript, offered his continued services in return for further financial support: BL, Add. MS 61650, fol. 64. A few weeks after com-pleting the second, noting 'how very generous you have already been', Tindal requested a further £400: BL, Add. MS 61650, fol. 87r. (In turn, Gordon ridiculed the 'ill success' of the 'ancient', mercenary, 'learned *Oxonian*' at attracting either readers or truly substantial reward: *BJ*, 26 Jan. 1723 [113].) Cf. Lalor, *Matthew Tindal*, 26–7, ch. 5; TNA, SP 35/23, fol. 101r (1720). After Sunderland's death, Tindal switched effortlessly to praise his successor, Walpole: [Tindal], *Corah and Moses*.

57 *other critics presumed*: *Applebee's*, 2 Sept. 1721; *A Letter to the Free-holder* (1722), viii–x.

58 *'maliciously or traitorously'*: *Applebee's*, 15 July 1721. Cf. [Defoe], *Commentator*, 15 Jan. 1720; *Historical View*; [James Ralph], *The Case of Authors by Profession* (1758), esp. 11, 19–20, 29–39.

58 *'common Hackney writers'* etc.: *Pasquin*, 13 May 1723, reprinted in [Gordon], *Humourist* (1724), 111–17. Cf. *LJ*, 6 May 1721 [28]; *The Works of Tacitus* [trans. and ed. Thomas Gordon], 2 vols (1728–31), 1: 35, 49–50.

58 *'made their peace'*: *Pasquin*, 27 May 1723.

58 *Channel Islands*: Ashworth P. Burke, *Family Records* (1897), 223–6. According to a modern genealogical database, Elizée was born on Guernsey in January 1692 and died in 1758 – both dates are plaus-ible, though this source cites no evidence and is incorrect about

other biographical details: ancestrylibrary.com/family-tree/person/tree/153233181/person/192282509215.

58 *His paper, barely a year old*: it began as the *Thursday's Journal* (6 Aug.– 24 Dec. 1719), then became the *London Journal; or the Thursday's Journal* (26 Dec. 1719–7 May 1720), and finally on 14 May 1720 was renamed the *London Journal*, at the same time as it changed publishers, presumably due to Dobrée's acquisition.

58 *'the only person'* etc.: E[lizée] D[obrée] to [Charles Delafaye, under-secretary of state and government spymaster] 8 Jan. 1721, TNA, SP 35/30, fol. 16 (in French). His unnamed relative was doubtless the merchant and banker William Dobrée (1674–1760), the first of the family to emigrate to London, who lost money in the South Sea crash and had moved to Botolph Lane in 1721 or 1722: see *Daily Post*, 3 Aug. 1720; *LJ*, 17 Aug. 1723; 'William Dobree, bankrupt, 1754', at priaulxlibrary. co.uk. Elizée always wrote to the government from this address, even after he and his wife had set up house in a much humbler location nearby; see Sun Insurance Office Policies, 1722–23, TLA, CLC/B/192/F/001/MS11936/014, 216, 286–87, and /MS11936/015, 120.

59 *Dobrée felt secure enough to marry*: the marriage of Elisha Dobrée and Elizabeth Lowther took place on 14 May 1721, as recorded in All Hallows register of marriages 1692–1732, TLA, P69/ALH5/A/007/MS05087; for his domestic life, see also Dobrée to Richard Peters, 28 Sept. 1741, RG-021-4, box 3, item 355, Pennsylvania State Archives, Harrisburg.

59 *the deal*: Letters from Dobrée to Delafaye, Jan.–May 1721, TNA, SP 35/30, fols 16, 28, 88–9, and TNA, SP 35/31, fols 32, 38, 81, 194, 204; statement of the *Journal*'s finances, 1721, TNA, SP 35/68/2, fol. 103; TNA, SP 43/66, 27–28 June 1723; T 1/255, fols 304–5; Realey, 'London Journal and Its Authors', 27–9, 33–4; K. L. Joshi, 'The London Journal, 1719–1738', *Journal of the University of Bombay* 9 (1940), 57–66; Simon Targett, 'A Pro-Government Newspaper During the Whig Ascendancy', *Journal of History & Politics* 7 (1989); Karl Tilman Winkler, *Handwerk und Markt . . . in London 1695–1750* (1993), 425–32; Lemmings, 'Dark Side of Enlightenment', 145–8.

59 *the second pair*: *BJ*, 20 Oct. 1722 [100] (quoted: 'what are usually called libels'); *BJ*, 27 Oct. 1722 [101].

59 *'extravagant, arbitrary, and violent'*: *BJ*, 29 Sept. 1722 [96].

59 *they continued publishing Cato's Letters*: *BJ*, 22 Sept.–13, 20 and 27 Oct. 1722; 27 July 1723 [96, 100, 101, 138]; see also *Cato's Letters* (3rd edn, 1733), 4: 289. Later in 1723, Gordon published several essays

under the pseudonym Criton: six of these were included in the 1733 and later editions of *Cato's Letters*.

59 *always been for sale*: for Gordon's early life and career, see esp. BL Add MS 70299, bundle 11 (unfoliated), T[homas G[ordon] to Robert Harley, [?]Jan. 1713]; Add MS 70198, fol. 146, [Thomas Gordon] to Robert Harley, 22 Feb. [1713]; Add MS 70032, fols 49r–50v, J. B. to Thomas Gordon, 11 Feb. 1713 [i.e. 1714]; Add MS 36772, correspondence of George Duckett MP, fols 194v, 198r–199v, 202–203v, 204r–205v, 210r–211v, letters from and about Gordon, 1719; Beinecke Library, Yale, MS Osborn c502 (dated 4 July 1713 but probably written between 1714 and 1719).

59 *unprincipled, mercenary hack*: *The Characters of Two Independent Whigs* (1720), 3–6.

60 *'constant overtures'* etc.: KUL, MS G23, fols 9r–10r, 30r–v.

60 *had written most of the Letters*: of the first 76 collected Letters, up to 12 May 1722, Gordon wrote 61 (and co-wrote a further 3 with Trenchard); of the ensuing 62, Gordon wrote only 17 (and co-wrote a further 2): *Cato's Letters* (1733 edn).

60 *switched to government propaganda*: for Gordon's secret juggling between ministerial propaganda and Cato's Letters, continued attacks on the latter by government papers, and contemporary speculation about Cato's 'Great Alteration' and quest 'for a Pension', see *St James's Journal*, 15 Nov., 1 Dec. 1722; 19 Jan., 18 May 1723; *Weekly Journal*, 15 June 1723; [Gordon], *Art of Railing*; *Pasquin*, Nov. 1722–Mar. 1724; *Letter to the Freeholder*, viii–x.

60 *'capacity and opportunity'* etc.: *St James's Journal*, 3 May 1722 (my italics), reprinted in [Gordon], *Humourist* (1724), 240–46.

61 *'Cato's Letter'* etc.: [Thomas Gordon], *A Short View of the Conspiracy* ([early May] 1723), half-title page, 7–8, 20, 28–9, 47–8, 58. Cf. *BJ*, 20 Apr., 4 May, 29 June 1723 [125, 127, 134]. In its last months, the column took a steadfastly anti-Jacobite, pro-Walpole line. Cf. McMahon, *Radical Whigs*, 170–74; Winkler, *Wörterkrieg*, 200–202, 360–62, 369–74.

61 *'he has gained his point'*: KUL, MS G23, fol. 44r.

61 *secret motives and quest for preferment*: even his critics conceded that 'Mr Trenchard is above all temptation' – he wrote from conviction, and could not be bought (KUL, MS G23, fol. 44r. Cf. ibid., fols 9r, 34r–v; *Historical View*, 15; *Characters of Two Independent Whigs*, 8–14; *Cato's Letters* (1724 edn), 1: xxvi–xxviii). Yet nonetheless the politics of Cato's Letters had from the outset been deeply shaped by his own

hidden animosities. Towards the end of his life, his one remaining ambition was to become a member of parliament, as his father had been
before him. In 1718 and 1719, he fruitlessly lobbied the Whig leader,
Lord Sunderland, to insert him into a safe seat, promising his 'attachment to the present ministry'. His profound 'personal resentment' at
being snubbed doubtless explains why, shortly afterwards, Cato's Letters began to assault Sunderland's government (KUL, MS G23, fols 19v,
22r–23r; [Tindal], 'Anti-Cato', 57r; BL, Add MS 61496, fol. 112r–v
(quoted: 'attachment to the present'); *Characters of Two Independent
Whigs*, 12–13; *Cato's Letters* (1724 edn), 1: xxvi (quoted: 'personal
resentment'); Romney Sedgwick (ed.), *The History of Parliament: The
House of Commons 1715–1754* (1970), s.v. 'Trenchard, John'; he
did finally enter parliament after the 1722 general election). The Letters' other immediate obsession was with punishing the culprits of the
South Sea crash. Cato's uniquely vicious, unrelenting hostility to stock
market profiteers and corrupt politicians spurred the column's growing popularity. Week after week it called for exemplary public justice,
even summary lynchings. 'Let us pursue to disgrace, destruction and
even death, those who have brought this ruin upon us, let them be ever
so great, or ever so many,' Trenchard urged his readers in early 1721.
What he never mentioned was that he'd personally lost a large sum in
the crash, through the shenanigans of his bankers. This episode clearly
rankled, and sharpened his animosity towards Sunderland's ministry.
Trenchard's two covert grievances thus became the targets of Cato's
initial wrath (*LJ* 11 Feb. 1721 [16] (quoted: 'Let us pursue'); KUL, MS
G23, fol. 12r; TNA, C 11/41/13, C 11/309/11, C 11/361/109; PROB
11/596/42; cf. *LJ* 10, 17 Mar., 25 Aug., 1 Sept. 1722 [69, 70, 91, 92]).

61 *'about Mr Walpole's keeping his promise'*: KUL, MS G23, fols 42r,
44r. Cf. *Cato's Letters* (1724 edn), 1: xlv. In 1733, Gordon disin-
genuously protested that the Letters had been ended 'without any
sordid Composition, and without any Consideration' except that he
and Trenchard had 'judged that the Public, after all its terrible Convulsions, was again become calm and safe': *Cato's Letters* (3rd edn,
1733), 1: x–xi.

61 *most trusted secret censor*: *Works of Tacitus* [trans. and ed. Gordon], 1:
dedication, 33–4; *Historical View*, 16–18; *The Yale Edition of Horace
Walpole's Correspondence*, ed. W. S. Lewis, 48 vols (1937–83), 13: 12;
15: 311; William Coxe, *Memoirs of the Life and Administration of Sir
Robert Walpole*, 3 vols (1798), 1: xx–xxi; John Nichols, *Literary Anecdotes of the Eighteenth Century*, 6 vols (1812), 1: 709; British Museum,

item no. 1902,0822.38; Hanson, *Government and the Press*, 79–82; Winkler, *Wörterkrieg*, 284–8.

62 *'following party'*: *Bob-Lynn against Franck-Lynn* (1732), 16, 20–21, 27–8; *The Universal Spy*, 6 May 1732; *Fog's Weekly Journal*, 30 Nov., 7 Dec. 1734; *The Works of Alexander Pope*, ed. Joseph Warton, 9 vols (1797), 4: 300; 5: 278–9; *Historical View*, 14–18; [Ralph], *Case*, 37–8. Henry Fielding underwent a very similar trajectory in his dealings with Walpole: Keymer, *Poetics of the Pillory*, 192–201.

62 *Modern scholars*: see e.g. Levy, *Emergence*, 109–18; Robbins, *Eighteenth-Century Commonwealthman*, 115–16; *English Libertarian Heritage*, ed. Jacobson, xxviii–xxx; McMahon, *Radical Whigs*, esp. 84–5; Winkler, *Wörterkrieg*, esp. 371; *ODNB* ; Tarantino, *Republicanism*, esp. xxii, 34–7.

62 *'tumultuously . . . to publish'*: *Works of Tacitus* [trans. and ed. Gordon], 1: 105–6. Cf. ibid., 2: 92–145; *BJ*, 2 Nov., 26 Dec. 1723.

62 *His post-1723 view*: National Library of Scotland, Adv.MS.23.3.26, fol. 64v; [Thomas Gordon], *An Appeal to the Unprejudiced* (1739); [Gordon?], *Warning to the Whigs* (1744); [Gordon], *Works of Sallust . . . with Political Discourses* (1744), xvi–xxi, 1–25, 58–9, 70–72, 83–5, 145–6, 168, 183–91; [Gordon], *An Essay on Government* (1747), ii–iii; [Gordon], *Independent Whig . . . vol. IV* (1747), 294–336 (quoted: 'ungrateful and licentious' etc.). Cf. Simon Varey, 'The Craftsman', *Prose Studies* 16 (1993), 66–7; Winkler, *Wörterkrieg*, esp. 289–308, 479–99, 635–43; Eckhart Hellmuth, 'Towards Hume – the Discourse of Liberty of the Press in the Age of Walpole', *History of European Ideas* 41 (2018); Marshall, *Political Journalism*, ch. 6.

63 *cobbled together by two hacks*: for their disdain of books and academic scholarship, see *Cato's Letters* (1724 edn), 1: xxxii–xxxvii; *Works of Tacitus* [trans. and ed. Gordon], 1: [A2r]; Nichols, *Literary Anecdotes*, 1: 709.

63 *taken up and developed*: see *The Country Journal: or, the Craftsman*, nos. 268–9, 272, 275, 278, 284, 288, 301, 303, 356, 372, 407–8, 426, 472, 583–4 (1731–37); Simon Robertson Varey, 'The Craftsman 1726–1752' (University of Cambridge PhD thesis, 1976).

63 *'bulwarks of liberty'*: from the 1720s onwards, that distinctive phrase had spread into general use; by the 1760s and 1770s, English-speaking authors everywhere treated it as a proverbial axiom: see e.g. *True Briton* 1 (3 June 1723); *A Third Letter* [Dublin, 1725]; *The Country Journal* 51 (24 June 1727); *The Bee* 14 (2 June 1733); *The Nature of the Charitable Corporation* (1732), 9; *The Sufferings of John Coustos* (1746),

xxiii; *A Letter to the Citizens of Dublin* (1749), 18–19; *A Letter to the Freeholders* (Boston, 1749), 8–10; *A Series of Letters Relating to the Antigallican* (1758), 84; T. C. Phillips, *An Apology* (1761), v; *North Briton* 1 (5 June 1762), 27 (4 Dec. 1762); John Wilkes, *A Letter to the Worthy Electors* ('London' [i.e. Paris?], 1764), 10; [Wilkes], *A Letter to the Right Honourable William Lord Mansfield* (1768), 24; *The Speeches of John Wilkes*, 3 vols (1777–8), 1: 82; cf. also *St James' Chronicle* (24 May 1763); *Debates Relative to the Affairs of Ireland*, 2 vols (1766), 1: 679–80; *The True Sentiments of America* (1768), 90; *Vox Senatus* (1771), 72; *Patriotism: A Political Satire* (1767), xvii; *Another Letter to Mr Almon* (1770), 6; *A Dialogue between a Country Farmer and a Juryman* (1770), title-page; *Letters Concerning the Present State of England* (1772), 14; *A Short Historical Account of Lochwinioch Parish* (Paisley, 1773), 28; *Essays Historical, Political and Moral*, 2 vols (Dublin [1774?]), xiv; *Letter Humbly Submitted* (1774), 45; John Carter, *The Reviewer Reviewed* (Norwich [1781]), 1.

63 *First Amendment*: the Bill of Rights as a whole embodied Cato's conception of fixed, constitutional 'checks and restraints' on government: Gary McDowell, 'The Language of Law and the Foundations of American Constitutionalism', *William and Mary Quarterly* 55 (1998).

65 *their own theories of speech*: Mark Zuckerberg, 'Standing for Voice and Free Expression' (speech at Georgetown University, 17 Oct. 2019); Mike Isaac, Sheera Frenkel and Kate Conger, 'Inside Mark Zuckerberg's Sprint to Remake Meta for the Trump Era', *New York Times*, 10 Jan. 2025.

4. THE SHAPES OF FREEDOM

66 *The Shapes of Freedom*: an earlier version of this chapter was published as Fara Dabhoiwala, 'Liberty, Slavery, and Biography', *Journal of British Studies* 62 (2023).

67 *tools of enslavement*: see Simon P. Newman, *Freedom Seekers* (2022); David Waldstreicher, 'Reading the Runaways', *William and Mary Quarterly* 56 (1999); Jordan E. Taylor, 'Enquire of the Printer', *Early American Studies* 18 (2020).

67 *wrote a letter as 'A Woman'*: LJ, 2 and 23 Dec. 1721 [later, in the collected editions, combined into Cato's Letter 58]. Unbeknown to its readers, this essay was an in-joke, composed on the anniversary of Trenchard's third marriage, with an encomium by Gordon.

68 *'public liberty'* etc.: LJ, 4 Feb. 1721 [15].

68 *'writing that hurts'* etc.: *LJ*, 10 June 1721 [32]. See also *BJ*, 20 Oct. 1722 [100].

68 *'treated them with great niceness'* etc.: *Cato's Letters*, 4 vols (1724 edn), 1: xxix–xxx. See also Thomas Gordon to William Simpson, 28 Dec. [1723], KUL, MS G23, fol. 42v.

68 *female speech*: see e.g. Jelle Haemers and Chanelle Delameillieure, 'Women and Contentious Speech in Fifteenth-century Brabant', *Continuity and Change* 32 (2017); Amanda Jane Whiting, *Women and Petitioning in the Seventeenth-Century English Revolution* (2015).

69 *'From the first dawn'* etc.: S[arah], F[yge], 'The Emulation' and 'The Liberty', in her *Poems on Several Occasions* (1703), 20–21, 108–9.

70 *'Wife and servant'*: Lady Chudleigh, 'To the Ladies', in her *Poems on Several Occasions* (1703), 40.

70 *women were central*: see documents relating to the printing and distribution of the *London Journal*, Aug. 1721, TNA, SP 35/28, fols 10, 13, 15, 18r–v; Karl Tilman Winkler, *Handwerk und Markt: Vetriebsewesen and Tagesschrifttum in London, 1695–1750* (1993), esp. chs 6–8; Paula McDowell, *The Women of Grub Street* (1998). In 1734–5, similarly, Catherine Zenger took over the printing of the *New-York Weekly Journal*, Cato's great American champion, while her husband, John Peter Zenger, was in jail awaiting trial for seditious libel.

70 *'the ladies ... turn their heads'*: Robert Molesworth, unpaginated dedicatory epistle to [Mary Monck], *Marinda: Poems and Translations Upon Several Occasions* (1716).

70 *female authorship* etc.: *The Cambridge History of the Book in Britain*, ed. John Barnard et al., 7 vols (1999–2019), 4: ch. 20; 5: ch. 6; Susan Staves, *A Literary History of Women's Writing in Britain, 1660–1789* (2006); Elaine Chalus, '"Ladies Are Often Very Good at Scaffoldings"', *Parliamentary History* 28 (2009).

71 *'private' and 'public'*: Jürgen Habermas, *The Structural Transformation of the Public Sphere*, trans. Thomas Burger and Frederick Lawrence (1989); Dario Castiglione and Lesley Sharpe (eds), *Shifting the Boundaries* (1995); Michèle Cohen, *Fashioning Masculinity* (1996); Philip Carter, *Men and the Emergence of Polite Society* (2001). For its many gendered ironies and contradictions, see Faramerz Dabhoiwala, *The Origins of Sex* (2012), 181–90.

71 *'deserved a statue'* etc.: Gordon to Trenchard, 1 Aug. [1721], KUL, MS G23, fol. 9v. See also *LJ*, 13 May, 22 July 1721 [29, 38].

72 *'that men and women'*: *Spectator*, 5 May 1711; see also *Spectator*, 2 June, 7 Dec. 1711, 13 Feb. 1712; Rachel Weil, *Political Passions* (1999).

72 *it was perennially contradicted*: Leonore Davidoff and Catherine Hall, *Family Fortunes* (1987); Kathryn Gleadle and Sarah Richardson (eds), *Women in British Politics, 1760–1860* (2000); Kathryn Gleadle, '"Opinions Deliver'd in Conversation"', in José Harris (ed.), *Civil Society in British History* (2003).

72 *'enslaved'* etc.: *LJ*, 4 Feb. 1721 [15].

73 *'all Asia and . . . all Africa'* etc.: *LJ*, 14 Oct. 1721 [48]. See also *LJ*, 22 July 1721 [38].

73 *employed the rhetoric of slavery*: see esp. David Armitage, 'John Locke, Carolina, and the *Two Treatises of* Government', *Political Theory* 32 (2004); James Farr, 'Locke, Natural Law, and New World Slavery', *Political Theory* 36 (2008); Holly Brewer, 'Slavery, Sovereignty, and "Inheritable Blood"', *American Historical Review* 122 (2017); Mark Goldie, 'John Locke and Empire', Carlyle Lectures, University of Oxford, 2021.

73 *British readers and writers*: see John Richardson, *Slavery and Augustan Literature* (2004), esp. ch. 1; Christopher Leslie Brown, *Moral Capital* (2006); Simon Gikandi, *Slavery and the Culture of Taste* (2011).

73 *'furnishing the plantations'* etc.: [Daniel Defoe], *An Essay Upon the Trade to Africa* (1711), 5, 34; see also Tim Keirn, 'Daniel Defoe and the Royal African Company', *Historical Research* 61 (1988).

73 *transatlantic slave trade*: William Pettigrew, *Freedom's Debt* (2013).

73 *London's newspapers openly celebrated*: see e.g. *LJ*, 3 June, 2 Sept. 1721; 3 Aug., 7 and 21 Sept. 1723; 22 Feb. 1729; *BJ*, 26 Dec. 1724; 'For Sale', *Runaway Slaves in Britain*, University of Glasgow, runaways.gla.ac.uk/for_sale/.

73 *'men are naturally equal'* etc.: *LJ*, 16 Sept. 1721 [45].

73 *'another species of mankind'* etc.: *LJ*, 20 Jan. 1722 [62].

74 *'slave' could refer*: Srividhya Swaminathan and Adam R. Beach (eds), *Invoking Slavery in the Eighteenth-Century British Imagination* (2013).

74 *'effeminate Asiaticks and Africans'*: Algernon Sidney, *Discourses Concerning Government* (1698), 6. See also Steven Jablonski, 'Ham's Vicious Race', *Studies in English Literature* 37 (1997).

74 *'Prince of Slaves'*: *LJ*, 14 Oct. 1721 [48]. See also Peter A. Dorsey, *Common Bondage* (2009).

74 *'English planters in America'* etc.: *LJ*, 24 Feb. 1722 [67].

74 *'colonies planted in proper climates'* etc.: *BJ*, 24 Nov. 1722 [106].

74 *enthused about the slave trade*: John Cary, *An Essay on the State of England* (Bristol, 1695), 47, 65–86; Jonathan Duke-Evans, 'The Political Theory and Practice of the English Commonwealthsmen, 1695–1725' (University of Oxford DPhil thesis, 1980), 22, 26; *ODNB*, s.v. 'Cary, John (1649–1719x22)'.

74 *South Sea Company*: Trenchard v. Wanley, 1721, TNA, C 11/41/13.

74 *in the hands of a millionaire*: 'Philip John Miles', LBS.

74 *spy to the East or West Indies*: T[homas] G[ordon], untitled retrospective account of his dealings with Harley, Beinecke Library, Yale University, MS Osborn c502, 59.

75 *one of the first books*: The Calve's-Head Club; or, A Modest Apology for Parson Alberoni (Kingston, Jamaica, 1719).

75 *Bill, sailed to India*: National Library of Scotland, Adv. MS.23.3.26, fol. 63r (1740); journal and pay ledger of the *Halifax*, 1740–1742, BL, IOR/L/MAR/B/651C and /651H; Anthony Farrington, *Catalogue of East India Company Ships' Journals and Logs, 1600–1834* (1999), 294. Bill was alive in 1750 but seemingly not by 1767 (will of Thomas Gordon, proved 8 Aug. 1750, TNA, PROB 11/781/344, and will of Thomas Gordon of Jamaica, proved 17 Dec. 1781, TNA, PROB 11/1085/244).

75 *Patty*: with her husband, Edward Bullock, Patty Gordon had two daughters. In 1765, she died giving birth to a son, who did not long survive her. Her husband then married his teenaged mistress, Elizabeth-Saville Trower, and fathered two more children before his own death in 1771; see will of Edward Bullock, proved 12 Dec. 1771, TNA, PROB 11/1084/356 (quoted: 'Negroes, mules'); will of Thomas Gordon of Jamaica, TNA, PROB 11/1085/244; inventory of the estate of Edward Bullock, 3 Feb. 1772, JA, 1B/11/3/52, fols 218b–223; inventory of the estate of Mary Bullock, 30 Apr. 1802, JA, 1B/11/3/95, fols 188v–190; inventory of the estate of Edward Bullock [Jnr], 13 Jan. 1827, JA, 1B/11/3/143, fols 52–3; inventory of James Jones, 6 Dec. 1838, JA, 1B/11/3/153, fols 195b–197; Accounts Produce Books 1773–1786, returns for Fair Prospect estate, JA, 1B/11/4/7–11; baptism of Elizabeth-Saville Trower, St Catherine's parish register, 4 Nov. 1751, JA, 1B/11/8/3/1; entries for 1, 24, 27 Sept. 1765; 7 Dec. 1768; 12 Feb. 1769; 15 Dec. 1771; and 24 Apr. 1772, St Catherine's parish register 1764–1808, JA, 1B/11/8/3/48; St Catherine's vestry minutes, 1759–1768, JA, 2/2/4; 'Edward Bullock of Kingston Jamaica, ????–1771', LBS; 'Edward Bullock, 1772–1824', LBS; 'Fair Prospect estate, St. Thomas-in-the East', LBS; Trevor Burnard, *Mastery, Tyranny, and Desire* (2004), 88.

75 *Her brother Tom*: Inventories of the estate of Thomas Gordon, 13 May and 24 Aug. 1772, JA, 1B/11/3/51, fols 73–7, 151–52b; Land Patents, JA, 1B/11/1/31, fols 98r–v (original foliation); Declarations of Lands Held, St Catherine's, JA, 2/2/26, p. 147; 'Thomas Gordon Esquire [3771]', LBS; 'Grace Gordon [3751]', LBS; *Gazette of Saint Jago de la Vega*, 3 May 1781, 13 Sept. 1781.

75 *He spent his life*: I have reconstructed Tom Gordon's career and outlook from the following: minutes of the Council, May 1760, JA, 1B/5/3/16; minutes of the Council, June 1765, Dec. 1766, Dec. 1767, JA, 1B/5/3/17; minutes of the Council, JA, 1B/5/3/18, fols 2, 5b, 11b, 65b–66b, JA; journals of the Council, JA, 1B/5/4/10–12; St Catherine's vestry minutes, 1759–1769, JA, 2/2/4–5; St Catherine's poll tax and deficiency rolls, JA, 2/2/22; St Catherine's list of freeholds, JA, 2/2/27, pp. 37, 59; Kingston vestry minutes, 1763–7, JA, 2/6/4, pp. 10, 27b, 31b, 71b, 108b, 145b; Kingston vestry minutes, 1768–70, JA, 2/6/5, pp. 9b, 38, 91b, 130b; Sir Archibald Grant to Thomas Gordon, 19 Dec. 1752, 17 July 1755, 31 May 1756, NRS, GD345/1161/4/65, /1163/3/102–3, /1164/3/38; Gordon to Sir Archibald Grant, 27 June 1752, 12 July 1753, 6 Jan. 1756, NRS, GD345/1162/4/7, /1162/5/28, /1164/3/38; John Gillespie to Sir Archibald Grant, 14 July 1763, NRS, GD345/1169/3/18; miscellaneous letters to Sir Archibald Grant, 1762 and 1766, NRS, GD345/1170/3 and /1171/5/75; census of St Jago de la Vega, 1754, East Sussex Record Office, SAS/RF/20/7, fol. 7r; Gordon to Rose Fuller, 28 Aug. 1755, East Sussex Record Office, SAS/RF 21/23; petition of inhabitants of St Jago de la Vega, TNA, CO 137/37, fol. 185r; Patrick Browne, *The Civil and Natural History of Jamaica* (1756), list of subscribers (unpaginated); *Journals of the Assembly of Jamaica*, 14 vols ([Kingston] Jamaica, 1811–1829), 4: 487, 528, 627–8, 650, 662–3, 672, 695, 700, 703, 714; 5: 247, 250–54, 447–49, 525, 532, 576, 599–603; 6: 112, 114, 116–17, 183; 'The Letters of Simon Taylor of Jamaica', ed. Betty Wood, in *Travel, Trade and Power in the Atlantic, 1765–1884*, ed. Betty Wood and Martin Lynn (2002), 49, 85, 106; *A Parcel of Ribbons*, ed. Anne M. Powers (n.p., 2012), 124, 147, 157, 160, 173.

75 *attorney-general of Jamaica*: he probably had known his father's fellow propagandist for Walpole in the late 1720s and early 1730s, Matthew Concanen, who served as Jamaica's attorney-general from 1732 to 1743 and then returned to London while Tom was training as a barrister. See *ODNB*, s.v. 'Concanen, Matthew (1701–1749)'; *Register of Admissions to the Honourable Society of the Middle Temple*, vol. 1, ed. H. A. C. Sturgess (1949), 327; Middle Temple, 'Minutes of Parliament, 1703–1747' (1970, typescript deposited at Middle Temple Archive, London), 388–9.

75 *in the Caribbean*: see Roderick Cave, *Printing and the Book Trade in the West Indies* (1987); James Robertson, 'Eighteenth-Century Jamaica's Ambivalent Cosmopolitanism', *History* 99 (2014). That liberty

of the press was, in general, a topic as keenly discussed in the West Indies as in Britain and North America, and that 'Cato' became a common reference there, too, is suggested, for example, by the *Barbados Gazette*, 6 Nov. 1731; *Remarks on Zenger's Tryal, Taken out of the Barbados Gazette's* ([Philadelphia], [1737]); *Antigua Gazette*, 12 Apr. 1755; *Dominica Mercury, or Free-Port Gazette*, 3 Sept. 1768; *Barbados Mercury*, 13 Oct. 1770.

75 *potent political ideal*: on race and freedom of speech, see Miles Ogborn, *The Freedom of Speech: Talk and Slavery in the Anglo-Caribbean World* (2019); Jack P. Greene, 'Liberty, Slavery, and the Transformation of British Identity in the Eighteenth-Century West Indies', *Slavery and Abolition* 21 (2000).

76 *eloquence of Africans*: for an early example, see *A Letter from a Merchant at Jamaica [. . .] To which is added, A Speech Made by a Black* (1709), 29.

76 *'naturally inferior'* etc.: David Hume, *Essays: Moral, Political, and Literary*, ed. Eugene F. Miller (1987 edn), 208, 629–30 (a note added in 1753 to an essay first published in 1748). His final, 1777 edition sharpened the anti-Black contrast by leaving out a passing reference to the 'four or five' other human 'species' to whom whites were also inherently superior. Despite professing 'disgust' at how 'domestic slavery, in the American colonies' corrupted slave owners, Hume also repeatedly adopted the perspectives of 'our planters' – for example, that 'we [are] obliged to exercise a rigorous military government over the negroes'. See ibid., 383–4, 389–90, 429, 639. For his contempt for Africans and support of slavery, see David Hume, *A Treatise of Human Nature*, ed. David Fate Norton and Mary J. Norton, 2 vols (2007), paras 2.2.8.14 and 3.2.3.10; *The Letters of David Hume*, ed. J. Y. T. Greig, 2 vols (1932), 2: 113–14; *Further Letters of David Hume*, ed. Felix Waldmann (2014), 65–8.

76 *Hume's assertion*: Richard H. Popkin, 'Hume's Racism', in Richard H. Popkin, *The High Road to Pyrrhonism*, ed. Richard Watson and James E. Force (1980), 251–66; Aaron Garrett and Silvia Sebastiani, 'David Hume on Race', in Naomi Zack (ed.), *The Oxford Handbook of Philosophy and Race* (2017).

76 *'ingenious gentleman'*: *LJ*, 21 Oct. 1721 [49]; see also minutes of ordinary meetings, 25 Oct. 1716, Royal Society Archives, London, JBO/12/86, and minutes of Council, 8 Nov. 1716, Royal Society Archives, CMO/2/268; *Gentleman's Magazine* 41 (1771); Ogborn, *Freedom of Speech*, 58–9; Vincent Carretta, 'Who Was Francis

Williams?', *Early American Literature* 38 (2003); John Gilmore, s.v. 'Williams, Francis (*c*.1690–1762)', *ODNB* ; idem, 'The British Empire and the Neo-Latin Tradition', in Barbara E. Goff (ed.), *Classics and Colonialism* (2005).

76 *his rhetorical skill*: Gillespie to Grant, 14 July 1763, NRS, GD 345/1169/3/18 (quoted: 'the ablest speaker'); minutes of the Council, 13 Dec. 1766, JA, 1B/5/3/17; *Gentleman's Magazine* 46 (1776), 37 (quoted: 'famed in wordy war'; 'eloquence [flowed] from his tongue'); 'very moving' is in all of the following: *New-York Gazette*, 11 June 1764; *Providence Gazette*, 16 June 1764; *Boston Evening-Post*, 18 June 1764; *Newport Mercury*, 18 June 1764; *New-London Gazette*, 22 June 1764; *Pennsylvania Gazette*, 28 June 1764.

76 *self-confident heir*: see Thomas Gordon, *A Cordial for Low Spirits*, 3 vols (3rd edn, 1763), 1: v; 'A Manuscript by Lord Adam Gordon', ed. Keith W. Murray, *Genealogist*, new series 14 (1898), 15.

76 *cornerstone of liberty*: see Jack P. Greene, *Negotiated Authorities* (1994), esp. chs 8, 14; idem, *Creating the British Atlantic* (2013), ch. 8.

76 *'had not the modesty'*: Edward Long, *The History of Jamaica*, 3 vols (1774), 2: 478.

77 *'virtue and understanding'*: ibid., 2: 480 (in Latin).

77 *successfully petitioned*: 'A Short State of the Case of Francis Williams of the Island of Jamaica', and ancillary documents, 1731, TNA, CO 137/19, fols 29r–35v, 73r–74v, at 29r; *Acts of the Privy Council of England: Colonial Series*, 6 vols (1910), 3: 344–5. See also Brooke N. Newman, 'Contesting "Black" Liberty and Subjecthood in the Anglophone Caribbean, 1730s–1780s', *Slavery and Abolition* 32 (2011). I am writing a biography of Williams.

77 *'petition of negro slaves'*: James Robertson, 'A 1748 "Petition of Negro Slaves" and the Local Politics of Slavery in Jamaica', *William and Mary Quarterly* 67 (2000).

77 *'sweets of liberty'* etc.: John Fielding, *Extracts from Such of the Penal Laws* (1762), 143–4. See also Ogborn, *Freedom of Speech*, 175.

77 *'which locked her mouth'*: Olaudah Equiano, *The Interesting Narrative and Other Writings*, ed. Vincent Carretta (1995), 63.

77 *'shit'* etc.: quoted in Burnard, *Mastery, Tyranny, and Desire*, 260–61.

78 *major plots*: dates compiled from Michael Craton, *Testing the Chains* (1982), and Vincent Brown, *Tacky's Revolt* (2020).

78 *Akan proverb*: Ogborn, *Freedom of Speech*, 41.

78 *slave talk*: Craton, *Testing the Chains*; Ogborn, *Freedom of Speech*; Brown, *Tacky's Revolt*.

78 *imbalances of power*: for the doubled erasure of enslaved female voices in the surviving records, see esp. Saidiya Hartman, 'Venus in Two Acts', *Small Axe* 26 (2008); Marisa J. Fuentes, *Dispossessed Lives* (2016).

78 *Equiano's words*: Equiano, *Interesting Narrative*, 94, 158–9; Vincent Carretta, *Equiano, the African* (2005); John Bugg, 'The Other Interesting Narrative', *PMLA* 121 (2006).

79 *gain more agency*: see e.g. Brown, *Tacky's Revolt*, 211; Philip D. Morgan, *Slave Counterpoint* (1998), esp. 313, 464, 560–80.

79 *spoke out defiantly*: Ogborn, *Freedom of Speech*, 91–108; Brown, *Tacky's Revolt*, 106–7, 111, 145, 155–6, 220, 242.

79 *forge passes for runaway slaves*: 'Confession of Scyrus a negro', 1733, TNA, CO 137/20, fol. 179r–v; [John Lindsay], 'A Few Conjectural Considerations Upon the Creation of the Humane Race', 1788, BL, Add. MS 12439, fol. 196v.

79 [footnote] *'Slavery'* etc.: *Boston Gazette*, 23 Aug. 1773; David Waldstreicher, *The Odyssey of Phillis Wheatley* (2023), 199–200.

79 *destabilized white efforts*: cf. Laurent Dubois, 'An Enslaved Enlightenment', *Social History* 31 (2006); Brown, *Tacky's Revolt*; Ogborn, *Freedom of Speech*, ch. 5.

80 *American popularity of Cato's Letters*: see e.g. Elizabeth Christine Cook, *Literary Influences in Colonial Newspapers, 1704–1750* (1912), esp. 81–3, 89–90, 106, 113, 125–6, 129, 137, 257, 263; Clinton Rossiter, *Seedtime of the Republic* (1953), 141–2, 145–7, 298–300, 357, 492 n. 120; *The English Libertarian Heritage*, ed. David L. Jacobson (1965), xlviii–lx; Bernard Bailyn, *The Ideological Origins of the American Revolution* (1992), esp. 35–7, 44–4, 52–3, 57–62, 86, 132–3; Chad Reid, '"Widely Read by American Patriots"', in Mark L. Kamrath and Sharon M. Harris (eds), *Periodical Literature in Eighteenth-Century America* (2005); Heather E. Barry, *A 'Dress Rehearsal' for Revolution* (2007).

80 *Benjamin Franklin*: *New-England Courant*, 11 Sept. 1721; 9 and 16 July 1722; J. A. Leo Lemay, *The Life of Benjamin Franklin*, 3 vols (2006–9), 1: 85, 111, 150, 155, 158–65, 188, 453.

80 *Andrew Bradford*: e.g. *American Weekly Mercury*, 26 Feb. 1723; 12 Mar., 4 and 25 Apr. 1734; 6 Nov. 1740.

80 *New-York Weekly Journal*: as Cosby himself noted of the 'weekly . . . false and scandalous libels printed in Zengers Journal', 'there is nothing more common with writers of seditious libels than for them to tell the world they speak the sentiments of the people': *Documents Relative to the Colonial History of the State of New-York*, ed. E. B. O'Callaghan, 15 vols (Albany, 1853–87), 6: 4–7.

80 *foundational moment*: James Alexander, *A Brief Narrative of the Case and Trial of John Peter Zenger* [1736], ed. Stanley Nider Katz (1963); *Freedom of the Press from Zenger to Jefferson*, ed. Leonard W. Levy (1966); see also Jill Lepore, *New York Burning* (2005).

81 *not original*: Karl Tilman Winkler, *Wörterkrieg: Politische Debattenkultur in England, 1689–1750* (1998), ch. 11; Simon Robertson Varey, 'The Craftsman, 1726–1752' (University of Cambridge PhD thesis, 1976); Alison Olson, 'The Zenger Case Revisited', *American Literature* 35 (2000), esp. 231–2.

81 *gained much more sway*: *New-York Gazette*, 4 Feb. 1733/4; *New-York Weekly Journal*, 11 Feb. 1733/4; see also *American Weekly Mercury*, 4 Nov. 1734.

81 *'colonies and plantations' etc.*: *New-York Weekly Journal*, 12–19 Nov. 1733.

81 *republished Trenchard and Gordon's columns*: *New-York Weekly Journal*, 11 Feb.–4 Mar. 1734; see also *New-York Weekly Journal*, 7–14 Jan., 15 Apr. 1734.

81 *reran Cato's defence of free speech*: *New-York Weekly Journal*, 11 Nov.–9 Dec. 1734; see also *New-York Weekly Journal*, 30 Dec. 1734, 27 Jan. 1735, 19 Dec. 1737–17 Jan. 1738.

81 *'This is a state of slavery'*: Alexander, *Brief Narrative*, 143.

81 *bolstered colonial press freedom*: Olson, 'Zenger Case Revisited'; Amy Watson, 'The New York Patriot Movement' *William and Mary Quarterly* 77 (2020).

82 *'Every man who prefers'*: Alexander, *Brief Narrative*, 99.

82 *Alongside its constant appeals*: see e.g. *New-York Weekly Journal*, 31 Dec. 1733–14 Jan. 1734; 28 Jan., 15 Apr., 22 July, 5–14 Oct. 1734; 27 Jan.–10 Feb., 28 Apr.–26 May 1735.

82 *owned and traded slaves*: see e.g. *South-Carolina Gazette*, 14 June 1740; Isaiah Thomas, *The History of Printing in America*, 2 vols (2nd edn, 1874), 1: xxv, 63, 99, 101, 130, 133, 163, 343–4; 2:48; Lepore, *New York Burning*, 72; Cave, *Printing and the Book Trade in the West Indies*, 31–3; Hennig Cohen, *The South-Carolina Gazette, 1732–1775* (1953), 6; David Waldstreicher, *Runaway America* (2004).

82 *publicly burned*: *New-York Weekly Journal*, 2 Dec. 1734.

82 *Alexander … Morris*: *New-York Weekly Journal*, 13 Feb. 1737/8 (quoted: 'the pampered insolence'); *ODNB*, s.v. 'Alexander, James (1691–1756)', 'Morris, Lewis (1671–1746)'; Eugene R. Sheridan, *Lewis Morris, 1671–1746* (1988), ch. 1 (quoted: 'devoted reader', 'Negroes'); Paul David Nelson, *William Alexander, Lord Stirling* (1987), 11–12.

Their great friend and patron Robert Hunter was the governor of Jamaica who oversaw its 1730 Act degrading the rights of Francis Williams and other free Blacks. For the historiography, see esp. Edmund S. Morgan, *American Slavery, American Freedom* (1975), 3–6; see also Lepore, *New York Burning*, xii, xx.

82 *Dobrée*: I have reconstructed Dobrée's trajectory in England from the following: Tower Ward Land Tax assessments 1722–5, TLA, CLC/525/MS11316/071, p. 52, /074, p. 50, /077, p. 53, /080, p. 49; baptism of Mary, daughter of Elisha Dobrée and Elizabeth, St Olave Hart Street, 16 September 1722, TLA, P69/OLA1/A/003/MS17818; baptism of James, son of Elisha Dobrée and Elizabeth, St Botolph without Aldgate, 25 Jan. 1729, TLA, P69/BOT2/A/008/MS09225/003; baptism of Susannah, daughter of Elisha Dobrée and Elizabeth, 7 June 1732, TLA, P69/MIC1/A/003/MS06988/01; Dobrée to Charles Delafaye, Undersecretary of State, with enclosures, 27–28 June 1723, TNA, SP 43/66; commission of bankruptcy against Elisha Dobrée, 30 July 1725, TNA, SP B4/5, 23; petition of Elisha Dobrée, TNA, SP 36/155/1/122A–123; *Whitehall Evening-Post*, 1 Dec. 1724; *London Gazette*, 7 Aug. 1724, 21 Aug. 1724, 30 Nov. 1725; *Philosophical Transactions* 33 (1726), 431; Dobrée to Benjamin Martyn, 9 July 1735, TNA, CO 5/637, fol. 177 (quoted: 'since my infancy').

83 *his extended family*: will of Michael Henry Pascal, proved 8 May 1786, TNA, PROB 11/1142/88; 'Bonamy Dobrée', LBS; 'Harry Hankey Dobrée', LBS; Voyage ID 77536, *Slave Voyages* (slavevoyages.org); Equiano, *Interesting Narrative*, 68–9, 91, 105, 255 n. 145, 270 n. 304; Doug Ford, 'A Respectable Trade or Against Human Dignity?', *Heritage Magazine* [Jersey] (2006), 7. Another branch of the family was based in Nantes, the French slaving capital: see Robert Stein, 'The Profitability of the Nantes Slave Trade, 1783–1792', *Journal of Economic History* 35 (1975).

83 *made for Charleston, South Carolina*: my account of Dobrée in South Carolina and Georgia is based primarily on the following: Georgia correspondence of the Board of Trade, 1734–46, TNA, CO 5/636–41; correspondence of the Trustees for Georgia 1732–40, TNA, CO 5/666–67; Georgia land grants, instructions, petitions, etc., 1732–52, TNA, CO 5/670–71; journal of the Trustees for Georgia, 1737–45, TNA, CO 5/687; minutes of the Council of the Trustees for Georgia, 1732–6, TNA, CO 5/689; Earl of Egmont papers, Hargrett Library, University of Georgia, Athens, MS 746; transcripts of the Earl of Egmont papers, Hargrett Library, MS 1786; *Colonial Records of the State of Georgia,*

1732–1784, ed. Allen D. Candler et al., 39 vols (1904–1989); Royal Commission on Historical Manuscripts, *Manuscripts of the Earl of Egmont: Diary of Viscount Percival afterwards first Earl of Egmont*, 3 vols (1920–1923); [Thomas Stephens], *A Brief Account of the Causes that have Retarded the Progress of the Colony of Georgia* (1743), 59; Francis Moore, *Travels into the Inland Parts of Africa* (1738); Francis Moore, *A Voyage to Georgia Begun in the Year 1735* (1744); *The Works of John Wesley*, vol. 18: *Journals and Diaries (1735–38)*, ed. W. Reginald Ward and Richard P. Heitzenrater (1988), 361, 408, 448; *The Works of John Wesley*, vol. 25: *Letters (1721–39)*, ed. Frank Baker (1980), 452–4.

83 *Things did not go well*: Messrs Beale and Cooper to Dobrée, 9 Nov. 1734, TNA, CO 5/636, fol. 57; Patrick Houston to Peter Gordon (1 Mar. 1735), and Gordon to Trustees (7 May 1735), TNA, CO 5/637, fols 11r–v, 18r; minutes of the Council of the Trustees for Georgia, 10 May 1735, TNA, CO 5/689, 176; 'A List of Persons Who Went from Europe to Georgia', Hargrett Library, MS 4132 (printed as *A List of the Early Settlers of Georgia*, ed. E. Melton Coulter and Albert Saye (1949)), entries for Dobrée and his seven servants; *South-Carolina Gazette*, 27 July 1734.

83 *'I . . . came into'*: Dobrée to Richard Peters, 28 Sept. 1741, Pennsylvania State Archives.

83 *'journal of events'*: Dobrée to Trustees, 13 Feb. and 28 Mar. 1735, TNA, CO 5/636, fols 201v, 300r.

83 *'penman'* etc.: Dobrée to Benjamin Martyn, 9 July 1735, TNA, CO 5/637, fols 177–8.

83 *'freedom in writing'*: for Dobrée's invocations of scribal freedom, see TNA, CO 5/636, fols 33, 106, 164, 190v, 300, and TNA, CO 5/637, fols 174, 177.

83 *South Carolina's laws*: quoting extracts printed in *South-Carolina Gazette*, 4 May 1734, while Dobrée was in Charleston; and see *The Statutes at Large of South Carolina*, ed. Thomas Cooper and David J. McCord, 10 vols (Columbia, SC, 1836–41), 7: 343–427; Philip D. Morgan, 'Black Life in Eighteenth-Century Charleston', *Perspectives in American History*, NS 1 (1984).

84 *'rights'*, *'privileges'* etc.: Andrew C. Lannen, 'Liberty and Slavery in Colonial America: The Case of Georgia, 1732–1770', *Historian* 79 (2017), 39–40, 47.

84 *everywhere in Georgia*: Betty Wood, *Slavery in Colonial Georgia, 1730–1775* (1984); Brown, *Moral Capital*, 78–87; Noeleen McIlvenna,

The Short Life of Free Georgia (2015); Anthony F. Moffett, 'Runaway Slaves and the Making of Georgia' (University of Florida PhD thesis, 2015), ch. 3.

84 *'liberty of getting Negroes'*: quoted in Wood, *Slavery in Colonial Georgia*, 18.

84 *business with slavers*: on Dobrée and slavery, see Dobrée to Trustees, 27 Jan., 6 Feb. 1735, [Feb.?] 1737, TNA, CO 5/636, fols 165, 190v, and TNA, CO 5/639, fols 178–9.

84 *'whimsical'*: *Manuscripts of the Earl of Egmont*, 2: 379; see also Harman Verelst to Dobrée, 19 Apr. 1737, TNA, CO 5/667, fol. 14v. Eliza Dobrée, born Elizabeth Lowther, who single-handedly maintained herself and their three children, may have been the 'Eliz[abe]th Dupre', aged seventy-eight, interred at Union Street Independent burial ground in Southwark on 22 July 1783 (register of burials, 1773–87, TNA, RG 4/4358).

84 *'the great damage'* etc.: Dobrée to Trustees, 15 Jan. 1735, TNA, CO 5/636, fol. 106r–v; see also 28 Mar. 1735, TNA, CO 5/636, fol. 300v; *South-Carolina Gazette*, 27 July 1734.

85 *He was right*: Benjamin Martyn to Bailiffs and Recorder of Savannah, 28 Oct. 1734, TNA, CO 5/666, fol. 38v; Cohen, *South-Carolina Gazette*, 10–11; Jeffery A. Smith, 'Impartiality and Revolutionary Ideology', *Journal of Southern History* 49 (1983).

85 *précis of Cato*: *South-Carolina Gazette*, 2 Feb. 1734 (approvingly reprinted by James Alexander in *New-York Weekly Journal*, 4 Mar. 1734).

85 *the Gazette's columns*: *South-Carolina Gazette*, 27 July 1734; 18 Jan. 1735 (quoted: 'Negro man, named Cato'); 12 June 1736 (quoted: 'the right of every man' etc.); 14 and 21 Aug. 1736; 16 July 1748.

85 *Affy Crawford*: will and probate of Affy Crawford, 1750, J0038-92, subseries 2, no. 511; will and probate of Hugh Crawford, 1745–49, J0038-92, subseries 2, no. 592, New York State Archives, Albany; *Minutes of the Common Council of the City of New York, 1675–1776*, 8 vols (1905), 5: 2, 45, 141, 143, 189, 194; *New York Genealogical and Biographical Record* 72, no. 4 (1941): 292–3, and 75, no. 1 (1944): 19.

85 *bloodiest racial episode*: see Lepore, *New York Burning*.

86 *'great deal of craft'*: [Daniel Horsmanden], *A Journal of the Proceedings in the Detection of the Conspiracy* (1744), iii.

86 *'for a long time argued with'* etc.: ibid., 32.

86 *white justice*: Lepore, *New York Burning*, esp. 163–5, 168, 173–5, 188–9.

87 *slave trials*: ibid., 79–83, 121, 165–6, 200, 212. Lepore's misinterpretation of Alexander's attitudes is corrected in Brendan McConville, 'Of Slavery and Sources', *Reviews in American History* 34 (2006), and proved by James and William Alexander Papers, New Jersey Historical Society, Newark, MG 70, box 3, esp. 71–2 [pencilled pagination].

87 *he met intermittently with Dobrée*: Lawrence Smyth to Alexander, 10 Mar. 1742, New-York Historical Society, MS 8; Small Scrapbook, New-York Historical Society, MS 531, items 75, 76, 80, 82, 83, 96, 98; General Board of Proprietors of the Eastern Division of New Jersey: deed books of exemplified copies (scribed by Dobrée), New Jersey State Archives, Trenton, PEASJ002, vols 1–10; Alexander Papers, New Jersey Historical Society, MG 70, box 3; James Alexander Papers, Princeton University Library, C0024, boxes 3–4; *The Minutes of the Board of Proprietors of the Eastern Division of New Jersey*, 4 vols (1949–85).

87 *what had happened in Stono*: Peter H. Wood, *Black Majority* (1974), ch. 12; John K. Thornton, 'African Dimensions of the Stono Rebellion', *American Historical Review* 96 (1991); *Stono*, ed. Mark M. Smith (2005); Peter Charles Hoffer, *Cry Liberty* (2010); Lepore, *New York Burning*, 53, 163; Jane Landers, *Black Society in Spanish Florida* (1999), chs 1–2. See also Oglethorpe to Trustees, 28 May 1742, TNA, CO 5/641, fol. 145.

88 *Other contemporary accounts*: *Stono*, ed. Smith, 8; *Boston Weekly News-Letter*, 8 Nov. 1739; *Pennsylvania Gazette*, 8 Nov. 1739.

88 *document penned by Elisha Dobrée*: 'An Account of the Negroe Insurrection in South Carolina', TNA, CO 5/640, fols 392–6, printed in (and previously known to historians only via) *Colonial Records of the State of Georgia*, 22: 232–6. It was enclosed in a letter (also scribed by Dobrée) of 9 Oct. 1739 from James Oglethorpe to Harman Verelst, accountant of Georgia's Trustees. Verelst received it on 13 Mar. 1740; it was printed in the following: the *London Daily Post*, 17 Mar. 1740; *Weekly Miscellany*, 22 Mar. 1740, *London Magazine* 9 (1740), 151–2; *Gentleman's Magazine* 10 (1740), 127–9.

88 *seventeenth-century English papers*: Newman, *Freedom Seekers* (2022).

89 *'Though he is my property'*: *South-Carolina Gazette*, 7–28 Nov. 1775. See also Waldstreicher, *Runaway America*, esp. ch. 1; Betty Wood, '"High Notions of Their Liberty"', in Philip Morgan (ed.), *African American Life in the Georgia Lowcountry* (2010).

89 'Servitude mars all genius': LJ, 3 Mar. 1721 [68]; see also LJ, 31 Mar. 1722 [70].

89 'wrote passes for slaves': quoted in Stono, ed. Smith, 55–6; David Ramsay, *The History of South Carolina*, 2 vols (Charleston, 1809), 1: 110–13, also records 'their black captain, named Cato'.

89 'a sensible cunning fellow': *New-York Gazette*, 7–21 July 1729.

89 Yaff: Yaff was born in America around 1694, apparently to a mother enslaved by Richard Ingoldsby, the governor of New York in 1691–2 and 1709–10, who died in 1719. He was subsequently made the butler and valet of a wealthy Philadelphia merchant and slave trader, William Trent, who had recently moved to New Jersey (where he established Trent-town, i.e. Trenton, now the state capital). After Trent's death in December 1724, Yaff was acquired by Alexander, one of Trent's executors, at some point after April 1726. See Lepore, *New York Burning*, 287 n. 39; and the documents and information about Trent and Yaff at the Trent House Association website, williamtrenthouse. org. For countless other similar examples, see Waldstreicher, 'Reading the Runaways'; *'Pretends to Be Free': Runaway Slave Advertisements from Colonial and Revolutionary New York and New Jersey*, ed. Graham Russell and Alan Edward Brown, rev. edn (2019); for a Jamaican instance, see *Daily Advertiser* [Kingston, Jamaica], 12–15 Jan. 1791.

5. ENLIGHTENED EXPERIMENTS

91 'the great advantages' etc.: printed in Juha Mustonen (ed.), *The World's First Freedom of Information Act* (2006), 8.

91 it must have influenced them: Henrik Horstbøll, Ulrik Langen and Frederik Stjernfelt, *Grov Konfækt: tre vilde år med trykkefrihed 1770–73*, 2 vols (2020), 1: 465.

91 'We have decided' etc.: *Kabinetsstyrelsen i Danmark, 1768–1772*, ed. Holger Hansen, 3 vols (1916–23), 1: 46–7; see also 1: 288 (explicitly extending print freedom to newspapers).

92 Swedish law: Juha Manninen, 'Anders Chydenius', in Mustonen (ed.), *World's First*, 22.

92 Danish and Norwegian codes: *The Danish Laws* (1756), 466–9; Norwegian code of 1687, bk 6, available at hf.uio.no/iakh/tjenester/kunnskap/samlinger/tingbok/lover-reskripter/chr5web/chr5register. html.

92 *staged verbal disputations*: Debora Shuger, 'St. Mary the Virgin and the Birth of the Public Sphere', *Huntington Library Quarterly* 72 (2009).

92 *republic of letters*: see e.g. Françoise Waquet, 'Qu'est ce que la République des Lettres?', *Bibliothèque de l'École des Chartes* 147 (1989); Hans Bots and Françoise Waquet, *La République des Lettres* (1997).

93 *'is an extremely free state'* etc.: Pierre Bayle, *Dictionnaire historique et critique* (Rotterdam, 1697), note to 'Catius'.

94 *'absolutely necessary'* etc.: Baruch Spinoza, *Tractatus Theologico-Politicus* (1670), ch. 20. I disagree with the interpretation of Spinoza as especially radical on this point that has been advanced by Jonathan I. Israel in his *Radical Enlightenment* (2001), 117, 270 and *passim*, and *Enlightenment Contested* (2006), 155–63.

94 *'must at all times'* etc.: Immanuel Kant, 'An Answer to the Question: What is Enlightenment?' (1784), in *What is Enlightenment?*, ed. and trans. James Schmidt (1996), 59, 60, 63.

95 *could still be banned*: the literature on the varieties of censorship is immense. Israel, *Radical Enlightenment*, ch. 5, surveys the main variations, trends and loopholes.

95 *obtain an official permit*: Hannah Marcus, *Forbidden Knowledge* (2020), esp. ch. 5.

95 *Italy's various states*: [Gabriel François Coyer], *Voyages d'Italie et de Hollande*, 2 vols (Paris, 1775), 2: 190–91; Edoardo Tortarolo, *The Invention of Free Press* (2016), ch. 5.

95 *ever more accessible*: see e.g. Hans Erich Bödeker, 'Journals and Public Opinion', in Eckhart Hellmuth (ed.), *The Transformation of Political Culture* (1990); Israel, *Radical Enlightenment*, ch. 7.

95 *'we believe'*: Denis Diderot and Jean le Rond d'Alembert, *Encyclopédie*, vol. 3 (Paris, 1753), xi.

96 *liberation from censorship*: Adrian Johns, *The Nature of the Book* (1998), 374–5, 378–9; Henrik Horstbøll, 'Anybody May Write Anything', in John T. Lauridsen and Margit Mogensen (eds) *Copenhagen: Gateway to Europe* (1996), 35.

96 *truth was being stifled*: [Louis-Sébastien Mercier], *Memoirs of the Year Two Thousand Five Hundred*, trans. W. Hooper, 2 vols (1772), 1: epistle dedicatory.

96 *'awakening Europe'*: Louis-Sébastien Mercier, *Tableau de Paris*, 12 vols (Amsterdam, 1781–8), 4: 258–9, trans. and quoted in Robert Darnton, *The Forbidden Best-Sellers of Pre-Revolutionary France* (1996), 229.

96 *'pure lights of reason'*: [Mercier], *Memoirs of the Year*, 1: 2.

96 *utopian year*: ibid., 1: ch. 11 and 2: ch. 2. (Mercier's original text was set in 2440; the English translation changed this to the year 2500.)

96 *'nothing leads the mind'*: ibid., 2: 2.

96 *'the true measure'*: ibid., 1: 60.

96 *'very few absurdities'*: ibid., 1: 62.

96 *'opinion of the public'* etc.: ibid., 1: 58–60; cf. Darnton, *Forbidden Best-Sellers*, ch. 4 and 226–31.

97 *'common good'* etc.: Jean-Jacques Rousseau, *The Social Contract*, trans. Maurice Cranston (2006), bk 4, ch. 1. See also [Paul Henry Thiry, Baron d'Holbach], *La Politique naturelle*, 2 vols (1773), 2: 78–88; William Godwin, *An Enquiry Concerning Political Justice*, 2 vols (1793), esp. bk 6, ch. 6, and bk 8, ch. 8; Javier Fernández Sebastián, 'From the "Voice of the People" to the Freedom of the Press', in Jesús Astigarraga (ed.), *The Spanish Enlightenment Revisited* (2015).

97 *struggles with censors*: on Rousseau and censorship, see Raymond Birn, 'Book Censorship in Eighteenth-Century France and Rousseau's Response', *Studies on Voltaire and the Eighteenth Century* (2005); Helena Rosenblatt, 'Rousseau, Constant, and the Emergence of the Modern Notion of Free Speech', in Elizabeth Powers (ed.), *Freedom of Speech: The History of an Idea* (2011), 140–45; Tortarolo, *Invention*, 87–94.

98 *'fourth estate'*: *Oxford English Dictionary* (oed.com), s.v. 'estate', 7b: 'the fourth estate'.

98 *Anglophone conservatives*: see Hellmuth (ed.), *Transformation*, ch. 19; see also Chapter 7 of this book.

98 *'previous restraints'*: William Blackstone, *Commentaries on the Laws of England*, 4 vols (Oxford, 1765–69), 4: 151. Cf. *Encyclopédie*, vol. 13 (1765), 320.

98 *'freedom of the press'* etc.: Tortarolo, *Invention*, 137–41 (quoting 141).

98 *'Books can do good'* etc.: Carlo Antonio Pilati, *On Reforming Italy* (1767), 220–21.

98 *official censors*: Alcesti Tarchetti, 'Paulo Frisi . . . il censore censurato', in Gennaro Barbarisi (ed.), *Ideologia e scienza nell'opera di Paolo Frisi* (1987); Ugo Baldini, 'Frisi, Paolo', in *Dizionario biografico degli Italiani* 50 (1998); Robert Darnton, *Censors at Work* (2014), pt 1; Ritchie Robertson, *The Enlightenment* (2020), 389–95.

99 *appealed to rulers*: see e.g. K. A. Papmehl, *Freedom of Expression in Eighteenth Century Russia* (1971); *Der Josephinismus*, ed. Harm Klueting (1995), 130, 215–18; Tortarolo, *Invention*, 141–5.

99 *'is established in England'*: [Voltaire], *L'A, B, C: Dialogue Curieux* ('London, 1762' [i.e. Geneva, 1768]), 88; see also Karl Friedrich Bahrdt, *On Freedom of the Press and its Limits* (Züllichau, 1787), 137–8, in *Early French and German Defenses of the Freedom of the Press*, ed. and trans. John Christian Laursen and John van der Zande (2003); Jean-Pierre Lavandier, *Le Livre au temps de Joseph II et de Léopold II* (1995), esp. 37–45. Cf. Richard Butterwick, *Poland's Last King and English Culture* (1998); Nicholas Cronk, 'Voltaire and the Uses of Censorship', in E. Joe Johnson and Byron R. Wells (eds), *An American Voltaire* (2009).

99 *Frederick the Great*: Tortarolo, *Invention*, 144–54.

99 *'Nothing surprised me more'*: quoted in Christopher Clark, *Iron Kingdom* (2006), 256–7.

99 *'Don't speak'* etc.: Lessing to Friedrich Nicolai, 28 Aug. 1769, in Lessing, *Werke und Briefe*, ed. Wilfried Barner et al., 12 vols (1985–2003), 11: letter 501. Cf. *Edict wegen der wiederhergestellten Censur* (Magdeburg, 1749); Ernst Ferdinand Klein, 'On Freedom of Thought and the Press' (1784), trans. John Christian Laursen, in *What is Enlightenment?*, ed. James Schmidt (1996).

99 *slower to develop*: cf. Bödeker, 'Journals and Public Opinion'.

100 *Christian Wolff*: Eckhart Hellmuth, 'Zur Diskussion um Presse- und Meinungsfreiheit', in Günter Birtsch (ed.), *Grund- und Freiheitsrechte im Wandel von Gesellschaft und Geschichte* (1981), 210–11. For similar views elsewhere, see Arlette Farge, *Subversive Words*, trans. Rosemary Morris (1994), 2; Ann Thomson, 'Defending the Truth', in Robert G. Ingram et al. (eds), *Freedom of Speech, 1500–1850* (2020).

100 *later German theorists*: more liberal German visions of press freedom were put forward in the 1780s, for example by the publisher Friedrich Nicolai, the philosopher Moses Mendelssohn, the scholar and statesman Wilhelm von Dohm and the journalist Wilhelm Ludwig Wekhrlin: see Eckhart Hellmuth, 'Enlightenment and Freedom of the Press', *History* 83 (1998), 429–30, 437; idem, 'Zur Diskussion', 215; Edoardo Tortarolo, 'Censorship and the Conception of the Public in Late Eighteenth-Century Germany', in Dario Castiglione and Lesley Sharpe (eds), *Shifting the Boundaries* (1995), 141–2; *Early French and German Defenses*, ed. and trans. Laursen and van der Zande, 94–8.

100 *'human right'* etc.: Bahrdt, *On Freedom*, 165. Cf. [Mathew Tindal], *Beweis daß das Christenthum so alt als die Welt sey* [trans. Johann Lorenz Schmidt] (Frankfurt and Leipzig, 1741), 8–103 (Schmidt's preface).

100 *'it must not transcend'*: Immanuel Kant, 'On the Common Saying: "This May be True in Theory, But it Does not Apply in Practice"', trans. H. B. Nisbet, in *Kant's Political Writings*, ed. Hans Reiss (1970), 85. Elsewhere, Kant presumes that the ideal is *'a constitution allowing the greatest possible human freedom* in accordance with laws which ensure *that the freedom of each can coexist with the freedom of all the others'*: Reiss, 'Introduction', ibid., 23. See also Peter Niesen, *Kants Theorie der Redefreiheit* (2008).

100 *Johann Gottlieb Fichte*: [J. G. Fichte], *Zurückforderung der Denkfreiheit* [Danzig, 1793]; Anthony J. La Vopa, 'The Revelatory Moment: Fichte and the French Revolution', *Central European History* 22 (1989), esp. 149–53; Anthony J. La Vopa, *Fichte* (2001), 92–4 and *passim*; Diethelm Klippel, 'The True Concept of Liberty', in Hellmuth (ed.), *Transformation*.

101 *trickle-down theory*: Horst Möller, 'Enlightened Societies', in Hellmuth (ed.), *Transformation*, 229–33; Sebastián, 'From the "Voice of the People"', 229. Sophia Rosenfeld, 'Writing the History of Censorship in the Age of Enlightenment', in Daniel Gordon (ed.), *Postmodernism and the Enlightenment* (2001), brilliantly situates late eighteenth-century French disputes over freedom of expression within a wider universe of intellectual concerns about the abuses and politics of language.

101 *'the gross ignorance'*: Adam Smith, *An Inquiry into the Nature and Causes of the Wealth of Nations*, 2 vols (1776), 2: 373.

101 *'Learning to read'* etc.: Heinrich Friedrich Diez, *Apologie der Duldung u. Preßfreiheit* (n.p., 1781), 42.

101 *Johann Friedrich Struensee*: for this and the following four paragraphs in this chapter, see [Balthasar] Münter, *A Faithful Narrative of the Conversion and Death of Count Struensee* [trans. G. F. A. Wendeborn] (1773); *Luxdorphiana, eller Bidrag til den danske Literairhistorie*, ed. Rasmus Nyerup (Copenhagen, 1791), 4–21; Jens Kragh Höst, *Der dänische Geheimcabinetsminister Graf Johann Friedrich Struensee* 2 vols (1826–7); [Georg] Hille, 'Struensee's literarische Thätigkeit', *Zeitschrift der Gesselschaft für Schleswig-Holstein- Lauenburgische Geschichte* 16 (1886), 275–99; Stefan Winkle, *Struensee und die Publizistik* (1982); idem, *Johann Friedrich Struensee* (1983); idem, *Die heimlichen Spinozisten in Altona und der Spinozastreit* (1988); Matthias Reiber, *Anatomie eines Bestsellers: Johann August Unzers Wochenschrift "Der Arzt" (1759–1764)* (1999), esp. 135–47, 225–9; Johan Schioldann, '"Struensée's Memoir on the Situation of the King" (1772): Christian VII of Denmark', *History of Psychiatry* 24 (2013); Rita Wöbkemeier,

'Johann Friedrich Struensee (1737–1772) als Artz und Mediziner', in Irmtraut Sahmland and Hans-Jürgen Schrader (eds), *Medizin- und kulturgeschichtliche Konnexe des Pietismus* (2016); Horstbøll et al., *Grov Konfækt*, ch. 23.

102 *'harmful or beneficial'* etc.: quoting a now lost 1760 essay: see Winkle, *Struensee und die Publizistik*, 87 n. 187.

103 *in 1769*: cf. Lessing's intriguing reference in the letter from Hamburg in August 1769 quoted above, to voices being raised in Denmark against despotism and exploitation.

103 *eighteen hundred decrees*: see *Kabinetsstyrelsen i Danmark, 1768–1772*, ed. Holger Hansen, 3 vols (1916–23); Winkle, *Johann Friedrich Struensee*, 201–31.

103 *Jens Schelderup Sneedorff and P. F. Suhm*: see Horstbøll et al., *Grov Konfækt*, 1: 466–9.

104 *'3. Another order'*: *Kabinetsstyrelsen*, ed. Hansen, 1: 46; Horstbøll et al., *Grov Konfækt*, 1: 13–15.

104 *culmination of decades*: cf. Anders Burius, *Ömhet om friheten* (1984), chs 8–9.

104 *rubber stamp*: Michael Roberts, *The Age of Liberty: Sweden, 1719–1772* (1986), 62.

104 *censorship*: Burius, *Ömhet om friheten*, chs 2–7, is the most detailed account, though I have relied mainly on English-language summaries: Ann Öhrberg, '"A Threat to Civic Coexistence"', in C. Appel and M. Fink-Jensen (eds), *Religious Reading in the Lutheran North* (2010); Rolf Nygren, 'The Freedom of the Press Act of 1766 in Its Historical and Legal Context', in Kristina Örtenhed and Bertil Wennberg (eds), *Press Freedom 250 Years* (2018).

104 *'ignorance is better'* etc.: quoted in Roberts, *Age of Liberty*, 69, 105.

104 *Count Carl Gyllenborg*: *Svenskt biografiskt lexikon*, 'Gyllenborg, Carl'; Jonathan Swift, *To the Count de Gyllenborg* [1719], ed. Hermann J. Real (2013).

105 *spirited discussion*: Thomas von Vegesack, 'Background', in Peter Forsskål, *Thoughts on Civil Liberty*, ed. David Goldberg et al. (2009), 29–31; Burius, *Ömhet om friheten*, 214–15.

106 *'That every citizen'*: *Sveriges riddarskaps och adels riksdags-protokoll: från och med år 1719*, 28 vols (Stockholm, 1875–1964), vol. 11, appendix B, no. 20; see also 11: 348–9, 363 (11–12 Apr. 1739).

106 *Anders Bachmanson*: *Borgarståndets riksdagsprotokoll från frihetstidens början*, ed. Nils Staf, 8 vols (1945–82), 3: 199–201 (11–15 Mar. 1727); Burius, *Ömhet om friheten*, 231–7; Lars Herlitz, 'Det civila

samhället och Sveriges underutveckling', *Scandia* 57 (1991), 284, 318 nn. 6–9, 322 n. 64.

106 *'against the will'*: Andreas Bachmanson, *Arcana oeconomiæ et commercii* (Stockholm, 1730), 132, [364].

106 *suppressed book of 1734*: Riksarkivet, Stockholm, Börstorpsamlingen vol. 62, E 3003 (unpaginated). The other texts were extracts from Eustace Budgell, *A Letter to Cleomenes* (1731), and selections from *The Craftsman*.

107 *government banned*: Marie-Christine Skuncke, 'Press Freedom in the Riksdag 1760–62 and 1765–66', in Örtenhed and Wennberg, *Press Freedom*, 112; 'Johan Ihre', *Svenskt biografiskt lexicon*.

107 *'should otherwise'*: Henrik Lagerlund, 'The Reception of David Hume's Philosophy in Sweden', in Peter Jones (ed.), *The Reception of David Hume in Europe* (2013), 225.

107 *'to let authors write'*: Ludvig Holberg, *Epistler*, Tom. *IV* (Copenhagen, 1749), 338 (= Epistola CCCXCV).

107 *Christian König*: Pentti Virrankoski, *Anders Chydenius: demokraattinen poliitikko valistuksen vuosisadalta* (1986), 185; E. P. Hutchinson, 'Swedish Population Thought in the Eighteenth Century', *Population Studies* 13 (1959).

107 *weekly newspaper*: Roberts, *Age of Liberty*, 152; Virrankoski, *Anders Chydenius*, 185–6; Burius, *Ömhet om friheten*, 237–9.

107 *Niclas von Oelreich*: Burius, *Ömhet om friheten*.

108 *'Free peoples'*: quoted in Jonas Nordin, 'From Seemly Subjects to Enlightened Citizens', in Örtenhed and Wennberg (eds), *Press Freedom*, 28.

108 *Nordencrantz*: *Til riksens höglofl. ständer församlade vid riksdagen år 1760* (1759), esp. 618–70; *Oförgripelige gentankar, om frihet i bruk, af förnuft, pennor och tryck* (1761); Lars Magnusson, 'Anders Nordencrantz', in Örtenhed and Wennberg (eds), *Press Freedom*; Skuncke, 'Press Freedom', 113–14; Burius, *Ömhet om Friheten*, 240ff.

108 *Peter Forsskål*: Petrus Forsskål, *Dubia de principiis philosophiae recentioris* (Göttingen, 1756); *Neueste Geschichte der Gelehrsamkeit in Schweden* 4 (1759), 549–76; Forsskål, *Dubia* (revised edn [Copenhagen, 1760]); Archives of the Linnean Society, London: Letter from Forsskål in Alexandria to Linnaeus in Uppsala, 20 Oct. 1761 (L2976); Ere Nokkala, 'Peter Forsskål', in Örtenhed and Wennberg (eds), *Press Freedom*.

108 *'that Swedish liberty'*: Johann David Michaelis, *Lebensbeschreibung* (Leipzig, 1793), 64–6.

109 *'If only'*: Neueste Geschichte, 553.

109 *he even helped him*: Rietje van Vliet, *Elie Luzac (1721–1796): Boekverkoper van de Verlichting* (2005), 109, 137–76 (Luzac and Michaelis later fell out).

109 *central figure*: for Luzac's pamphlet and career, see Elie Luzac, *Het gedrag der stadhouders-gezinden, verdedigt* (1754); van Vliet, *Luzac*, chs 1, 2, 5.

110 *L'Homme machine*: for this and the following two paragraphs in this chapter, see [Elie Luzac], *Essai sur la liberté de produire ses sentimens* ([Amsterdam?], 1749); Wyger R. E. Velema, *Enlightenment and Conservatism in the Dutch Republic* (1993), esp. ch. 1; *Early French and German Defenses*, ed. and trans. Laursen and van der Zande; van Vliet, *Luzac*, esp. 62–75.

111 *'books full of indecent'*: [Luzac], *Essai*, 86.

111 *'not accustomed'*: van Vliet, *Luzac*, 212.

111 *well known in Holland*: *Brieven door een voornaam Lord . . . op den naam van Cato* (Delft, 1722); *Brieven over de Vryheid*, 3 vols (Alkmaar and Amsterdam, 1752–5; 2nd edn Utrecht, 1766); S. R. E. Klein, *Patriots Republikanisme* (1995), esp. 72–3.

111 *German translation*: *Cato, oder Briefe von der Freyheit*, trans. Johann Gottfried Gellius, 4 vols (Göttingen, 1756–7); Forsskål, *Dubia* (1756 edn); Rietje van Vliet, ''1756–1757: Elie Luzac geeft de republikeinse Cato's Letters uit', *Mededelingen van de Stichting Jacob Campo Weyerman* 26 (2003).

111 *advance the cause*: for this and the following paragraph in this chapter, see [Peter Forsskål], *Tankar om borgerliga friheten* (Stockholm, 1759); Forsskål, *Civil Liberty*, ed. Goldberg et al.; Jonas Nordin and John Christian Laursen, 'Northern Declarations of Freedom of the Press', *Journal of the History of Ideas* 81 (2020).

112 *scientific expedition*: L. J. Baack, 'A Naturalist of the Northern Enlightenment', *Archives of Natural History* 40 (2013).

112 *'How fares'*: Forsskål to Linnaeus, 20 Oct. 1761; see also 2 Apr. 1762 (L3065).

112 *Riksdag*: for the 1760 Riksdag, see *Politska Skrifter af Anders Chydenius*, ed E. G. Palmen (1880), xciv–c; Virrankoski, *Anders Chydenius*, 186–9; Skuncke, 'Press Freedom', 114–16 (quoted: 'the lowliest congregation').

113 *overriding problem*: cf. Carl Wennerlind, 'Atlantis Restored', *American Historical Review* 127 (2023).

113 *'to loosen the bonds'* etc.: *Anticipating the Wealth of Nations: The Selected Works of Anders Chydenius*, ed. Maren Jonasson et al. (2012), 228, 233.

114 *many more months*: for this and the following four paragraphs in this chapter, see Virrankoski, *Anders Chydenius*, 189–209; *Anticipating the Wealth of Nations*, esp. pt 2; Manninen, 'Anders Chydenius'; Skuncke, 'Press Freedom', 117–34. In a prize essay of 1763, published in 1765, Chydenius had already listed 'constraints on reasoning, writing and printing' as one of the causes of mass emigration from Sweden: *Anticipating*, 96–8.

114 *'letting what is said here'*: *Sveriges Ridderskaps . . . Riksdags-Protokoll*, 23: 44 (29 Jan. 1762).

114 *'The public consists of a multitude'*: quoted in Skuncke, 'Press Freedom', 128.

114 *Even in England*: ibid., 129.

114 *'the public is an enlightened judge'*: quoted ibid., 128.

114 *no one even raised*: *Anticipating the Wealth of Nations*, 221–5.

114 *'truths exercise a persuasive power'* etc.: quoted ibid., 241; see generally ibid., ch. 7.

114 *abolishing censorship*: ibid., chs 4, 11; Gustav Björkstrand, 'Anders Chydenius', in Örtenhed and Wennberg (eds), *Press Freedom*, 99–100.

115 *Act of 1766*: Kongl. Maj:ts Nådige Förordning, Angående Skrif- och Tryck-friheten (Stockholm, 1766); Roberts, *Age of Liberty*, 106–7.

116 *the example of the Chinese*: Anders Chydenius, *Berättelse om Chinesiska Skrif-friheten* (Stockholm, 1766); *Anticipating the Wealth of Nations*, 224–5, 344; Nokkala, 'Forsskål', 71–2; Skuncke, 'Press Freedom', 118–19. Cf. Jonathan D. Spence, *Treason by the Book* (2001).

116 *'the freedom to speak'*: Voltaire, *L'A, B, C* [1768], in *Les Œuvres complètes de Voltaire*, 65A (2011).

116 *'there is no freedom'*: Voltaire, 'Epître au roi de Danemark' (1771), in *Les Œuvres complètes de Voltaire*, 73 (2004); cf. *Hr. F. A. d. Voltaires Brev til Hans Majestæt Kongen af Danmark* (Copenhagen [1771]).

116 *'through the spread of suspicions'*: quoted in Vegesack, 'Background', 35.

116 *increasingly critical of Struensee*: Horstbøll et al., *Grov Konfækt*.

116 *'press freedom must not be abused'* etc.: *Kabinetsstyrelsen*, ed. Hansen, 1: 176–7.

117 *'press freedom is more extensive'*: *Gustave III par ses lettres*, ed. Gunnar von Proschwitz (1986), 151.

117 *he steadily curtailed it*: Stig Boberg, *Gustav III och Tryckfriheten, 1774-1787* (1951); H. Arnold Barton, 'Gustav III of Sweden and the Enlightenment', *Eighteenth-Century Studies* (1972).

117 *'the liberty to think'* etc.: Jens Møller, 'P. F. Suhms regeringsregler 1774', *Historisk Tidsskrift* 12 (1972), and 'P. F. Suhms *Euphron*', *Historisk Tidsskrift* 12 (1973); see also Horstbøll et al., *Grov Konfækt*, ch. 21. The manifesto was, though, a document essentially addressed to the king, and presumed a traditional, monarchical form of rule. The novel and manifesto were also translated into German in 1776.

117 *East Asia*: Lin Yutang, *A History of the Press and Public Opinion in China* (1936), 1–73; Richard H. Mitchell, *Censorship in Imperial Japan* (1976), 1–12; Joseph Needham (ed.), *Science and Civilisation in China*, vol. 5, pt 1 (1985), 360–83; Tortarolo, *Invention*, xxi–xxv.

117 *Ottoman Empire and much of the Americas*: Christoph K. Neumann, 'Book and Newspaper Printing in Turkish', in Eva Hanebutt-Benz et al. (eds), *Middle Eastern Languages and the Print Revolution* (2002); Orlin Sübev, *Waiting for Müteferrika: Glimpses of Ottoman Print Culture* (2018); Nir Shafir, *The Order and Disorder of Communication* (2024); J. H. Elliott, *Empires of the Atlantic World* (2006), 205, 329.

117 *Brazil*: Valeria Gauz, 'Early Printing in Brazil', *Bulletin du bibliophile* (2013).

117 *international terms*: cf. the essays in Elizabeth Powers (ed.), *Freedom of Speech: The History of an Idea* (2011).

117 *Netherlands*: Joris van Eijenatten, 'Van godsdienstvrijheid naar mensenrecht', *BMGN* (2003).

118 *news of the Scandinavian innovations*: Boberg, *Gustav III och Tryckfriheten*, 39, 60–61; John Christian Laursen, 'Censorship in the Nordic Countries, ca. 1750–1890', *Journal of Modern European History* 3 (2005), 106–10.

118 *the basic, individual right of all citizens*: Horstbøll et al., *Grov Konfækt*, chs 37–40; Laursen, 'Censorship in the Nordic Countries'.

118 *Nowadays*: every single one of the 192 national constitutions currently in force around the world includes a guarantee of freedom of expression: https://constituteproject.org/.

6. THE ACCIDENTAL EXCEPTIONALISM OF THE FIRST AMENDMENT

119 *'the moment you limit free speech'*: Salman Rushdie, remarks after lecture at the University of Vermont, 14 Jan. 2015.

120 *'freedom is indivisible'*: ibid.

120 *'weaponizing' of free speech*: *Janus v. State, County, and Municipal Employees*, 585 US __ (2018), dissents by Sotomayor, and by Kagan joined by Ginsburg, Breyer and Sotomayor; Adam Liptak, 'How Conservatives Weaponized the First Amendment', *New York Times*, 30 June 2018.

121 *written constitutions*: Linda Colley, *The Gun, the Ship, and the Pen* (2021), 127–8.

121 *free-speech laws everywhere else*: as far as I know, the only exception is the post-war constitution of Japan, which states: 'Freedom of assembly and association as well as speech, press and all other forms of expression are guaranteed. No censorship shall be maintained, nor shall the secrecy of any means of communication be violated.' But this too is essentially an American text, which was hurriedly drafted and imposed by the US occupation force in 1946–7. By contrast, Japan's own first written constitution (1889–1947) had specified that 'Japanese subjects shall, within the limits of law, enjoy the liberty of speech, writing, publication, public meetings and associations' (Article 29). My point extends also to the legal approach of nations like the United Kingdom and Australia whose constitutions (unwritten or written) contain no explicit guarantee of freedom of expression; and to that of Canada, whose 1960 Bill of Rights includes 'freedom of speech' and 'freedom of the press' without any further qualification, but whose jurisprudence nonetheless takes an avowedly balancing approach.

122 *1798 Sedition Act*: the most detailed accounts are *Freedom of the Press from Zenger to Jefferson*, ed. Leonard W. Levy (1966); idem, *Emergence of a Free Press* (1985); Wendell Bird, *Press and Speech Under Assault* (2016); idem, *Criminal Dissent: Prosecutions Under the Alien and Sedition Acts of 1798* (2020); idem, *The Revolution in Freedoms of Speech and Press* (2020).

122 *Supreme Court*: *Schenck v. United States* (1919); *Gitlow v. New York* (1925).

122 *intervening period*: see esp. Michael T. Gibson, 'The Supreme Court and Freedom of Expression from 1791 to 1917', *Fordham Law Review* 55 (1986); Mark A. Graber, *Transforming Free Speech* (1991); Michael Kent Curtis, *Free Speech, 'The People's Darling Privilege'* (2000); Geoffrey R. Stone, *Perilous Times* (2004). The outstanding exception is David M. Rabban, *Free Speech in Its Forgotten Years* (1997).

123 *declarations of rights*: Of the thirteen rebellious colonies, Connecticut and Rhode Island only amended their existing charters, rather than

drawing up new constitutions. The constitutions of New Hampshire (1776), South Carolina (1776), New Jersey (1776) and New York (1777) initially omitted any declarations of rights; South Carolina added one in 1778, New Hampshire in 1783. My discussion will leave aside the additional, more conventional provisions that some state constitutions (and the federal constitution of 1787) made for 'freedom of speech' during legislative deliberations.

124 *American printing*: Arthur M. Schlesinger, *Prelude to Independence* (1958); Levy, *Emergence*, chs 2–6; Bird, *Revolution*, ch. 7.

124 *'The importance of this'*: Dunlap's *Pennsylvania Packet*, 4 Nov. 1774.

124 *essentially libertarian*: Eckhart Hellmuth, '"The Palladium of all other English Liberties"', in idem (ed.), *The Transformation of Political Culture* (1990); Mark Knights, *Trust and Distrust* (2021), ch. 9.

125 *Patriot rebels celebrated*: Bird, *Revolution*, chs 7–9 (292–3 for Cato's Letters).

125 *first colonial 'declaration of rights'*: PGM, 1: 271–91. In other states, too, the early constitutional press clauses seem to have been accepted without discussion, even when the exact wording of other rights was keenly debated: *An Essay of a Declaration of Rights* [Philadelphia, 1776]; *The Proceedings Relative to Calling the Conventions of 1776 and 1790* (Harrisburg, PA, 1825), pt 2; *Proceedings of the Convention of the Province of Maryland ... August, 1776* (Annapolis, MD [1776]).

125 *'spreading false news'* etc.: William Blackstone, *Commentaries on the Laws of England*, 4 vols (1765–9), 4: 149–53; see also 3: 123–6.

126 *two new state declarations*: in 1779, the lawyer, pamphleteer and leading Patriot politician John Adams, whose 1798 Sedition Act was later to encapsulate his own Blackstonian view of libels, drafted the Massachusetts constitution. His proposed article on press liberty simply followed that of Pennsylvania's 1776 declaration, but when it was discussed in the convention, this text caused 'a large debate', and was referred to a committee of three delegates. They subsequently proposed the wording that was eventually (with two small stylistic tweaks) adopted. This removed the first clause Adams had proposed, and replaced it with the new, Blackstonian phrase: *Papers of John Adams*, ed. Robert J. Taylor et al. (1977–), 8: 240, 263–4; *Journal of the Convention for Framing a Constitution ... 1780* (Boston, MA, 1832), 39, 41. The wording of New Hampshire's press clause was agreed by a convention in the summer of 1781 and adopted in 1783; press liberty had not been included in the state's initial, very brief, proposed declaration of rights: *A Declaration*

of Rights ... for the State of New-Hampshire (Exeter, NH, 1779); *An Address of the Convention for Framing a New Constitution* (Portsmouth, NH, 1781), 24. See also Hellmuth, '"Palladium"', 478–86.

126 *political opponents*: John Adam Treutlen to John Hancock, 19 June 1777, quoted in *American National Biography*, 'John Adam Treutlen' ('Enemies of American Freedom'); [Joseph Galloway], *A Candid Examination of the Mutual Claims of Great-Britain, and the Colonies* (New York, 1775), 1 (quoted: 'We see freedom of speech'); Schlesinger, *Prelude*, 222–7, 239–41; Levy, *Emergence*, 75–81, 173–86 (quoting 174: 'wrong sentiments').

127 *'writing or speaking' etc.: An Act of Assembly ... for restraining and punishing Persons, who are inimical to the Liberties ...* [New London, CT, 1775].

127 *'well-meaning, but uninformed people' etc.: Journals of the Continental Congress, 1774–1789*, ed. Worthington Chauncey Ford et al., 34 vols (1904–37), 4: 18–21 (2 Jan. 1776).

127 *criminalizing Loyalist opinions*: Levy, *Emergence*, 176–7; Bird, *Revolution*, 341.

127 *'The liberty of the press' etc.: Pennsylvania Evening Post*, 16 Nov. 1776.

128 *'UNLAWFULLY endeavouring': By his Honour John-Adam Treutlen* [Savannah, GA, 1777].

128 *new constitutions*: Levy, *Emergence*, 197–8.

128 *'seditious libel'*: see e.g. Zechariah Chafee, *Free Speech in the United States* (1941); Leonard W. Levy, *Legacy of Suppression* (1960); idem, *Emergence*; Bird, *Revolution*. More illuminating is the approach of Jud Campbell, 'Natural Rights and the First Amendment', *Yale Law Journal* 127 (2017).

128 *list of rights*: Max Farrand, *The Records of the Federal Convention*, 4 vols (1911–37), 2: 334 (quoted: 'the liberty of the press'), 340–42; cf. ibid., 3: 122 and appendix D.

128 *'He wished' etc.*: ibid., 2: 587–8; see also 582–3.

129 *'to insert a declaration' etc.*: ibid., 2: 611, 617–18, 620; see also 3: 143–4, 161–2, 290–91.

129 [footnote] *'generally begin'*: Farrand, *Records*, 3: 256.

129 *'There is no declaration' etc.*: ibid., 2: 637, 640; see also 3: 102, 128, 135–6; *PGM*, 3: 991–1003, 1041–4.

129 *several state conventions: The Ratifications of the New Fœderal Constitution, together with the Amendments, Proposed by the Several States* (Richmond, VA, 1788); Pauline Maier, *Ratification: The People Debate the Constitution, 1787–88* (2010).

129 *'among other essential rights'* etc.: *Debates and Other Proceedings of the Convention of Virginia* (2nd edn, Richmond VA, 1805), 466; see also 467–77; *PGM*, 3: 1041–4, 1054–7, 1070–72, 1118–23; J. Gordon Hylton, 'Virginia and the Ratification of the Bill of Rights, 1789–1791', *University of Richmond Law Review* 25 (1991).

130 *'That the people'*: *Debates and Other Proceedings*, 473.

130 *'essential'* etc.: *PJM*, 8: 351.

130 *'For why declare'* etc.: *Federalist Papers* no. 84 (first published in the *Independent Journal*, 16 and 26 July 1788); cf. Bird, *Revolution*, chs 9–10.

130 *'parchment barriers'*: *Federalist Papers* no. 48 (first published in the *New York Packet*, 1 Feb. 1788). Madison used the same image in a letter to Jefferson on 17 Oct. 1788 (*PJM*, 11: 295–300), and when introducing his proposed Bill of Rights to Congress in June 1789 (*Congressional Register*, 4 vols (1789–90), 1: 431).

131 *'ought to be revised'*: *PJM*, 11: 404; see also 295–300, 415–18, 428–9.

131 *How lawmakers altered*: for the drafting and absolutist rhetorical framework of the First Amendment, see Neil H. Cogan, *The Complete Bill of Rights* (2015 edn), ch 2. For hints of alternative approaches, see Helen E. Veit et al., *Creating the Bill of Rights* (1991), 267, 293: in late July, Roger Sherman proposed the formulation that the people's natural rights included 'Speaking, writing and publishing their Sentiments *with decency* and freedom' (my emphasis); while in early September it was reported (perhaps semi-facetiously) that some members of Congress 'warmly favoured that liberty of Speach and of the press may be stricken out [of the proposed amendments], as they only tend to promote licentiousness'.

133 *'waiting for the declaration'*: Louis Gottschalk, *Lafayette Between the American and the French Revolution* (1950), 53–4.

133 *Lafayette finally received*: for this paragraph and the next one in this chapter, see *PTJ*, 12: 149–50, 438–40 (quoting 440: 'a bill of rights'), 460–61, 558, 568–71, 583; 13: 4–8, 124–9, 440–43 and *passim*; 14: 650; Gottschalk, *Lafayette Between*, 364–5, 367–8, 374; *The Letters of Lafayette to Washington, 1777–1799*, ed. Louis Gottschalk (2nd edn, 1976), quoting letters 201, 203.

133 *spring of 1788*: *PTJ*, 13: 188–90, 455, 458; Gottschalk, *Lafayette Between*, chs 23 and 24.

134 *'all the world'*: *PTJ*, 14: 365.

134 *examples of such drafts*: ibid., 14: 370, 436–9; 15: 127, 231–3.

134 *Condorcet published his own plan*: [Marie Jean Antoine Nicolas de Caritat, Marquis de Condorcet], *Déclaration des droits, traduite de l'anglois* [trans. Richard Gem?] (1789).

134 *Declaration of the Rights of Man*: *PTJ*, 15: 165–8, 230–33, 249–50, 255; *L'An 1 des droits de l'homme*, ed. Antoine de Baecque, Wolfgang Schmale and Michel Vovelle (1988). The most detailed study of its speech and press provisions is Charles Walton, *Policing Public Opinion in the French Revolution* (2009), ch. 4.

134 *America's state constitutions*: *Examen du gouvernement d'Angleterre, comparé aux constitutions des États-Unis* (1789), 241, 267–87; Marcel Gauchet, *La Révolution des droits de l'homme* (1989), 52–4; cf. *PTJ*, 15: 366.

134 *the crown renewed*: Walton, *Policing*, 87.

134 *Article 10*: essentially following the same model as Virginia's 1786 Statute for Religious Freedom, drafted by Jefferson and championed by Madison.

135 *a necessary restraint*: for the sovereignty of the nation and the power of the law, see Dale Van Kley (ed.), *The French Idea of Freedom* (1994).

135 *not liberties to be protected*: for the French approach to rights, see Dan Edelstein, *On the Spirit of Rights* (2019), esp. ch. 7.

135 *British, not transatlantic*: *L'An 1*, ed. de Baecque, Schmale and Vovelle, 60, 127 and *passim*; cf. [Jean-Paul] Rabaut de Saint-Etienne, *Projet du préliminaire de la constitution françoise* (Versailles, 1789), iv; Gauchet, *Révolution*, ch. 2.

136 *right to free speech*: Walton, *Policing*, chs 3–4.

136 *he and other francophone authors*: Mirabeau, *Aux Bataves sur le Stathoudérat* ('London' [i.e. Paris?], 1788), 81; idem, *Sur la liberté de la presse* ('London' [i.e. Paris?], 1788); Wybo Jan Goslinga, *De rechten van den mensch en burger* (1936), 26–36; Walton, *Policing*, 91, 116, 196–7.

136 *'the degree'*: *PTJ*, 14: 443–4 (my italics); see also 439.

136 *'No man can be molested'*: ibid., 439.

136 *'Charter of Rights'* etc.: ibid., 15: 168.

136 *Lafayette scrapped*: for Lafayette's drafts, see ibid., 230–33; *L'An 1*, ed. de Baecque, Schmale and Vovelle, 65–6.

136 *dozens of other proposals*: *L'An 1*, ed. de Baecque, Schmale and Vovelle, 87 and *passim*; Raymond Birn, 'Religious Toleration and Freedom of Expression', in Van Kley (ed.), *French Idea*.

137 *'the press shall be free'* etc.: [Condorcet], *Déclaration . . . Traduite*, 42, and idem, *Déclaration des Droits* (1789), 10; for the chronology of these texts, see Jean-Claude Gaudebout, 'Les deux déclarations des

droits de Condorcet en 1789 et la physiocratie', *Annales historiques de la Révolution française* 402 (2020).

137　*Article 11: L'An 1*, ed. de Baecque, Schmale and Vovelle, 182–6 and *passim*; Gauchet, *Révolution*, 174–8; Walton, *Policing*, 86–91.

137　*letter from Madison: PTJ*, 15: 180–81.

138　*'Their declaration of rights'* etc.: ibid., 364–9.

138　*proposals he sent them*: ibid., 1: 329–86, quoting 344 ('Printing presses shall be free') – the first of at least three different drafts that Jefferson composed.

138　*favouring a balanced articulation*: ibid., 6: 278–317 (quoting 304, 316: 'Printing presses shall be subject'; 'an innovation') (cf. *PJM*, 10: 205–20; 11: 213, 295–300; *Congressional Register*, 1: 431). This was possibly the origin of a Virginia anti-Federalist proposal in spring 1788 for a national Bill of Rights to guarantee that 'printing presses shall not be subject to restraint, other than liableness to legal prosecution, for false facts printed and published': *The Documentary History of the Ratification of the Constitution*, ed. John P Kaminski et al., 26 vols (1976–2013), 9: 773. Jefferson's suggested wording for the French free-press clause in June 1789 evidently drew on these precedents. After he became president in 1801, he repeatedly lamented that 'the abuses of the freedom of the press here have been carried to a length never before known or borne by any civilized nation', and that American newspapers, instead of being confined to 'true facts', were filled only with lies and errors – 'nothing can now be believed which is seen in a newspaper. Truth itself becomes suspicious by being put into that polluted vehicle' (letters to Marc Auguste Pictet, 5 Feb. 1803, and John Norvell, 11 June 1807).

139　*'the first Declaration'* etc.: *American Herald and the Worcester Recorder*, 1 Oct. 1789.

139　*journals up and down the coast*: e.g. *New-York Daily Gazette* (17 Oct.); *Pennsylvania Packet* (21 Oct.); *Federal Gazette and Philadelphia Evening Post* (22 Oct.); *Independent Gazetteer* [Philadelphia] (22 Oct.); *Pennsylvania Gazette* (28 Oct.); *Newport Herald* (29 Oct.); *United States Chronicle* [Providence, RI] (5 Nov.); *Massachusetts Spy* [Worcester, MA] (5 Nov.); *City Gazette* [Charleston, SC] (10 Nov.); *Freeman's Journal* [Philadelphia] (11 Nov.); *Salem Mercury* (17 Nov.); *Independent Chronicle* [Boston] (19 Nov.); *Carlisle Gazette* (25 Nov.).

139　*virtually every other state*: for the sole exception, see Hylton, 'Virginia and the Ratification'.

139 *first ten amendments*: debate of the two other proposed amendments, and the formal process of approval, took longer: *Extracts from the Diary of Jacob Hiltzheimer*, ed. Jacob Cox Parsons (1893), 157; *Minutes of the First Session of the Fourteenth General Assembly* (Philadelphia, 1789); *Minutes of the Second Session of the Fourteenth General Assembly* (Philadelphia, 1790).

139 *the special convention*: unless otherwise noted, my account of its proceedings is based on *Minutes of the Convention of the Commonwealth of Pennsylvania* (Philadelphia, '1789' [i.e. 1790]); *Minutes of the Grand Committee of the Whole Convention of the Commonwealth of Pennsylvania* (Philadelphia [1790]); *Diary of Jacob Hiltzheimer*, ed. Cox Parsons; 'Pennsylvania Weather Records, 1644–1835', *Pennsylvania Magazine of History* 15 (1891).

140 *almost entirely overlooked*: Levy, *Emergence*, 211–12, and Bird, *Revolution*, 174–6, make brief passing references to them, without noticing their significance.

140 *Robespierre's stirring speech*: e.g. *Pennsylvania Mercury*, 3 Dec. 1789; *Independent Gazetteer*, 7 Dec. 1789; *Freeman's Journal*, 9 Dec. 1789. These articles notably interpolate passages not included in the French transcript, and omit his praise of American press-freedom laws: *Archives parlementaires de 1787 à 1860*, ed. J. Mavidal and E. Laurent, 1st series, 82 vols (1867–1990), 29: 631–3; Gauchet, *Revolution*, 176–8.

141 *'an explicit law'* etc.: *Federal Gazette and Philadelphia Evening Post*, 12 Sept. 1789. Cf. *Freeman's Journal*, 30 Oct. 1782.

141 *'I confess'* etc.: *Federal Gazette and Philadelphia Evening Post*, 24 Oct. 1789.

143 *how to define 'truth'*: informing this debate was the widely publicized recent conviction, without a jury trial, of the printer and publisher of Philadelphia's anti-Federalist *Independent Gazetteer* by the Supreme Court of Pennsylvania, which turned in part on the meaning of 'the freedom of the press' in the state's existing Bill of Rights, and its inapplicability to 'slanderous words' intended to 'delude and defame': *Respublica v. Oswald*, 1 US 319 (1788).

144 *'The citizen'*: *Collected Works of James Wilson*, ed. Kermit L. Hall and Mark David Hall (2007), 1046 (my italics); see also 1136.

144 *long-running political struggles*: Terry Bouton, *Taming Democracy* (2007), esp. ch. 8; Kenneth Owen, *Political Community in Revolutionary Pennsylvania, 1774–1800* (2018), esp. ch. 3; Angus Harwood Brown, 'The Pennsylvania Council of Censors', *American Journal of Legal History* 64 (2024).

145 *'There being no restraint'* etc.: Massachusetts citizens quoted in Clyde Augustus Duniway, *The Development of Freedom of the Press in Massachusetts* (1906), 134-6.

145 *'sentiments, concerning'*: *The Constitution of Vermont* (1786), 8 (ch. 1, art. 15).

145 *Delaware's legislators*: *Proceedings of the House of Assembly of the Delaware State, 1781-1792, and of the Constitutional Convention of 1792*, ed. Claudia L. Bushman et al. (1988), 784, 908.

145 *every single territory*: leaving aside Vermont, which joined the Union in 1791 but has never amended its 1786 formulation.

147 *'While we deny'* etc.: *PTJ*, 44: 379-81.

147 *most modern scholarship*: rare exceptions are Rabban, *Free Speech*; Lyndsay Mills Campbell, 'Truth and Consequences: The Legal and Extralegal Regulation of Expression in Massachusetts and Nova Scotia, 1820-1840' (PhD thesis, University of California, Berkeley, 2008), chs 5-7.

147 *Hawaii became the first*: *Proceedings of the Constitutional Convention of Hawaii 1950* (1960), esp. 301, 420. Between 1921 and 1933, successive editions of the *Model State Constitution*, composed by a national committee of experts and issued by the National Municipal League, recommended the wording 'Every person may freely speak, write and publish on all subjects, being responsible for the abuse of that liberty; and in all trials for libel, both civil and criminal, the truth when published with good motives and for justifiable ends, shall be sufficient defense'. In 1941 this was changed to conform to the national constitution: 'There shall be no law passed nor executive action taken abridging the freedom of speech or of the press.' The final edition, issued in 1963, combined this and other clauses into a simple copy of the First Amendment, boasting that the result was 'more traditional in its conformity to basic American political ideas than either its predecessor *Models* or most existing state constitutions', which had suffered from 'unclear thinking and bungling workmanship'.

147 *If James Madison*: *PJM*, 10: 205-220; *Congressional Register*, 1: 423-37 (quoting 435: 'I think there').

149 *state constitutions do so more generally*: for state constitutions and jurisprudence, see e.g. Margaret A. Blanchard, 'Filling in the Void: Speech and Press in State Courts Prior to *Gitlow*' and appendix, in Bill F. Chamberlin and Charlene J. Brown (eds), *The First Amendment Reconsidered* (1982); G. Alan Tarr, 'State Constitutionalism and "First Amendment" Rights', in Stanley H. Friedelbaum (ed.), *Human Rights*

in the States (1988), and *Understanding State Constitutions* (1998), 168–9, 196–7; Charles N. Davis and Paul H. Gates Jnr, 'Superseding the Federal Constitution: The New Federalism, State Constitutional Supremacy and First Amendment Jurisprudence', *Communications and the Law* 17 (1995); Jennifer A. Klear, 'Comparison of the Federal Courts' and the New Jersey Supreme Court's Treatments of Free Speech on Private Property', *Rutgers Law Journal* 33 (2002); 'Exceeding Federal Standards', *Albany Law Review* 77 (2014); Elijah O'Kelley, 'State Constitutions as a Check on . . . Social Media Platforms', *Emory Law Journal* 69 (2019).

149 *'It would be quite as significant'*: *Federalist Papers* no. 84 (first published in the *Independent Journal*, 16 and 26 July 1788).

149 *'free people of color'* etc.: Meinrad Greiner, *The Louisiana Digest, Embracing the Laws of the Legislature* (New Orleans, 1841), 220, 521.

150 *'the political truths'*: *PJM*, 11: 298–99.

151 *'under the First Amendment'*: *Gertz v. Robert Welch, Inc.*, 418 US 323 (1974).

7. LEGITIMATE AND ILLEGITIMATE EXPRESSIONS

152 *global political ideal*: cf. Linda Colley, *The Gun, the Ship, and the Pen* (2021), esp. chs 3, 5.

153 *Alexander Radishchev*: Douglas Smith, 'Alexander Radishchev's *Journey from St Petersburg to Moscow*', in Elizabeth Powers (ed.), *Freedom of Speech: The History of an Idea* (2011).

153 *'the only support'* etc.: [Joan Derk van der Capellen tot den Pol], *Aan het volk van Nederland* (1781), 75–6; cf. *Handboekje voor Nederland* (Amsterdam, 1786), 38–40, 92–3. For the Patriots' reading and publicizing of Cato's Letters and other English texts, and Dutch press ideals and practices in the 1780s, see A. C. Duke and C. A. Tamse (eds), *Too Mighty to be Free* (1987), ch. 6; M. Evers, 'Angelsaksische inspiratiebronnen voor de patriottische denkbeelden van Joan Derk van der Capellen', in Th. S. M. van der Zee et al. (eds), *1787: De Nederlandse Revolutie?* (1988); S. R. E. Klein, *Patriots Republikanisme* (1995), 72–3, 91–127; Joris van Eijenatten, 'Van godsdienstvrijheid naar mensenrecht', *BMGN* (2003); Janet Polasky, 'Revolutionaries Between Nations, 1776–1789', *Past and Present* (2016).

154 *translation of Luzac*: *Onderzoek over de Vryheid, Van zyne Gevoelens mede te deelen* (Amsterdam, 1782).

154 *'Newspaper writers'*: Wyger R. E. Velema, *Enlightenment and Conservatism in the Dutch Republic* (1993), 165–6; and generally ch. 5.

154 *'that have no other purpose'*: Rietje van Vliet, *Elie Luzac (1721–1796)*, 386; and generally ch. 6.

154 *'the unlimited liberty'* etc.: M. Mercier, *New Picture of Paris*, 2 vols (1800), 1: xiii; 2: 190–93, 203–5.

155 *a bishop in Brittany*: Charles Walton, *Policing Public Opinion in the French Revolution* (2009), 98–100.

155 *successive Acts*: for 1790s French laws, see ibid., ch. 5 (quoting 123–4, 129, 132–5).

155 *Dutch Republic*: Duke and Tamse (eds), *Too Mighty*, 115–22 (quoting 125 n. 62: 'his thoughts and feelings'); W. R. E. Velema, 'Politiek, pers en publieke opinie', in *Grondwetgeving 1795–1806* (1997).

155 *'no law would dare'*: quoted in Walton, *Policing*, 134.

156 *'If every individual'*: quoted ibid., 132–3.

156 *'intolerable 'licentiousness'*: *American Citizen* [New York], 20 Oct. 1806.

156 *'no limitation'* etc.: articles 353 and 355 of the 1795 French constitution.

156 *'Today we can hazard'* etc.: Walton, *Policing*, 232 and 'Conclusion'.

156 *embraced a similar approach*: see e.g. Duke and Tamse (eds), *Too Mighty*, 122 and n. 82; Clarice Neal, 'Freedom of the Press in New Spain', in Nettie Lee Benson (ed.), *Mexico and the Spanish Cortes, 1810–1822* (1966); Javier Fernández Sebastián, 'Toleration and Freedom of Expression in the Hispanic World Between Enlightenment and Liberalism', *Past and Present* 211 (2011); idem, 'From the "Voice of the People" to the Freedom of the Press', in Jesús Astigarraga (ed.), *The Spanish Enlightenment Revisited* (2015); Helena Rosenblatt, 'Rousseau, Constant, and the Emergence of the Modern Notion of Free Speech', in Powers (ed.), *Freedom of Speech*, 148–9; Corinna Zeltsman, *Ink Under the Fingernails* (2021).

156 *English-speaking world*: *A Representation of the Present State of Religion* (1711); Geoff Kemp, 'The "End of Censorship" and the Politics of Toleration', *Parliamentary History* 31 (2012); Eckhart Hellmuth, '"The Press Ought to be Open to All", in Gordon Pentland and Michael T. Davis (eds), *England and Scotland, 1688–1815* (2016), 10–11, 14–19; Wendell Bird, *The Revolution in Freedoms of Speech and Press* (2020), ch. 3.

157 *'strictly forbidden'* etc.: *Journals of the House of Representatives of Massachusetts*, 55 vols (1919–90), 4: 72, 208–9.

157 *'every man has the liberty'*: Voltaire, *Letters Concerning the English Nation* (1733), 193 (Letter XX).

157 *van Effen*: *De Hollandsche Spectator* 220 (4 Dec. 1733); P. J. Buijn-
    sters, *Justus van Effen 1684–1735: leven en werk* (1992).

157 *Gellius*: *Cato, oder Briefe von der Freyheit*, trans. Johann Gottfried
    Gellius, 4 vols (Göttingen, 1756–7), 1: 65–70.

158 *'freedom of the press'*: quoted in Sebastián, 'Toleration and Freedom of
    Expression', 168–9.

158 *absence of 'prior restraint'*: Bird, *Revolution*, charts the evolving
    shape of this transatlantic discourse, stressing the extent to which the
    influential focus on prior restraint of William Blackstone and other
    conservatives from the 1760s onwards was, in fact, a deliberate distrac-
    tion from the real disagreements in contemporary press-liberty debates.

158 *Niclas von Oelreich*: Marie-Christine Skuncke, 'Press Freedom in
    the Riksdag 1760–62 and 1765–66', in Kristina Örtenhed and Bertil
    Wennberg (eds), *Press Freedom 250 Years* (2018), 130.

158 *Defoe*: Daniel Defoe, *Essay on the Regulation of the Press* (1704), 15.

158 *'The liberty'*: *The Correspondence of Jeremy Bentham*, ed. T. L. S. Sprigge
    et al., 13 vols (1968–2024), 8: 429–30 (Bentham to Jean Antoine Gauvain
    Gallois, Sept. 1814).

158 *British Isles*: Duke and Tamse (eds), *Too Mighty*, ch. 5; Eckhart Hell-
    muth, '"The Palladium of all other English Liberties"', in idem (ed.),
    The Transformation of Political Culture (1990); James Kelley, 'Regu-
    lating Print', *Eighteenth-Century Ireland* 23 (2008); Thomas Keymer,
    Poetics of the Pillory (2019).

158 *1760s*: John Brewer, *Party Ideology and Popular Politics at the Acces-
    sion of George III* (1976), esp. chs 8, 11.

159 *parliamentary proceedings*: Peter D. G. Thomas, 'The Beginning of Par-
    liamentary Reporting in Newspapers, 1768–1774', *English Historical
    Review* (1959).

159 *new Libel Act*: Thomas Andrew Green, *Verdict According to Con-
    science* (1985), ch. 8.

159 *draconian new statutes*: on British repression, see Eckhart Hellmuth,
    'After Fox's Libel Act', in Ulrich Broich et al. (eds), *Reactions to Rev-
    olutions* (quoting 143–4); Robert Pigot, *Liberty of the Press* (1790);
    Cobbett's Weekly Political Register, 13 Aug. 1814 (quoted: 'all is left');
    Trials for Treason and Sedition, 1792–1794, ed. John Barrell and Jon
    Mee, 8 vols (2006–7); Clive Emsley, 'An Aspect of Pitt's "Terror"',
    Social History (1981), and 'Repression, "Terror", and the Rule of Law
    in England During the Decade of the French Revolution', *English His-
    torical Review* (1985); Philip Harling, 'The Law of Libel and the Limits
    of Repression, 1790–1832', *Historical Journal* (2001); Vic Gatrell,

Conspiracy on Cato Street (2022), 125–8 (for visual imagery of the trope) and *passim*.

160 *In the United States*: see Michael Kent Curtis, *Free Speech, 'The People's Darling Privilege'* (2000); Geoffrey R. Stone, *Perilous Times* (2004).

160 *re-enslaved and sold*: Michael J. Crawford, *The Having of Negroes is Become a Burden* (2010).

161 *'cause slaves'* etc.: quoted in Kent Curtis, *Free Speech*, 125–6.

161 *free Black petitions*: this and the following two paragraphs of this chapter draw on: *Annals of Congress*, 30 Jan. 1797, 2–3 Jan. 1800; George F. Bragg, *History of the Afro-American Group of the Episcopal Church* (1922), chs 3–5; William C. diGiacomantonio, '"For the Gratification of a Volunteering Society"', *Journal of the Early Republic* 15 (1995); Crawford, *Having of Negroes*; Nicholas P. Wood, 'A "class of Citizens"', *William and Mary Quarterly* 74 (2017).

163 *'most dangerous'* etc.: *Columbian Centinel*, 29 Aug. 1835.

163 *'We are told'*: quoted in Kent Curtis, *Free Speech*, 153; see generally ibid., chs 4–13.

163 *'gag rule'* etc.: quoted ibid., 177–8.

164 *'truths confined'* etc.: Sebastián, 'Toleration', 178.

164 *'but this freedom'*: *Christianity Vindicated* (1797), 4.

164 *'dearest privilege'*: *The Celebrated Speech of the Hon. T. Erskine* (Edinburgh, 1793), 65. Erskine's entirely secular reading of *Areopagitica* incidentally epitomizes how by the eighteenth century Milton's text had come to be regarded, as it still is, as a clarion call for political free speech: cf. Hellmuth, 'After Fox's Libel Act', 152–6.

166 *'would be confined'* etc.: *R v. Paine* (1792), in *A Complete Collection of State Trials*, vol. 22, ed. T .B. Howell and Thomas Jones Howell (1817), cols 381–3.

166 *'An intellectual book'* etc.: *Christianity Vindicated*, 6–7, 11. See more generally John Spurr, 'The Manner of English Blasphemy, 1676–2008', in Stewart J. Brown et al. (eds), *Religion, Identity and Conflict in Britain* (2013).

167 *Thomas Anketell*: the account in this paragraph draws on TNA, CO 71/19, Jan.–Feb. 1791 [unfoliated] and CO 71/20; *Charibbean Register*, 26 Mar. 1791; *L'Ami de la Liberté*, 8 Jan., 22 Feb. 1791; *Dunlap's Daily American Advertiser*, 11 May 1791; John Anketell, *Poems on Several Subjects* (Dublin, 1793), list of subscribers; Janet Polasky, *Revolutions without Borders* (2015), ch. 5; Julius S. Scott, *The Common Wind* (2018), ch. 4.

167 *'the privilege of representation'* etc.: *Annals of Congress*, 30 Jan. 1797, col. 2018.

167 *'dark-complexioned citizens'* etc.: *Annals of Congress*, 27 Nov. 1797, col. 658; 30 Jan. 1797, col. 2021–2.

168 *'a class of citizens'* etc.: Wood, 'A "class of Citizens"', 111; *Annals of Congress*, 2 Jan. 1800, cols 229, 235.

168 *'The Negroes'*: Alexis de Tocqueville, *Democracy in America*, trans. Henry Reeve (1838), 242n.

168 *contesting such racial discrimination*: David Waldstreicher, 'Racism, Black Voices, Emancipation, and Constitution-Making in Massachusetts, 1778', *Journal of American Constitutional History* 2 (2024).

168 *'The free negroes'* etc.: quoted in Douglas Bradburn, *The Citizenship Revolution* (2009), 235; and see generally ibid., ch. 7; Robert G. Parkinson, *The Common Cause* (2016), 630–40.

168 *'If they are slaves'*: *Annals of Congress*, 30 Jan. 1797, col. 2020.

169 *'black gentlemen'* etc.: *Annals of Congress*, 2 Jan. 1800, col. 230. This edition was prepared in the 1830s from contemporaneous reports; in at least one of those, the whole of 'black gentlemen' and 'Thank God they are!' was italicized for emphasis: *Philadelphia Gazette*, 16 Jan. 1800.

169 *'Because many of those people'*: ibid., col. 242.

169 *'us and the rest'* etc.: ibid., col. 235.

169 *'those people'* etc.: ibid., col. 231.

170 *'slaves do not possess'*: *Register of Debates in Congress*, 13: col. 1733, 12 Feb. 1837; see also cols 1708–38.

170 *'While we would maintain'* etc.: *Albany Argus*, 8 Sept. 1835.

170 *'It has, indeed'* etc.: ibid. I have elided the final phrase before the question mark at the end of Dix's quoted speech – the original reads '. . . in the south, the general society of which they may constitute but an inconsiderable part?'

171 *'Slavery cannot tolerate free speech'* etc.: speech in Boston, 9 Dec. 1860, in *The Frederick Douglass Papers*, ed. John W. Blassingame et al., 1st series, 5 vols (1979–92), 3: 422–3.

171 *he observed in 1863*: 'The Proclamation and a Negro Army', address in New York, 6 Feb. 1863, ibid., 3: 549–69.

171 *many politicians and citizens*: on the First and Fourteenth Amendments, see Kent Curtis, *Free Speech*.

172 *women as slaves*: see e.g. Hasana Sharp, 'Slavery and Servitude in Seventeenth-Century Feminism', in Karen Detlefsen and Lisa Shapiro (eds), *The Routledge Handbook of Women and Early Modern Philosophy* (2023).

172 *'towards women as towards slaves'*: [Margaret Fuller], 'The Great Lawsuit', *The Dial*, July 1843, 12.

172 *the first theorist*: though Condorcet in the 1780s and 1790s also advocated in general for both the abolition of slavery and the rights of women.

173 '*X. No one shall be disquieted*' etc.: Olympe de Gouges, *Déclaration des droits de la femme et de la citoyenne*, in *Oeuvres*, ed. Benoîte Groult (1986), 104–5.

174 '*Many of these petitions*' etc.: *Speech of John Quincy Adams . . . on the Freedom of Speech* (Washington, DC, 1838), 15.

174 *the first large-scale women's petitions*: Alisse Portnoy, *Their Right to Speak* (2005), chs 1–2.

174 *female activists*: see e.g. Elizabeth Cady Stanton et al., *History of Women Suffrage*, 6 vols (New York, 1881–1922), 1: 39–40, 52–3; Portnoy, *Their Right to Speak*, ch. 6; *American National Biography* (1999), s.v. 'Foster, Abby Kelley'.

174 '*female petitioners*': Portnoy, *Their Right to Speak*, 229.

175 '*In this country*': Catharine E. Beecher, *An Essay on Slavery and Abolitionism, with Reference to the Duty of American Females* (1837), 104–5. Towards the end of her life, Beecher was nonetheless to draft and circulate a women's anti-suffrage petition that was presented to Congress: *Godey's Lady's Book and Magazine* 82: 491 (May 1871), 476–7.

175 '*The investigation of the rights*' etc.: A. E. Grimké, *Letters to Catherine E. Beecher* (1838), 114–19.

175 '*slaves were not excluded*': *Speech of John Quincy Adams*, 57–61; *Congressional Globe* (1838), 6: 474.

175 '*the People of the United States*' etc.: *Speech of John Quincy Adams*, 76–7; *Congressional Globe* (1838), 6: 480, 483.

175 '*fenced off*': Stanton et al., *History of Women Suffrage*, 1: 60.

176 '*to hold a women's rights convention*': ibid., 1: 61.

176 '*In advocating liberty*': ibid., 1: 53.

177 *into the 1960s*: see e.g. *The Lady Chatterley's Lover Trial*, ed. H. Montgomery Hyde (1990), 62; Christopher Hilliard, *A Matter of Obscenity* (2021).

177 *feminist theorists*: on feminism and pornography, see e.g. Andrea Dworkin, *Pornography: Men Possessing Women* (1981); Catharine A. MacKinnon, *Only Words* (1993).

177 '*dangerous confusion*': Ronald Dworkin, 'Liberty and Pornography', *New York Review of Books*, 15 Aug. 1991; cf. ibid., 21 Oct. 1993 and 3 Mar. 1994.

177 '*an attack*': Ronald Dworkin, 'Foreword', in Ivan Hare and James Weinstein (eds), *Extreme Speech and Democracy* (2009), vi. For a more

nuanced view, see Bernard Williams, 'Drawing Lines', *London Review of Books*, 12 May 1994. Cf. Hilliard, *Obscenity*, 207–10, 215–16.

179 *'nigger'*: see esp. Randall Kennedy, *Nigger: The Strange Career of a Troublesome Word* (2002).

180 *A Jewish comedian*: for instructive cases regarding comedy and anti-semitism, see e.g. *M'Bala M'Bala v. France*, European Court of Human Rights, application no. 25239/13 (2015); David Baddiel, 'Free Speech and Nazi Dogs', *Times Literary Supplement*, 10 Apr 2018.

8. IMPERIAL ENTANGLEMENTS

181 *printed in English*: C. A. Bayly, *The Birth of the Modern World 1780–1914* (2004), 19.

182 *how imperial rule was justified*: see e.g. Catherine Hall, *Macaulay and Son* (2012); Priya Satia, *Time's Monster* (2020).

183 *'dragging . . . people through dirt'* etc.: Karl Marx, *New-York Daily Tribune*, 8 Aug. 1853.

183 *'Whatever may have been'*: ibid., 25 June 1853.

183 *'merely birthing pain'*: Satia, *Time's Monster*, 145.

183 *'folly and injustice'* etc.: Adam Smith, *An Enquiry into the Nature and Causes of the Wealth of Nations*, ed. R. H. Campbell and A. S. Skinner, 2 vols (1976), 2: 588.

183 *critical of imperialism*: Sankar Muthu, *Enlightenment Against Empire* (2003); Jennifer Pitts, *A Turn to Empire* (2005), chs 2–4; Uday S. Mehta, 'Edmund Burke on Empire', in Sankar Muthu (ed.), *Empire and Modern Political Thought* (2012).

184 *East India Company*: Nicholas B. Dirks, *The Scandal of Empire* (2006); Philip J. Stern, *The Company State* (2011); William Dalrymple, *The Anarchy: The Relentless Rise of the East India Company* (2019).

184 *'We have murdered'*: *The Yale Edition of Horace Walpole's Correspondence*, ed. W. S. Lewis et al., 48 vols (1937–83), 23: 387.

184 *high moral purpose*: Hall, *Macaulay and Son*, 73–9 and *passim*; Padraic X. Scanlan, *Slave Empire* (2020).

185 *'rude and uninstructed'* etc.: James Mill, *The History of British India*, 6 vols (2nd edn, 1820), 1: 403, 412–13, 416–18, 419–20, 422; 2: 76, 134, 158.

185 *'a general disposition'*: ibid., 2: 188.

185 *'habitual contempt'* etc.: ibid., 1: 386, 388.

185 *'many gloomy and malignant'* etc.: ibid., 1: 403.

185 *'made but a few'*: ibid., 2: 135; see also 137.

185 *'superior character'* etc.: ibid., 2: 186–8. Mill conceded only Indians' pre-eminence in 'the more delicate manufactures' of fine textiles, the fabrication of 'trinkets' and 'the art of polishing and setting the precious stones': 2: 187.

185 *'to make war'* etc.: evidence of James Mill, 16 Feb. 1832, in *Minutes of Evidence Taken Before the Select Committee on the Affairs of the East India Company*, House of Commons Papers 1831–2, 735-VI: 8.

186 *'happiness and welfare'*: *ODNB*, s.v. 'Campbell, Sir George'.

186 *'elevated'*: George Campbell, *White and Black* (1879), 121.

186 *'assimilated'*: George Campbell, *India as It May Be* (1853), xii.

186 *'benefits'* etc.: Campbell, *India as It May Be*, xii, xxv. Karl Marx's 1853 comments on India for the *New-York Daily Tribune* drew on Campbell's newly published book.

186 *'English government in India'* etc.: James Mill, 'Review of *Voyage aux Indes orientales*, by Le P. Paulin De S. Barthélemy, Missionary', *Edinburgh Review* 15 (1810), 371.

187 *'duplicity and hypocrisy'* etc.: Pitts, *Turn to Empire*, 223. Tocqueville himself staunchly championed his own nation's brutal colonization of Algeria, and agreed with his friend John Stuart Mill that 'backward' and 'declining' peoples, destined to be subordinated and civilized by 'enlightened' and 'progressing' ones, could not be permitted the same rights as Europeans. Even French colonists themselves in Africa constituted only a society in its 'infancy', not yet mature enough to be permitted freedom of the press or other 'political liberties': see Pitts, *Turn to Empire*, ch. 7; Alexis de Tocqueville, *Writings on Empire and Slavery*, trans. and ed. Jennifer Pitts, esp. 10, 24, 60–61, 111–12, 130, 138, 140, 142, 166.

187 *the most convenient answer*: Karuna Mantena, *Alibis of Empire* (2010).

187 *'the Aryan stock'* etc.: quoted in Satia, *Time's Monster*, 134.

188 *'indirect' forms of governance*: Mantena, *Alibis*.

189 *reading and writing were highly valued*: C. A. Bayly, *Empire and Information* (1996).

189 *communication systems of the East India Company*: see Miles Ogborn, *Indian Ink* (2007).

189 *experiments in printing*: Anant Kakba Priolkar, *The Printing Press in India* (1958). The East India Company in Madras from 1761 possessed a press captured from the French in Pondicherry, which was used for administrative and missionary work, as well as some commercial printing: Graham Shaw, *Printing in Calcutta to 1800* (1981),

ix, 16–17. Margarita Barns, *The Indian Press* (1940), 44, notes that in 1674 the East India Company sent a press to Bombay but in 1753 reported that 'the printing houses were in a very bad condition and unfit for use'. Most likely such machines would have been used mainly to produce forms, receipts and other administrative paperwork, rather than communicative public texts. The earliest-surviving Bombay imprint dates from 1772.

189 *Halhed*: Nathaniel Brassey Halhed, *A Code of Gentoo Laws* (1776); *ODNB*, s.v. 'Halhed, Nathaniel Brassey'.

190 *'a general medium'* etc.: Nathaniel Brassey Halhed, *A Grammar of the Bengal Language* (Hoogly, Bengal, 1778), ii.

190 *'the illiterate and careless'* etc.: ibid., 23.

190 *'the conquest of India'*: Bernard S. Cohn, *Colonialism and Its Forms of Knowledge* (1996), 16; and generally ch. 2.

190 *'Great Britain'*: Halhed, *Grammar*, xxiv–xxv. For the wider context, see Joshua Ehrlich, *The East India Company and the Politics of Knowledge* (2023).

190 *James Hicky*: Andrew Otis, *Hicky's Bengal Gazette* (2018), is an indispensable and detailed account, though I differ from it on several points of interpretation. Also invaluable is P. Thankappan Nair, *A History of the Calcutta Press* (1987).

190 *typical imperial entrepreneur*: *Memoirs of William Hickey*, ed. Alfred Spencer, 4 vols (1919–25), 2: 175–6; Otis, *Gazette*; *HBG*, 4 and 11 Nov. 1780; Nair, *Calcutta Press*, 34.

191 *'First, and late printer'*: colophon added to *HBG* from the issue of 8 Apr. 1780

191 *'to print a newspaper'*: quoted in Otis, *Gazette*, 268–9 n. 99.

191 *'for the more speedy'*: *HBG*, 8 Apr. 1780; see also 25 Mar. 1780.

191 *'Chief intention'* etc.: *Proposals for Printing a News-Paper, in Bengal, to be published every Saturday, by J. A. Hicky* [Calcutta, 1779?], broadsheet (University of Melbourne Library); *HBG*, 22 Apr. 1780.

192 *first eleven months*: Otis, *Gazette*, 290 n. 369.

192 *better-capitalized rivals*: *HBG*, 24 June 1780, 5 May 1781; *India Gazette*, surviving issues of 25 Nov. 1780 (no. 2) onwards; Otis, *Gazette*, 92–7.

192 *embittered political crusader*: see *HBG*, 4 Nov. 1780 onwards. Otis, *Gazette*, 290 n. 369, quantifies the change: there was a tenfold increase in opinion articles, and press freedom became one of their main subjects. For Hicky's violent and resentful temper, see *Memoirs of William Hickey*, ed. Spencer, 2: 173–4, 3: 160–63.

192   *non-stop polemic*: already between July and October 1780, as Hicky anticipated the launch of the rival paper, he had begun to carry more political news. During September he reprinted (presumably from a London paper) a speech made at Westminster by Charles James Fox on 2 February 1780, attacking ministerial corruption and mismanagement. This included passing references to the governance of India, and to John Wilkes's travails in the 1760s: *HBG*, 2, 9, 16 and 23 Sept. 1780.

192   *His last Gazette*: *HBG*, 23 and 30 Mar. 1782 (which specifies that his press and types were seized from prison on Tuesday 26 March).

193   *public auction of his press*: *India Gazette*, 6 Apr. 1782; Otis, *Gazette*, 202. (For Wilkins's work as Company printer during these years, see Ogborn, *Indian Ink*, 226–30.) After Hastings, on the eve of his departure for England, allowed Hicky to be released, around Christmas 1784, Hicky changed his attitude and was ever after his 'warm and zealous defender': *Memoirs of William Hickey*, ed. Spencer, 3: 262. He briefly resurrected his paper, but then returned to his practice as a surgeon and apothecary: Otis, *Gazette*, 314–15 n. 706; Nair, *Calcutta Press*, 33–5.

193   *newspapers in the West Indies*: *Proposals for Printing a News-Paper, in Bengal*.

193   *adverts for local slaves*: e.g. *HBG* 1 and 8 Apr., 16, 23 and 30 Dec. 1780; 27 Jan., 10, 17 and 24 Feb., 1, 8 and 22 Sept. 1781

193   *'open to all parties'*: Hicky first used the motto in his issue of *HBG*, 27 May 1780, together with the *Public Ledger*'s subtitle, 'A Daily Political and Commercial Paper' (changing 'Daily' to 'Weekly'). See *Public Ledger*, 7 June 1766; *Hampshire Chronicle*, 24 Apr. 1775, 3; Jordan E. Taylor, 'A Revolution in Mottoes', *Journal of the American Revolution* (2018).

193   *worldwide channels*: *HBG*, *passim*; Otis, *Gazette*, 82 and 284–5 nn. 292–4.

194   *resonated across*: Ben Gilding, 'The Rise and Fall of *Hicky's Bengal Gazette* (1780–2): A Study in Transoceanic Political Culture', *Journal of Imperial and Commonwealth History* 47 (2019); Mark Knights, *Trust and Distrust* (2021), ch. 9.

194   *invocations and examples*: e.g. *HBG*, 18 and 25 Nov., 2 and 23 Dec. 1780; 28 Apr., 16 June, 7 July 1781.

194   *'The case of Mr HICKY'*: *HBG*, 25 Nov. 1780; Otis, *Gazette*, 203–5, 306–7 n. 586.

195   *'a weekly paper'* etc.: quoted in Otis, *Gazette*, 186.

195 *'This is the boasted liberty'*: quoted ibid., 174.

195 *'Freedom of the press'*: *India Gazette*, 2 Dec. 1780.

195 *'I really wonder'* etc.: quoted in Otis, *Gazette*, 131. Cf. Barns, *Indian Press*, 66.

196 *regulated printers*: Kirsten MacKenzie, *Imperial Underworld* (2016), esp. chs 6–7.

196 *censorship of newspapers*: Barns, *Indian Press*, chs 4–5 (quoting p. 75: 'the conduct of government' etc.).

196 *exceptional spaces*: cf. Partha Chatterjee, *The Black Hole of Empire* (2012).

196 *overwhelmingly European medium*: Shaw, *Printing in Calcutta*; but for examples of the early indigenous use of print, see e.g. Barns, *Indian Press*, 44, 111–12; Miles Ogborn, 'The Amusements of Posterity', in Charles W. J. Withers and Miles Ogborn (eds), *Geographies of the Book* (2010).

196 *Bengali, Persian and Gujarati*: Barns, *Indian Press*, 58–9; Shaw, *Printing in Calcutta*, 18, 32–4, 235 and checklist; private communication from Robert Travers.

196 *Indian employees*: Ogborn, *Indian Ink*, ch. 6, esp. 234–44, 264.

196 *owned and edited by white men*: *East India Periodical Publications, and Licensed Printing Presses . . . for the Years 1814, 1820, and 1830*, House of Commons Papers 1831–2, 37: 1–6 [compiled by James Mill]; Nair, *Calcutta Press*, xi, xiii–xv, chs 5–6 (esp. 215–16); Barns, *Indian Press*, 57–9.

196 *Commons debate*: for the quoted extracts from the Commons debate of March 1811, see *Hansard's Parliamentary Debates*, 1st series, 19: cols 462–76 (21 Mar. 1811); see also R. G. Thorne (ed.), *The History of Parliament: The House of Commons 1790–1820* (1986), s.v. 'Dundas [afterwards Saunders Dundas], Robert (1771–1851)'; C. A. Bayly, *Recovering Liberties* (2012), 79.

197 *'Duty of this country'*: East India Company Act, 53 Geo. III, c. 155 (1813), paragraph xxxiii.

197 *'God-like bounty'* etc.: *Asiatic Journal* 5 (1818), 174–5.

198 *ended pre-publication censorship*: for the controversial politics of Hastings's policy and his public remarks on this subject, which were widely publicized and frequently reprinted, see A. F. Salahuddin Ahmed, *Social Ideas and Social Change in Bengal, 1818–1835* (2nd edn, 1976), 59–67. The same regulations were adopted the following year in Bombay.

198 *Indians had maintained*: on Indian cultures of communication and adoption of print, see Bayly, *Empire and Information*, esp. 204, 212–20, 238–43, 266, 298 (quoting 214: 'implies other means'); Anindita

Ghosh, *Power in Print* (2006), explores the indigenous social, cultural and linguistic impact of Bengali print into the later nineteenth century.

198 *Large numbers of printed books*: just between 1810 and 1820, it was estimated that over 15,000 volumes had been printed and sold in the Bengali language alone, mainly on Indian-owned presses: Ahmed, *Social Ideas*, 90.

198 *thriving centre*: ibid., esp. chs 3–4; Sisir Kumar Das, *A History of Indian Literature 1800–1910* (1991), 23–83, 419–56; Bayly, *Recovering Liberties*, 79; idem, 'Empires and Indian Liberals', in Catherine Hall and Keith McClelland, *Race, Nation and Empire* (2010), 79; James Long, *Hand-Book of Bengal Missions ... Together with an Account of General Educational Efforts in North India* (1848), 472–3. Das records several Indian-owned presses in Calcutta and elsewhere between 1807 and 1818 (*History*, 426, 431, 435); the first Bengali newspaper appears to have been the *Bengal Gazetti* (1818), published by Gangadhar Bhattacharya.

198 *Kasiprasad Ghosh*: *Asiatic Journal* 26 (1828), 317–20; Long, *Hand-Book of Bengal Missions*, esp. 472, appendices B and D; Rosinka Chaudhuri, 'Orientalist Themes and English Verse in Nineteenth-Century India' (University of Oxford DPhil thesis, 1995).

198 *agitating since the 1810s*: Bayly, 'Empires and Indian Liberals', 80–81.

198 *'We are here in India'* etc.: minute by James Farish (acting governor), 28 Aug. 1838, quoted in B. K. Boman-Behram, *Educational Controversies in India* (Bombay, [1943]), 236–7.

199 *'a medium through which'* etc.: quoted in Priolkar, *Printing Press in India*, 114–17; see also 109–10, 119–20, 122–5; Barns, *Indian Press*, 134–5.

200 *James Silk Buckingham*: Ralph E. Turner, *James Silk Buckingham* (1934); *ODNB*, s.v. 'Buckingham, James Silk'.

200 *Calcutta Journal*: for this and the following two paragraphs of this chapter, see BL, MSS Eur F140/61(a): copies of papers relating to the press in India, 1819–22; BL, MSS IOR/P10/55: Bengal government Council minutes and memoranda about the press, 1822; *1834 CJ Report*; Barns, *Indian Press*, chs 6, 8 (quoting 115: 'political events or transactions' – new regulations of 4 Apr. 1823). Similar regulations were adopted in Bombay in 1825 and 1827: Priolkar, *Printing Press in India*, 131–40.

200 *dealing with troublesome print*: Ritika Prasad, 'Imprimatur as Adversary', *Modern Asian Studies* 55 (2021).

200 *'affect the British power'* etc.: *1834 CJ Report*, appendix: 41.

201 *'will rebound hither'*: quoted in Lynn Zastoupil, *Rammohun Roy and the Making of Victorian Britain* (2010), 101. See also BL, MSS Eur

F140/63, for discussions on the subject between the government, company and new governor-general.

201 *Commons select committee*: *1834 CJ Report.*

201 *Rammohun Roy*: unless otherwise specified, materials relating to Roy are drawn from James Silk Buckingham, 'Sketch of the Life, Writings, and Character of Ram Mohan Roy', *Parliamentary Review* 4: 32 (1 Feb. 1833), 113–20; *English Works of Raja Rammohun* Roy, ed. Jogendra Chunder Ghose, 3 vols (1901 edn); *Letters and Documents Relating to the Life of Raja Rammohun Roy*, ed. Rama Prasad Chanda and Jatindra Kumar Majumdar (1938); J. K. Majumdar, *Raja Rammohun Roy and Progressive Movements in India* (1941); Bruce Carlisle Robertson, *Raja Rammohan Ray* (1995); Zastoupil, *Rammohun Roy*, esp. ch. 6.

202 *As a writer*: see e.g. Ram Mohun Roy, *A Defence of Hindoo Theism* (Calcutta, 1817); Rammohun Roy, *A Second Defence of the Monotheistical System* (Calcutta, 1817); idem, *Translation of an Abridgment of the Vedant* (1817); [Roy], *Translation of a Conference* [Calcutta, 1818]; Zastoupil, *Rammohun Roy*, 25–8; *ODNB*, s.v. 'Roy, Rammohun', for his Sanskrit publications. The opening issue of Roy's *Mirat* announced that the paper would constantly bear in mind 'the saying of the Poet, that "the wounds of the spear may be healed, but a wound inflicted by the tongue is incurable" ' (Majumdar, *Raja Rammohun Roy*, 299). Roy was a dedicated student of the Christian Bible, and that sounds remarkably like a paraphrase of the Old Testament verse contrasting the stroke of the whip with the stroke of the tongue (Ecclesiastes 28:17).

202 *'on all occasions'*: [George Augustus Frederick Munster, Earl of] Fitzclarence, *Journal of a Route across India* (1819), 106.

202 *a frequent contributor*: Buckingham, 'Sketch of the Life', 115.

202 *Roy himself founded two weeklies* etc: Majumdar, *Raja Rammohun Roy*, 283–336; Zastoupil, *Rammohun Roy*, 99–100 (quoted: 'the benefits to be expected').

203 *his own press*: Buckingham, 'Sketch of the Life', 116

203 *'If it be true'*: *Calcutta Journal*, 31 Jan. 1822, quoted in Majumdar, *Raja Rammohun Roy*, 285.

203 *'powerful engine'*: *Calcutta Journal*, 14 Feb. 1823, quoted in Majumdar, *Raja Rammohun Roy*, 315.

203 *closed down in his paper*: Majumdar, *Raja Rammohun Roy*, 319–23.

203 *Dwarkanath Tagore*: Kissory Chand Mitra, *Memoir of Dwarkanath Tagore* (Calcutta, 1870), 39–48; *ODNB*, s.v. 'Tagore, Dwarkanath'.

203 *'to punish millions'*: Roy, *English Works*, ed. Ghose, 2: 312.

203　*their arguments*: ibid., 2: 278–319; *Asiatic Journal* 16 (1823), 581–95; 'Letter of certain natives of India, to Mr Canning' [Nov. 1824], *Oriental Herald* 7 (1825), 193–4.

203　*'shackled' and 'enslaved' etc.*: Jugunnouth Mugmoodare, 'Letter of a Native of India', *Oriental Herald* 7 (1825), 188–92.

203　*'Asiatic'*: Roy, *English Works*, ed. Ghose, 2: 285.

203　*'people placed under'*: ibid., 285–6.

203　*'the natives of India' etc.*: ibid., 288–9.

204　*'already served'*: ibid., 282.

204　*'unlimited confidence'*: ibid., 279.

204　*'the most precious'*: ibid., 285.

204　*'suddenly' and illegally 'invaded'*: ibid., 287, 291–2.

204　*'assured of the possession'*: ibid., 281.

204　*legally difficult*: see e.g. *1834 CJ Report*, appendix: 54–5, 123–8, 131–9.

204　*'Inhabitants of Calcutta' etc.*: Roy, *English Works*, ed. Ghose, 2: 285. The practical basis of this claim was the fact that, unlike Indians in the interior territories, all inhabitants of Calcutta were under the jurisdiction of the English-law Supreme Court that the British had established at Fort William. For other notable examples of Roy's arguing against discriminatory British-Indian laws and practices, and in favour of the equal treatment of Indians and Europeans, non-Christians and Christians, see *The Correspondence of Raja Rammohan Roy*, vol. 1: *1809–1831*, ed. Dilip Kumar Biswas (1992), 1–19, 356–86; Chatterjee, *Black Hole of Empire*, ch. 5.

204　*'to preserve the union' etc.*: Roy, *English Works*, ed. Ghose, 2: 309.

205　*'great aversion'*: *Asiatic Journal*, new series 12 (1833), 197. For Roy's views on the spiritual superiority of ancient Hindu revelation and culture over its European equivalents, see Robertson, *Raja Rammohan Ray*.

205　*'greatly attached to us' etc.*: *The Correspondence of Jeremy Bentham*, ed. T. L. S. Sprigge et al., 13 vols (1968–2024), 13: 59, 472 (James Young to Bentham, 30 Sept. 1828 and 14 Nov. 1830); see generally Bayly, *Recovering Liberties*, 11, 101–2.

205　*'error in managing' etc.*: Roy, *English Works*, 2: 283, 286; see also 299 and 'Letter of certain natives'.

205　*When the Mirat condemned*: for these examples, see Majumdar, *Raja Rammohun Roy*, 299–300; Chatterjee, *Black Hole of Empire*, 148; Bayly, *Recovering Liberties*, 77–8.

205　*'public remark' etc.*: Roy, *English Works*, ed. Ghose, 2: 298–305.

205 *'slaves'* etc.: ibid., 306, 309. An 1826 petition which Roy also promoted likewise complained that under British rule Indians had been reduced to 'a state of political degradation which is absolutely without a parallel in their former history': *Correspondence*, vol. 1, ed. Biswas, 364.

206 *the position of Roy*: though it's notable that in 1831, giving evidence to parliament in Britain, Roy was more circumspect, arguing for 'the importance of the fullest publicity being afforded to judicial proceedings by means of the press', and the vital role of the 'superintendence of public opinion' over public officials, yet demurring that 'I have no reference to the question of a free press, for the discussion of local politics, a point on which I do not mean to touch': Roy, *English Works*, ed. Ghose, 2: 14. By this time, he and Tagore had both helped found new papers in Calcutta: Majumdar, *Raja Rammohun Roy*, 326ff.

206 *Buckingham* etc.: for Buckingham, Bentham and others, see e.g. Buckingham, 'Examination of the Arguments Against a Free Press in India', *Oriental Herald and Colonial Review* 1: 2 (Feb. 1824), 197–224 and 18: 57 (Sept. 1828), 442–61; Zastoupil, *Rammohun Roy*, ch. 9; *Correspondence of Jeremy Bentham*, 12: 58 (Bentham to Sir Francis Burdett, 23 Sept. 1824); Bayly, *Recovering Liberties*, 121–2.

206 *'The cause is noble'*: Leicester Stanhope, *Sketch of the History and Influence of the Press in British India* (1823), foreword.

206 *'the people of India'*: ibid., 6.

206 *'our fellow-subjects'*: ibid., foreword. Twenty million pounds was a gigantic sum, equivalent to almost half of the annual budget of the British government at this time.

206 *'mental despotism'*: ibid., 52.

206 *'Do not treat'* etc.: ibid., 183.

206 *'the Typographical Colonel'*: ODNB, s.v. 'Stanhope, Leicester Fitzgerald Charles, fifth earl of Harrington'.

207 *openness of discussion*: see e.g. Seid Gholam Hossein Khan, *The Seir Mutaqherin, or Review of Modern Times*, [trans. Haji Mustapha], 3 vols (Calcutta, 1789–90), 1: 22–3 of Translator's Preface; 2: 406–7, 545–6, 550–51, 566–9, 596–8, and 21, 25 of second pagination; Bayly, *Recovering Liberties*, 80–81; Robert Travers, 'Indian Petitioning and Colonial State-Formation in Eighteenth-Century Bengal', *Modern Asian Studies* 53 (2019), 113–16.

207 *collective petitioning*: Stanhope, *Sketch*, 5; *Petitioning and Political Cultures in South Asia*, special issue of *Modern Asian Studies* 53 (2019).

207 *other side of the debate*: see e.g. Stanhope, *Sketch*, 70–71; Ahmed, *Social Ideas*, 72. When, a few months after Buckingham's deportation, the *Calcutta Journal* dared to start publishing extracts from Stanhope's pamphlet, the government of Bengal shut the paper down for good: ibid., 73.

207 *'Political discussion'*: quoted in Majumdar, *Raja Rammohun Roy*, 283–4.

207 *'depends not'* etc.: *Asiatic Journal* 14 (1822), 138*.

208 *'a presumptuous "Black Man"'*: *Correspondence of Jeremy Bentham*, 13: 58 (James Young to Bentham, 30 Sept. 1828); for another example, see Sophia Dobson Collet, *The Life and Letters of Raja Rammohun Roy*, ed. Dilip Kumar Biswas and Prabhat Chandra Ganguli (1962), 326.

208 *'for the purpose of fomenting'*: *Asiatic Journal* 14 (1822), 139.

208 *'like permitting the approach'*: Stanhope, *Sketch*, 73, quoting a speech by Charles Grant, the influential former chairman of the East India Company's Board of Directors.

208 *'our peculiar situation'* etc.: BL, MSS Eur F140/61(b): copy of a minute by Sir Thomas Munro to the Board of Directors of the East India Company, on the liberty of the Indian press, April 1822.

208 *'must be force'* etc.: BL, MSS Eur F140/60(a): memorandum by B. H. Jones for Lord Amherst on the 'Political State of India', Nov. 1822, 208–9 (quoting an earlier memo from Sir Thomas Munro to Lord Hastings).

208 *'but in no sense'* etc.: letter from the chairman and deputy chairman of the East India Company to the president of the Board of Control, 17 Jan. 1823, in *1834 CJ Report*, appendix: 124–5. Like all the other presumptions surveyed here, this was a much-repeated notion.

209 *'conquered people'* etc.: ibid., 132–3, memorandum by Sir John Malcom on liberty of the press in India, 12 Apr. 1822.

209 *'black' Indians and 'half-castes'* etc.: BL, MSS Eur F140/56: Sir Thomas Reid to Lord Amherst, 28 Nov. 1822.

209 *'notions of their own importance'*: letter from the chairman and deputy chairman of the East India Company to the president of the Board of Control, 17 Jan. 1823, *1834 CJ Report*, appendix: 126.

209 *'the rights of man'* etc.: BL, MSS Eur F140/56: Sir Thomas Reid to Lord Amherst, 28 Nov. 1822.

209 *'lower the European character'*: letter from the chairman and deputy chairman of the East India Company to the president of the Board of Control, 17 Jan. 1823, in *1834 CJ Report*, appendix: 125.

209 *'the evils'*: [John Adam], *Statement of Facts Relative to the Removal from India of Mr. Buckingham* (Calcutta, 1823), 57; cf. BL, MSS IOR/

P10/55: minute of William Bayley about press liberty and the native press, 10 Oct. 1822; Zastoupil, *Rammohun Roy*, 101, 140–41.

210 *'that if full licence'*: CW, 30: 70.

210 *offered him a seat*: on Mill and India, see CW, 1: 82–7, 247–9 ('I had given enough of my life to India' is how he revealingly described in his autobiography his decline of the offer of a seat on the Council of India: CW, 1: 249); CW, 30.

210 *'enlightened'* etc.: ibid., 79–80, 93, 103; see also same sentiments at 164.

210 *much illuminating recent work*: see esp. Lynn Zastoupil, *John Stuart Mill and India* (1994); Martin I. Moir et al. (eds), *J. S. Mill's Encounter with India* (1999); Pitts, *Turn to Empire*, ch. 5; Karuna Mantena, 'Mill and the Imperial Predicament', in Nadia Urbinati and Alex Zakaras, *J. S. Mill's Political Thought* (2007).

211 *powerful imperial agent*: ODNB, s.v. 'Mill, James'; CW, 1: 6–7, 82–4; CW, 30. 'The happiness and misery of so many millions are affected by what I write,' he boasted to a friend in 1819 about his extraordinary new sway over the peoples of India: quoted in Pitts, *Turn to Empire*, 125.

211 *'I am going'*: *Correspondence of Jeremy Bentham*, 12: 458 (Bentham to James Young, 28 Dec. 1827). For further testimony of Mill's great influence on Indian policy, see ibid., 12: 447–51 (Bentham to Rammohun Roy, Dec. 1827? and 8 Feb. 1828); ibid., 13: 14 (Bentham to Richard Clark, Aug. 1828); CW, 1: 28–9.

211 *foundations of his own education*: on James and John Stuart Mill, see CW, 1: 6–9, 10 n., 16, 27–9, 562, 582.

211 *'infancy'* etc.: quoted in Pitts, *Turn to Empire*, 123, 127–33, 139.

212 *plenty of commentators criticized*: see e.g. *Asiatic Journal* 25 (1828), 596–602; 26 (1828), 317–20; 27 (1829), 525–38, 665–78; 28 (1829), 1–14, 257–67, 513–25; 29 (1830) 81–91, 191–8; J. V. Naik, 'Instant Indian Nationalist Reaction to James Mill's *The History of British India*', Proceedings of the Indian History Congress 63 (2002); Bayly, 'Empires and Indian Liberals', 78–9.

212 *repudiated his father's views*: see e.g. Lynn Zastoupil, 'India, J. S. Mill, and "Western" Culture', in Moir et al. (eds), *J. S. Mill's Encounter*, 136–9.

212 *'the eldest son'* etc.: CW, 1: 26–9, 212–13.

212 *'independent negro commonwealth'*: CW, 1: 304–5 (1824); for Mill's later crusades against bigotry, see e.g. Pitts, *Turn to Empire*, 161–2.

212 *'the passive and slavish'* etc.: CW, 30: 30, 93, 117, 165. For the general point, see esp. Pitts, *Turn to Empire*, 133–44; Catherine Hall, 'The

Nation Within and Without', in idem et al. (eds), *Defining the Victorian Nation* (2000), 188–91; Mantena, 'Mill and the Imperial Predicament', 307–10.

213 '*the more powerful race*' etc.: C W, 30: 13–15.

213 *system of colonial rule*: only occasionally, after the rebellion of 1857, did Mill ever acknowledge that in some respects British policies in India 'have done, and are still doing, irreparable mischief'. But even such injustice he invariably exculpated as 'committed with the most generous intentions', or done 'for the most part innocently': C W, 30: 222, 93.

213 *Mill's views*: cf. Christopher Barker, 'Unfree, Unequal, Unempirical', in Robert G. Ingram et al. (eds), *Freedom of Speech, 1500–1850* (2020), esp. 242–5 (though 246 wrongly ascribes to Mill statements by others, which Mill was only signing to certify them as being true copies of Company papers).

213 '*intelligent natives*' etc.: C W, 30: 51, 64–5.

213 '*a people most difficult*' etc.: ibid., 155, 176; see also 201.

213 '*I myself*': ibid., 12: 365.

213 '*the public of India*': ibid., 30: 49.

214 '*organ exclusively of individual interests*' etc.: ibid., 70–71, 165; see also 201–2.

214 '*some Indian malcontent*': ibid., 165.

214 '*Indian malcontents*' etc.: ibid., 198.

215 '*a society in which*': quoted in Kris Grint, 'The Freedom of the Press in James Mill's Political Thought', *Historical Journal* 60 (2017), 363.

215 '*Utterly out of the question*': *Hansard's Parliamentary Debates*, 3rd series, 19: 513: Thomas Babington Macaulay quoted Mill thus in a Commons speech of 10 July 1833; the latter's original exchange of 21 Feb. 1832 is printed in *Report from the Select Committee on the Affairs of the East India Company*, House of Commons Papers 1831–2, 735–I: 49.

215 *his basic theory*: Grint, 'Freedom of the Press'; [James Mill], 'Liberty of the Press', *Edinburgh Review* 18 (1811); [James Mill], 'Liberty of the Continental Press', *Edinburgh Review* 25 (1815); James Mill, 'Liberty of the Press' (1821), *Supplement to the Fourth, Fifth, and Sixth Editions of the Encyclopaedia Britannica*, 6 vols (Edinburgh, 1815–24), 5: 258–72; transcripts of vols 1–4 of his commonplace books, at intellectualhistory.net/mill.

215 '*this best bulwark*': [Mill], 'Liberty of the Press' (1811), 98.

215 *'institutions and functionaries'*: Mill, 'Liberty of the Press' (1821), 270.

215 *'it would be impossible'*: [Mill], 'Liberty of the Press' (1811), 121.

216 *'direct exhortation'* etc.: Mill, 'Liberty of the Press' (1821), 263–4.

216 *'false facts'*: ibid., 269–70.

216 *So did that of Bentham*: Jeremy Bentham, *On the Liberty of the Press, and Public Discussion* (1821), 9–15.

216 *'private men'*: Mill, 'Liberty of the Press' (1821), 269.

216 *'private rights'*: ibid., 258.

216 *'for protecting the rights'*: ibid., 263.

216 *'the people'*: e.g. [Mill], 'Liberty of the Press' (1811), 116, 121; [idem], 'Liberty of the Continental Press', 116, 125–6, 133.

216 *'human improvement'*: ibid., 113; cf. ibid., 112, 127–8; [Mill], 'Liberty of the Press' (1811), 98.

216 *'the real point of importance'*: Mill, 'Liberty of the Press' (1821), 268.

216 *'correct opinions'* etc.: ibid., 267–8.

216 *'freedom of discussion'*: ibid., 270.

216 *'there is no possible means'* etc.: [Mill], 'Liberty of the Continental Press', 132.

217 *Westminster Review*: [John Stuart Mill], 'Law of Libel and Liberty of the Press', *Westminster Review* 3 (1825), 285–321 (quoting 285: 'abominations'). James Mill's 1821 article was reprinted unchanged in the seventh and eighth editions of the *Encyclopaedia Britannica*, which appeared in 1842 and 1857 respectively. The ninth edition, completed in 1888, no longer included an article on 'Liberty of the Press', substituting instead brief entries on 'Press Laws' and 'Libel'.

217 *further thought*: for one likely influence on John Stuart Mill's later thought, see Samuel Bailey, *Essays on the Formation and Publication of Opinions* (1821); and for this and other strands of early nineteenth-century British arguments about free speech, and Mill's relationship to them, see Gregory Conti, 'What's Not in *On Liberty*', *Journal of British Studies* 55 (2016); idem, 'Before – and Beyond – *On Liberty*', in Ingram et al. (eds), *Freedom of Speech*; K. C. O'Rourke, *John Stuart Mill and Freedom of Expression* (2001), pt 1.

217 *'"liberty of the press"'* etc.: CW, 18: 228. In his footnote, Mill was referring to two cases in 1858 when the British government had (though ultimately unsuccessfully) prosecuted London publications that seemed to justify a recent assassination attempt against Napoleon III in Paris.

217 *'thought and discussion'* etc.: ibid.

218 *'mental development'* etc.: ibid., 219–20, 241–2.

218 *'necessity to the mental well-being'*: ibid., 257. Cf. Pierre Bourdieu, *Language and Symbolic Power*, ed. John B. Thompson, trans. Gino Raymond and Matthew Adamson (1991), ch. 6.

218 *'if it is not fully'* etc.: CW, 18: 243, 262.

218 *'to enable average'* etc.: ibid., 243.

218 *'abstract right'*: ibid., 224.

218 *'moral, social'*: ibid., 15: 581 (Mill to Theodor Gomperz, 4 Dec. 1858).

219 *'the dictum that truth'*: ibid., 18: 238.

219 *'as mankind improve'* etc.: ibid., 250.

220 *'the propagation of doctrines'* etc.: ibid., 231.

220 *'which concerns others'* etc.: ibid., 223–4.

220 *'self-regarding conduct'* etc.: for this principle, which Mill often refers to, though without fully addressing its implications for all manner of speech, see e.g. ibid., 296.

220 *'liberty of thought and discussion'* etc.: ibid., 225–6; see also 227: 'the Liberty of Thought: from which it is impossible to separate the cognate liberty of speaking and writing'.

221 *'even opinions lose their immunity'* etc.: ibid., 260–61.

221 *'not a place'*: ibid., 241.

222 *'No one can be a great thinker'*: ibid., 242; cf. 268 on 'genius'.

222 *'World history travels'* etc.: Georg Wilhelm Friedrich Hegel, *Lectures on the Philosophy of World History*, trans. H. B. Nisbet (1975), 190, 197.

222 *Auguste Comte*: Georgios Varouxakis, 'The Godfather of "Occidentality"', *Modern Intellectual History* 16 (2019), and 'When did Britain Join the Occident?', *History of European Ideas* 46 (2020).

222 *'in modern Europe'*: CW, 18: 120–21 ('Civilization', 1836).

222 *'magnificent palaces'* etc.: ibid., 243.

222 *'well-developed human beings'* etc.: ibid., 267, 274.

222 *'the absolute and essential'*: ibid., 215.

223 *'public opinion'* etc.: ibid., 268–9, 272–4.

223 *pessimism of late middle age*: ibid., lxxxi.

224 *history, 'progress'*, etc.: for Mill's frequent earlier rehearsal of these themes, see e.g. ibid., 119ff., 'Civilization' (1836); 155ff., 'De Tocqueville on Democracy in America [II]' (1840).

224 *'human beings in the maturity'*: CW, 18: 224.

224 *'we may leave out'*: ibid. The Mughal emperor of India, Akbar (1542–1605), who ruled before the arrival of the British East India Company, was famous for his military conquests, successful government and intellectual open mindedness. The only other explicit reference to India

in *On Liberty* came in a factually dubious footnote about the dietary customs of its different religions (18: 285 n.).

224 *'the stage of progress'* etc.: *CW*, 18: 217, 224. See also ibid., 223: 'any member of a civilized community', and 19: 39–5, 567–8, 568–77 (*Considerations on Representative Government*, 1861).

225 *'India (for example) is not fit'*: ibid., 568.

225 *'I am not aware'*: ibid., 18: 291.

225 *'with which an intelligent'*: 'Limitations of Indian Liberty', *Calcutta Review* 34 (1860), 101.

9. COLONIAL AND POSTCOLONIAL UNFREEDOMS

227 *James Fitzjames Stephen*: *ODNB*, s.v. 'Stephen, Sir James Fitzjames, first baronet (1829–1894)', 'Stephen, James (1758–1832)' (grandfather), 'Stephen, Sir James (1789–1859)' (father).

228 *disciple of John Stuart Mill*: 'Mr Mill on Political Liberty', *Saturday Review*, 12 and 19 Feb. 1859; K. C. O'Rourke, *John Stuart Mill and Freedom of Expression* (2001), 94, 101–4.

228 *rejection of Mill's influential theory*: *LEF*, xxi n. 10, 24–5; *ODNB*. Stephen's book also took aim at Mill's essays *Utilitarianism* (1862) and *The Subjection of Women* (1869). It originally appeared as a series of articles in the *Pall Mall Gazette*, between November 1872 and January 1873, and then was published as a book in April 1873; Mill died on 7 May of that year.

228 *'my Indian experience'*: *LEF*, 3.

228 *'If Mr. Mill'* etc.: ibid., 40–41.

228 *'To publish opinions'* etc.: ibid., 64, 92.

229 *'irrational'* etc.: ibid., 47–50.

229 *'the minority are wise'*: ibid., 10.

229 *'the wise minority'*: ibid., 10; see also 39, 45–6.

229 *'have become capable'* etc.: ibid., 34–9.

229 *'very small minority'* etc.: ibid., 87–8.

229 *'rough'* and *'civilized'*: ibid., 36.

229 *'that force is used'*: ibid., 37.

230 *'were brought about'*: ibid., 31–3.

230 *'forced upon the people'* etc.: ibid., 49–53.

230 *'the subjects'* etc.: John Bruce Norton, *The Administration of Justice in Southern India* (Madras, 1853), 8.

230 *After the rebellion*: John Bruce Norton, *Topics for Indian Statesmen*, ed. G. R. Norton (1858), ch. 11 (mainly, though not exclusively, concerned

with the English, rather than the vernacular press; 346 for the critique of Mill); *ODNB*, s.v. 'Norton, John Bruce (1815–1883)'.

231 *directly exposed to print*: C. A. Bayly, *Recovering Liberties* (2012), 79; Robert Darnton, *Censors at Work* (2014), 91–5, 119.

231 *'townsmen of Bombay'*: J[ohn] Chapman, preface to Nowrozjee Furdoonjee, *On the Civil Administration of the Bombay Presidency* (1853), iv (and see 17); *ODNB*, s.v. 'Chapman, John (1801–1854)'.

231 *indigenous eyes*: Furdoonjee, *Civil Administration*, viii, 1–2, 9, 25.

231 *strategically choosing*: Bayly, *Recovering Liberties*, 12–13, 201; see also S. Ambirajan, 'John Stuart Mill and India', in Martin I. Moir et al. (eds), *J. S. Mill's Encounter with India* (1999), 245–57.

231 *'John Stuart Mill is the greatest'* etc.: Ashutosh Mookerjea, 'Liberty, Equality, Fraternity', *Mookerjee's Magazine* 2 (1873), 372, 377, 381, 391–2; see also Bayly, *Recovering Liberties*, 202–3, 210–11, 346.

232 *'in the British colonies'*: 'Press Laws in the British Colonies and India', *Encyclopaedia Britannica*, 25 vols (9th edn, 1875–89), 19: 722.

232 *1820s regulations were repealed*: 'Printing-Presses', Act no. XI of 1835; cf. *A Penal Code Prepared by the Indian Law Commissioners* (Calcutta, 1837), clauses 291–3 and Note L; A. F. Salahuddin Ahmed, *Social Ideas and Social Change in Bengal, 1818–1835* (2nd edn, 1976), 85–9.

232 *vast network of surveillance*: Darnton, *Censors at Work*, 101 ('censorship overlaid with protests denying its existence', as he beautifully epitomizes the resulting system).

232 *'a modern war of propaganda'*: C. A. Bayly, *Empire and Information* (1996), 319; see also 319–23, 329–31, 335–45, 350–51, 361, 366.

232 *'to excite feelings'*: Act no. XXVIII of 1870, amending the penal code (the text of this provision was based on clause 113 of Macaulay's 1837 draft code, whose presumptions are analysed later in this chapter).

232 *'read by and disseminated'* etc.: quoted in Margarita Barns, *The Indian Press* (1940), 279–88.

232 *'disaffection to the government'* etc.: ibid., 304–6.

233 *'to split up'*: quoted in Sumit Sarkar, *The Swadeshi Movement in Bengal 1903–1908* (1973), 18.

233 *'both by openly seditious'*: Darnton, *Censors at Work*, 127, quoting the explanatory text published with the 1910 Indian Press Act; see also Barns, *Indian Press*, chs 13–17, appendices 1–3.

233 *'nothing can be further'* etc.: quoted in Darnton, *Censors at Work*, 273 n. 35.

233 *'We must take'*: quoted ibid., 124.

233 *'free expression of opinion'*: Shiva Rao, *The Framing of India's Constitution*, 5 vols (1966-8), 1: 44, 59 – in 1924-5, the 'Declaration of Rights' of a proposed constitution included the right to 'free expression of opinion and the right of assembly peaceably and without arms'; in a 1928 draft constitution, this was amended to: 'The right of free expression of opinion, as well as the right to assemble peaceably and without arms, and to form associations or unions, is hereby guaranteed for purposes not opposed to public order or morality.'

233 *This pattern*: see e.g. Aurobindo Mazumdar, *Indian Press and Freedom Struggle* (1993).

234 *'harm the reputation'* etc.: *A Penal Code Prepared by the Indian Law Commissioners* (Calcutta, 1837), quoting clauses 282 and 469; see also clause 485 and Notes J and R.

234 *Mill, reviewing Macaulay's text*: CW, 30: 29.

234 *'monstrous superstition'* etc.: *Penal Code*, Note J.

234 *'the peculiar circumstances'* etc.: ibid., Note R.

234 *'Religious discussion'*: ibid., Note J.

234 *'wounding'* etc.: ibid., Note M.

235 *'there is probably no country'* etc. : ibid., Note J.

235 *'discussions having a tendency'*: *1834 CJ Report*, appendix: 41; Barns, *Indian Press*, 115-23. Macaulay described his own appointment to the Council as to be 'the guardian of the people of India against the European settlers': *The Letters of Thomas Babington Macaulay*, ed. Thomas Pinney, 6 vols (1974-81), 2: 340 (to Hannah Macaulay, 22 Nov. 1833).

235 *Mill's early dispatches*: Penelope Carson, 'Golden Casket or Pebbles and Trash?', in Moir et al. (eds), *J. S. Mill's Encounter*, 160-66.

235 *'irritating and insulting remarks'*: *English Works of Raja Rammohun Roy*, ed. Jogendra Chunder Ghose, 3 vols (1901 edn), 2: 297.

235 *'no alarm whatever prevails'* etc.: ibid., 300; see also Bayly, *Empire and Information*, 191.

236 *far longer tradition*: Leicester Stanhope, *Sketch of the History and Influence of the Press in British India* (1823), 84-8, 153-4.

236 *their own weekly publications*: see e.g. Ahmed, *Social Ideas*, 34-5.

236 *'To assert'* etc.: Stanhope, *Sketch*, 184.

236 *the young Tom Macaulay*: Catherine Hall, *Macaulay and Son* (2012), 73-9, 204-14, 239-40; *Hansard's Parliamentary Debates*, 3rd series, 19: 513 (speech by Macaulay, 10 July 1833).

236 *'a very remarkable man'*: *Letters*, ed. Pinney, 2: 47.

237 *'I am plagued'* etc.: Macaulay to Hannah Macaulay, 21 May 1833: *Letters*, ed. Pinney, 2: 242; for similar sentiments, see also 2: 245–6, 283.

237 *'a decomposed society'* etc.: *Hansard's Parliamentary Debates*, 3rd series, 19: 503–36 (speech by Macaulay, 10 July 1833). He thought it 'the best speech, by general agreement, and in my own opinion, that I ever made in my life': *Letters*, ed. Pinney, 2: 268; see also 283. Twenty years later, in one of his final interventions as an MP, he argued (as John Stuart Mill also had done, the previous year) that no natives had yet been admitted to the ranks of India's administration simply because not a single Indian was as yet intellectually qualified to serve in it: *Hansard's Parliamentary Debates*, 3rd series, 128: col. 757 (24 June 1853).

237 *'legislating for a conquered race'*: quoted in Hall, *Macaulay*, 215; see also 127; *Hansard's Parliamentary Debates*, 3rd series, 19: 503–36 (speech of 10 July 1833); *Letters*, ed. Pinney, 2: 329, 365, 367 (for James Mill's support); 3: 193, 345, and *passim* for his taking the job to gain financial independence.

237 *'absolutely immeasurable'*: Macaulay, minute on education, 2 Feb 1835, printed in G. O. Trevelyan, *The Competition Wallah* (1864), 414.

237 *'sound and useful'* etc.: Macaulay to James Mill, 24 Aug. 1835: *Letters*, ed. Pinney, 3: 150.

237 *'a single shelf'* etc.: Macaulay, minute on education, in Trevelyan, *Competition Wallah*, 413, 415.

238 *he also pushed his colleagues*: George Otto Trevelyan, *Life and Letters of Lord Macaulay*, 2 vols (1876), 1: 344–8.

238 *'the Bengalee'* etc.: Hall, *Macaulay and Son*, 248; see also chs 5 and 6.

238 *penal code*: for its long gestation and ignoring of Indian opinion, see Atul Chandra Patra, 'An Historical Introduction to the Indian Penal Code', *Journal of the Indian Law Institute* 3 (1961); K. J. M. Smith, 'Macaulay's "Utilitarian" Indian Penal Code', in W. M. Gordon and T. D. Fergus, *Legal History in the Making* (1991). It came into operation on 1 Jan. 1862.

238 *particular criticism*: T. B. Macaulay et al., *The Indian Penal Code, as Originally Framed in 1837* (Madras, 1888), 409–17.

238 *in the end*: 1860 penal code, clauses 298 and 499 (though the truth defence was restricted to matters concerning 'the public good'); the sedition clause, 124A, expanding Macaulay's 1837 clause 113, was added in 1870.

238 *'gesture or sound'* etc.: Macaulay et al., *Indian Penal Code, as Originally Framed*, 409–10.

239 *created more religious conflict*: Asad Ali Ahmed, 'Specters of Macaulay', in Raminder Kaur and William Mazzarella (eds), *Censorship in South Asia* (2009).

239 *'and which might lead'*: James Fitzjames Stephen, *A History of the Criminal Law of England*, 3 vols (1883), 3: 312–13; see also idem, 'Codification in India and England', *Fortnightly Review* 18 (1872), 654. In 1870, Stephen was responsible for adding Section 124A to the penal code.

239 *'to promote feelings of enmity'*: section 153A, added by the Indian Penal Code (Amendment) Act, 1898; cf. Abhinav Chandrachud, *Republic of Rhetoric* (2017), 227.

240 *to punish 'insult'*: Neeti Nair, 'Beyond the Communal 1920s', *Indian Economic and Social History* 50 (2013).

240 *'sectarian animosity'* etc.: for this and the following three paragraphs of this chapter, see *Abstract of the Proceedings of the Council of the Governor General of India, Assembled for the Purpose of Making Laws and Regulations, 1898*, 37 (Calcutta, 1899), 31–51 (18 Feb. 1898); here quoting 31–6 (Mackenzie Dalzell Chalmers).

240 *'over 250 millions'* etc.: ibid., 49 (Sir Griffith Evans); see also 48 (James La Touche), 65–7 (H. E. M. James).

240 *'the tendency'*: ibid., 90–91 (Sir Alexander Mackenzie).

241 *'we want simply'*: ibid., 36 (Chalmers); see also 69 (C. C. Stevens), 95 (Mackenzie), 152 (Viceroy Lord Elgin).

241 *'philosophic treatises'*: ibid., 67 (James); see also 51 (Evans), 53–4 (La Touche).

241 *'semi-educated'* etc.: ibid., 92–3 (Mackenzie).

241 *'disaffection'* etc.: ibid., 37–42 (quoting 40).

241 *'over-zealous police-official'* etc.: ibid., 147 (Chitnavis). See also Chandrachud, *Republic of Rhetoric*, 227.

242 *'who else are fit'*: *Abstract of the Proceedings of the Council*, 60.

242 *'faulty and unfounded'* etc.: ibid., 60, 63; cf. e.g. Sailendra Nath Sircar, 'Liberty of the Press', *National Magazine* 12 (1898), 71–5; A. Stephen, 'John [sic] Silk Buckingham and the Liberty of the Indian Press', *National Magazine* 13 (1898), 106–13.

242 *'obnoxious'* etc.: *Abstract of the Proceedings of the Council*, 74, 75 (Bishambar Nath); see also 72–5, 145.

242 *'the general native public'*: ibid., 77 (Ramhimtulla Mohamed Sayani); see also 75–83. The Maharaja of Darbhanga, Lakshmeshwar Singh, a new member attending his first meeting of the Council, first voted in

favour of the measure, but then introduced several unsuccessful opposition amendments to reduce the scope of section 124A: ibid., 106–16, 116–30.

242 *'religious beliefs'* etc.: quoted in Nair, 'Beyond the Communal 1920s', 334; for the debates, see *Legislative Assembly Debates (Official Report): First Session of the Third Legislative Assembly, 1927* (Delhi, 1927–8). Once again, the proposed text was not circulated in vernacular languages; once again, it faced strong public opposition.

242 *'Many of the greatest'* etc.: *Legislative Assembly Debates . . . 1927*, 4460.

242 *'most dangerous'* etc.: ibid., 4469, 4474, 4478.

242 *'alien'* etc.: ibid., 4478–80; see also 4467, 4469–74.

243 *'to preach disaffection'* etc.: quoted in Chandrachud, *Republic of Rhetoric*, 39–40.

244 *'could safely trample'* etc.: Nathuram Godse quoted in Neeti Nair, *Hurt Sentiments* (2023), 31; see generally ibid., ch. 1.

244 *'No law shall be made'*: quoted in Rao, *Framing*, 2: 87.

244 *'right to freedom of speech'* etc.: quoted ibid., 5: 755; for the creation of India's new constitution, see generally ibid., vols 2–5.

244 *further laws*: e.g. section 153B, added in 1972, against speech 'prejudicial to national integration'. In 2017 the Law Commission of India recommended the addition of two further clauses (153C and 505A), prohibiting 'incitement to hatred' and 'causing fear, alarm, or provocation of violence'.

244 *past two decades*: see e.g. Siddharth Narrain, 'Law, Language and Community Sentiment', in Janny H.C. Leung and Alan Durant, *Meaning and Power in the Language of Law* (2018); Amrita Basu, 'Changing Modalities of Violence', in Karen Barkey et al. (eds), *Negotiating Democracy and Religious Pluralism* (2021); Nair, *Hurt Sentiments*.

245 *further afield*: on adoption of versions of the penal code beyond India, see Mirjam Maters, *Van zachte wenk tot harde hand* (1998), esp. chs 3 and 7; H. F. Morris, 'A History of the Adoption of Codes of Criminal Law and Procedure in British Colonial Africa, 1876–1935', *Journal of African Law* 6 (1974); M. L. Friedland, 'R. S. Wright's Model Code', *Oxford Journal of Legal Studies* 1 (1981). The version of the Indian penal code adopted in Sudan in 1899 omitted its provisions against religiously hurtful words.

245 *model criminal code*: R. S. Wright, *Drafts of a Criminal Code and a Code of Criminal Procedure*, Parliamentary Papers, 1877, C–1893; Friedland, 'R. S. Wright's Model Criminal Code'. It was eventually

adopted only in British Honduras, Tobago, St Lucia, British Guiana and the Gold Coast.

245 *penal code for England*: *Criminal Code (Indictable Offences) Bill* (Bill 178, 41 Vict.; 1878), sections 41, 55-6, 98, 176-85.

246 *revised version of this code*: *Report of the Royal Commission Appointed to Consider Indictable Offences: With . . . A Draft Code*, Parliamentary Papers, 1879, C-2345, sections 102-3, 141 (adding 'in decent language' to the good faith exemption for blasphemy), 227-43.

246 *fairly random*: Morris, 'History of the Adoption of Codes of Criminal Law'; Friedland, 'R. S. Wright's Model Code'.

246 *early European theorists*: Jeremy Waldron, *The Harm in Hate Speech* (2012), ch. 8; Teresa M. Bejan, *Mere Civility* (2017).

248 *Southern US states*: see e.g. *The Code of Tennessee 1932* (1931), paras 2343-5 (in force until 1967); *Mississippi Code of 1930 of the Public Statute Laws of the State of Mississippi*, paras 7315-16 (in force until 1968). Similar statutes were enacted in Oklahoma (1923-5), and Arkansas (1928-68). All such laws were ruled unconstitutional by the Supreme Court in *Epperson v. Arkansas*, 393 US 97 (1968).

248 *Germany*: Daniel Riesman, 'Democracy and Defamation: Control of Group Libel', *Columbia Law Review* 42 (1942), 729 n. 15, 741-2, 744.

248 *France*: Waldron, *Harm in Hate Speech*, 40.

248 *1930s onwards*: cf. Karl Loewenstein, 'Militant Democracy and Fundamental Rights', *American Political Science Review* 31 (1937), 651-4; idem, 'Legislative Control of Political Extremism in European Democracies', *Columbia Law Review* 38 (1938), 746-9.

248 *South West Africa*: David Fraser, *Nazi Antisemitism and Jewish Legal Self-Defence* (2024), ch. 5.

248 *South America*: see e.g. the 1940 Brazilian penal code, Article 140, which penalized insulting someone's dignity on the basis of race, colour, ethnicity, religion or origin.

249 *'with intent to create ill-will'*: *The Times*, 19 Sept. 1936; see also ibid., 15 Aug. 1936; TNA, KV 2/1365, 94a: Security Service memo by T. M. Shelford, 'The Imperial Fascist League' (1942).

249 *'attack on free speech'* etc.: Arnold S. Leese, *My Irrelevant Defence* (1938), introduction.

249 *'public mischief'* etc.: *The Times*, 22 Sept. 1936.

249 *'would be biting'* etc.: see Christopher Hilliard, 'Words that Disturb the State', *Journal of Modern History* 88 (2016), 786, 789, and generally, for this and the following two paragraphs of this chapter.

249 *'Group Defamation'* etc.: *Report of the Committee on the Law of Defamation* (1948), 11.

249 *'calculated to incite'*: quoted in Gisela C. Lebzelter, *Political Anti-Semitism in England 1918–1939* (1978), 131.

250 *'words calculated'*: quoted ibid., 140.

250 *'the fact that'*: quoted in Hilliard, 'Words', 770–71.

250 *'In the light of'* etc.: quoted ibid., 786.

250 *'on grounds of colour'*: Race Relations Act (1965), clause 6.

250 *'to prevent arising'*: quoted in Hilliard, 'Words', 787.

251 *'by which a group'*: Danish penal code, paragraph 266b.

251 *'arguments or suggestions'*: *Laws of the State of Mississippi Passed at a Regular Session* (1920), 307 (ch. 214); *Mississippi Code of 1930 of the Public Statute Laws of the State of Mississippi*, section 1103.

251 *legal redress for personal libel*: see Riesman, 'Democracy and Defamation: Control', 747 n. 104; idem, 'Democracy and Defamation: Fair Game and Fair Comment' [in two parts], *Columbia Law Review* 42 (1942).

251 *some new statutes*: on American group libel laws, see e.g. C. Cahill and Basil Jones, *Callaghan's Illinois Statutes Annotated, 1917–1920* (1920), 614, 657–8; Joseph Tanenhaus, 'Group Libel', *Cornell Law Quarterly* 35 (1949), 271–2, 286–7.

251 *Anti-Defamation League*: on Jewish activism and group libel laws, most of which were soon challenged and struck down, see Morton Rosenstock, *Louis Marshall* (1965), 149–50, 167–8; Howard M. Sachar, *A History of the Jews in America* (1992), 315–16; Evan P. Schultz, 'Group Rights, American Jews, and the Failure of Group Libel Laws, 1913–1952', *Brooklyn Law Review* 66 (2000), 104–6.

251 *'a class of citizens'* etc.: *Revised Statutes of the State of Illinois 1917* (1918), 999–1000 (i.e. criminal code, sections 224a and 224b); see also *Beauharnais v. Illinois*, 343 US 250 (1952), 258–61; Samantha Barbas, 'The Story of *Beauharnais v. Illinois*', *Journal of Free Speech Law* (2023), 426–7.

252 *'deliberately to slander and vilify'*: Nickieann Fleener-Marzec, 'D. W. Griffith's *The Birth of a Nation* . . . and the First Amendment' (University of Wisconsin–Madison PhD thesis, 1977), 8 and *passim*.

252 *experimentation with group libel laws*: see e.g. Riesman, 'Democracy and Defamation: Control', 733; 'Statutory Prohibition of Group Defamation', *Columbia Law Review* 47 (1947); Tanenhaus, 'Group Libel'; idem, 'Group Libel and Free Speech', *Phylon: The Atlanta Review of Race and Culture* 13 (1952); 'Group Libel Laws', *Yale Law Journal* 61

(1952); Samuel Walker, *Hate Speech* (1994), 82–6; David Goodman, 'Before Hate Speech', *Patterns of Prejudice* 49 (2015), 208; Samantha Barbas, 'The Rise and Fall of Group Libel', *Loyola University Chicago Law Journal* 54 (2022).

252   *in force today*: Connecticut General Statutes section 53-37 (2022); Massachusetts General Laws, ch. 272, section 98c (2022); Minnesota Statute section 609.765 (2022); West Virginia Code section 61-10-16 (covering any public 'picture or theatrical act') (2022).

252   *'This is a white man's country'*: quoted in *The Worker: Illinois Edition*, 14 May 1950, 10.

253   *supported Beauharnais's argument*: on the Beauharnais case, see Federal Bureau of Investigation, file no. 105–291: the White Circle League of Chicago (at archive.org); *Beauharnais v. Illinois*, 343 US 250 (1952); Barbas, 'The Story of *Beauharnais v. Illinois*'; Erika J. Pribanic-Smith and Jared Schroeder, 'Breaking the White Circle', *American Journalism*, 38 (2021).

253   *'the Founders'* etc.: quoting from *Beauharnais v. Illinois*, 267–75 (Black's dissent).

253   *'unseemly language'* etc.: quoting from ibid., 284–7 (Douglas's dissent); though it's notable that Douglas also, somewhat contradictorily, joined the dissent by Reed (see note below), which did explicitly acknowledge the power of states to pass group libel laws.

253   *'reckless and vicious libel'* etc.: quoting from ibid., 287–305 (Jackson's dissent).

253   *'the constitutional power'*: quoting from ibid., 277–84 (Reed's dissent – joined by Douglas).

254   *'personal abuse'* etc.: quoting from ibid., 251–67 (majority opinion written by Felix Frankfurter). The last phrase, 'the systemic avalanche of falsehoods' (from 261 n. 16), is Frankfurter quoting his former student David Riesman, who had clerked for Justice Brandeis in the later 1930s, and whose 1942 articles on group libel laws evidently influenced the court's decision. For Riesman, see Daniel Horowitz, 'David Riesman', *Buffalo Law Review* 58 (2010).

254   [footnote] *'libelous'* and *'insulting'* words: *Chaplinsky v. New Hampshire*, 315 US 568 (1942).

255   *the rights of the speaker*: for this argument, see Ronald Dworkin, 'Foreword', in Ivan Hare and James Weinstein (eds), *Extreme Speech and Democracy* (2009).

256   *hard social and legal problem*: see e.g. Hare and Weinstein (eds), *Extreme Speech*, part 2; Michael Herz and Peter Molnar, *The Content*

and *Context of Hate Speech* (2012); Timothy Garton Ash, *Free Speech* (2016), chs 2, 5.

10. THE MARKETPLACE OF IDEAS

257 *foundational documents*: see e.g. the constitutions of the USSR (1936), Article 125; Cuba (2019), Articles 54–5; China (1982), Article 35; Democratic People's Republic of Korea (2019), Article 67. The same guarantees are also included in the current constitution of the Russian Federation, the successor state of the Soviet Union.

259 *printing presses, books and pamphlets*: see e.g. Michael Harris, *London Newspapers in the Age of Walpole* (1987); Charles E. Clark, *The Public Prints* (1994); Joad Raymond (ed.), *News, Newspapers and Society in Early Modern England* (1999); Hannah Barker, *Newspapers, Politics and English Society, 1695–1855* (2000); James Raven, *The Business of Books* (2007); Michael F. Suarez and Michael L. Turner (eds), *The Cambridge History of the Book in Britain*, vol. 5: *1695–1830* (2009).

260 *suing each other for verbal insults*: see e.g. Martin Ingram, *Church Courts, Sex, and Marriage in England, 1570–1640* (1987), 374; J. A. Sharpe, *Defamation and Sexual Slander in Early Modern England* (1980), 9; Tim Meldrum, 'A Woman's Court in London', *London Journal* 19 (1994), 2–4; Robert Shoemaker, *The London Mob* (2007), ch. 3; Jane Kamensky, *Governing the Tongue* (1997), 186–91, 201; Lyndsay Mills Campbell, 'Truth and Consequences: The Legal and Extralegal Regulation of Expression in Massachusetts and Nova Scotia, 1820–1840' (University of California, Berkeley, PhD thesis, 2008), 50.

260 *scandalum magnatum*: John Lassiter, 'Defamation of Peers: The Rise and Decline of the Action for *Scandalum Magnatum*, 1497–1773', *American Journal of Legal History* 22 (1978).

260 *prosecutions for seditious words*: Larry Eldridge, *A Distant Heritage* (1994); David Cressy, *Dangerous Talk* (2010), ch. 11; Peter Rushton and Gwenda Morgan, *Treason and Rebellion in the British Atlantic, 1685–1800* (2020), 81–8.

260 *punished for spoken sedition*: Clive Emsley, 'An Aspect of Pitt's "Terror"', *Social History* (1981), appendix B; idem, 'Repression, "Terror", and the Rule of Law in England During the Decade of the French Revolution', *English Historical Review* (1985), 807, 822.

260 *how language was produced*: Kamensky, *Governing the Tongue*, 191; Roy Porter, *Enlightenment* (2000), 235–9.

260 *'the government of the tongue'*: the best-selling tracts of William Per-
kins, *A Direction for the Government of the Tongue According to Gods
Word* (1593), and Richard Allestree, *The Government of the Tongue*
(Oxford, 1674), alone went through over thirty editions: English Short-
Title Catalogue (estc.bl.uk).

260 *art of conversation*: cf. Peter Burke, *The Art of Conversation* (1993),
esp. 109ff.; Philip Carter, *Men and the Emergence of Polite Society*
(2001), 62ff.

261 *'enjoyment'* etc.: Joseph Butler, 'Upon the Government of the Tongue',
in *Fifteen Sermons* (1726), 57, 59, 65; cf. also John Barnard, *A Present
for an Apprentice* (1740).

261 *distinguish speech from other kinds of action*: Shoemaker, *London
Mob*, 68–73.

261 *'speaking falsely'* etc.: *London Journal*, 10 June 1721 [Cato's Letters,
no. 32].

261 *'from house to house'* etc.: John Milton, *Areopagitica* (1644), 47. Cf.
Kamensky, *Governing the Tongue*, 187–8. A lone late exception was
David Hume's 1741 assertion in his essay on the liberty of the press,
probably channelling Milton on this point, that 'a whisper may fly as
quick, and be as pernicious as a pamphlet', or more so: *Essays Moral
and Political* (Edinburgh, 1741), 15–16.

261 *'because such are public'*: *Rex v. Darby* (1687), 3 Mod. 139, and *Eng-
lish Reports Full Reprint* 87: 89–90. See also 'The Pre-*Thorley v. Kerry*
Case Law of the Libel-Slander Distinction', *University of Chicago Law
Review*, 23 (1955), esp. 138–45.

262 *Treason Acts*: C. H. Firth and R. S. Rait, *Acts and Ordinances of the
Interregnum, 1642–1660* (1911), 120–21, 193–4, 831–5. The 1661
Treason Act also explicitly extended to 'words alone', and to 'malicious
or advised speaking'.

262 *royal proclamation in Scotland*: *Proclamation Against Slanderers and
Leasing-makers*, 16 June 1686.

262 *criminalizing Loyalist speech*: see Chapter 6 of this book.

262 *Virginia passed an Act*: *The Revised Code of the Laws of Virginia*
(1819), 553; Julius S. Scott, *The Common Wind* (2018), 141–2.

262 *Russia*: K. A. Papmehl, *Freedom of Expression in Eighteenth-Century
Russia* (1971), ch. 1 (quoting p. 2: 'behind locked doors'). An exception
to the criminalization of private writing was made for religious teachers.

263 *eighteenth-century laws*: this is evident already in *By the Queen, a
Proclamation for Restraining the Spreading False News* (1702), which
starts by reciting medieval statutes against false tales, and includes a

single mention of 'writing, printing, or speaking' sedition, but whose substance is essentially directed against writing and printing, rather than verbal utterances.

263 *Henry Sacheverell*: Geoffrey Holmes, *The Trial of Doctor Sacheverell* (1973), ch. 3.

263 *After 1800*: Cressy, *Dangerous Talk*, 251-4 (quoting 253: 'the cutting off').

263 *Sedition Act of 1798: An Act in Addition to the Act, Entitled 'An Act for the Punishment of Certain Crimes Against the United States'*, approved 14 July 1798 (my italics).

263 *'words vanish in air'* etc.: [James Sullivan], *A Dissertation Upon the Constitutional Freedom of the Press in the United States* (Boston, 1801), 12.

263 *Britain*: for the 1792 and 1795 laws, see *A Proclamation . . . [Against] Wicked and Seditious Writings*, 21 May 1792; *Treasonable and Seditious Practices Act*, 36 Geo. III, c. 7 (1795).

264 *oaths, promises*: see e.g. John Spurr, 'Perjury, Profanity and Politics', *The Seventeenth Century* 8 (1993).

264 *essentially harmless*: cf. Frederick Schauer, 'Harm(s) and the First Amendment', *Supreme Court Review* (2012).

264 *'sticks and stones'*: first recorded in the American abolitionist journals *Christian Recorder*, 22 Mar. 1862, and *Liberator*, 2 Jan. 1863.

265 *'the stroke of the tongue'*: Ecclesiastes 28:17. See Chapter 1 of this book.

265 *'the press – and of late'* etc.: CW, 18: 162, 165.

265 *'public opinion'*: ibid., 228 (*On Liberty*).

265 *'The more I think'*: ibid., 14: 332.

266 *pre-dated the printing press*: see Andrew Pettegree, *The Invention of News* (2014).

266 *market for news*: for the facts in this and the next paragraph of this chapter, see Ivon Asquith, 'The Structure, Ownership and Control of the Press, 1780–1855', in George Boyce et al. (eds), *Newspaper History* (1978); James Curran and Jean Seaton, *Power Without Responsibility* (8th edn, 2018), chs 1–3. See also A. Aspinall, *Politics and the Press, c. 1780–1850* (1949); Victoria E. M. Gardner, *The Business of News in England, 1760–1820* (2016).

267 *'The corruption and baseness'*: Cobbett's *Weekly Political Register*, 11 Apr. 1807.

267 *'mechanical age'*: Thomas Carlyle, 'Signs of the Times', in *Critical and Miscellaneous Essays II*, ed. Henry Duff Traill (2010), 59.

267 *similar arguments*: on Carlyle and Balzac, see Lothar Müller, *White Magic: The Age of Paper*, trans. Jessica Spengler (2015), 140–63. See also [Edward Bulwer Lytton], *England and the English*, 2 vols (1833) 2: 7–36.

267 *'to perpetuate the slavery'*: *Poor Man's Guardian*, 26 Dec. 1835.

267 *'capitalists, idlers'*: ibid., 21 Nov. 1835.

268 *'either for good or evil'* etc.: ibid., 28 Nov. 1835.

268 *'accelerating'*: ibid., 26 Dec. 1835.

268 *first major political essay*: 'Remarks on the Latest Prussian Censorship Instruction' (written 1842; published 1843), in Karl Marx, *On Freedom of the Press and Censorship*, trans. Saul K. Padover (1974), 89–108.

268 *'the voice of the people'* etc.: ibid., 43, 181, 77.

269 *'revolutionary terrorism'* etc.: ibid., 154.

269 *'the first duty'*: ibid., 144. From London, Marx briefly resurrected the paper as a monthly journal, which lasted until November 1850.

269 *'The first freedom'* etc.: ibid., 41.

269 *'not subject'*: ibid., 33. For his disdain of profit as a motive, see ibid., xxvii–xxviii, 181.

269 *'the difference between'* etc.: *Northern Star*, 4 Apr. 1846.

270 *'the possibility of appealing'* etc.: Ferdinand Lassalle, *The Working-Man's Programme*, trans. Edward Peters (1884), 41, 46.

270 *'world-historical'* etc.: Karl Knies, *Der Telegraph als Verkehrsmittel: Mit Erörterungen über den Nachrichtenverkehr überhaupt* (Tübingen, 1857), iii, 61; on Knies, see also Ronald A. Fullerton, 'A Prophet of Modern Advertising', *Journal of Advertising* 27 (1998); Hanno Hardt, *Social Theories of the Press* (2nd edn, 2001), ch. 4; Jean-Michel Johnston, *Networks of Modernity* (2021), ch. 4.

271 *Schäffle*: Albert Schäffle, *Bau und Leben des socialen Körpers*, 4 vols (Tübingen, 1881), esp. 1: 432–66 (quoting 452: 'the most powerful means').

271 *'newspapers only address'*: Karl Bücher, 'Zur Frage der Pressreform', *Zeitschrift für die gesamte Staatswissenschaft* 76 (1921), 307; see generally Hardt, *Social Theories*, chs 3, 5–7.

271 *'the uninhibited pursuit'* etc.: Knies, *Telegraph*, 248–51.

272 *So important was the struggle*: Karl Kautsky, *Das Erfurter Programm* (1892), 216–19.

272 *German Social Democratic Party*: for recurrent disputes within the party about the limits of critical free speech, see Maria Löblich and Niklas Venema, 'Die SPD, die Meinungsfreiheit und die Konsequenzen der Massenpresse im Kaiserreich', *Publizistik* 65 (2020).

272 *Lenin*: Lars T. Lih, *Lenin Rediscovered: What Is to Be Done? In Context* (2006), 11–12, 59, 149 (quoted: 'the revolutionary newspaper'), 403, 418–19, 422, 435, 455–6, 585, 604–7, 819–36; idem, *Lenin* (2011), chs 1–3.

273 *'freedom for the rich'*: Albert Resis, 'Lenin on Freedom of the Press', *Russian Review* 36 (1977), 282; see also 274–84.

273 *'the counter-revolutionary press'* etc.: 'Decree on the Press', 27 Oct. [Old Style] / 9 Nov. [New Style] 1917 (from Feb. 1918, when the calendar was reformed, all dates were New Style), *ДЕКРЕТЫ СОВЕТСКОЙ ВЛАСТИ* [*Decrees of the Soviet Government*] (1957–97), 1: 24–5 (at hist.msu.ru). The translation of this first decree is from soviethistory. msu.edu.

273 *'will be granted'* etc.: ibid.

274 *'attempted counterrevolution'* etc: *The Debate on Soviet Power: Minutes of the All-Russian Central Executive Committee of Soviets, Second Convocation, October 1917–January 1918*, ed. John L. H. Keep (1979), 70 (debates of 4 Nov. / 17 Nov.).

274 4 Nov. decree: 'All-Russian Central Executive Committee Resolution on the Press', 4 Nov. / 17 Nov. 1917, *ДЕКРЕТЫ*, 1: 43–4.

274 *Three days later*: 'Decree on the Introduction of a State Monopoly on Announcements', 7 Nov. / 20 Nov. 1917, *ДЕКРЕТЫ*, 1: 55–6.

274 *'Revolutionary Press Tribunal'* etc.: 'Decree on the Revolutionary Press Tribunal', 28 Jan. / 10 Feb. 1918, *ДЕКРЕТЫ*, 1: 432–4. See also *Bolshevik Revolution, 1917–1918: Documents and Materials*, ed. James Bunyan and H. H. Fisher (1934), 280, 297–8.

274 *'popular editions'* etc.: 'Decree on the State Publishing House', 29 Dec. 1917 / 11 Jan. 1918, in *Bolshevik Revolution*, ed. Bunyan and Fisher, 595–6.

274 *'For the purpose'*: *The Russian Constitution* (1919), 7.

275 *dissenting voices*: *Bolshevik Revolution*, ed. Bunyan and Fisher, 199–208, 219–24, 342, 345, 347, 351; *The Debate on Soviet Power*, ed. Keep, 68–79, 91–3, 140–41, 148, 167, 249, 272–3.

275 *'tangle of venomous snakes'*: Maxim Gorky, *Untimely Thoughts*, trans. Herman Ermolaev (1995 edn), 50; see also 51–2.

275 *'shameful attitude'* etc.: ibid., 85, 183; see also 85–92, 182–4.

275 *dictatorial power grab*: Karl Kautsky, *The Dictatorship of the Proletariat*, trans. H. J. Stenning [1919?], esp. 3, 21, 27, 33–8, 45, 90, 124, 132–3, 144–8; idem, *Terrorism and Communism*, trans. W. H. Kerridge (1920), 175–7, 188, 208, 211–12, 221.

275 *'we defend press freedom'* etc.: *The Debate on Soviet Power*, ed. Keep, 70–75; see also *Bolshevik Revolution*, ed. Bunyan and Fisher, 560, 564; V. I. Lenin, *Collected Works*, 45 vols (1960–78), 28: 108, 248, 370, 460–61; Nikolai Bukharin, 'Programme of the Communists (Bolsheviks)' (1919), reprinted in *Revolutionary Radicalism: Its History, Purpose and Tactics*, 4 vols (1920), 2: 1701–7; L. Trotsky, *The Defence of Terrorism* (1921), 56–9.

277 *'Citizens of the People's Republic'* etc.: constitution of the People's Republic of China (1982).

277 *heavily monitored and censored*: Li Yuan, 'Censoring China's Internet', *New York Times*, 2 Jan. 2019; Yuyu Chen and David Y. Yang, 'The Impact of Media Censorship', *American Economic Review* 109 (2019); James Griffiths, *The Great Firewall of China* (2019). Wikipedia has a notably full series of up-to-date articles on Chinese internet surveillance and censorship.

277 *'anti-proletarian'* etc.: Letter to G. Myasnikov, 5 Aug. 1921, Lenin, *Collected Works*, 32: 504–9.

278 *'Western anti-China forces'* etc.: 'Communiqué on the Current State of the Ideological Sphere' (aka 'Document 9'), April 2013, translation at chinafile.com.

278 *'to give freedom of speech'*: Sarah Davies, *Popular Opinion in Stalin's Russia* (1997), 104.

278 *Gavril Myasnikov*: Paul Avrich, 'Bolshevik Opposition to Lenin', *Russian Review* 43 (1984).

279 *'in conformity'*: constitution of the USSR (1936), Article 125.

279 *'bourgeois' conception*: J. Arch Getty, 'State and Society Under Stalin', *Slavic Review* 50 (1991), 25–7; Davies, *Popular Opinion*, 105–8, 123.

279 *embedded in social systems*: *The Programme of the Communist Party of the Soviet Union* (1985), 72–83.

279 *'the deliberate opium'* etc.: Andrei Sakharov, 'Thoughts on Progress, Peaceful Coexistence and Intellectual Freedom' (1968), translation at sakharov.space; for more on communist dissenters, see Benjamin Nathans, 'Soviet Rights-Talk in the Post-Stalin Era', in Stefan-Ludwig Hoffmann (ed.), *Human Rights in the Twentieth Century* (2011), 173–83; idem, *To the Success of Our Hopeless Cause* (2024).

280 *'Literature in the GDR'* etc.: quoted in Darnton, *Censors at Work*, 199, 202; see generally ibid., pt 3 and 'Conclusion'.

280 *'No form of censorship'* etc.: quoted in Richard Zipser (ed.), *Fragebogen: Zensur* (1995), 43–5, 120; see also e.g. 9–10, 31, 34–6, 70, 73–4, 78.

282 *'real opposition'* etc.: quoted in Michael Lewis, 'Has Anyone Seen the President?', *Bloomberg.com*, 9 Feb. 2018.

283 *'conscientiously opposed to war'* etc.: flyer quoted from *Transcript of Record: Supreme Court of the United States: October Term, 1918*, cases 437 and 438 (1918); see also *Camden Daily Courier*, 18 Feb. 1914; *Philadelphia Inquirer*, 28 Feb., 7 and 24 Mar. 1914, 19 and 26 Apr. 1919; *Cincinnati Enquirer*, 5 July 1914; *Evening Public Ledger* (Philadelphia), 19 Sept. 1916; *Detroit Free Press*, 29 Oct. 1916; *Daily Herald* (Gulfport, Mississippi), 11 June 1917; *New Yorker Volkszeitung*, 26 Apr. and 28 June 1919; *Daily Worker* (New York), 14 Mar. 1939; *Plainfield Courier-News*, 27 Jan. 1943.

284 *'false reports'* etc.: 1917 Espionage Act; 1918 Sedition Act.

284 *protection of controversial speech*: on US free-speech campaigners in the late nineteenth and early twentieth century, see David M. Rabban, *Free Speech in Its Forgotten Years* (1997), ch. 1.

285 *'free speech fights'* etc.: Rabban, *Free Speech*, 83, 87; see generally ibid., ch. 2; IWW History Project at depts.washington.edu/iww/.

285 *took the same line*: see e.g. *Debs and the War* [1922], 7–8, 14, 19–20, 35, 37–40, 53.

286 *'absolute and complete'* etc.: *In the Supreme Court of the United States, October Term, A.D. 1903: No. 561: United States ex rel. John Turner vs William Williams . . . Argument of Appellant* [1903], 37, 49.

286 *'the vital issue'* etc.: quoted in Rabban, *Free Speech*, 272.

286 *'denial of constitutional rights'* etc.: *Report of Harris Weinstock* (1912), 3, 9–11, 22.

286 *same issues were raised*: Rabban, *Free Speech*, ch. 3.

287 *'liberty of the press'* etc.: *Patterson v. Colorado*, 205 US 454 (1907), 462, 465.

287 *didn't only prohibit 'previous restraints'* etc.: *Schenck v. United States*, 249 US 47 (1919), 51–2.

288 *duly locked up* etc.: Richard Polenberg, *Fighting Faiths* (1987).

288 *'the Free Speech Century'*: see e.g. Anthony Lewis, *Freedom for the Thought That We Hate* (2007); Vincent Blasi, *Ideas of the First Amendment* (2nd edn, 2012); Lee C. Bollinger and Geoffrey R. Stone (eds), *The Free Speech Century* (2019), xv (quoted: 'the Supreme Court's').

288 *studied his writings*: on Holmes and Mill, see *Holmes–Laski Letters*, ed. Mark DeWolfe Howe, 2 vols (1963), 2: 841, 1208; G. Edward White, *Justice Oliver Wendell Holmes* (1993), 94, 96–7, 510 n. 36, 517 n. 23.

289 *'safeguard of progress'*: Harold Laski, *Authority in the Modern State* (1919), 280.

289 *evolved from his earlier views*: a useful compilation is *The Fundamental Holmes*, ed. Ronald K. L. Collins (2010).

289 *'opinions and speech'*: Sheldon M. Novick, 'The Unrevised Holmes and Freedom of Expression', *Supreme Court Review* (1991), 389.

289 *Brandeis in another case*: Sugarman v. United States, 249 US 182 (1919).

289 *'Only the present danger'* etc.: *Abrams v. United States*, 250 US 616 (1919), dissent by Holmes, joined by Brandeis.

289 *'there was no evidence'* etc.: *Gitlow v. New York*, 268 US 652 (1925), quoting 652, 656 (see also 664), majority opinion; and 673, dissent of Holmes, joined by Brandeis.

290 *'No danger flowing'*: Whitney v. California, 274 US 357 (1927), quoting 377, concurrence of Brandeis, joined by Holmes.

290 *'marketplace of ideas'*: Sam Lebovic, *Free Speech and Unfree News* (2016), 258 n. 33.

291 *'the right of an ass'*: Holmes–Laski Letters, ed. DeWolfe, 1: 752. For the sincere pacifist, see *United States v. Schwimmer*, 279 U.S. 644 (1929); in *Whitney v. California*, their now famous words about 'more speech, not enforced silence', previously quoted, emphatically did not apply to the defendant, the communist Anita Whitney: they *upheld* her conviction.

292 *two intertwined stories*: brilliantly illuminated by Laura Weinrib, *The Taming of Free Speech* (2016), and Lebovic, *Free Speech*, to whose arguments my analysis is greatly indebted.

292 *'exaggerates private right'*: Roscoe Pound, 'Liberty of Contract', *Yale Law Journal* 18 (1909), 461.

292 *'the individual interest in free belief'*: Roscoe Pound, 'Interests of Personality', *Harvard Law Review* 28 (1915), 454.

293 *'to serve the cause'* etc.: 'Suggestions for Reorganization of the National Civil Liberties Bureau' (1920), Princeton University Mudd Library, ACLU Papers, 120: 32–7.

293 *'a class government'* etc.: *The Fight for Free Speech* (1921), 4–6.

293 *'the expression of all opinions'*: ibid., 15.

293 *'the overthrow'*: quoted in Weinrib, *Taming*, 181.

293 *singled out the Ku Klux Klan* etc.: *Fight for Free Speech*, 4, 7, 13; Dwight Macdonald, 'The Defense of Everybody – I', *New Yorker* (11 July 1953), 35.

293 *defending the rights of antisemites*: Samantha Barbas, *The Rise and Fall of Morris Ernst, Free Speech Renegade* (2021), 142–5.

435

293 *'Is it not clear'*: *Shall We Defend Free Speech for Nazis in America?* (1934), 2-3.

294 *'If I aid'*: quoted in Dwight Macdonald, 'The Defense of Everybody – II', *New Yorker* 18 Jul 1953, 44-5.

294 *'To defend the rights of Nazis'*: John Palmer Gavit to Roger Baldwin, 8 Nov. 1934: Princeton University Mudd Library, ACLU Papers, 700 [unpaginated].

294 *ACLU's shift in principles*: for this and the following paragraph in this chapter, see Weinrib, *Taming*, chs 7, 8, epilogue (quoting 311: 'to link free enterprise'); idem, 'Rethinking the Myth of the Modern First Amendment', in Bollinger and Stone (eds), *Free Speech Century*, 62, 67.

295 *'the corporate takeover'*: John C. Coates IV, 'Corporate Speech and the First Amendment', *Constitutional Commentary* 30 (2015), 275.

296 *'a monopoly market'*: Weinrib, 'Rethinking the Myth', 67.

296 *the American newspaper scene*: Alexis de Tocqueville, *Democracy in America*, trans. Henry Reeve (New York, 1838), ch. 11.

296 *'most parts'* etc.: George Campbell, *White and Black* (1879), 28.

297 *'to expect a newspaper magnate'*: Edward Alsworth Ross, 'The Suppression of Important News', *Atlantic Monthly* (Mar. 1910), 310.

297 *'the newspaper-owner'*: Edward Alsworth Ross, 'Social Decadence', *American Journal of Sociology* 23 (1918), 630.

297 [footnote] *'free trade in ideas'* etc.: White, *Justice Oliver Wendell Holmes*, 515 n. 119.

297 *non-profit newspapers*: Victor S. Yarros, 'A Neglected Opportunity and Duty in Journalism', *American Journal of Sociology* 22 (1916); idem, *My 11 Years with Clarence Darrow* (1950); Ross, 'Suppression', 310-11; Upton Sinclair, *The Brass Check: A Study of American Journalism* (1920 edn), 438-43.

297 *'misleading'* etc.: Walter Lippmann, *Liberty and the News* (1920), 35, 63.

297 *'the protection'*: ibid., 62-3; see also Lebovic, *Free Speech*, ch. 1.

298 *'the problem'*: quoted in Lebovic, *Free Speech*, 3.

298 *'interest in freedom of the news'* etc.: *New York Times*, 13 Jan. 1939; *Time*, 23 Jan. and 6 Nov. 1939; Lebovic, *Free Speech*, ch. 2.

298 *Most Americans agreed*: Stephen Bates, *An Aristocracy of Critics* (2020), 40.

298 *'I can see nothing'*: quoted ibid., 24.

298 *economic reforms*: Lebovic, *Free Speech*, ch. 3.

298 *statute contravened*: *Near v. Minnesota*, 238 US 697 (1931); Lebovic, *Free Speech*, 42-9.

299 *'lead to or approximate censorship'*: quoted in Lebovic, *Free Speech*, 67.

299 *'government-controlled'*: quoted ibid., 66.

299 *'a public service institution'* etc.: quoted ibid., 59, 61, 68–9, 74–5; see also 56–63, 72–6, 85–7.

299 *'the freedom, functions'*: William Ernest Hocking, *Freedom of the Press* (1947), iv.

300 *'planning for'* etc.: Alexander Meiklejohn, *Free Speech and Its Relation to Self-Government* (1948), 39, 104. For equivalent British views, see e.g. Hermon Ould (ed.), *Freedom of Expression* (1944), 27–8.

300 *Associated Press ruling*: *United States v. Associated Press*, 52 F. Supp. 362 (SDNY 1943); *Associated Press et al. v. United States*, 326 US 1 (1945).

300 *'too simple'*: quoted in Lebovic, *Free Speech*, 141.

300 *'the right of the citizen'* etc.: *A Free and Responsible Press* (1947), 18.

300 *'vigorous, continuous'*: quoted in Bates, *Aristocracy*, 106.

300 *'totalitarianism'* etc.: *Free and Responsible Press*, 5, 128–31; see also Hocking, *Freedom of the Press*; idem, *Freedom of the Press in America* (1947); Lebovic, *Free Speech*, 140–45.

301 *power with 'social responsibility'*: for this last point, see Bates, *Aristocracy*, ch. 18.

301 *'In the United States the battle'*: Earl L. Vance, 'Freedom of the Press for Whom?', *Virginia Quarterly Review* 21 (1945), 342.

301 *left-wing American thinkers*: see e.g. Herbert Marcuse, 'Repressive Tolerance', in Robert Paul Wolff et al. (eds), *A Critique of Pure Tolerance* (1969 edn); Edward S. Herman and Noam Chomsky, *Manufacturing Consent* (1988).

302 *'At the present moment'* etc.: Truman speech to Congress, 12 Mar. 1947.

302 *'freedom of enterprise'*: Weinrib, *Taming*, 223, quoting the industrialist Walter Kohler in 1937.

302 *'Free people'* etc.: address of Robert H. Jackson to the Council of State Governments, 21 Jan. 1941, 11–14 (at justice.gov); see also Louis Menand, *The Free World* (2021), 352, 703.

302 *'advocacy'* etc.: Smith Act of 1940, 18 US Code section 2385 (2000).

303 *'those abuses'* etc.: *Dennis v. United States*, 341 US 494 (1951).

303 *majority had shifted*: *Yates v. United States*, 354 US 298 (1957).

303 *occupied Germany*: see e.g. TNA, FO 1049/115 and 116 (1945); FO 1060/1125 and 1126 (1945–9).

304 *drafting of international conventions*: Sarah H. Cleveland, 'Hate Speech at Home and Abroad', in Bollinger and Stone (eds), *Free Speech Century*, esp. 224; United Nations Commission on Human Rights, eighth

session, summary record of 321st meeting, 4 June 1952 (E/CN.4/ SR.321).

305 *'the rights of free speech'* etc.: quoted in Samantha Barbas, *Actual Malice* (2023), 171.

306 *'deliberately and maliciously false'*: *New York Times Co. v. Sullivan*, 376 US 254 (1964), 300.

306 *'debate on public issues'*: ibid., 270.

306 *'dampens the vigor'*: ibid., 279.

306 *'public persons'*: see e.g. Frederick Schauer, 'Public Figures', *William and Mary Law Review* 25 (1984); Samantha Barbas, *Newsworthy* (2017).

307 *'revengeance'* etc.: *Brandenburg v. Ohio*, 395 US 444 (1969).

307 *the right of American Nazis*: *National Socialist Party of America v. Village of Skokie*, 432 US 43 (1977).

307 *'anger, alarm, or resentment'*: *R.A.V. v. St Paul*, 505 US 377 (1992).

307 *'protecting the community'*: ibid.

308 *'Expose through discussion'*: *Whitney v. California*, 377.

308 *Is this faith justified*: cf. Frederick Schauer, 'Facts and the First Amendment', *UCLA Law Review* 57 (2010).

308 *collateral damage*: cf. Schauer, 'Harm(s) and the First Amendment'.

308 *philosophical defenders*: see e.g. Ronald Dworkin, 'Foreword', in Ivan Hare and James Weinstein (eds), *Extreme Speech and Democracy* (2009).

309 *American legal scholars*: Rabban, *Free Speech*, ch. 4.

309 *'the First Amendment's unequivocal command'*: *Konigsberg v. State Bar*, 366 US 36 (1961), quoting dissent by Black, 61; cf. *District of Columbia v. Heller*, 554 US 570 (2008); *United States v. Stevens*, 559 US 460 (2010).

310 *'governmental interest'*: *Buckley v. Valeo*, 424 US 1 (1976), 48–9. For the contingent historical roots of this trajectory, see also Mark A. Graber, *Transforming Free Speech* (1991).

310 *'The whole point'*: *McCutcheon v. Federal Election Commission*, 572 US 185 (2014), 187; see also *Citizens United v. FEC*, 558 US 310 (2010).

310 *far from linear or consensual*: see e.g. the contrasting views on display in Geoffrey R. Stone et al. (eds), *The Bill of Rights in the Modern State* (1992), as well as in Bollinger and Stone (eds), *Free Speech Century*.

310 *'striking chiefly'*: Robert Post, 'Recuperating First Amendment Doctrine', *Stanford Law Review* 47 (1995), 1250; see also idem, 'Reconciling Theory and Doctrine in First Amendment Jurisprudence', *California Law Review* 88 (2000); Frederick Schauer, 'Towards an Institutional First Amendment', *Minnesota Law Review* 89 (2005).

310 *narrow and abstract conception*: see e.g. Genevieve Lakier, 'The First Amendment's Real *Lochner* Problem', *University of Chicago Law Review* 87 (2020).

310 *'worthless'* etc.: *R.A.V. v. St. Paul*, 400, 416.

311 *'blinkered and aphoristic'* etc.: *Citizens United v. Federal Election Commission*, 558 US 310 (2010), 475.

311 *'not only the individual's right'*: *McCutcheon v. Federal Election Commission*, 237.

311 *'goes wrong'* etc.: *Janus v. American Federation*, 585 US __ (2018).

311 *location and shape of those boundaries*: see e.g. *New York v. Ferber* 458 US 747 (1982); Frederick Schauer, 'The Boundaries of the First Amendment', *Harvard Law Review* 17 (2004); *Citizens United v. Federal Election Commission*, 419–25; Deborah Pearlstein, *Democracy Harms and the First Amendment*, Knight First Amendment Institute Essay (2022), 8–11.

312 *disdained to consider*: this reluctance is not limited to its free-speech jurisprudence: Frank I. Michelman, 'Integrity-Anxiety?', in Michael Ignatieff (ed.), *American Exceptionalism and Human Rights* (2005).

312 *the rest of the world*: cf. Frederick Schauer, 'The Exceptional First Amendment', in Ignatieff (ed.), *American Exceptionalism*.

312 *Historical approaches*: see e.g. Anthony Lewis, *Make No Law: The Sullivan Case and the First Amendment* (2011); Barbas, *Actual Malice*; idem, *Newsworthy*.

313 *'the First Amendment'*: *Beauharnais v. Illinois*, 275 (dissent by Black).

314 *'to withdraw from the Government'*: Hugo L. Black, 'The Bill of Rights', *New York University Law Review* 35 (1960), 874–5.

314 *carried a copy of the constitution*: Tracy S. Uebelhor (ed.), *The Truman Years* (2006), 42; David L. Lange and H. Jefferson Powell, *No Law* (2009), ch. 10; Barbas, *Actual Malice*, 152–4.

314 *in Black's view*: for Black's exceptions to the First Amendment, see *Tinker v. Des Moines Independent Community School District*, 393 US 503 (1969), dissent by Black (armbands); *Cohen v. California*, 403 US 15 (1971), minority dissent (jacket); *Time Magazine*, 5 Apr. 1968 (marching, picketing, flag-burning).

314 *a card that trumps*: see e.g. *303 Creative LLC v. Elenis*, 600 US __ (2023); *Defense Distributed v. United States*, No. 18-50811 (5th Cir. 2020); *Bernstein v. US Dept. of State*, 945 F. Supp. 1279 (ND Cal. 1996); Andrew Solomon, 'The Shape of Love', *New Yorker*, 22 Mar. 2021. Cf. Frederick Schauer, 'First Amendment Opportunism', in Lee C. Bollinger and Geoffrey R. Stone (eds), *Eternally Vigilant* (2002);

idem, 'The Politics and Incentives of First Amendment Coverage', *William and Mary Law Review* 56 (2015).

314 *'ad hoc balancing'*: in practice, despite this rhetoric, the court does tolerate a fair amount of such balancing: for this point, and the broader insufficiency of the court's approach to free speech and democracy, see Pearlstein, *Democracy Harms*; and see also Schauer, 'Towards an Institutional First Amendment'.

315 *'the alternative to private control'*: David Cole, 'Why We Must Still Defend Free Speech', *New York Review of Books*, 28 Sept. 2017.

316 *'the exhibition of moving pictures'*: Mutual Film Corporation v. *Industrial Commission of Ohio*, 236 US 230 (1915), 230–31. In 1952, the court changed its mind on this point, ruling that films, even though 'a large-scale business conducted for private profit', fell under the protection of the First Amendment: *Joseph Burstyn, Inc. v. Wilson*, 343 US 495 (1952).

317 *'is not engaged'*: Meiklejohn, *Free Speech*, 104.

317 *Federal Communications Commission*: 1934 Communications Act. Section 326 of this act, deploring 'censorship', forbad the FCC to 'interfere with the right of free speech'; its final clause (repealed in 1948) prohibited 'obscene, indecent, or profane language' on the radio.

317 *segregationist Mississippi television station*: see https://en.wikipedia. org/wiki/WLBT.

317 *'First Amendment is relevant'*: Red Lion Broadcasting Co., Inc. v. FCC, 395 US 367 (1969), 368.

317 *'a responsible press'*: Miami Herald Pub. Co. v. Tornillo, 418 US 241 (1974), 256. A subsidiary argument during these decades was that government regulation of radio and television was justified because the number of usable transmission frequencies was not limitless, and the broadcast spectrum was therefore a scarce public resource.

318 *'the First Amendment was adopted'*: Federal Communications Commission Record 2 (1987), 5057; see generally Paul Matzko, *The Radio Right* (2020); Kathryn Cramer Brownell, 24/7 *Politics: Cable Television and the Fragmenting of America from Watergate to Fox News* (2023).

318 *communications revolution, the internet*: for this and the next three paragraphs in this chapter, see 1996 Telecommunications Act; Jeff Kosseff, *The Twenty-Six Words that Created the Internet* (2019); idem, 'A User's Guide to Section 230', *Berkeley Technology Law Journal* 37 (2022); Colin Crowell, 'Reflections on the 25th Anniversary of the Telecommunications Act of 1996', *medium.com* (2021).

319 *'end of history'*: Francis Fukuyama, 'The End of History?', *The National Interest* 16 (1989).

319 *'We know how much'* etc.: speech by Bill Clinton at Johns Hopkins University, 8 Mar. 2000.

321 *potential issues of free speech and harm*: see Susan J. Brison and Katharine Gelber (eds), *Free Speech in the Digital Age* (2019).

322 *'the incentives of business'*: Monika Bickert, 'Defining the Boundaries of Free Speech on Social Media', in Bollinger and Stone (eds), *Free Speech Century*, 271.

322 [footnote] *'American companies'*: Senator Edward Markey, quoted in Bobby Allyn, 'President Biden Signs Law to Ban TikTok', *NPR*, 24 Apr. 2024.

323 *dirty work*: see e.g. David Pilling, 'The Young People Sifting Through the Internet's Worst Horrors', *Financial Times*, 11 Jan. 2024.

323 *shibboleths of their own*: for related divergences between European and American attitudes, see James Q. Whitman, 'The Two Western Cultures of Privacy', *Yale Law Journal* 113 (2004).

324 *Facebook entered Myanmar*: see e.g. Megan Specia and Paul Mozur, 'A War of Words Puts Facebook at the Center of Myanmar's Rohingya', *New York Times*, 27 Oct. 2017; Paul Mozur, 'A Genocide Incited on Facebook, With Posts from Myanmar's Military', *New York Times*, 15 Oct. 2018. Similar things happened in Cambodia: Megha Rajagopalan, 'This Country's Democracy Has Fallen Apart', *BuzzFeed News*, 21 Jan. 2018.

324 *'We had just promised'*: quoted in Joseph Menn and Gerry Shih, 'Under India's Pressure, Facebook Let Propaganda and Hate Speech Thrive', *Washington Post*, 26 Sept. 2023.

324 *spreading deliberate lies online*: see e.g. Stuart A. Thompson, 'Fake News Still Has a Home on Facebook', *New York Times*, 13 June 2024.

325 *backed itself into a corner*: for recent American judicial and legislative moves to address some of these issues, see Kosseff, 'User's Guide to Section 230'.

326 *'everyone has the right'* etc.: Universal Declaration of Human Rights (1948), articles 19, 29, 30.

326 *'the task of ensuring'*: Official Minutes of the 65th Plenary Meeting of the General Assembly of the United Nations, 14 Dec. 1946: UN Digital Library, A/PV.65, 1379.

327 *the European Convention's creators* etc.: Council of Europe, confidential memo DH (56) 15 on 'Preparatory Work on Article 10 of the European Convention on Human Rights', 17 Aug. 1956, at coe.int/en/web/human-rights-convention/preparatory-works.

AFTERWORD: FROM THE PAST TO THE FUTURE

331 *a clear line*: a valiant attempt to write a global history of free speech in this vein is Jacob Mchangama, *Free Speech: A History from Socrates to Social Media* (2022).

331 *The alternative answer*: an especially influential version of this argument is Tim Wu, 'Is the First Amendment Obsolete?', *Michigan Law Review* 117 (2018).

332 *freedom for the wolves*: Isaiah Berlin, 'On the Pursuit of the Ideal', *New York Review of Books*, 17 Mar. 1988; idem, 'The First and the Last', *New York Review of Books*, 14 May 1998; cf. Joseph E. Stiglitz, *The Road to Freedom* (2024), esp. ch. 9.

332 *outrageous bullshit*: see Harry Frankfurt, *On Bullshit* (2005), on why 'bullshit is a greater enemy of the truth than lies are' (61).

333 *'Much that he has said'* etc.: *United States of America v. Donald J. Trump*, US District Court, District of Columbia, case 23-cr-257-TSC: Amici Curiae brief by the American Civil Liberties Union, 25 Oct. 2023.

334 *workplace harassment*: see Frederick Schauer, 'The Speech-ing of Sexual Harassment', Robert Post, 'Sexual Harassment and the First Amendment', and Jack M. Balkin, 'Free Speech and Hostile Environments', in Catharine A. MacKinnon and Reva B. Siegel (eds), *Directions in Sexual Harassment Law* (2004).

335 *boycotting*: see e.g. Andrew Phemister, '"The Surging Tide of Pauper Democracy"', *Radical History Review* 134 (2019).

336 *university campuses*: an incisive introduction to the issues is Ulrich Baer, *What Snowflakes Get Right* (2019).

337 *how best to regulate or incentivize*: cf. Jack Balkin, 'Free Speech versus the First Amendment', *UCLA Law Review* 70 (2023).

338 *'we're for free speech'*: Stanley Fish, *There's No Such Thing as Free Speech* (1994), 16; see also idem, *The First* (2019), chs 1-2; Charlotte Lydia Riley (ed.), *The Free Speech Wars* (2021).

338 *unwarranted 'censorship'*: see e.g. Steven Lee Myers, 'State Department's Fight Against Disinformation Comes Under Attack', *New York Times*, 14 Dec. 2023.

339 *governmental censorship*: see e.g. Fabio Bertoni, 'Florida Takes Aim at the First Amendment', *newyorker.com*, 6 Mar. 2023; idem, 'How Would This Supreme Court Rule on Book Banning?', *newyorker.com*, 7 Dec. 2023.

341   *'academic freedom'*: for differing arguments about the relationship between freedom of speech and academic freedom, see e.g. Frederick Schauer, 'Is there a Right to Academic Freedom?', *University of Colorado Law Review* 77 (2006); Robert Post, 'Academic Freedom and the Constitution', in Akeel Bilgrami and Jonathan Cole (eds), *Who's Afraid of Academic Freedom?* (2015); Keith E. Whittington, *You Can't Teach That!* (2024); David Rabban, *Academic Freedom* (2024).

Acknowledgements

My first debt is to my colleagues in the department of history at Princeton, for luring me across the Atlantic and providing me with the freedom and resources to write this book.

Though little has been published on the history of free speech outside the United States, I am obliged to the authors of the hundreds of local studies of censorship, speech regulation, laws, press, broadcasting, the internet and related subjects, around the world, upon whose work I have gratefully drawn – as well as to generations of First Amendment scholars and other theorists of free speech. Without them my forays into many areas previously unfamiliar to me would have been impossible. For the sake of general readers, I've not cluttered the narrative with historiographical interventions; but I trust that specialists in particular fields will be able to judge from the text and notes how far my interpretations match or differ from their own.

When I first began working on free speech, it was a revelation to discover the pellucid theoretical work of Frederick Schauer, the greatest First Amendment scholar of our time. After I had finished writing this book, I was thrilled to learn (once the refereeing process was complete, and he had kindly waived his anonymity) that he had written a deeply flattering report for my publishers about its manuscript. I am greatly saddened that he did not live to see its publication.

I thank the archivists and librarians across the world who facilitated my access to their collections, as well as the many people who have helped me with references and suggestions, especially the editors of journals and participants in seminars and conferences who allowed me to try out my ideas on them. I am also profoundly grateful to the kind friends and relations, talented students and excellent colleagues who generously read draft chapters at different stages of this project, or cheered me on through their benevolence and example – especially Aditi Rao, Ben Nathans, Carl Wennerlind, David Bell, David Cannadine, David Rabban, David Wootton, Debora Shuger, Deborah Pearlstein, Jacob Neis, Jan-Werner Müller, Jocelyn Pickard, John Harpham, Linda Colley, Nick Irvin, Peter Brown, Robert Travers, Sophie Rosenfeld and Zoë Pickard.

It has been a privilege to work again with my peerless editor at Penguin Random House, Stuart Proffitt, and his superb colleagues. I am indebted to James Pullen and to Ian Malcolm for their great support of this project, and to Sharmila Sen and her excellent team at Harvard University Press for enthusiastically championing it. Lisa Kraege helped me knock the notes into shape, Kate Parker was a wonderful copyeditor, and Paula Clarke Bain kindly created the index.

My lover, the brilliant scientist Jo Dunkley, has prohibited me from publishing the minutely detailed catalogue of her amazingness that I have been secretly compiling throughout the writing of this book – even though I have tried to assert my right to free speech, and to rally our adorable children to my cause. So I can only say that I live to talk with her about everything, and to make her laugh. All that I do is sustained by the warmth of her love, and the daily joy of our life together.

Index